THE RENAISSANCE IMAGINATION

THE
RENAISSANCE
IMAGINATION

Essays and Lectures by
D. J. GORDON

Collected and Edited by
STEPHEN ORGEL

University of California Press
Berkeley   Los Angeles   London

University of California Press
Berkeley and Los Angeles, California
University of California Press, Ltd.
London, England
"Roles and Mysteries" and "Ripa's Fate" copyright © 1975
by D. J. Gordon and Stephen Orgel
All other essays in this volume, copyright © 1975 by D. J. Gordon
ISBN 0-520-02817-1
Library of Congress Catalog Card Number: 74-81432
Printed in the United States of America
Designed by Michael Bass
and Lorena Laforest

D. D.

J. B. TRAPP

VIRORUM DOCTORUM AMICO DOCTIORI

STUDIISQUE HUMANITATIS AMICISSIMO

Contents

Preface

This volume contains every major article on the Renaissance by D. J. Gordon, including three that are previously unpublished, and one that has appeared only in a French translation. All these studies are concerned with the Renaissance imagination: the nature of its imagery and symbolism, the relation between its art and literature, its attitudes toward the ancient world and toward its own history. All of the essays are seminal or pioneering investigations; most are classics of their kind. They are here collected for the first time.

Having said so much, I shall allow the book to speak for itself—to do anything else would be presumptuous. But a word about my responsibilities in the project may be in order. The three opening pieces are hitherto unpublished. *Roles and Mysteries* and *Ripa's Fate* were conceived as introductory lectures on the nature of Renaissance imagery, and as such seemed to me an admirable introduction to the more specialized essays that comprise the bulk of the volume. *Rubens and the Whitehall Ceiling* was addressed to a more homogeneous audience of art-historians and scholars, but it is nevertheless similarly broad in its applications. Only the Rubens lecture was in finished form, and I have printed it without substantial alterations, though I have conflated material from two separate versions of the paper. The other two lectures exist only in a variety of rough drafts; and here my responsibility has been greater. The lines of argument are unchanged, and I have added very little to the evidence adduced; but it has been necessary to expand and clarify in a number of places, and the prose is often, unavoidably, more mine than my author's. Quotations in these lectures are given in English, and though I have cited the original texts in the notes, it has seemed sensible to retain the translations.

I have made only minor alterations in the published material, generally of an editorial nature. Except in cases where it would have been perverse or misleading not to do so, I have not attempted to bring the documentation up to date; but in fact, the reader will find little in this book that has been superseded by subsequent scholarship. I should add that there are points I disagree with from time to time here, and these have been allowed to pass without comment.

The published texts include a large number of Latin and Italian passages. Translations have been provided for all of these, with the exception of a few brief citations whose meaning is obvious in context. (For longer passages, the originals appear at the bottom of the page.) The English versions have been prepared by the editor and Mr. J. B. Trapp, with the generous, and ultimately indispensable, assistance of Dr. D. P. Walker, who is chiefly responsible for the Ficino translations. As for the documentation, however, I found myself feeling about it as Dr. Johnson felt about *Paradise Lost*—that nobody could wish it longer than it is—and I have therefore allowed quotations in the Appendices and Notes to remain only in the original languages. I hope it is not rash to assume that the only readers who will wish to return to the sources will be those equipped to read them.

I have undertaken to refer citations of Renaissance works to the same editions throughout the volume. This is more difficult than it may sound, because the texts of writers like Conti (who has been allowed to be called both Conti and Comes here, with only an occasional fussy reminder from the editor that they are the same person) and Cartari vary, sometimes very widely, from edition to edition. Insofar as it has proved feasible, it has been done. The text of Ficino used throughout is that of Basel, 1576. This was the standard sixteenth-century edition, and has the additional advantage of being very nearly identical in its pagination with several subsequent reprintings. It also has the disadvantage of a relatively large number of misprints; but its convenience seemed to outweigh its unreliability, and when errors occur in citations from it, I have silently (or nearly so) corrected them.

I am indebted in various ways to Lionel and Jane Kelly, to Mrs. J. Chennells and Mrs. P. Medhurst for searching files and answering endless transatlantic queries, to Sir Oliver Millar for information and encouragement at a crucial moment; but most of all to Mr. J. B. Trapp.

In addition to the copyright owners listed below, I have also to thank the following for generously supplying photographs: the University of Reading, the Photographic Service of the University of California Library, the Warburg Institute, the director of the Rubenshaus, Antwerp, and Mr. John Harris.

The previously published essays in this volume first appeared in the following journals or collections:

"Poet and Architect," *Journal of the Warburg and Courtauld Institutes* [hereafter cited as *JWCI*], XII, 1949.

"The Renaissance Poet as Classicist," under the title "Chapman's *Hero and Leander*," *English Miscellany* (Rome), V, 1954.

"The Imagery of *Blacknesse* and *Beautie*," *JWCI*, VI, 1943; reprinted in the revised version used here in *England and the Mediterranean Tradition*, 1945.

"*Hymenaei*," *JWCI*, VIII, 1945.

"Jonson's *Haddington Masque*," *Modern Language Review*, XLII, 1947.

"Chapman's *Memorable Masque*," in a French translation without notes, in *Les Fêtes de la Renaissance*, ed. Jean Jacquot, Paris 1956. The original version is hitherto unpublished.

"Name and Fame," *Papers Mainly Shakespearean*, ed. G. I. Duthie, Aberdeen University Studies, 1964, reprinted with kind permission.

"*Veritas Filia Temporis*," *JWCI*, III, 1939–40.

"Giannotti, Michelangelo and the Cult of Brutus," *Fritz Saxl, 1890–1948, a Volume of Memorial Essays*, ed. D. J. Gordon, 1957.

"Academicians Build a Theatre," *Friendship's Garland, Essays Presented to Mario Praz*, ed. V. Gabrieli, Rome 1966.

Drawings by Inigo Jones in the Devonshire Collection at Chatsworth are reproduced by kind permission of the Trustees of the Chatsworth Settlement.

Photographs in this volume are reproduced by permission of the following copyright owners:

A.C.L. Bruxelles   36

Alinari / Mansell Collection, London   73

James Austin   37

Bancroft Library, University of California, Berkeley   30, 38, 39, 40, 41, 42, 43, 44, 50, 52, 53, 63

Bodleian Library   11, 12

Courtauld Institute, University of London   9, 10, 56, 57

Kunsthistorisches Museum, Vienna   32

Louvre, Paris   18, 19, 54

Jean de Maeyer, Antwerp   16

National Gallery, London   1, 17

Warburg Institute, University of London   20, 33b, 34, 74

(Every effort has been made to locate the copyright holders of the photos used. In a few cases, however, this has proved impossible, and individuals not cited above who believe their work has been reproduced here are requested to communicate with either the editor or the University of California Press.)

S. O.

THREE LECTURES
ON
RENAISSANCE IMAGERY

1. Rubens, *War and Peace* (London, National Gallery).

Roles and Mysteries

I

When Rubens departed from London in March, 1630, he left as a farewell gift to his royal patron a picture representing Minerva—wisdom, prudence—aided by the rod of Mercury averting the threat of Mars from a scene of love, peace, plenty; the figures are placed in a pastoral landscape where the traditional enemies—the lustful satyr, the savage tiger—are tamed and at play (Figure 1). The painting records a political reality: peace between England and Spain, the specific, emergent occasion of Rubens' visit and of his diplomatic activities, had been concluded. So the artist had served as the architect of the king's peace; he was shortly to create, in a series of heroic paintings, the apotheosis of the rule of Charles I and the Stuart dynasty. The canvasses were installed in the ceiling of the king's Banqueting House in 1635, the year when France and Spain declared war, and the Thirty Years' War went into its final phase of general destruction. Five years later the last of the annual court masques, celebrations of the royal wisdom and power, was presented at Whitehall: *Salmacida Spolia*, the work of Inigo Jones and Sir William Davenant. Charles's peace ended with the Scottish war in 1639, and his eleven years of personal rule with the summoning of the Short Parliament in April 1640, dissolved after three weeks, and finally with the entry of the Scottish army into London and the summoning of Parliament again, the Long Parliament, in November 1640. It was from a window of the Banqueting House, the most significant artistic embodiment of the ideals of the Caroline monarchy, that Charles was to pass to the scaffold.

Salmacida Spolia belongs to the vexed, tormented, short passage of time when Charles

sought expedients—for making war, for averting war, for avoiding a Parliament domi-
nated by the opposition. As Rubens' ceiling expresses the triumph of Charles's autocracy,
Salmacida Spolia expresses its tragedy. Ceiling and masque speak a common figurative
language, at times revealing a relationship so close as to suggest that Jones and Davenent,
composing their entertainment, had the programme of the ceiling before them. History
has denied us one act of the drama: *Salmacida Spolia* was performed not in the Banqueting
House under Rubens' canvasses, but in a masquing hall specially constructed two years
before, lest the smoke of torches and candles damage the great panels. But ceiling and
masque go together, exemplifying in their symbols and allegories not only the glory of
Caroline rule, but more generally a mode of thought that was central to all the arts of the
European Renaissance.

2. ". . . much majesty in her aspect . . . and
a bridle in her hand, representing Reason."
(Engraving by S. Gribelin, 1720, after
Rubens, the Whitehall ceiling, detail.)[a]

3. ". . . winged children, one riding a furious
lion, which he seems to tame with reins and
with a bit . . ."

I wish to consider through a series of particular examples this mode of thought, and
its expression, and its fate. It is convenient to begin with the masque, for the text of
Salmacida Spolia tells us what it means, and may thus serve us as a guide to the non-verbal
arts. Jones designed a very elaborate proscenium arch for his production. No drawings of
this survive, but the architect's own detailed description is prefixed to the published
version. He calls this proscenium "a frontispiece to the whole work," explicitly relating
the arch framing the action both to the façade of a building (the original meaning of
frontispiece) and to those complex emblematic titlepages—for example to Ralegh's *History
of the World* and Ben Jonson's *Works*—that set out visually and verbally the burden or aim
of the volume that follows.

[a]Gribelin's eighteenth-century engraving of the ceiling has been used throughout, rather than
photographs of the paintings, because of its greater clarity of detail.

4. ". . . another bearing an antique ensign . . ."

Here is Inigo Jones's proscenium:

In the border that enclosed the scenes and made a frontispiece to all the work, in a square niche on the right hand stood two figures of women, one of them expressing much majesty in her aspect, apparelled in sky colour, with a crown of gold on her head, and a bridle in her hand, representing Reason (Figure 2): the other, embracing her, was in changeable silk with wings at her shoulders, figured for Intellectual Appetite, who while she embraceth Reason, all the actions of men are rightly governed. Above these, in a second order, were winged children, one riding on a furious lion, which he seems to tame with reins and with a bit (Figure 3): another bearing an antique ensign (Figure 4): the third hovering above with a branch of palm in his hand (Figure 5), expressing the victory over the perturbations. In a niche on the other side stood two figures joining hands, one a grave old man in a robe of purple, with a heart of gold in

6. ". . . the bird of Pallas, figured for Prudence . . ."

5. ". . . the third hovering above with a branch of palm in his hand, expressing the victory over the perturbations."

7. "...a third...with a lighted torch in his hand, representing the intellectual light ..."

a chain about his neck, figured for Counsel; the other a woman, in a garment of cloth of gold, in her hand a sword with a serpent winding about the blade, representing Resolution, both these being necessary to the good means of arriving to a virtuous end.

Over these and answering to the other side was a round altar raised high, and on it the bird of Pallas, figured for Prudence (Figure 6); on either side were children with wings, one in act of adoration, another holding a book, and a third flying over their heads with a lighted torch in his hand (Figure 7), representing the intellectual light accompanied with Doctrine and Discipline, and alluding to the figures below, as those on the other side.

8. "Forgetfulness of Injuries, extinguishing a flaming torch on an armour..." (Rubens' figure, however, is burning the armour.)

The rest of this frieze was composed of children, with significant signs to express their several qualities; Forgetfulness of Injuries, extinguishing a flaming torch on an armour (Figure 8); Commerce, with ears of corn; Felicity, with a basket of lilies; Affection to the Country, holding a grass-hopper; Prosperous Success, with the rudder of a ship; Innocence, with a branch of fern: all these expressing the several goods, followers of Peace and Concord, and forerunners of human felicity: so as the work of this front, consisting of picture qualified with moral philosophy, tempered delight with profit.

In the midst of the aforesaid compartment in an oval table was written: SALMACIDA SPOLIA. (22–70)[1]

Salmacida Spolia alludes to an adage:

Salmacida spolia sine sanguine sine sudore, potius quam Cadmia victoria, ubi ipsos victores pernicies opprimit.

[Better the spoils of Salmacis, won without blood or sweat, than Cadmian victories, which hurl destruction on the victors themselves.]

The classical stories are then set out in detail. Here is the account of the subject of the masque:

Discord, a malicious fury, appears in a storm, and by the invocation of malignant spirits proper for her evil use, having already put most of the world into disorder, endeavours to disturb these parts, envying the blessings and tranquility we have long enjoyed.

These incantations are expressed by those spirits in an antimasque: who on a sudden are surprised, and stopped in their motion by a secret power, whose wisdom they tremble at, and depart as foreknowing that Wisdom will change all their malicious hope of these disorders into a sudden calm, which after their departure is prepared by a dispersed harmony of music.

This secret wisdom, in the person of the king attended by his nobles, and under the name of Philogenes, or Lover of his People, hath his appearance prepared by a chorus, representing the beloved people, and is instantly discovered, environed with those nobles in the throne of Honour.

Then the queen personating the chief heroine, with her martial ladies, is sent down from heaven by Pallas as a reward of his prudence, for reducing the threatening storm into the following calm. (1–21)

What the spectator sees is this: first a scene of storm and tempest, with a globe of earth that turns into fire and from which a Fury emerges. The figure is familiar, with her torch and serpent hair. She invokes violence and destruction on "this over-lucky, too much happy isle," and Furies to arouse peccant humours and "incense / The guilty, and disorder innocence." Three Furies enter and dance the first anti-masque. The scene then changes to a pastoral, with Zephyr blowing, and "all such things as might express a country in peace, rich and fruitful"—corn, trees with vines, distant villages. From a silver chariot descend two figures, one representing Concord, the other the Good Genius of Great Britain. In a dialogue the Genius begs Concord to abide here for the sake of the good King Philogenes. To this plea Concord accedes, and they sing:

> O who but he could thus endure
> To live and govern in a sullen age,
> When it is harder far to cure
> The people's folly than resist their rage.
> (196–99)

No fewer than twenty entries of anti-masques follow, anatomizing the people's folly. They are led by Wolfgangus Vandergoose, "Operator to the Invisible Lady, styled the Magical Sister of the Rosicross," who promises miraculous cures for all the defects of nature. All the estates of the island are then represented: old men, young soldiers, children, a shepherd, a farmer and his wife, a country gentleman with his wife and bailiff—a society that should exist in perfect concord. Next come our ancestors who have been—or should be—reconciled at last: an ancient Irishman, Scotsman, Englishman. Then follies, first native—an amorous courtier, two roaring boys, four mad lovers—then foreign, for Discord is calling foreign follies to our island—a jealous Dutchman, his wife and her Italian lover, three Swiss, one of whom, a little boy, plays tricks on the other two as they sleep. Next appear four antique cavaliers, imitating a *manège* and tilting, representing true knightly chivalry; they are followed finally by their modern parody, a fashionable riding master. Two new entries then prepare the way for the vision of the Throne of Honour (Figure 9). Concord and the Good Genius, who have returned with the chorus of Beloved People, welcome the king as he appears with his lords. The emblems of the throne are classical heroes surmounting bound captives lying on trophies of armour, shields, antique weapons: the costumes of the masquers are also intended to suggest ancient valour or chivalry. A cloud machine now descends, sent (we have been told in the prefatory note) by Pallas, as patroness of Prudence. The cloud displaces the rocky Throne of Honour, and from it the queen and her companions emerge. Their dress is martial, Amazonian. The two sets of masquers, lords and ladies, dance their entry. Then the king and queen withdraw to their seats under the state, and the scene changes again to the prospect of a great, rich busy city—the urban counterpart of the prosperous pastoral we have seen earlier (Figure 10). And finally

> from the highest part of the heavens came forth a cloud . . . in which were eight persons
> . . . representing the spheres; this joining with two other clouds which appeared at that instant
> full of music, covered all the upper part of the scene, and, at that instant beyond all these, a
> heaven opened full of deities, which celestial prospect with the chorus below filled all the
> whole scene with apparitions and harmony. (458–64)

The "picture qualified with moral philosophy" of the proscenium, we recall, set out a scheme of virtues for the proper government of men's actions. The scheme is both personal, concerned with individual virtue, and public or political; it does not admit the

9. Inigo Jones: "scene of mountaines the way to the seat of honour." Setting for *Salmacida Spolia*, 1640. (Devonshire Collection, Chatsworth.)

10. ". . . the scene was changed into magnificent buildings . . . in the furthest part was a bridge over a river, where many people, coaches, horses, and such like, were seen to pass to and fro. Beyond this on the shore were buildings in perspective, which shooting far from the eye showed as the suburbs of a great city." (*Salmacida Spolia*, Inigo Jones's design for the final scene— the drawing is apparently a copy by John Webb. Devonshire Collection, Chatsworth.)

separation of those domains. Both sets of virtues are summed up in the king's "secret wisdom," the true knowledge to which the false mysteries of Vandergoose the Rosicrucian, leader of the anti-masque, are contrasted. The royal wisdom, moreover, is not only intellectual but also active, a heroic virtue; the king and his companions in the Throne of Honour are knights of old, and the rewards Pallas sends them, the ladies, are Amazonian heroines. The union of Philogenes' wisdom with the gifts of Pallas issues finally in the vision of the great, peaceful city: the masquers celebrate a concord that links men with gods and human activity with the harmony of the spheres. The final song, addressed "by a chorus of all" to the king and queen, begins:

> So musical as to all ears
> Doth seem the music of the spheres,
> Are you unto each other still,
> Tuning your thoughts to either's will.
> All that are harsh, all that are rude,
> Are by your harmony subdued,
> Yet so into obedience wrought,
> As if not forced to it, but taught.
>
> (467–74)

The love of the royal pair embodies the universal concord, and obedience is not forced, but taught. Better the quiet bloodless victory than the destructive glories of war:

> This you discerned, and by your mercy taught,
> Would not, like monarchs that severe have been,
> Invent imperial arts to question thought,
> Nor punish vulgar sickness as a sin.
>
> Nor would your valour, when it might subdue,
> Be hindered of the pleasure to forgive;
> They're worse than overcome, your wisdom knew,
> That needed mercy to have leave to live.

> Since strength of virtues gained you Honour's throne,
> Accept our wonder, and enjoy our praise;
> He's fit to govern there and rule alone
> Whom inward helps, not outward force doth raise.
>
> (368–79)

The masque concludes with reconciliation and forgiveness, insistent themes also of Rubens' ceiling.

II

It is possible that some of the figures on Jones's frontispiece had identifying labels. But how many of the audience, or of the masquers, recognized that a grasshopper was a significant sign expressing *Affection to the Country*, or understood the reference to *Salmacida Spolia*, which is nowhere explained in the text as performed? The changes of scene and the action are reasonably perspicuous; we are given enough in what is spoken or sung to identify the king as Philogenes and Wisdom, the throne as that of Honour—but not enough for us to know the crucial fact that the ladies are the gifts of Pallas, and therefore rewards for the royal virtue of prudence. There is some evidence to suggest that very occasionally at masques copies of the text or descriptions were available, like librettos at opera houses; but such cases were unusual, and the question remains.

Modern readers can, with diligence and luck, read the signification of Renaissance masque figures by tracing their origins in contemporary source-books, or establishing their relationships with other figures that we do understand. Very rarely can we determine what any member of the audience, any contemporary not involved in the planning of the production, made of it all. The very notion of a Renaissance audience is problematical for us. We tend to think of it as constant, culturally homogeneous, functioning as a unit and impervious to the passing of decades. It is true that the audiences for Jacobean and Caroline masques, though hardly unaffected by the passage of forty years, were in certain respects homogeneous, and there are important senses in which any audience functions as a unit. But none of this has to do with the degree of preparation its individual members bring to particular productions. The problem, of course, is not ours alone as we consider certain late Renaissance uses of imagery. It belongs as well to the medievalist: if Panofsky is right, how many people understood the Abbot Suger's endeavours at the Sainte Chapelle? How many could read the programmes of Chartres—or even see all the figures? And yet, each of these artistic phenomena was conceived with the presence of an audience in mind. The English court masque is a special application of a visual language found throughout Europe in ceiling or wall paintings, in churches, palaces, or the most private cabinets of princes, in jewels and embroideries, in all manner of shows, processions, pageants, triumphal entries, or royal funerals.

Modern study of these phenomena, their serious consideration as part of the life of society, and therefore as proper objects of historical attention, first came in 1860, in Jacob

Burckhardt's great *Civilization of the Renaissance in Italy*. Burckhardt was haunted by the idea that in Italy, unlike the north, there already existed a nation and a national culture based on "the free intercourse of all classes."[2] Festivals are, for him, "a higher phase in the life of the people, in which its religious, moral and political ideas took visible shape."[3] Burckhardt dealt with the problem of audiences this way: in Italy, he argued, the populace were universally familiar with the poetical basis of the shows, because they were familiar with their own poetic heritage, celebrating religious and secular heroes. "The majority, too, of the spectators—at least in the cities—understood the meaning of mythological figures, and could guess without much difficulty at the allegorical and historical, which were drawn from sources familiar to the mass of Italians."[4] Burckhardt in 1860 was not really fond of allegory, but the Italian shows had a special quality for him as an index to the nature of the audiences: "the public required them to be clearly and vividly characteristic, since its previous training had fitted it to be a competent critic."[5]

After Burckhardt, the pioneering detailed study of a Renaissance festival was Aby Warburg's essay on the Florentine *intermezzi* produced in 1589 to celebrate the wedding of Ferdinando de' Medici. Like Burckhardt, Warburg found himself confronting the problem of the audience and its response to the allegories; the audience in this case was a special one, since such performances were courtly and not public. For example, the first *intermezzo* showed, with learned reference to Plato, the harmony of the spheres. But Warburg felt that neither the action nor the words could have made the episode intelligible, nor could the splendid symbolic costumes of the actors. "The designer with his exaggerated search for attributes fell into combinations that are both arbitrary and obscure."[6] And contemporary records that Warburg discovered clearly demonstrate that even the courtly spectators, accomplished as they must have been, made little sense of the symbolism. All this Warburg found unsympathetic; he disliked what he calls "the torture of classical texts"[7] that goes into the making of such allegories. Both Warburg and Burckhardt viewed Renaissance mythology and symbolism with firm convictions about what constituted the truly classical; but their discontent with Renaissance spectacles, and their concomitant assumptions about the nature of Renaissance audiences, go deeper, to the very nature of the imagery itself.

III

Let us now turn to two Renaissance opinions; for in fact discontent of this sort was not new. The greatest of the Stuart processions was the royal entry of King James into the city of London in 1604. The City companies, on whom most of the expenses fell, commissioned Ben Jonson and Thomas Dekker to devise the shows that greeted the king as he passed through the streets. These were, for the most part, triumphal arches, what the Elizabethans understood as classical emblems suitable to a conquering emperor, together with brief poems or songs to explain the meaning of the displays. The first of Dekker's devices (it was not in fact used) involved a meeting of reconciliation between Saints

11. Stephen Harrison, *The Archs of Triumph . . . at his Maiesties Entrance and passage through his Honorable Citty & chamber of London vpon the 13th day of march 1603.* The Fenchurch arch, representing London.

George and Andrew, patron saints of England and Scotland respectively, and a speech of welcome by the *Genius Loci*, the spirit of London. When Dekker published his account of the show, he wrote as follows about his figure of *Genius*:

> To make a false flourish here with the borrowed weapons of all the old Maisters of the noble Science of Poesie, and to keepe a tyrannical coyle, in Anatomizing *Genius*, from head to foote, (only to shew how nimbly we can carve up the whole messe of the Poets) were to play the Executioner, and to lay our Cities household God on the rack, to make him confesse, how many paire of Latin sheets, we have shaken and cut into shreds to make him a garment. Such feates of Activitie are stale, and common among Schollears, (before whome it is protested we come not now (in a Pageant) to Play a Maisters prize). For *Nunc ego ventosae Plebis suffragia venor* [it is the votes of the windy people I am hunting now].
>
> The multitude is now to be our Audience, whose heads would miserably runne a wooll-gathering, if we doo but offer to breake them with hard words.[8]

Erudition and historical accuracy, Dekker claims, and their attendant obscurities, are self-defeating in this sort of entertainment. Dekker had apparently been criticised for making his *Genius* into a woman, hence the defensiveness of the tone. But the passage is not merely defensive; it is also an energetic attack on the poetic methods of his collaborator Jonson. In Jonson's Fenchurch arch, which represented London (Figure 11), the *Genius of the City* is, correctly, male (Figure 12). He carries a careful selection of attributes derived, Jonson explains in the published account, from Giraldi's encyclopedia of classical mythology and Rosinus' compendium on the antiquities of Rome. The scholarly requirements are scrupulously observed; this is a point to which I shall return.

12. The Genius of London. (Detail of Figure 11.)

Here we should note only that there is nothing at all defensive about Jonson's exposition of his aims:

> Neither was it becoming, or could it stand with the dignitie of these shewes (after the most miserable and desperate shift of the Puppits) to require a Truch-man [narrator], or (with the ignorant Painter) one to write, *This is a Dog*; or, *This is a Hare*: but so to be presented, as upon the view, they might, without cloud, or obscuritie, declare themselues to the sharpe and learned: And for the multitude, no doubt but their grounded iudgements did gaze, said it was fine, and were satisfied.[9]

Clearly Jonson's sense of his audience differs radically from Dekker's. But the common-sense tone of this passage conceals some very interesting assumptions. Why *should* the ignorant multitude have said that Jonson's arcane and scholarly symbolism "was fine"? Reaction to the incomprehensible, after all, can be resentment, and despite the crowds of commoners, the show was designed for royal and courtly eyes. An even stranger case is presented by the annual Lord Mayor's Shows in the City, pageantry designed not for the nobility, but for the citizens of London. This audience was not courtly or learned, yet as the century progresses we see in these celebrations the development of an increasingly esoteric imagery. In Middleton's *Triumphs of Truth* in 1613, for example, the figures included an emblem of ferocity—the rhinoceros—from Valeriano's *Hieroglyphica*, the animals symbolizing the five senses—the eagle, hart, spider, ape, dog—from Ripa's *Iconologia*, and the central figure of Truth, deriving from one of Jonson's most elaborate court allegories, and laden with abstruse attributes.[10] If indeed the multitude "said it was fine, and were satisfied" that is an important fact about English Renaissance culture: in an age when the marvelous was a subject of the highest poetic theorizing, the appeal of mysteries and wonders at this level should not be underestimated. Nor the marvelous quality of matters associated with the learned and the courtly; nor is it unlikely that ambitious Lord Mayors and ambitious City companies should wish to deploy imagery associated with the court, still the central social phenomenon of the age.

IV

I wish to turn now to a different kind of illustrative example, an anecdote from a collection of *Imprese* published by a Venetian man of letters, Camillo Camilli, in 1586. It concerns an English gentleman named Sir Arrigo Lee, who can only be Elizabeth's famous courtier Sir Henry Lee, though the story appears to have escaped his biographers. Lee had been in Venice and the Veneto several times, and it is perfectly possible that Camilli had met him; I am concerned here, however, not with questions of biographical veracity, but with the style and mode of thought revealed by the story. At Elizabeth's court Sir Henry Lee was the master of the Italianate arts of pageantry; he was responsible for devising and promoting the most important ceremonial occasions devoted to the glorification of the queen, particularly the annual tilts celebrating her accession day.

Here is Sir Arrigo's *impresa*, or device (Figure 13). Camilli explains it as follows:

> The passion of love belongs not only to the concupiscible part of the soul, but also to the irascible. Experience teaches us, indeed, that we are more roused to anger by persons whom we love than by those with whom we are not united or linked by some bond of love or friendship. It often happens, however, that anger does not drive love from the heart, but has power only to enter there and make war with love. Hence rises in the souls of lovers battles and reversals of position between those two most powerful passions, as one struggles for mastery over the other. And hence it often happens that from anger or the acts of anger a lover passes once again to redoubled and stronger acts of love. Hence the comic poet wrote, "The wrath of lovers is the

renewal of love." Love kept for a time within limits by its opposite revives when its strength returns with increased ardour, and rules more powerfully than before in the heart where it resides . . . . I have said so much as is relevant to my explanation of what the individual who

13. Sir Henry Lee's *impresa*,
from Camillo Camilli, *Imprese*, Venice 1586.

uses the *impresa* intends. For I know that it was invented by its author in a period when he found himself in just such an agitation of mind, that between love and hate; body and soul seemed at war. It was clearly invented by him when anger had mastery over love and made him long for freedom, and not when love had mastery over anger and made him wish a reconciliation. I should tell you that some years ago this noble knight left his native England and came to Italy, hoping perhaps, under the pretence of a search for pleasure, that distance would strengthen his anger and so free him from the snares of love. After a few months' sojourn here he returned to England. A short time passed and he came back again to Italy, went to stay in Venice, remained for a short time; and one day, on the spur of the moment, not one of his friends having any idea why, decided to depart and go to England. During his journey he took for his *impresa* this greyhound dragging its chain behind it and carrying in its mouth one of those caps that were once called Liberty Caps. He added this motto: *E Temo Non Adopre* [I fear he will not use it]. From what I have told you it is evident that he figured himself in the dog, dragging that chain in the act of flight with a cap of liberty in its mouth, to show his hope that this heart was justifiably alienated from some lady he had been in love with, but that he also did not feel himself so free from that passion that he was not hourly, against his will, forced to love her still. And this much is shown too by those two journeys made so quickly, one after another, to Italy. Finding after the second that he could no longer hold out, nor live any longer far away from his beloved; caught between feeling himself free and feeling himself driven afresh to see her, he wished by his choice of that motto to declare that he now despaired of being able to sustain that freedom which he had gained for himself by flight and distance; and yet that he knew he had almost won it. The figure of the dog that has escaped and has the cap in its mouth, but still drags the chain, which makes it easier to recapture, declares or delineates (and is a most admirable comparison for) the state and the soul of a person who, being almost free, is terrified of falling yet again into the slavery of love, and who, as the words of the motto indicate, has no power to sustain the freedom he has recovered, and is in danger of losing it again.[11]

Sir Henry Lee's image is technically an *impresa*, a term for which no precise English equivalent ever became current. John Florio in his Italian-English dictionary *Queen Anna's New World of Words* (1611) defines *impresa* thus: "An attempt, an enterprise, an undertaking. Also an impresse, a word, a mot or emblem. Also a jewell worne in ones hat, with some devise in it."[12] We may see from this how fluid the terminology was. The kind of imagery we are considering comes from many sources: books on classical myth, usually intended as general handbooks and containing allegorical expositions of the gods and their stories; monographs or encyclopedias of classical antiquities, coins and medals, works of art; collections of images—hieroglyphs, emblems, *imprese*—and iconologies, systems of images. All these kinds flow into each other, as do the sources and traditions they exploit; it is a mistake to be too curious in distinguishing the kinds. A vast literature has grown up about hieroglyphs, *imprese*, emblems, in which distinctions are sought, multiplied, abandoned; but the breadth of Florio's definition speaks for itself.

The first meaning of the term is *attempt, enterprise, undertaking*; in some way this form is for the Renaissance as the *essay* is to a later age. Florio then equates it with *emblem*; what the two had in common was the combination of picture and motto or legend; but Florio also treats *impresa* as synonymous with *word* or *mot*—with the motto itself. And finally, an *impresa* is a *device*—or rather the jewel that bears the device—to wear in one's hat. We might compare this brief variety of definitions with the much grander claims made by the most important encyclopedia of imagery in the age, Giovanni Pierio Valeriano's *Hieroglyphica*, first published in 1556 and frequently reissued in increasingly expanded editions. The title-page includes a passage that reads as follows:

> In this book of commentaries you have an explication not only of various pictures, coins and ancient inscriptions, but also, what is more, of the Egyptian and most other mysteries, as well as, to add to your entertainment, an immense store of commonplaces [i.e. *topoi*]; further, a curious interpretation of holy scripture, in which not infrequently we find both Christ himself and the apostles and prophets making use of expressions of this kind; so that, most significantly, you may understand how Pythagoras, Plato, and other illustrious men went to the Egyptians for their manner of teaching, inasmuch as to speak in hieroglyphs is to reveal the nature of things human and divine.

The great vogue for hieroglyphs dates from early in the sixteenth century, with the publication of a collection of genuine though late Egyptian images, *The Hieroglyphics of Horapollo*, together with their interpretations—though the latter were, for the most part, incorrect. By the end of the century, as the wonderful compendiousness of Valeriano's title-page demonstrates, the hieroglyph had become the centre of an extraordinary variety of intellectual and spiritual traditions: "to speak in hieroglyphs is to reveal the nature of things human and divine." Or rather, we may feel, to conceal it; the attraction of these figures for the Renaissance lay in their obscurity, the necessity for interpretation. They were held to be images devised by the Egyptian priests to preserve, and convey secretly, a hidden wisdom too sacred to be revealed to the multitude. From them, says Valeriano's publisher, Plato and Pythagoras learned. Sustaining all this is the powerful notion of the other hidden wisdom, clothed also in myth, which God had divulged to the gentiles, and which prefigures his sacred revelations. The parables and dark sayings of scripture are also hieroglyphs. We should note too the significant conjunction of this imagery with the commonplaces of rhetoric, a point to which we shall return.

Recent criticism has correctly focused on the concept of hidden wisdom in the Renaissance, and with this has come a re-emphasis—in effect a re-discovery—of the hermetic tradition, specifically magical and religious, in which the role of the image is a powerful one. Probably the most influential single study of the image and its meaning in the period has been E. H. Gombrich's essay *Icones Symbolicae: The Visual Image in Neo-Platonic Thought* (1948).[13] Gombrich is concerned to show that in the hermetic tradition visual imagery has a particular sacredness; that the image not only *represents*, but captures something of, or participates in the nature of, what is represented. Such a belief depends on seeing the universe as a single hierarchical structure, a unified whole. What had troubled Burckhardt and Warburg about the abstruseness of Renaissance symbolism, about the insistent preference throughout the ages for arcane imagery over explanation, is at the heart of Gombrich's argument:

> The vogue of the hieroglyph and emblem and the whole wealth of pictorial symbolism which followed on the Neo-Platonic movement can hardly be understood except against this background. The gravity with which the casuistry of the emblem and device was discussed by otherwise perfectly sane and intelligent people remains an inexplicable freak of fashion unless we understand that for them a truth condensed into a visual image was somehow nearer the realm of absolute truth than one explained in words. It was not what these images said that made them important, but the fact that what was said was also "represented".[14]

Renaissance iconographic methodology was, of course, much less straightforward than this passage suggests. For example, Tasso, in a treatise on *imprese*, explains that to represent things divine one must use dissimilars, not likenesses, because as Dionysius the Areopagite has shown, it is *negations* that are true of God, not affirmations—the divine is the most hidden, *Deus Absconditus*.[15] Tasso instances the Egyptian representation of God by a crocodile: when the crocodile is underwater a subtle veil falls from its forehead, so that while it can see, it cannot be seen. This is appropriate for God, who sees but is unseen.[16] The example illustrates, among other things, the difficulties of taking Renaissance theoretical statements on such matters at face value. We begin with the definition of the divine through dissimilars; but however unlike God a crocodile may initially appear to be, we in fact end with a rationalistic explanation of their similarities, and it is on this that the appropriateness of the hieroglyph depends. Tasso has, of course, misunderstood the Areopagite's dictum, which says simply that God is *not like anything*; but his own point is that even the most unlikely juxtapositions may serve as revelations of the essential unity of creation.

V

These are the methods that Camillo Camilli used, too, when he set out to expound Sir Henry Lee's device. The exposition of sacred mysteries, the revelation of "the nature of things human and divine," was equally relevant to less solemn matters. The notion of style, the concepts of roles and play are relevant here. In strongly hierarchical societies, the principle of decorum has ethical and political implications, as well as artistic and social ones, and roles are, in a sense, prescribed, necessary. Camilli's Italy and Lee's England were societies of this kind. In such a hierarchy it follows that the *class* is more important than the individual whose role is to be a member of it; the behaviour of fathers, sons, lovers, princes is generalized and abstracted, and only thereby known and comprehended. But individuals are not abstractions; and so individuals in such societies are most often presented not as representatives of particular classes, but as personifications: the abstract society—its ethics, morals, politics—is reconstituted through figures like Paternal Care, Filial Piety, True Love, Magnanimity—or Britomart, Gloriana, Astraea. With the social hierarchy goes a hierarchical scheme of values, the faculties, appetites, vices, virtues. Some of these are tied to certain particular classes, some are of universal application. The hierarchies fit together, their unity dependent on a coherent scheme of abstraction; and the translation of the whole abstract system into a set of *roles* is not only easy but necessary if the society is to function.

Now let us look again at Sir Henry Lee's device. It would be wrong, I think, to say that the emblem *expresses* his situation as lover, seeking to be free yet fearing that he is not. Rather it externalizes or dramatizes his situation, establishing a role that is both representative of similarly unhappy lovers and capable of being related to a body of relevant abstractions. To draw this relationship is the purpose of Camilli's preliminary remarks about love and hate. Of course this sort of thing will make sense only within a particular kind of group—one that is willing to accept externalizations of this kind as meaningful, to take them as definitions of real situations. For the device does not exist by itself; it has to be read; moreover, it has to be difficult to read. To read it is a kind of play, and its function is to define the group that *can* play—to establish the group's sense of coherence, identity, and security. Hence the *impresa*'s associations with chivalry, with antiquity, with hieroglyphs and the shared rituals of ancient mysteries: all are elitist, abstruse, exclusive.

Abstractions are not only pictorial. Tasso talks about his crocodile not so much as an image but as a figure in rhetoric; this is how Camilli deals with Lee's device as well. And we recall that the title page of Valeriano's *Hieroglyphica* includes a reference to the figurative language of scripture, and the promise of a storehouse of rhetorical commonplaces or *topoi*. On the title page of the most influential of all collections of images, Cesare Ripa's *Iconologia*, first published in 1593, the author asserts that it will be useful to poets, as well as to painters and sculptors, for the representation of the virtues, vices, affections and passions. Gombrich alludes to the existence of the rhetorical tradition in iconology, but does not explore it. Nevertheless, the assimilation of the visual image to the verbal figure is, for the age, a crucial point.

VI

Masques should provide us with extreme cases of the functioning of such imagery, but in fact they are very difficult to deal with. First of all we are hampered by an unusual scantiness of theoretical discussion; and then the masque, being a mixed and unstable form, tends to defy generalization. The most coherent body of masques was created by Ben Jonson, and it is difficult to avoid taking the Jonsonian masque as the norm, and, even more problematically, taking the texts of the masques as the masques themselves. The very distinction of recent literary studies in this area brings home to us the limits of what one can do with words alone. The masque was not only verbal—it was not even primarily verbal. It was spectacular, it was choreographic, it was musical. The masque audience was also very special; at court the presence of royalty, both as active masquers and seated in state, created a unique situation. The interaction of audience and entertainment at such a production was an enormously complex phenomenon.

If, with Gombrich in mind, we are looking for a coherent, widely accepted Renaissance theory of the image and its role in the masque, we shall not find one. Nor shall we even find much help in explaining the relationship between visual and verbal elements: the texts rarely move beyond descriptions of costumes and settings. Ben Jonson and Inigo Jones, poet and designer, had a famous quarrel about their respective parts and responsibilities in the masques on which they collaborated. I have written in detail about this, and I shall only briefly touch on the main points here: the crux of the argument was that both were in effect making the same claims, claims to *invention*. Invention is the word for finding the subject of the masque; this comes from the technical vocabulary of rhetoric, and as such belonged to the poet: *inventio* was the first and most difficult part of poetry. But Inigo Jones, an architect on the new model, profoundly influenced by Italian discussions about architecture as a liberal art, claimed the same vocabulary: *invention* belonged to him too, and so did a newer and grander word, *design*, which meant the idea, the first mental act, of which any structure was only the embodiment. Collaborators like Sir William Davenant and Aurelian Townshend were willing to let Jones claim the invention of their masques. George Chapman described his one collaboration with the architect, *The Memorable Masque of the Middle Temple and Lincoln's Inn*, as "ancient and authentical poesy," but also said that it had been "invented and fashioned" by Jones. Jonson, at least to begin with, was cautious in his assertions. There is a celebrated passage in *Hymenaei* (1606) in which the relationships of verbal and visual are discussed:

It is a noble and iust aduantage, that the things subiected to vnderstanding haue of those which are obiected to sense, that the one sort are but momentarie, and meerely taking; the other impressing, and lasting: Else the glorie of all these solemnities had perish'd like a blaze, and gone out, in the beholders eyes. So short-liu'd are the bodies of all things, in comparison of their soules. And, though bodies oft-times haue the ill luck to be sensually preferr'd, they find afterwards, the good fortune (when soules liue) to be vtterly forgotten. This it is hath made the most royall Princes, and greatest persons (who are commonly the personaters of these actions) not onely studious of riches and magnificence in the outward celebration, or shew; (which rightly becomes them) but curious after the most high, and heartie inuentions, to furnish the inward parts: (and those grounded vpon antiquitie, and solide learnings) which, though their voyce be taught to sound to present occasions, their sense, or doth, or should alwayes lay hold on more remov'd mysteries. And, howsoeuer some may squemishly crie out, that all endeuour of learning, and sharpnesse in these transitorie deuices especially, where it steps beyond their little, or (let me wrong 'hem) no braine at all, is superfluous; I am contented, these fastidious stomachs should leaue my full tables, and enioy at home, their cleane emptie trenchers, fittest for such ayrie tasts: where perhaps a few Italian herbs, pick'd vp, and made into a sallade, may find sweeter acceptance, than all, the most nourishing, and sound meates of the world.[17]

The central body-soul figure here comes from theoretical literature on *imprese* or emblems, where it has a sharp technical significance: the body is the visual image, the soul is the motto or legend accompanying it. Jonson is talking about the masque as a kind of emblem, only in this case the picture is transitory and the words remain. The term *soul* also appears in treatises on poetics as equivalent to *invention*, or *fiction*, or *fable*. So far Jonson's case seems clear; but the figure, if we press further, grows more complex.[18] It is true that the soul, in Platonic and Platonized Christian terms, is the *form* of the body, and souls are thus doubtless superior to bodies; yet, as Aquinas often tells us, the soul requires the body in order to achieve the true perfection if its nature—we are created *body and soul*. As to the primacy of the image over the word, there is in fact little support for Gombrich's thesis among the emblem writers—Tasso even asserts that Egyptian hieroglyphs, the very language of images, may well have been accompanied by words.[19] Renaissance treatises on psychology and perception disagree on the matter. On the one hand, sight is regularly ranked highest among the senses; on the other, speech is the vehicle of *ratio*, reason, our highest faculty. Hooker argues that important public actions must be marked by "some visible solemnity" because "words, both because they are common, and do not so strongly move the fancy of man, are for the most part but slightly heard,"[20] and Jonson himself says of painting that "it doth so enter, and penetrate the inmost affection . . . as sometimes it orecomes the power of speech, and oratory."[21] Ficino, nevertheless, is quite unequivocal: the Word is higher than the Image.[22] Nothing in Shakespeare's use of "image," "imagine," "imagination" suggests the presence in England of any widespread feeling about images of the sort that Gombrich describes. Part of the trouble is, of course, that we know so little about the etymology of these words (in any language); and from the beginning, even in antiquity, the terminology for talking about artefacts, representations, verbal constructs and mental happenings involves a bewildering confusion of synonyms. What is one to make, for example, of a passage like this: "The conceits of the mind are Pictures of things, and the tongue is the Interpreter of those Pictures . . ."?[23]

There was certainly, for the Elizabethans, an area of ambiguity, powerful in its applications, about the relationship between name and thing, representation and object—even name and person. And there were no doubt extreme cases: Chapman may well have thought his dark conceits imbued with the divine, and Ficino may, in some real sense, have worshipped Apollo and believed in amulets. But I suspect that such instances are extraordinary, and that the "removed mysteries" which Jonson held that masques dealt with are more readily explained. For if the relation between *name* and *thing* is not quite clear in the period, neither is the relation between *image* and what the image is *of*: an image does not exist by itself; it is an image *of* something. The preposition takes on a peculiar force when we are dealing with dramatized and enacted images, especially in such a group as performed and observed the masque.

The question of illusion in the masque is very complex. Let us look again at *Salmacida Spolia*: is there not a paradox in Inigo Jones's decision to produce so elaborately symbolic a statement in so strikingly realistic a setting? The tempest, the pastoral, the cityscape were obviously triumphs of theatrical illusion; but they functioned like the whole action, emblematically or allegorically, not realistically. Their true reality, that is, lay in their *meaning*. This quality is, in fact, basic to the nature of the masque as a form. In the same way, the king impersonates Philogenes, and Secret Wisdom, and an antique hero; the queen and her ladies, in their martial dress, are ancient heroines and the gifts of Pallas. But every member of the audience knows who they "really" are, and it is that knowledge, indeed, that gives their symbolic roles their meaning. After the final dance the hero and heroine move out of the action by taking their places as king and queen under the state; so far we should say the theatrical illusion is broken. But the masque continues; the final song is sung to them, hailing them as types and teachers, through their own concord, of domestic and social harmony. Has the illusion been broken? Should we not rather say that through their status as man and wife, personifications of true love, king and queen, the masque has extended itself beyond the theatre? Even the roles are still visible; Charles and Henrietta Maria are still dressed as ancient hero and Amazonian heroine.

The masque is a form in which the audience is required to be aware, consciously, all the time, of the performer beneath the role; to know that the king is king, and to take his various impersonations as translations of that basic, true identity. The roles he takes are real—as real as the role of king—because they are ways of defining his identity within the society; every role is true, in the sense that it is an abstraction, a personification of his qualities. The audience's participation is crucial; even if they do not join in the dance, they join in the play. They are bound together by their capacity to understand, and the masque, like the *impresa* on a smaller scale, functions to define their identity too, to assert their existence as a social group, and to guarantee—even in 1640—their security.

Finally let us confront yet again the most difficult question of all: what did such images, such disguises, confer on those who used them? Masques are often described by modern critics as acts of mimetic magic, as exorcism. This seems to me utterly misguided. I take as my general case the assumption of the forms of classical antiquity, and Rubens once more as my specific instance.

14. Portrait of Gaspar de Guzman, Count of Olivares. (Engraving by P. Pontius after Rubens.)

Here is an engraved portrait Rubens did for the Spanish minister Count Olivares (Figure 14). The statesman is supported by emblems of Minerva (spear, shield, owl) and Hercules (club and lion's skin). And here is Olivares' letter to Rubens, showing that he knew how to read the emblems of the goddess and the hero:

> As for the emblems, I can tell you that now I am freed of temporal and personal cares I am more than ever obliged to give a good account of the public affairs that have been entrusted to me. May God grant me the light and the strength needed for my task, and then I think I shall prize the portrait at its worth, and that its auguries are not entirely false.[24]

Are the emblems in this portrait anything more than conventional signs for abstract concepts? Were the figures of Hercules and Minerva merely clues to be deciphered and discarded, while the statesman's compliment or adjuration remained? I read in them something more. Rubens placed a similar conjunction of deities on his own house in Antwerp, itself a physical sign of the artist's conquest of his social world: it is crowned with the figures of Mercury and Minerva, persistent emblems throughout the imagery of Rubens' entire *oeuvre*. What more did these figures express than eloquence and wisdom; how were they more than such a motto as "Better diplomacy than war"?

We may start with simple things. To dominate his home Rubens chose two classical statues; he had long been a collector of antiquities, and wished his house to echo, in its northern way, something of the antique. We can see in this the externalization, the signalling, of a role: the collector, the rich amateur, the diplomatist—an extraordinary role for a painter, and one that Rubens made acceptable in the world of Renaissance Flanders.

But Rubens was more than a collector: he was a scholar as well, a classicist in the sense that Jonson was. Both artists had learned the great lesson of Renaissance humanist scholarship: that the ancient world existed as an entity, a separate, distanced, autonomous cultural domain—not merely a compendium from which fragments could be taken over and transmogrified, with no sense of context, of historical and cultural distance. This attitude toward the past was, in the period, relatively new. Rubens' passionate wish to grasp and revivify that past, of which, through rediscovery and effort he was a legitimate heir, is consonant with Jonson's passionate wish to hold Rome and London together in a single image, and to re-enact in England the role of Roman poet. It is terribly difficult for us to feel the force of that re-enactment, to sense the passion and the validity of the effort. Jonson had to get the figure of Genius on his Fenchurch arch right according to all the most learned authorities, not for magical or allegorical reasons, but for historical ones. And so with his mythologies: anything else was a falsification, and the Renaissance classicist was prepared to exploit, but not to falsify antiquity. The classical world, that most prized of ancient cultures, had to be got right because it was real and recoverable. Olivares' emblems were those of Hercules and Minerva not as simple allegorical signs, but because they carried with them the weight of history, and of the historical imagination, to admonish and aggrandize this particular modern statesman by giving him a role in that realized past. Rubens' household god and goddess are of the same order. They are not signs. They are figures that embody, as much through their accuracy as through their grace and grandeur, the power of that true, historical, ideal domain—the power of *sancrosancta vetustas*, holy antiquity. Crowning his house with them, Rubens asserts his role, and thereby his identity. This is not an act of allegory or magic. It is a declaration, a substantiation, the creation of a self.

Rubens and the Whitehall Ceiling

I

In 1620 Thomas Howard, Earl of Arundel, commissioned a portrait of his wife by Rubens. The choice of the painter reveals both taste and awareness; Arundel was the first great English collector and patron in the modern sense, the man whom Horace Walpole was to call "the father of *vertu* in England."[1] In his own time he was recognized as a connoisseur of ancient and modern art, and his house was an important centre for artistic activity. Four years before Arundel employed Rubens, in 1616, a certain William Smith, an English artist unknown to fame—and the name itself seems to introduce the plain realities of English life—wrote to the Earl requesting his patronage:

> Rememberinge the great love and affection which your Honor beareth to the misterie of paintinge (which I profess) . . . I make bould at this tyme, havinge seene the best workman-shippe in france, Germany and Italien, and beinge at this instante at Rome . . . to make tender of my selfe and service unto your Lordship, as that noble personadge whom I most honor. In that misterie, I am sure, I can doe somethinge . . . . I will be readye if your Honor have any occasion to use payntinge, or Statues in stone, or metall, to showe as well the readines of my affection, as the best of my skill . . . .[2]

Let us pause over that word *mystery*; William Smith may serve as the index to a significant transition in the history of art. In 1620, in Florence, the decorations of the Casa Buonarotti were being completed, devised and supervised by Michelangelo's nephew; this was the first house contrived as a museum and memorial to a painter. The decorative scheme was programmatic, designed (as Professor Wittkower has shown) to perpetuate a version of

ESEQVIE DEL DIVINO
MICHELAGNOLO
BVONARROTI
Celebrate in Firenze dall'Accademia de
Pittori, scultori, & Ar-
chitettori.
Nella Chiesa di S.Lorenzo il di 14 Luglio
MDLXIIII.

IN FIRENZE
Appresso i Giunti 1564.
Con Priuilegio.

15. *Obsequies of the Divine
Michelangelo*: title-page.

Michelangelo's achievement; it took its inspiration from the extraordinary celebrations of Michelangelo's death in 1564 – extraordinary because these were devised for an artist, sculptor, painter, architect, poet.[3] The title page of the pamphlet describing those obsequies characterizes the artist as "The *Divine* Michelangelo" (Figure 15): the epithet, more than mere hyperbole, preserves something very serious. Behind it lies principally the great polemical and theoretical endeavour that informs Vasari's *Lives*, that astonishing document which was to dominate, even in reactions against it, European views of the history of the arts and the role of the artist for centuries to come. The epithet *divine* reflects not only Vasari's view of Michelangelo as the supreme artist, but a complex of powerful ethical, psychological, metaphysical, theological assumptions as well, relating the artist to the *demiurge*, partaking, in his role of seer and image-maker, of the nature of the creator of all images.

In those elaborate obsequies staged in the church of San Lorenzo, Benedetto Varchi, official rhetorician for the Medici and for the role of poet and artist, described how Michelangelo habitually passed his time "all by himself, contemplating now the most secret mysteries of art and now the mysterious secrets of nature."[4] Painting for Varchi is a mystery, as it is for William Smith; but the two are worlds apart. Smith is using *mystery* in its medieval sense, relating to the organization of craftsmen into a guild, primarily for protection. In England the painters and stainers had amalgamated in 1502, and this company was active, at least during the Jacobean and Caroline years, principally in attempts to prevent lucrative commissions from going to imported European artists.

Michelangelo's obsequies too were intimately connected with the politics of a guild of artists.[5] But this body based its claims on very different premises. The celebrants of the ceremonies describe themselves as "the Academy of Painters, Sculptors and Architects"; this was the *Accademia del Disegno*, founded in 1563, the year before Michelangelo's death. It was an *academy*, not a guild, based on the model of the many literary and learned academies that had already become such important institutions in the organization of Italian intellectual life; and it embodied the claim that artists belonged to the world of the liberal arts, not to the world of crafts or mechanics. Behind this claim was a long and important dispute. The word *disegno*, now taken as the gift that unites painting, sculpture and architecture, and validates their assertion of the status of *arts*, bears in the Renaissance a complex weight of doctrine. In the England of James and Charles the term *design* figures largely (and contemptuously) as a new-fangled bit of jargon in Ben Jonson's long quarrel with Inigo Jones, the first English artist to claim this new role after the Italian fashion. Their quarrel was a version of earlier Italian disputes, and Jonson's intention in it was to strip away Jones's pretences to the liberal arts and reduce him to his proper role as craftsman—or, as Jonson put it, carpenter.

In Italy, the new artists won—officially in 1571. Members of the Academy were exempted from membership in the guilds, and the institutionalization of the special role of "artist" was formally effected. Thus the general theme of the paintings unveiled in the Casa Buonarotti in 1620 was not simply the glorification of the artist, but more particularly the assertion of his social status. For example, we may see there Michelangelo being received in Venice by the Doge himself, or again, Michelangelo showing Pope Julius III an architectural model: the artist is seated alongside the Pope, while the entourage of high prelates and gentlemen stand.

II

"In manner," we are told of Rubens, "he was impressive—yet human—and *nobile*; he usually wore a gold chain round his neck; and he would go riding through the city like other *Cavalieri* and persons of title; and by this sort of decorum Rubens sustained in Flanders the nobility of the name of painter."[6] And about 1628, so a scholar official of Antwerp wrote, noting the city's right to be proud of citizens like Rubens and the humanist Balthasar Moretus, "their houses will evoke the astonishment of the visitors as well as their admiration"[7] (Figure 16). Indeed, that god-crowned portico, souvenir of Italy, leading into Rubens' house, demonstrates notions of the artist and his role that are exceedingly remote from England—from anything that, say, New Place in Stratford demonstrated, except in one respect: success. In 1635 Rubens became a country gentleman as well with the purchase of the Château de Steen. This was the year his ceiling was installed in the Banqueting House at Whitehall; five years earlier Charles I had knighted him, the first artist to be so honoured.

That description of Rubens' state and decorum comes from Bellori's life of him; and the whole burden and tenor of Bellori's biography, in 1672, is the position of the artist. His account is directed to those claims long since made in Italy, and is stated in terms of

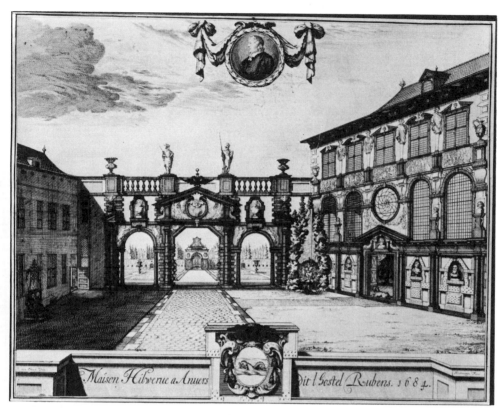

16. Rubens' house in 1684.
Engraving by Harrewyn. (Antwerp, Rubenshaus.)

the old dispute about whether painting is a *liberal* or a *mechanical* art. In ancient times, Bellori tells us, painting was honoured as "something divine." The Athenians, wisest of the Greeks, numbered painting with the liberal arts. In modern times, in spite of the honours painting has won, it is too often considered *mechanical* and *vile*.[8] But Rubens for Bellori is a great example of one who ennobled painting. In fact, Rubens was a very remarkable case in the story of the relationship between artist and patron. Learned, a scholar and friend of scholars, a gentleman, living like a gentleman, his career could be seen as enacting those new claims for the arts, which did or should have affected the style of that whole relationship. And there is something more. Much though he loved and honoured painting, and although he was to give a knighthood to Van Dyck, Charles's knighthood for Rubens in 1630 is not to be seen as the equivalent of Philip of Spain stooping to pick up Titian's brush, or of Francesco de'Medici offering a chair to Michelangelo, those favourite exempla in the history of the treatment of great artists by their patrons. Writing in the last years of his life, in the late 1890's, in that singularly beautiful little book *A Memoir on Rubens*, Jacob Burckhardt admonished his readers thus:

> The historians of art have to resign themselves to the fact that one of the greatest of their luminaries was indeed a clear, a *shining* figure, not mysterious, not 'numinous'. His very

appearance inspired confidence and understanding. He was a man of wide and general education, able to establish contact with important people in all walks of life.[9]

It is true that the skill with which Rubens so clearly arranged his life and his work extended to a peculiar ability in the negotiating of public affairs; and involved a deep concern, I believe, for some parts of them, that is not to be attributed only to ambition, even though success was clearly dear to him. Rubens' career as diplomatist and negotiator began early; and it was on the diplomatist as much as on the painter—or primarily on the diplomatist—that Charles conferred his English title. There were to be later, but much later, artists who occupied the kind of social position that Bellori admired, but I cannot think of one whose status was precisely like that of Rubens for so much of his life: whose genius and role as painter fed into this particular sort of political activity; and whose political activity fed into his art, not simply in the sense of getting him great commissions, but informing the manner and meaning of those great paintings that resulted. For a Marie de Medici or a Charles I, to commission some great conspicuous suite of state paintings from Rubens was a delicate, complex affair.

III

It is of course still, even now, notoriously hard for us to believe that a great painting can have, could ever have had, a political purpose. Notoriously hard, equally, even now, for us to read, let alone take seriously, the language of such paintings. There is an allegory now in the National Gallery, that Rubens painted before he left London in March 1630, as a farewell present for Charles I (see Figure 1). It should be compared with another allegory, painted about 1637/8, and commonly known as *The Horrors of War* (Figure 17). The latter picture is the subject of a very well known letter from Rubens to a fellow painter, which I must quote at length.

> As for the subject of the picture, it is very clear, so that with the little I wrote to you about it at the beginning, the remainder will perhaps make itself better understood to your experienced eye, than through my explanation. Nevertheless, in order to obey you, I will describe it in a few words.
>
> The principal figure is Mars, who has left the open temple of Janus (which in time of peace, according to Roman custom, remained closed) and rushes forth with shield and bloodstained sword, threatening the people with great disaster. He pays little heed to Venus, his mistress, who, accompanied by her Amors and Cupids, strives with caresses and embraces to hold him. From the other side, Mars is dragged forward by the Fury Alekto, with a torch in her hand. Nearby are monsters personifying Pestilence and Famine, those inseparable partners of War. On the ground, turning her back, lies a woman with a broken lute, representing Harmony, which is incompatible with the discord of War. There is also a mother with her child in her arms, indicating that fecundity, procreation, and charity are thwarted by War, which corrupts and destroys everything. In addition, one sees an architect thrown on his back with his instruments in his hand, to show that that which in time of peace is constructed for the use and

ornamentation of the City, is hurled to the ground by the force of arms and falls to ruin. I believe, if I remember rightly, that you will find on the ground under the feet of Mars a book as well as a drawing on paper, to imply that he treads underfoot all the arts and letters. There ought also to be a bundle of darts or arrows, with the band which held them together undone; these when bound form the symbol of Concord. Beside them is the *caduceus* and olive-branch, attributes of Peace; these also are cast aside. That grief-stricken woman clothed in black, with torn veil, robbed of all her jewels and other ornaments, is the unfortunate Europe who, for so many years now, has suffered plunder, outrage and misery, which are so injurious to everyone that it is unnecessary to go into detail. Europe's attribute is the globe, borne by a small angel or genius, and surmounted by the cross, to symbolize the Christian world.[10]

17. Rubens, *The Horrors of War*. (London, National Gallery.)

That such an explanation should have been required at all involves questions that I can hardly touch on here; and I bring forward this letter only to show *how* we are to read the figurative language of such paintings. The peace of the Christian world, all the creations of the civil, the human life, are shattered by War. Look now at Rubens' gift to Charles I (Figure 1). There is little authority for the titles of so many of Rubens' pictures, and I call this *Prudence* (or *Wisdom*) *Defending Peace from War*. Minerva — *Prudence* or *Wisdom* — is turning a reluctant Mars, accompanied by some horrid Fury, away from his intended victims, the children who are being crowned by the torch-bearing Love, and are being offered the fruits of plenty by a domesticated satyr, while a leopard, tame as a cat, plays with the cornucopia. The wild creatures are innocent. The central figure, the woman feeding the child, carries on the theme of the family and of love: iconographically she is Charity.

But we have not only the rich gifts of the cultivated and peaceful land, we have also the rich gifts of *Liberality*, the goblets and jewels in the splendid vessel she is carrying. And the woman with the timbrel must figure Harmony or Joy. A little flying *putto* is holding out the *Caduceus*, above Minerva's head. The *caduceus*, Mercury's wand, stands for *peaceful suasion*, the effect and power of *eloquence*; and although Minerva is armed, she is not using violence against Mars: he is being quite gently turned away.

Rubens had come back to Antwerp in 1609, when the 12 years' truce between Spain and the United Provinces brought peace to his own city and the Spanish Netherlands. He was trusted by the Archduke and his successor, the Infanta Isabella, and even eventually by the Court of Spain, which at first hardly welcomed the presence of a professional painter in high councils. Peace and war, and peace by negotiation, were the burden of those intense periods of diplomatic activity—secret and open—that occupied Rubens in Antwerp, Paris, Madrid and London from the end of the peace of the Netherlands in 1621 until 1633 or 1634, just before the Infanta's death, when he renounced all political diplomatic activity, and found, he writes, by divine grace, peace of mind.[11] But there was no external peace. All these activities of Rubens, including those that involved England, were, of course, episodes in the failed diplomacy of the Thirty Years War. That canvas of the destruction of the peace of the Christian world (1637–8) is Rubens' image of what a very unemotional modern historian, who dates the last phases of the conflict from 1635, when France and Spain went to war, has called the "desolation unutterable" of Europe.[12] The subject preoccupied Rubens in his retirement. There is, for example, a splendid rapid gouache of 1635/7 that shows Minerva and Hercules—a significant conjunction of deities—repelling Mars, accompanied by a Fury, savaging his prey, women and children (Figure 18). And in that bad year 1635 Rubens designed the great pageant that welcomed the Infanta's successor, the Cardinal Infant Ferdinand, to Antwerp. Good government, the restoration of prosperity, peace are the major themes of the iconography. Hopes for

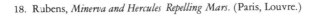

18. Rubens, *Minerva and Hercules Repelling Mars*. (Paris, Louvre.)

peace echo through Rubens' letters, as he watches the rashness of princes, and the ruin of his beloved Antwerp: "we find ourselves without peace, rather than at war; or to put it better, we have the inconveniences of war without the advantage of peace. This city, at least, languishes like a consumptive body, declining bit by bit. Every day sees the population going down, for these unhappy people have no means of supporting themselves either by industrial skill or trade." And "I should like the whole world to be in peace, that we might live in a golden age instead of an age of iron."[13]

That gift in 1630 to Charles is both hope and admonition. Rubens' contacts with English diplomatic personalities had begun about 1620, and had become very serious a few years later, from 1625, when he met the then all-powerful and quite disastrous Duke of Buckingham in Paris during the celebrations of Charles's marriage. Tortuous, intricate, these movements' object at least was clear. It was the negotiation of peace between England and Spain—with all its implications, so far as Rubens was concerned, for the neutralizing of the United Provinces and the peace of his own Netherlands. In 1628 Buckingham was murdered. By this time Rubens was already on his way to England, by way of Madrid; he arrived in London in June, 1629, not as ambassador of Spain or plenipotentiary—though Philip, to raise his status had made him Secretary of his Privy Council of the Netherlands—but as "envoy empowered to negotiate a truce preparatory to the exchange of Ambassadors and the conclusion of peace." All this was eventually successful, ambassadors were agreed on, and exchanged; but it took the best part of a year, and it was March 1630 before Rubens was free to depart from London, leaving his gift behind him. And indeed, so far, the hope was justified: for the moment, Minerva and Mercury won; prudence and suasion made a peace between England and Spain in the last months of 1630. Rubens also left England commissioned to paint a ceiling for the king's Banqueting House in Whitehall.

The old Banqueting House in the palace of Whitehall had burned down in January 1619, and had been rebuilt by Inigo Jones, Surveyor of the King's Works, by March 1622. As early as the summer of 1621, before the death of James, Rubens had been approached to do something on the grand scale—perhaps the ceiling—for the new House. But nothing came of this. There must have been discussions during Rubens' London visit, and possibly too, during the four to five years that elapsed before the ceiling panels were completed and installed. We have a marvellous series of preliminary sketches, but there is absolutely no literary documentation of discussions, plans, programme.[14]

Charles was the only English monarch who ever loved and had the highest taste in painting (his only rivals are George IV and Prince Albert, which doubtless points some unpleasant moral). We can only grieve when we read, for example, of the seven Titians that Van Dyck saw in the first of Charles's privy chambers, or of Buckingham's collections, or of Arundel's. The wish for a great monumental work by Rubens corresponded, obviously, to a true, deeply felt, personal impulse (and the approach to Rubens in 1621 must surely be attributed to Charles and Buckingham, not to James). But nothing was simple. What the king had in his private cabinet was one thing. A monumental work in his Banqueting House was another. The name of that building is apt to mislead us: this was, in that ramshackle palace, the principal room of state, where the most solemn and ceremonious appearances of royalty were enacted. The great masques were performed there until the ceiling was installed—and they should not be excluded from the list of solemn acts; but this was also, for example, the room to which foreign envoys and ambassadors were led, with high ceremonial, to the king in state: where king met king. The decoration of such a room was a public and political act: a declaration of the meaning of the ruler's kingship. Here Charles, child of the James who had constantly declared, in no blasphemous gesture, kings to be God on earth, and sustained by the iterations of the most powerful Anglican divines, might move, an image, among images, in that late Renaissance world where the relationship between image and what was imaged, sign and what was signified, was still patient of ambiguous readings, and in part powerful by very reason of that ambiguity. Here a king might move delicately but potently between fiction, representation, enaction, identification or participation. This was a world where the "real," the "historical," could cohabit with the feigned, where the hard political programme could, without distortion, undergo translation into symbol; and where, in particular, the images of classical antiquity could serve, without profanity or incongruity, as double vehicles, carrying the felt greatness of the antique world as revelation and aggrandizement of human achievement, heightened by a sense of rediscovery and re-enactment, and carrying also, in the minds of some, for validation, the knowledge that these were signs permitted by God to the people that walked in darkness, a wisdom allowed to the ancients. If we persist, in a later mode, in being scandalized about boundaries between the sacred and profane, or the "real" and the "feigned," we can never understand or feel the power of such great public images; nor can we feel it if, in a modern, sentimental way, we prefer to forget that great hard-headedness is needed for the organization and administration of mysteries.

A political act is aimed at the present. If history, the past, is involved in that act, it is history directed to the present, to the emergent occasions that Ben Jonson said masques were directed to, though they also enclosed more removed mysteries. The emergent occasion here is the position of the patron at the time, and what he needs history for. The subject chosen for the Whitehall ceiling was the reign, the acts, the glorification of James I. We have to consider, then, James I, and "history"; but we have to consider what version of this seemed desirable to Charles and his advisers in 1629–30 (and what would still be acceptable four or five years later); and we have to consider Rubens.

When Rubens came to England he was no novice in such a situation. On the contrary. In 1625 he had completed what he was allowed to complete of the greatest of all such monumental representations of royalty and royal acts: the sequence on the life and acts of Marie de Medici in her new palace of the Luxemburg in Paris. This had been an affair of the greatest political importance, complexity, and delicacy, not to say danger, both in the choice and treatment of subjects. And about this we do know something, if not everything. We know who the queen's adviser was; we know about the role of Rubens' learned friend, Peiresc, and about the interventions of Richelieu, who had his own game to play. We also know how actively involved Rubens himself was, that he was no mere executant of some programme drawn up by a patron or a learned adviser. Here is Rubens giving an account of the young king's visit to the pictures—an awkward moment, considering his relationships with his mother:

19. Rubens, *The Felicity of the Queen's Regency*, from the Marie de Medici series.
(Paris, Louvre.)

His Majesty showed complete satisfaction with our pictures, from the reports of all who were present, particularly M. de St. Ambroise. *He* served as interpreter of the subjects, changing or concealing the meaning with great skill. I believe I've written you that a picture representing *The Departure of the Queen for Paris* has been removed, and in its place I have painted an entirely new one, representing *The Felicity of Her Regency* [Figure 19]. This shows the flowering of the Kingdom of France, with the revival of the sciences and the arts through the Liberality and Splendour of her Majesty, who sits upon a shining throne and holds a scale in her hands, keeping the world in equilibrium by her prudence and equity. This subject which does not specifically touch upon the *raison d'état* of this reign, or apply to any individual, has evoked much pleasure, and I believe that if the other subjects had been entrusted entirely to us, they would have passed as far as the Court is concerned, without any scandal or murmur [the Cardinal perceived this too late, and was very much annoyed to see that the other new subjects were taken amiss]. For the future I believe there will not fail to be difficulties over the subjects of the other gallery, which ought to be easy and free from scruples [i.e. the Henri IV gallery, which was never finished] .... But Monsignor the Cardinal de Richelieu, although I have given him a concise programme in writing, is so occupied with the government of the state that he has not had time to look at it even once ....[15]

What an admirable insight into what was involved for the painter of state subjects that passage offers! The problem of the Whitehall ceiling was not in any way so complex. But how we wish we had such a "concise programme in writing" for it! For some agreement must have been reached. Rubens had, after all, to be told something about James I, and about how his patron wished that subject to be treated. Charles himself must surely have had some adviser: Inigo Jones and Archbishop Laud present themselves as reasonable possibilities, but we have no information on the matter. As for Rubens' own role, we can show how close the subject and iconography are to preoccupations of his own. But let me repeat that we have nothing like a contemporary account of the scheme; that the scheme was not understood when Gribelin engraved the ceiling in 1720; or when Joseph Spence wrote about it in the mid-18th century; and that theirs is the tradition that penetrated authoritative and still influential descriptions, like Rooses', or the account in the L.C.C.'s Survey volume.[16]

I believe that some of our difficulties have come from looking too precisely for references to specific actions. Although most certainly directed to *emergent occasions* I think the imagery is far more generalized than it was intended to be in the Medici cycle, generalized in that sort of way of which Rubens himself talks in his letter about the episode called *The Felicity of the Queen's Regency*.

IV

In 1628 came the Petition of Right. In 1629—just three months before Rubens arrived in England—Charles had dissolved Parliament by force, complaining of the "vipers" who had misled his Commons. For the next eleven years there was to be no Parliament. Those months of Rubens' stay mark the beginning of the period of Charles's personal rule, when he tried to realize the ideal and style of kingship bequeathed to him by his father and sustained by his divines. One frame of reference for the ceiling, then, is the concept of the absolute king, made by God a little God on earth (in James's own words), endowed with specific virtues and powers, exalted. It is from such a king that blessings flow to his people; and these principal blessings are specific and issue from specific kingly virtues. This is the other burden of the ceiling: the blessings or gifts of the divine king to his people are peace and the fruits of peace. And these come from the union in the king of *active wisdom* or *prudence* with the *power of peaceful suasion*: this notion of kingship was European, and its language was familiar to Rubens. The fact that peace, abroad and at home, was a political necessity to Charles, need not involve us here in disputes about degrees or kinds of "belief" on the part either of the creators of the ceiling or of those who saw it. It was opportune to make such a statement; but questions about relationships between a sense of the opportune and a sense of the "true" are mostly impossible formulations. It is essential to realize that this version of James's reign and of his virtues is to be read as referring to Charles and his reign. It is the availability and the currency of this version that concerns us. And it was no new *ad hoc* version. James himself had been actively concerned to prepare it, years before. King of Peace was one of his favourite roles.

When James came to England in 1603 he came in peace—"contrary to the fears at home and the hopes abroad," wrote Laud, remembering that troubled time when, on James's death, he came to prepare a list of the most notable features of his character and reign.[17] In James's first address to Parliament he had said that these were the gifts he brought: peace at home and peace abroad. One of his favourite honorifics was *Rex Pacificus*. His mottoes were *Beati Pacifici* and he appropriated to himself the Virgilian verses:

> Hae tibi erunt artes: pacisque imponere morem
> Parcere subiectis et debellare superbos.

The preacher at James's funeral, alluding to James as the British *Solomon* (another of his favourite roles), said, "Every man liu'd in peace under his vine and his *figge tree* in the daies of Salomon . . . . And so they did in the blessed daies of King James."[18] It was a text that the poets, who for twenty years had been singing of his peace, had loved to apply to James. And Laud, more soberly, noted:

> The continuance of full twenty-two years' reign all in peace, without war from foreign enemy or rebellion at home.[19]

V. The Apotheosis

"His rest, no question, is in Abraham's bosom, and his crown changed into a crown of glory." So Laud of the dead king. The central, oval, panel in the ceiling shows the apotheosis of James (Figures 20 and 21). He ascends to heaven surrounded by the classical symbols of apotheosis. His foot on the globe, he rises on the outstretched wings of the eagle. *Putti* take from him his imperial orb and crown: his head is bare for another crowning. Justice raises him by his left arm. At his right Piety, adoring, kneels by her flaming altar. And Religion with the Book—it is inscribed *In Principio erat Verbum*—raises

her eyes to God. Above James, Peace with the wand of Mercury joins hands with the armed maiden to hold the laurel, emblem both of victory and peace. *Putti* hold the *corona civica*, the crown of oak given to the man who had saved a fellow citizen, which Augustus had placed as emblem on his coins. Other *putti* carry the palm branches of victory and the trumpets of fame.

The king can rise to heaven in his imperial robes, because his kingship itself is sacred; and with those symbols of apotheosis because the Roman *imperium* was divinely ordered, a foreshadowing of the Christian order that was to come: Augustus, first and parent of the line, round whom the formulations of the *imperium* and the imperial virtues crystallized, was author of the peace in which Christ was born. The king is the instrument through which the secular order is incorporated with the divine will. The two virtues of the king which sum up his duties to each sphere are Religion and Justice—"This great comprising Kingly virtue without which there can be no religious peaceable government"—so Laud. In those are expressed his relationship to secular and sacred, and the means whereby he united secular and sacred. Religion expressed his relationship to God, Justice his relationship to man. James calls the first book of his *Basilicon Doron*, "Of a King's Christian

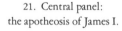

21. Central panel: the apotheosis of James I.

20. *Opposite*: The Whitehall ceiling, showing the position of the individual panels. In this and subsequent illustrations Simon Gribelin's 1720 engraving has been used for clarity, although it misrepresents the direction in which several of the panels face.

Duty towards God," and the second, "Of a King's Duty in his Office." The first deals with religion; the second with justice: the first with service to God; the second with service to Man.

> . . . In two degrees standeth the whole seruice of God by man: interior, or upwarde; exterior or downewarde: the first by prayer in faith towardes God: the next by workes flowing therefrom before the worlde: which is nothing else, but the exercise of Religion towardes God, and of equitie towardes your neighbour.

James divides Religion into two parts. The first is the "worship of God according to his revealed will" which is "wholly grounded upon the Scripture . . . quickened by faith and conserved by conscience." Then there is prayer—for only by prayer is faith nourished.[20] The two figures, Religion and Piety, which go together to make a complex image of Religion express this; they show knowledge based on the Bible accompanied by prayer and adoration. And the king's justice, like God's, acts swiftly, terribly, without respect of person. Perhaps it is to express this that Justice here carries, as well as her scales, Jove's thunderbolt. James was not only King or Prince of Peace. He was, famously, the British Solomon. James was identifying himself with that king whose typical act was *judgement*, whose role was wisdom. And Laud wrote of him, "He was the justest man that could sit between parties, and as patient to hear."[21] It is from *Justice* that *Peace* springs, as the divines remind us. Peace—and they recall Hesiod—is the daughter of Law.

This panel is central to the composition. Here are the virtues that have earned James, the sacred, just, religious monarch, his apotheosis. This is the consummation. The other parts of the programme show how these gifts and graces had worked to the happiness of his kingdom, and by reference, how the rule of Charles works and will work.

VI. The Crowned Child or The New Birth

One of the pair of supporting panels certainly points to a specific act. It has bothered, in detail, commentators a good deal (Figure 22). And I report my own reading—though Oliver Millar has called it fanciful[22]—because quite independently Fritz Saxl had arrived at the same conclusion. James is enthroned and crowned, in his left hand the orb, in his right the sceptre. With the sceptre James points to a naked child. Over the child's head two women are holding two crowns. An armed maiden is binding them together. Over this group *putti* support the royal arms. Below the group, and at the foot of the throne, a *putto* sets fire with a torch to a pile of arms. This strange event is being watched by four people: in the background by two men in contemporary dress, whose heads only can be seen; by a soldier standing at the side of the throne; and by another officer in very different dress sitting at his feet. Behind James's throne, barely visible, is a sphinx.

The central problem is, obviously, who or what is the child, and what is this crowning? There has been traditional agreement that the two women must represent England and Scotland, and this is obviously right. Tradition has insisted that the child

22. North panel: the crowned child.

must be Charles, and that the scene must represent James designating Charles as his successor, or perhaps creating him Prince of Wales. Such an interpretation, however, is really untenable.

Saxl's most notable contribution to our understanding of the ceiling was to point this out and offer a more persuasive interpretation. "But who is the child?" Saxl asked. "It has been said to be Charles. He had certainly not been crowned as a child, and it is unlikely that the ruling monarch would be presented in his Banqueting Hall as an ecstatic baby." I had already come to the same conclusion, moved by the obvious travesty of facts known intimately to all England that such a representation of Charles would imply. Charles was *not* born James's heir and never seemed as a child to have the smallest chance of being Prince of Wales. His elder brother, the Prince Henry of whom so much was hoped, died in 1612 when he was eighteen years old, already a man, ready for marriage, and a political power in his own right. At that time Charles was twelve years old; he did not become Prince of Wales till four years later when he was sixteen. Although political paintings could supply devious versions of history, I do not believe that facts of this order would be blatantly violated to show Charles crowned by the wisdom of James as heir, or Prince of Wales while he was still a baby. And Saxl continued: "The naked child painted in analogy to the Christ child must be an allegorical being representing the happy birth of the United Kingdom. It was James's will—and therefore all eyes are turned toward him—that the

Stuarts should, by wisdom's direction, rule over a united island and thus promote eternal peace: a *putto* in the foreground is busy setting fire to armour. Thus the . . . picture represents the enthronement of James's successors as the peaceable monarchs of this united island, a deed over which Wisdom presides."[23]

This is surely right. James in his own person united the crowns of England and Scotland. But he did more. We see here that the binding together of the two crowns is being carried out by Minerva–she has been called Britannia, but Minerva seems more obvious and more likely–at James's bidding. This is an act of his wisdom; and that sphinx behind the throne–a figure associated with Minerva by mythographers–emphasizes his wisdom as king (and adds another idea very characteristic of James: that the special wisdom of kings, which is statecraft, is above the comprehension of the vulgar). The binding together of the crowns is defined by the royal arms. We are so familiar with those that we forget what they are. They are the new arms assumed by James when he took the style, in 1604, by proclamation, of *King of Great Britain*, after a propaganda campaign, and in spite of the objections of the Commons. They are now the arms and that is now the style of Charles. James was defeated in his attempt to bring about a full legal union of the two kingdoms. But in his wisdom he did effect their union under one name, Great Britain, and thus the creation of a new kingdom (or, in a favoured version, the re-uniting of an old). This is the union and the birth that is celebrated here. And it is a union and a birth that James's wisdom has effected in peace, and his is a line established in peace: the *putto* setting fire to the arms is a familiar emblem of peace.

> And verily the uniting the two Kingdomes into the name of Britaine is not unlike (Essay [Isaiah] 21) that chariot, drawne with two horsemen, mentioned in Esay; at sight whereof, the watchman cryed, Babilon is fallen, Babilon is fallen, and all the images of her Gods are smitten downe to the ground. For so (except we will smother the childe of Union in his first birth,) both English, and Scottish, will soone heare him sound aloude into the whole world, that all great Britaine is like Jerusalem, which is, as a City, at unity with it selfe; and Babilon, even division, disorder, discord.
>
> Thus we say, and thus we sing, *Redeunt Saturnia regna*, even the golden age of Britaine's Monarchy is come againe: Alter Tiphis, et altera, quae vehat Argos, / delectos Heroes: atque iterum ad Trojam / magnus mittetur Achilles.[24]

I have quoted this from one of James's divines to show the way in which the union was regarded by a contemporary, to show that the child image was a perfectly possible one, and to convey this sense of the accomplishment of prophecy, of destiny fulfilled, of the inauguration of a new era that attended James's coming and his assumption of the style that sealed the meaning of his coming.

I now think, following Oliver Millar, that the rather shaggy figure seated on the steps of the throne is a Sergeant-at-Arms carrying his ceremonial mace: his dress is an approximation to the familiar uniform of the royal bodyguard; he shows on his back the Tudor rose. The Sergeant-at-Arms was a figure from high, court ceremony, and in keeping at such an act. The soldier supports the throne: this is the function of a soldier. His dress, neither modern nor ancient, belongs to the world both in and out of time to which the whole composition belongs. For the two modern figures watching from the other side of the throne I can offer only a suggestion. Both Saxl and I thought they must be intended as portraits; both of us would have liked to recognize in them Charles accompanied by Buckingham, the dear favourite of two kings. But we could not honestly say that we could make a very convincing case. And undoubtedly the composition of the panel, based though it seems to be on a ceiling painting by Veronese showing Esther before Ahasuerus, recalls something wholly in keeping with the context: a judgement of Solomon.[25]

VII. The Refusal To Accept Victory through War

A third panel completes the central axis of the ceiling (Figure 23). Formally it balances the scene of *The Crowned Child*; and it is tempting to refer it to a specific act. This has, indeed, been done, and Saxl accepted a reference here to the Gunpowder Plot. I think myself that the imagery is too generalized to be pinned down in this way—generalized like that Regency episode in the Medici cycle. I should take this as a general statement about, again, James's peace, and about a prominent and relevant characteristic of his rule. We might call this panel *The Refusal to accept Victory through War*.

23. South panel: the refusal to accept victory through war.

In front of the king throned in an architectural screen we see a familiar motif: a victor triumphing over his subjugated enemy. The enemy is an evil figure: in his right hand he has the serpent of envy, hate. But the victor is himself dangerous; he is a barbaric figure carrying the flaming torch of destruction or discord. He is a Mars offering his victory to the king. But the king turns away from him and stretches a protecting arm to the embracing figures of Peace and Plenty.

This sort of victory must be refused, for it brings with it destroying flames and threatens peace and plenty, which the throned king must guard. And so his wisdom or prudence is personified, and interposes to ward off this Mars with a Medusa shield. The personification is Minerva, the warrior maid, armed too, with Jove's thunderbolt—not the most usual attribute for her, but sanctioned by scholars and used elsewhere by Rubens. With Minerva goes Mercury, god of embassies and eloquence, who stretches his *caduceus* to the supine enemy: Mercury reconciles by peaceful suasion. The dangerous victories of war, then, are rejected in favour of the victories of wisdom or prudence and peaceful suasion. So James did, so Charles will do.

VIII. Virtues and Vices

Those two scenes are flanked by panels each representing a *Virtue* conquering a *Vice*. We should be able to read each pair in conjunction with the scene it goes with. And as all four also enclose the whole scheme, standing as they do at the four corners, they should apply to the whole ceiling. Yet they are troublesome. The trouble is not about the virtues but about what specific vices are opposed to them; they are mostly very *generalized* images, suitable for many contexts.

The scene of the New Birth, or accomplishment of the Union, is supported by a panel of Hercules striking down with his club a female figure with snaky hair and a snake wound round her right arm (Figure 24), and by a panel of Minerva vanquishing an ugly nude female figure with her lance; above, her owl holds the conqueror's laurel wreath (Figure 25). The Hercules has been called Heroic Virtue, his defeated enemy, Envy, who is Rebellion in the political sense. Hercules is certainly Heroic Virtue. Minerva has been called Chastity, and her enemy Lust. This latter reading I do not think likely. I think we must read the two figures, Hercules and Minerva together. We are helped once again by the portrait Rubens did, for engraving, of the great Spanish Minister, Olivares, in which Olivares appears supported by the emblems of Minerva, spear, shield, and owl, and of Hercules, the club and the lion's skin (see Figure 14). Here again is Olivares' acknowledgement:

> As for the emblems, I can tell you that now I am freed of temporal and personal cares I am more than ever obliged to give a good account of the public affairs that have been entrusted to me. May God grant me the *light* and the *strength* needed for my task and then I think I shall prize the portrait at its worth and that its auguries are not entirely false.[26]

24. and 25. North side panels: Hercules and Minerva.

Light and Strength: this is the union of Minerva and Hercules. These two must, like Mercury and Minerva, be united, for Heroic Virtue cannot stand without the helping presence of Wisdom. Mythologically, it was Minerva who advised Hercules and helped him to achieve his labours, that most familiar allegory of heroic virtue. And it is appropriate that these virtues should support the scene of the Union, perfected and maintained by the Wisdom and Heroic Virtue of James.

In the panels at the other corners, supporting the scene of James's refusal of the victories of war and his protection of Peace and Plenty, even the identification of the Virtues is doubtful. A female, crowned with laurel, glory round her head, pouring precious objects from a great horn, has commonly been called Liberality (Figure 26). The light would be because Liberality is effulgent, and the laurel because Liberality goes with Peace. The enemy may indeed be Avarice as she has been called. For the other female Virtue I propose the name either of Reason (which would link her with Minerva) or

26. and 27. South side panels: Liberality and Reason (?).

Temperance, in our sense of moderation: this because of her attribute, the reins, and head-harness of a horse–these, Renaissance authorities say, go with either virtue, to show that she masters appetites (Figure 27). If we take them so, the pair can be read together, like Hercules and Minerva, and read also in conjunction with the scene they frame, James's *Wisdom* or *Prudence* refusing war, taming his enemies peacefully, and protecting Peace and Plenty. Liberality is a necessary kingly virtue, and of course can go only with Peace; but it was well known that unless controlled by Reason or Temperance, Liberality passed into its corresponding Vice, Profligacy. James himself had stressed this point when instructing his son in the kingly virtues in *Basilicon Doron*; and of James, Laud had written in that compendium of memorabilia which I have quoted before: "He was bountiful to the highest pitch of a King." The objects poured from the corncupia are royal: orb, sceptre, crown, coins.

IX. A Golden Age

What gifts the virtues of the king, and his government, have brought to his country are displayed in the two lateral panels. These frame the New Birth or Union scene, and show what has followed this creation. They are vigorous, rich and animated processions of *putti* (Figures 28 and 29). The *putti* are taming wild beasts; they carry and play with horns of plenty and an enormous profusion of the fruits of the earth. They realize the peace and plenty that James–and Charles–have brought to their not very grateful subjects. One *putto* rides on a tiger; a chariot is drawn by a lion and a bear; to another chariot a wolf and a sheep are yoked. We are dealing here with Loves, and should remember such a familiar emblem of the power of love as Alciati's of Cupid as master of the lions who draw his chariot (Figure 30). And we should remember those so often conflated visions of Isaiah and Virgil. Saxl called the child in the Union panel *nova progenies*; I have cited one of the passages showing how easily the prophecies of the Union and the king who would effect it and usher in a new age could be assimilated to the Virgilian vision: *redeunt Saturnia regna*. Thoughts of the peace of James almost inevitably carried such images, and we can feel the presence of such allusions in these panels.

28. and 29. Central side panels: putti exemplifying peace and plenty.

X. Hermathena

The imagery with which Rubens rendered the Stuart rule was international, both in sources and applications. I suggested, at the start, that for Rubens, there was a genuinely

30. The Power of Love, from Andrea
Alciati, *Emblemata*, Padua 1621.

personal mode of statement involved in this formal iconography; and I pointed to this in connexion with those representations of Peace and War.

For a moment I should like to return to this, and pick out one single feature of his iconography which by its rarity and its placing suggests that it held a personal importance for Rubens. The key to this is Rubens' use of Minerva, whose attributes and presence have come into this discussion again and again; and Rubens' use of this not unusual figure is not, in fact, altogether usual. I should think that the formal source of the composition of *Peace defended from War* which Rubens gave to Charles as a present is an allegorical painting by Tintoretto in the Doge's Palace in Venice–the monument above all others where Rubens learned the art of political painting (Figure 31). A contemporary title was, apparently, *Pallas drives Mars away while Peace and Plenty embrace*, and this explains the simple subject well enough (the allegory figures of course the peaceful policy of the Republic). The tale of the enmity between Minerva and Mars goes back to the *Iliad*, and it was primarily from Homer (read of course through the work of commentators and

31. Tintoretto, *Pallas Repelling Mars while Peace and Plenty Embrace.* (Venice, Palazzo Ducale.) At one point in its history the picture was moved and, presumably at that time, badly cut down: most of the figure of Peace has gone. The original composition can still be seen, and was widely known in Europe in the late sixteenth century, from an engraving by Agostino Carracci.

sixteenth-century scholars) that Rubens' Minerva comes (Figure 32). In this splendid picture in Vienna, whose drama is almost lost in reproduction, Victory is crowning the triumphant hero with laurel—which is also Minerva's sign of peace. The hero's expression is grave, thoughtful, not the ugly distorted face of Mars, for he is looking upwards for his inspiration; and at his ear is Minerva. This is the characteristic role of Minerva in Homer: she is the adviser, the counsellor of warriors. Rubens' Minerva is not primarily Wisdom in the sense of contemplative wisdom, but rather Prudence, an active virtue, a practical sagacity. Minerva, patroness of olive and distaff, of the useful arts of peace, was also equipped with terrible force, which Rubens shows by giving her her father's thunderbolt, really an unclassical attribute, justified by commentators from a passage in the *Aeneid*, but

32. Rubens, *Victory Crowning the Hero*. (Vienna, Kunsthistorisches Museum.)

very rarely used in painting. She is counselling Rubens' hero, as she counselled the demi-god Hercules: Heroic Virtue cannot succeed unless guided by her *light*—as Olivares understood when Rubens offered him the combined emblems of Hercules and Minerva. Similarly, again and again Rubens joins Minerva and Mercury, either as two figures acting together, or by a conjunction of their attributes—the *caduceus*, the snaky winged wand, will stand, for example, for *Mercury*. Now, the weight of this conjunction is something very special to Rubens, I believe. The idea comes from the books of the sixteenth-century mythographers and antiquaries, who found in two of Cicero's letters reference to a figure called the *Hermathena*: very obscure passages and so the more easily subjected to elabora-

33a. Hermathena, from Vincenzo Cartari, *Imagines*, 1581. (*Above*).

33b. Hermathena, from Vincenzo Cartari, *Imagini*, 1615. (*Top Right*).

34. Hermathena, from Otho Vaenius, *Emblemata*, 1607. (*Below Right*).

tion, and indeed invention. This deity could be shown either as the two gods in conjunction or as Athene with attributes of Hermes. Illustrations from different editions of one of the most popular handbooks of mythology, Cartari's *Images of the Gods of the Ancients*, show both forms (Figure 33, a and b). We can see the two gods in a source very close indeed to Rubens, in a book of emblems by his friend and first teacher of painting, Otho van Veen (or Vænius) (Figure 34). Or a much earlier version may be relevant. In Achille Bocchi's *Symbolicæ quæstiones*, famous for its engravings by Giulio Bonasone, the two gods stand at the angle of a wall, as herms, their arms linked. Between, a *putto*, standing on a lion's head, and bridling it to show his mastery of it, points up to the gods whence his mastery comes: the motto is *sic monstra domantur* (Figure 35). To combine Prudence or active sagacity with the suasions of eloquence for the taming of monsters: what else had Rubens tried to urge on rulers? And what else had been the aim of so much of that active, laborious public life of his? And so, building his house in Antwerp, which announced his worldly success, he set on that grand portico, as presiding deities, Mercury and Minerva (Figure 36).

35. Hermathena, from Achille Bocchi, *Symbolicae quaestiones . . .* , 1574.
The motto reads, "Sapientiam
modestia, progressio eloquentiam,
felicitatem haec perficit." The engraving is by Giulio Bonasone.

36. The figures of Mercury and Minerva on the portico of Rubens' house in
Antwerp. These are modern copies by E. Deckers of the originals, which were
replaced in 1939.

XI

To commission the Banqueting House ceiling was imaginative, bold, like Charles's private collecting. As an act of state it was, at best, irrelevant. At the heart of Whitehall the Stuart rule is displayed in an international imagery forged for the great absolute Catholic rulers; at the heart of the great scheme James is shown rising to heaven in a type of representation evolved, primarily, for the Assumption of the Virgin; for that, formally, is where the apotheosis comes from. With the imagery of the ceiling we are in the world of the last court masques, a *Triumph of Peace* or a *Salmacida Spolia*. In this latter masque Jones's emblematic proscenium arch carried figures strikingly reminiscent of the ceiling; as also was the motto of the masque itself, *Salmacida spolia sine sanguine sine sudore, potius quam Cadmia victoria, ubi ipsos victores pernicies opprimit*: "the allusion is that his Majesty, out of his mercy and clemency approving the first proverb, seeks by all means to reduce tempestuous and turbulent natures into a sweet calm of civil concord." The bloody victories of war have been rejected in favour of victory over the perturbations, supported by Reason joined with Intellectual Appetite, of Prudence, Doctrine and Discipline, supported by Counsel and Resolution. This English world has become such that all the troubles of the kingdom can be shown as snaky figures of discord controlled by Mercury's wand and the harmonies of the royal dance. "A kind of exorcism" that last masque has been called: if this is so, it is a singularly ineffectual kind. Imagery and style work together only to sustain a group's image of itself, in effect to point to and sustain its frightening isolation. Outside Whitehall a far different vocabulary was formulating and directing thought and act.

Ripa's Fate

In 1922 Emile Mâle went to Rome to study the iconography of Christian art after the Council of Trent. Five years later he described his initial bewilderment in Rome's swarm of churches among swarming allegories that he could not read. The account of his enlightenment is worth citing at length:

> Some time later, while I was studying Bernini at the Villa Borghese, I was surprised to see that that beautiful *Truth* of his, all quivering with life, is holding in one hand a kind of sun shooting out his rays, and has a globe under one foot (Figure 37). How were such attributes to be read? What meaning lay hidden in them by Bernini who had, we know, conceived this statue in a moment of deep melancholy? And was it really he who had invented these strange attributes? I came to doubt it that day when still in Rome, in the church of *Santo Spirito* of the Neapolitans, I noticed on the tomb of Cardinal Giovanni Battista de Luca a *Truth* with a sun in her hand and a globe under her foot. Was there a rule, then, that *Truth* should be represented in this way? And if there was a rule, where did it come from? I seemed to be glimpsing a kind of language of allegory with its own vocabulary and laws.[1]

It soon became clear to Mâle, he goes on,

> that these artists had not only a tradition, but a book, a kind of dictionary of allegory that they consulted whenever they had to personify an abstract idea. It remained to discover that book . . . .
>
> The library of the Roman College, which had belonged to the Jesuits, is today the National Library of Italy. There, everything recalls the past. In these sombre galleries, under their parchment bindings, you are almost sure to find all the books that excited Europe in the 16th and 17th centuries. And it was there that I found an Italian book, once celebrated, now

37. Bernini, *Truth*. (Rome, Villa Borghese.)

SIMVLACRVM·VERITATIS·TEMPORE·DETEGENDAE
QVOD·LAVRENTIVS·BERNINIVS·EQVES
OLIM·CALVMNIA·ADPETITVS
IN·SOLATIVM·DOLORIS·INSCVLPSIT
ET·TRANSMITTI·POSTERIS·SVIS·IN·PERPETVVM·IVSSIT
QVO·PRAESENTE·ADMONERENTVR
INIVRIAS·FERENDAS·POENAS·NON·EXPETENDAS

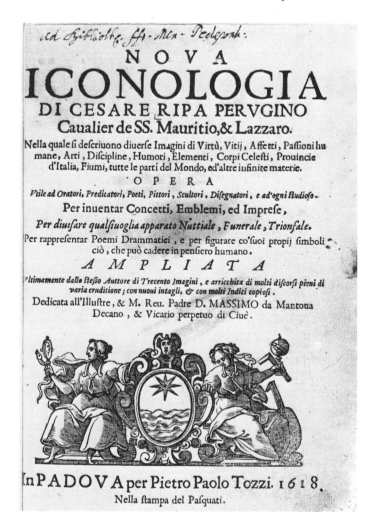

38. Cesare Ripa, *Iconologia*:
title-page.

deep in oblivion: the *Iconologia* of the Cavalier Cesare Ripa (Figure 38). This is an illustrated dictionary of allegories where the author teaches you how to personify abstract ideas. I was turning over the pages rather idly without even a notion of its interest when an image of *Truth* woke my attention (Figure 39). Naked, and altogether like Bernini's *Truth*, she had a sun in her hand and a globe under her foot. And underneath I read in Ripa's Italian commentary this: "Truth is represented quite naked because simplicity is her nature . . . . She carries the sun to show that she loves light, that she herself is light . . . , she has the globe of the world under her feet to show that she is more precious than any worldly thing: which is why Menander says she is a citizen of the skies."

"It was," says Mâle, "an encouraging start":

Instead of turning Ripa's pages I began to read him with the greatest attention; and it was not long before I realized that with Ripa in my hand I could explain most of the allegories that adorn the palaces and churches of Rome.[2]

39. Ripa, *Truth*.

It is undeniably an enormously dramatic rendering—the scholar wandering through the hundreds of churches, oratories, palaces of Rome, confronting those plastic riddles, realizing that there is before him a whole world speaking an unknown language, and suddenly, in that musty library, by no tedious process of decipherment, but at one blow, indeed by chance, finding the one key to this language of art, not simply in post-Tridentine Rome, but in all of western Europe; for, Mâle came to see, code and key were international.

Emile Mâle had a genuine gift for self-dramatization, and a real command of narrative eloquence. I have quoted at such length because we really do have in this passage a moment recorded, the sense of a moment of discovery when a whole great chapter of human effort is given meaning. Mâle published his essay in 1927; the complete book appeared five years later. And the very odd thing is that his claim to discovery was almost justified. A few scholars, notably Paul Reyher and Erwin Panofsky, had used Ripa before this time, the former primarily as illustrative material for a study of the English masque, the latter more extensively. But it really does seem to have been Mâle who, after 1927, made Ripa inescapable for anyone concerned with the art of the Renaissance.

A question Mâle did not ask was why it should have been left for him to discover this forgotten book in that dusty gallery. Mâle himself finds traces of it far into the eighteenth century, even in revolutionary France. It was first published in Rome in 1593, first published with illustrations in 1603, translated into the major languages, reprinted in a huge variety of versions and forms; it is impossible to determine when its printing history really ends. Though it was well-known in England, the first English version did not appear until 1709, the second and last, produced by an architect called Richardson, in 1777–9, reprinted in 1785; and this may, indeed, be the final version. A vast affair produced by Boudard in Parma in five volumes between 1764 and 1767 was in a sense the ultimate Ripa, the book in its most compendious form. For the bibliographies mask an essential fact: Ripa's text was never stable; every edition contains alterations and amplifications. What happened to this encyclopedia in the course of two centuries of revision is a real question in cultural history. And why that gap of another century and a half until Mâle found a copy? Why did Ripa disappear?

The case of Ripa's *Iconology* is a clamant example in a large history. Whatever happened to all the Renaissance encyclopedias of classical mythology, those great, familiar repositories of allegorical information? Why was it possible, for example, for a scholar in 1938 to publish a dictionary of classical myth in the works of Ben Jonson based on the assumption that Jonson knew only the classical texts as established in Leipzig and Oxford? Or, to state the problem another way, since 1908 everyone who has been concerned with the history of classical scholarship has gone, rightly, to the three volumes which John Edwin Sandys published under that title. Yet Sandys does not even mention the three most important Renaissance studies of classical mythology, that by Lilio Gregorio Giraldi (1548), that by Natales Comes (or Conti) (1551), or the most popular, particularly addressed to poets and artists, that by Vincenzo Cartari (1556). Sandys was himself an encyclopedist, but those compilations, despite innumerable users over more than two centuries, did not concern him. In 1908 they were not knowledge; for the world of scholarship they did not exist.

II

From the real moment of Mâle's discovery of Ripa let us turn back to an imagined moment. A learned gentleman called Polymetis and his genial guests conduct a dialogue in a garden. The scene takes place in that most ambitious work *Polymetis*, first published in 1747, by the mild and amiable, the Reverend Joseph Spence, Fellow of New College, country parson, tutor and bear-leader to young gentlemen, miscellaneous writer, Professor of Poetry and Regius Professor of Modern History at Oxford, and—it is as well for his fame—friend of Pope. The topic of Dialogue 18 in *Polymetis* is "The use of this Enquiry, in particular, and of the defects of the Modern Artists in Allegorical Subjects," and, like Mâle's revelation, it defines a cultural attitude and must be quoted at length. Polymetis begins:

> Any one that has been much used to see the works of the modern sculptors, will I believe be very ready to acknowledge that in the allegorical figures of their own invention, we are frequently at a loss to know what they mean. I could give you various instances of this, even from the gardens of Versailles, and the collections in Rome itself; but I rather chuse to refer you to a number of instances, that lay all together: in a book published by Cavalier Ripa, to direct our modern artists in subjects of this kind; and which, it seems has been so generally regarded as a good model, that it has been translated into no less than seven different languages.
>
> —You need not refer me to that, as a new thing to me, says Mysagetes; Ripa is my old acquaintance. I used to divert myself with the oddness of his figures, when I was a boy; and remember several of them still. I know you have got his book here, in your study; and tho' you did not care perhaps to own it, I shall (with your leave) take it down from that shelf: if it were

40. Ripa, *Flattery*.

only out of pure malice, to puzzle Philander; in setting him to guess, what some of his figures mean. Here I have it: and (to go on regularly) will give Philander ten minutes, to name who this lady is toward the beginning of the book, with a flute in her hand, and a stag at her feet (Figure 40).

By her flute, says Philander, I should be apt to take it for a muse; but by the stag, it should be a Diana.

It is neither the one, nor the other, answered Mysagetes; and you are yet very wide of the person intended. This lady is a very gentle lady called Flattery; and she is represented with a flute and stag, because, (as some authors say,) stags are naturally very great lovers of music; and will suffer themselves to be taken, if you will but play upon a flute to them.—I hope you will have better luck with the next. Who is this naked lady, whose body is encompassed all round with light, and whose head is hid in the clouds? (Figure 41).

Ay this, says Philander, is not so difficult as the former: for by the circumstances you have just mentioned, and by the globe and compasses there in her right hand, the known emblems of Urania, you will at least allow this to be that Muse.

I find, replied Mysagetes, that you would be for making a Muse of every figure you see. No, Sir; this is Beauty: and her head is all involved in clouds, because there is nothing so difficult to be conceived by the human mind, as the true idea of beauty. —Once more: Who is this man, with a pair of bellows in one hand, and a spur in the other? (Figure 42).

I must give out, answered Philander, for I never had any happiness in solving riddles; and these I think are rather more intricate, than any I ever yet tried at.

Well, says Mysagetes, since you find them so knotty, I will trouble you with no more trials . . . . This man then is, Caprice; and he is marked out by his bellows and spur, as my author says, because the capricious are sometimes very ready to blow up people's virtues; and at others, as ready to strike at their vices . . . . All these surely are instances of improper and

41. Ripa, *Beauty*.

unnatural allegories, in this work of the Cavalier Ripa . . . . Such is the model which has been given, from Rome itself, for our modern artists! and such the work, which has been translated into the languages of, at least, seven different nations![3]

42. Ripa, *Caprice*.

43. Vaenius, *Pulvis et Umbra Sumus*, from *Horatii
Emblemata*, 1607.

So Spence dismisses Ripa. He goes on to dismiss one of the most popular of all emblem books, Otho Vænius' emblematized Horace. If Ripa is far-fetched, obscure, absurd, unnatural, Vænius pictorializes his Horace too literally and minutely, and therefore frivolously. Thus "*Pulvis et umbra sumus*" becomes "a dark burying-vault, with dust sprinkled about the floor; and a shadow, walking upright, between two ranges of urns"[4] (Figure 43).

Spence then confronts a larger name, Rubens himself. Rubens' allegories in the most sumptuous of late Renaissance pageants, the entry of Ferdinand of Austria into Antwerp in 1635, are discussed and found wanting. The two great showpieces of political allegory, the Whitehall ceiling and the Marie de Medici series, are pronounced absurd.[5] Then turning from designers and painters, Spence illustrates the *Defects of our modern poets in their allegories* by considering some well-chosen examples from *The Faerie Queene*.

III

Spence's dismissal of Ripa and his inability to read modern allegories depend on historiographical premises that are also value judgements. These inform his very notions of the ancient and the modern. The ancient is prescriptive for the modern, because the ancient is better; questions of historical definition become inextricably linked with questions of value. *Polymetis* is described on its title-page as "An enquiry concerning the agreement between the works of the Roman poets and the remains of the antient artists, being an attempt to illustrate them mutually from one another." By *ancient* Spence meant Roman, not Greek. His enquiry necessitated setting up a corpus of ancient art–sculpture, gems, coins–and is related to a number of other such attempts in the period, notably to the newest and most generally accepted corpus, the fifteen folio volumes of the Abbé Bernard de Montfaucon, *L'Antiquité Expliquée* (1719). Spence's method involved iconographical descriptions of the ancient remains, and here a debt is acknowledged to Addison's posthumously published *Dialogues on the Usefulness of Ancient Medals* (1721). But Spence has other overt purposes as well. His book belongs to the traditional discussion about the relationships between poetry and the visual arts, primarily painting–the *ut pictura poesis* discussion. It is also directed to the modern artist, whether painter, poet, or sculptor, and is intended as a guide and handbook for him, to take the place of the sixteenth- and seventeenth-century manuals that Mysagetes found so "improper and unnatural." Most important of all it sets forth certain basic assumptions, the notions of the defining excellencies of ancient art and poetry that inform the whole work; and these cannot be separated from Spence's concept of what scholarship or learning is, what constitutes *fact* or *accuracy*. The central questions turn out to be enormously intricate ones: what is *really* Roman? What monuments are truly ancient? By what criteria do we determine this and set up our corpus and canon? And having done so, by what criteria do we read those remains?

On the first score Spence accused Montfaucon of being indiscriminate:

> We are much obliged to him for his industry; but his choice is rather too loose and unconfined. You have, even in the better part of his collection, Tuscan gods mixt with Roman; old Gallick figures, with those of Syria; and the monsters of Egypt, with the deities of Athens.[6]

To this Mysagetes replies approvingly,

> I am very glad . . . to hear that you have decimated your gods: for I should have been heartily vext to see a deity with a dog's head or a hawk's head, upon its shoulders.[7]

The Egyptian shapes are therefore dismissed, all such figures as the sixteenth century knew from Cartari, and were freely admitted by Montfaucon (Figures 44 to 47). This purging of the pantheon is done in the name of historicism, of adherence to what is really Roman.

The basic question, then, becomes one of authority, and Spence, Montfaucon and Addison are alike in their distrust of written records, and their concern instead with monuments and objects. "It is much safer," said Addison, "to quote a Medal than an Author."[8] "By Antiquity," said Montfaucon, "I mean only what may be the Object of the

44. Cartari, the Egyptian Diana and Apollo. (*Imagines* 1581.)

45. Cartari, various representations of Mercury; note the dog-headed version in the foreground. (*Imagines* 1581.)

Sight, and may be represented by Figures."[9] For Spence, "our eyes . . . are much more faithful and true to us than our ears"; or again, "the figures of the things themselves speak to the eyes; and are less equivocal, and more expressive, than the clearest language can possibly be."[10]

The general problem for the student of classical culture in the age was formulated in precisely these terms, in a debate between the antiquary and the historian, between the object, the *antiquity*, and the written record.[11] It turned on a growing scepticism, from the late seventeenth century onward, about the value of literary materials as authorities. But what safe evidence have we, then, for reading the monuments themselves? Spence's only claim for poets follows Addison's, and it is a modest one: that the poets lived at the same time and shared the same ideas as the artists, and therefore must be the best commentators on them. All three writers have only contempt for later commentators or exegetes, and especially for the mythologists. Here is a characteristic passage from Montfaucon on a figure of Jupiter Ammon (Figure 48):

> The whole is symbolical, and perhaps hath mysterious significations. One might give a hundred different interpretations of these sorts of mysteries, and all equally uncertain.[12]

Addison was similarly conscious of the medallist's vulnerability. His studies might be quite useless; he might become a *mere* antiquary, a virtuoso, a "critic in rust."[13] Or he might fall into the errors of literary commentators, misreading his medals precisely as critics have misread, or over-read, the poets. There are mystical antiquaries or "visionaries," who "will find a mystery in every tooth of Neptune's trident"; such men "fancy an interpretation vulgar when it is natural."[14] An example is cited: the representation of the three Graces:

> What could have been more proper to shew the beauty and friendship of the three Graces, than to represent them naked and knitt together in a kind of dance? It is thus they always appear in ancient sculpture.[15]

Addison goes on to ridicule the medallists who have found in this dance an allegory of the nature of gratitude, and reserves a special sneer for Seneca's moralization of the scene in *De Beneficiis*, concluding,

> It is an easy thing . . . to find out designs that never entered into the thoughts of the sculptor or the coiner. I dare say, the same Gentlemen who have fixed this piece of morality on the three naked sisters dancing hand in hand, would have found out as good a one for them, had there been four of them sitting at a distance from each other, and covered from head to foot.[16]

With this mockery a canonical Renaissance text is dismissed, and an allegory that had been fertile in innumerable Renaissance works of arts is pronounced meaningless. In place of ancient wisdom Addison offers common sense.

Spence was equally impatient with the commentators:

46. Montfaucon, Anubis-Mercury.
(*L'Antiquité Expliquée*, 1719.)

47. Montfaucon, Osiris.
(*L'Antiquiteé Expliquée*, 1719.)

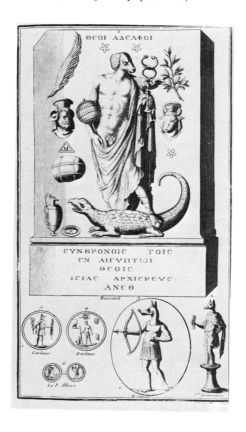

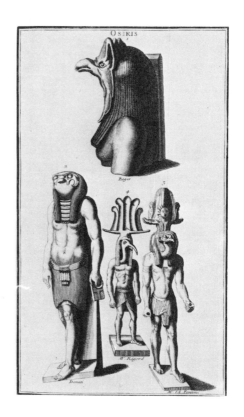

48. Montfaucon, various representations of Jupiter Ammon.
(*L'Antiquité Expliquée*, 1719.)

There has never been a more wrong-headed set of men upon earth . . . . Their usual aim seems to be, to shew their own erudition . . . . When you consult them, their answers are for the most part as dark, and as equivocal, as those of oracles.[17]

Even the authority of the poets has to be carefully weighed:

There is a great deal of difference in the authority of a poet near the second Punic war, and one who lived in Augustus's time. This must naturally be settled according to the growth of poetry, and the improvement of the arts among the Romans.[18]

This is illuminating. The historiographical decision about what text or object has most authority, which presents itself as a decision about time or chronology, is in fact a value judgment: it hinges on the question of what is most *truly* Roman. This is the issue in Spence's charge of indiscriminateness against Montfaucon, and it justifies his own decimation of the gods. Spence's controlling premises emerge in the account of the progress of poetry and the arts in Rome with which he introduces his book. The story is the familiar one of rise, peak, decline; the first age, dating from the first Punic War, was merely preparatory to the second, the age of Augustus, the truly authoritative age, the essential ancient Roman epoch; the third, the decline, ran from the beginning of Nero's reign to the end of Hadrian's.

Spence characterizes the three ages through formulaic accounts of their literary styles. Of Terence, in the first epoch, he writes, "There is a beautiful simplicity, which reigns thro' all his works. There is no searching after wit, and no ostentation of ornament in him";[19] and the age in general was "more remarkable for strength, than for refinement in writing."[20] In the Augustan age, Virgil is "correct"–the word is several times reiterated –in a time when "all false thoughts and idle ornaments in writing were discouraged."[21] What marked their sudden decline was "a desire of writing smartly, and an affectation of shining, . . . prettiness, and glitter, and luxuriance of ornaments . . . ; and their poetry was quite lost in high flights and obscurity."[22] None of this, of course, is original with Spence. What is important to observe is how criteria of value and scholarly criteria work together to create a canonical definition of ancient art and a strict delimitation of the ancient world.

Spence characterizes modern allegories with words like confusion, darkness, multiplicity, impropriety, riddle. Ripa is described as a book of puzzles. I believe that this vocabulary was first systematically applied to allegory by the Abbé Jean-Baptiste du Bos in his *Reflexions Critiques sur la Poésie et sur le Peinture* (1719). It was very widely read in England; and *Polymetis*, both as a contribution to the *ut pictura poesis* literature and as a prescriptive work for the modern artist must be related to it. Neatly encapsulated in du Bos, Spence and other English writers found those criteria for the limitation and proper use of allegory which we know so well from, say, Johnson. Du Bos is concerned with works produced in the past hundred years, and his continual refrain in his discussion of the modern turns upon riddles, enigmas, ciphers to which no one has the key–which, indeed, very few people would want.[23] Rubens in the Medici cycle and Le Brun at Versailles are his chief villains; for him the *reductio ad absurdum* of the modern situation is that at Versailles there are, lying on the tables, little books to tell us what the pictures are about. Du Bos has one central idea to explain all this: during the last hundred years artists have been governed by *esprit*. *Esprit* is the desire to be clever at all costs. In the name of *esprit* modern artists have abandoned the language of the passions common to all men to invent a language above the reach of ordinary comprehension. In du Bos's account, *esprit* is precisely analogous to those terms Spence found to characterize the declining arts of Rome: affectation, false ornament, and the rest. To du Bos, moreover, the cultivation of *esprit* accompanies a cultural decline and fall; for he is working within a historiographical scheme of the *modern*.

Du Bos's *modern* is based on a relatively new concept of art history, devised in Italy and France in the seventeenth century, and superseding Vasari's notion of the progress of the arts. Briefly, the new scheme sees the high point of modern art in Raphael. From him there is a decline punctuated by a few great exceptions, for example Poussin—and Spence adds Domenichino, "for justness and correctness":[24] this is Spence's scheme of the modern too. Poussin and Domenichino are the great *correct* painters, as Virgil was correct; they are being judged in relation to the ancient.

The two schemes of ancient and modern work together to control Spence's readings of Renaissance allegories. Of the Rubens Whitehall ceiling he writes: "I cannot well guess why the Cupids, in one of these pannels, are to conduct a triumphal sort of car, drawn by wild lions; and much less, why the triumphal car in the other, is drawn by a lamb and a bear."[25] Spence has, in fact, abandoned any possible interpretive tools; there were a number of places he might have gone for assistance. Here again, from Alciati's *Emblems*, is one of Rubens' sources (Figure 49).

The power of love tames the fiercest creatures and triumphs over them; the source adduced for the image is classical verse. Love bridles the lion; the pastoral ram is yoked together with the savage bear; the fruits of the earth are displayed in rich profusion. The imagery echoes familiar texts from Virgil and Isaiah: this is the golden age of peace and plenty, and through it Rubens figures the reign of James, and by implication of Charles.

Or again, in Rubens' Antwerp pageant, one of the personified winds baffles Spence: "that very strange one in particular; whose arms end in a sort of finny wings, from the elbow; and whose legs are of so strange a figure, that it would puzzle one to find out any name for it."[26] And again, though Spence is perfectly well aware of interpretive handbooks like the despised Ripa, it never occurs to him to turn to them for help. Here is the wind, in Cartari's *Images* (Figure 50). He is Boreas, and Cartari refers to a well-known passage in Pausanias as authority for his having a serpent's tail instead of feet.

49. Alciati, The Power of Love.
(*Emblemata*, 1621.)

50. Cartari, the four winds. Boreas is at the upper right, carrying off Orithyia.

Apart from Rubens, Spence chooses for particular criticism four very famous modern allegories by the otherwise admirable Domenichino, of the Cardinal Virtues, painted between 1628 and 1630 in the pendentives of the dome of San Carlo ai Catinari in Rome. Let us consider only one, Fortitude (Figure 51). "Fortitude, is with a sword and a shield; supported by a man with a dart in his hand, and a lion: on her right hand, is the motto of the Jesuits; and on her left, a column; not erect."[27] The motto, *Umilitas*, is more properly the *impresa* of San Carlo Borromeo, to whom the church was dedicated. The allegories in fact wittily employ, with double meanings, several personal and family devices of the saint, but of this Spence is ignorant. Nor does he seem to have known the standard account of the allegories in Bellori's seventeenth-century life of Domenichino.

Now Emile Mâle picked on these paintings too. Maintaining that Bellori's account was insufficient, he chose them to illustrate the importance of Ripa. Domenichino's *Fortitude*, Mâle points out, is Ripa's armed Minerva-like figure *Fortezza* (Figure 52). The column is added because Ripa says the column is the strongest feature of a building and supports all the others. Ripa puts a lion on Fortezza's shield (in some versions it is at her feet) because the lion was the Egyptian hieroglyph for strength. In Domenichino the lion is at her feet, being bridled by a young man who threatens it with an uplifted weapon. Mâle shows that the bridling and goading of the lion are taken from Ripa's figure of *Dominio di*

51. Domenichino, *Fortitude*. (Rome, San Carlo ai Catinari.)

Stesso, self-mastery (Figure 53) – the lion because the Egyptians also used it to figure the soul. Ripa took the whole figure from Valeriano's *Hieroglyphs*, where it means that self-mastery must restrain the soul when it is too ardent, and goad it when it is slow and sluggish. Mâle regards his whole discussion, not unreasonably, as a triumphant vindication of his claims for the handbooks.[28]

This is precisely the sort of analysis that Spence avoids: when Mysagetes and Philander engage in it, they do so only to dismiss it. Spence has no interest in understanding Domenichino's intentions; he is exclusively concerned to contrast Domenichino's Cardinal Virtues with the ancient images of them that he has found. For the ancients Fortitude, "who is to act," has her sword; that is enough for her. What Spence wishes to emphasize is what he terms the *simplicity* of the ancients in such representations, "that simplicity, which indeed runs generally through all their designs." If simplicity is the mark of canonical art and its allegories, then Alciati and Ripa are absurd. What is more, if ancient art is simple, then beast-headed gods or fish-tailed winds are not ancient; and so they are excluded from the corpus – they cease to exist and cannot be recognized.

52. Ripa, *Fortezza.*
(*Iconologia*, 1618.)

53. Ripa, *Dominio di Stesso.*
(*Iconologia*, 1618.)

IV

We can see how curiously placed Spence is when we turn to the question of poetry and consider his attitude toward Spenser. *Polymetis* in both its editions, 1747 and 1755, belongs to an immensely important period in the history of Spenser criticism. Hughes' edition with his remarkable essay on allegorical poetry had been published in 1715, and was reprinted in 1750. Jortin's *Remarks on the Faerie Queene* appeared in 1734. In 1754, Warton's first version of his *Observations on the Faerie Queene* was published, and the second, revised and expanded, in 1762. 1758 saw the first annotated edition, John Upton's, which with all its faults remained the best commentary until this century. Hurd's *Letters on Chivalry and Romance* came in 1762.

Not surprisingly, Spence applied to Spenser the same terminology he used to characterise Ripa or Vænius; there is much talk of fancifulness, whims, lack of clarity. These are the faults, for example, of the procession of the months from the *Mutability Cantos*—Spence finds this an instance of "ridiculous Imagination." Principles of coherence in the scene utterly elude him: "February is introduced in a waggon, drawn by two fishes; May, as riding on Castor and Pollux: June is mounted on a crab; October, on a scorpion: and November comes in, on a Centaur, all in a sweat; because, (as the poet observes,) he had just been fatting his hogs."[29] Apparently Spence did not even recognise that the months are shown in the procession of the zodiacal year and associated with the labours appropriate to each month. One would think that the signs of the Zodiac were clear enough, even if the traditional scheme *sign-month-labour* proved elusive, but Spence finds it all utterly baffling. For a case of over-amplification, Spence chooses the procession of Pride in Book I. Here again, he finds nothing but muddle: "she has so many different things and attributes about her; that was this shew to be represented, (in the manner of our old pageants,) they would rather set one a guessing what they meant themselves, than serve to point out who the principle figure should be."[30] He is unaware that the Vices in the procession are the seven deadly sins, that they attend on Pride because Pride is the chief of the sins and comprises all the others. Upton, commenting on these passages ten years later, knows all about the Zodiac and the deadly sins. But the medieval was out of Spence's reach, and he was therefore cut off from one of the main sources for contemporary re-interpretation of Spenser.

Spence also complains that Spenser misrepresents "the stories, and allegorical personages, of the antients."[31] This was a matter of general concern, but other critics were prepared to allow a certain "freedom," and "his own mythology" to Spenser. Spence's charges are based specifically on ancient authorities, but his canon is not the same as that employed by other commentators. For example, he is worried by Spenser's sirens, who are half fish (*FQ* 2.12.30–31). This, Spence says, is not ancient, and cites a gem, Martial, and Ovid. "The moderns, by some mistake or other, have turned their lower parts into fish; and so made of them the very same sort of monster, which Horace speaks of, in the beginning of his Art of Poetry."[32]

Renaissance mythographers like Cartari record two traditions about the sirens, one that they are bird-footed, the other that they are fish-tailed, and generally refuse to decide the issue. Upton, unlike Spence, is unperturbed:

> These poetical beings have the feet of birds, and the upper parts of a virgin. But should you ask why did not Spenser follow the ancient poets and mythologists, than the moderns in making them Mermaids? My answer is, Spenser has a mythology of his own: nor would he leave his brethren the romance writers, where merely authority is to be put against authority. Boccace has given a sanction to this description. *Geneal*[*ogia*] *Deorum, Lib.* vii *Cap.* 20. Let me add our old poets, as Gower, . . . and Chaucer . . . . Vossius has followed it too . . . .[33]

In this same elaborate note Upton refers also to Comes' *Mythologiae*. Comes had not been quite forgotten: Jortin had already used him, and so had Hughes and Warton, though as an authority on genealogy, not on allegory. But Warton goes a step further than the other commentators. After referring to Comes for Spenser's list of sea-gods, he writes in 1754:

> Spenser probably took his catalogue from this mythologist; I think he has given us no names (Albion excepted) but what are found in that author . . . .[34]

For Spence Comes carries no authority at all, not being ancient. For the other commentators he is one authority among many, old and new, not differentiated. For Warton he is the *source*: an historiographical process is at work. In 1762, Warton's revised edition adds this: "Natalis Comes was then just published, and, I suppose, a popular book."[35] Here I think we catch a moment; the methods of the historians of antiquity are being applied to a sixteenth-century poet. Spence could not do this, any more than he could use Ripa for Domenichino. He knew two worlds only, the truly ancient and the modern. Spenser is a modern, and the modern is defined only by its relationship to the ancient.

V

> The last and most eminent characteristic of the Greek works is a noble simplicity and sedate grandeur in Gesture and Expression.

With this sentence, in 1755, the year of Spence's second edition, from the depths of rococo Germany, Johann Joachim Winckelmann announced to Europe both the primacy and character of the classical ideal, inventing Greek art before he had seen any; and poor, fierce, desperate, obsessed, self-destroying, demonic, inventing that ideal, so powerful for so long, out of his own antitheses. I have quoted from the translation of the *Gedanken*, *Reflections on the Painting and Sculpture of the Greeks*, published in London in 1765 by Winckelmann's disciple Henry Fuseli.[36]

Like Spence's, Winckelmann's aim is prescriptive. The use of *simple* and *simplicity* as criteria of value has been adopted and given an almost technical application to a newly restricted corpus of the truly ancient. This is part of Winckelmann's achievement. His passionate scholarship was directed to establishing a canon for contemporary art; and he wanted, as much as Spence did, a new system of allegory. He shared, too, with Spence and the rest, that scheme of the modern arts declining from Raphael—for him Bernini is the chief enemy.

We tend to think of the consequences of Winckelmann, of the "Greek simplicity," in terms of Canova, or Flaxman, or David. To a certain extent this is justified; such a painting as David's *Leonidas before Thermopylae* renders precisely Winckelmann's nude heroic Greece (Figure 54). "I wish," said David of this painting, "neither movement nor impassioned expression."[37] Indeed the pose of Leonidas is derived from a cameo that Winckelmann had published (Figure 55). Or we might take the work of Thomas Banks, generally considered the first truly neo-classic sculptor in England, a protégé of Fuseli, and thus directly influenced by Winckelmann's ideas. Here is his monument to Mrs. Petrie in the Parish Church at Lewisham (Figure 56). The virtues who attend the dying woman, faith, hope, and charity are personified in as simple and clear embodiments as even Spence could have wished. This particular application of allegory was explicitly allowed by the new theorists. "I agree therefore," du Bos had written—and Thomas Warton quoted the passage—"to let them draw Faith and Hope supporting a dying person."[38] Reynolds said of Banks that he was "the first British sculptor who had produced works of classic grace":[39] and there at last is the adjective being used as a measure of value.

But there was another side to Winckelmann's nature, and it has been tactfully overlooked by his disciples and commentators. In the *Reflections* Winckelmann had set out the artist's need for some satisfactory "learned apparatus, by whose stores he might be enabled to invest abstracted ideas with sensible and meaning images. . . . Nothing has yet been published of this kind, to satisfy a rational being . . . . The artist himself knows best in what degree he is satisfied with Ripa's Iconology."[40] In 1766 Winckelmann published his own *Attempt at an Allegory Principally for the Use of Artists*.[41] All the world, he says, knows the standard books of allegories. These are Valeriano's *Hieroglyphica*, Ripa, and Boudard (the last, of course, is really an expanded version of Ripa). Each is dismissed: Valeriano for

54. J. L. David, *Léonide aux Thermopyles* (detail): the figure of Leonidas. (Paris, Louvre.)

55. A cameo with the figure of Ajax Oïleus engraved on it, from J. J. Winckelmann, *Monumenti Antichi*, Rome 1821.

56. Thomas Banks, funeral monument to Mrs. Petrie. (Lewisham Parish Church.)

offering nothing but feeble conjectures and useless discourses, Boudard for plagiarism and inaccuracy. Ripa's treatment is less summary but no more sympathetic: the fact that the book should have become the artist's manual only reveals to Winckelmann how depraved was the taste of the eras after the golden age of Raphael. What was original with Ripa, and not copied from the emblem books, demonstrated that he had not the remotest acquaintance with sculptures, gems, reliefs, medals, antique monuments of any kind. Very few of his images are suitable for use in painting, and some, indeed, are patently ridiculous. Had Ripa known the Italian proverb *to piss in a sieve* (to take useless trouble) he would doubtless have tried to render that too.

A categorical dismissal, so it would seem. Winckelmann goes on to lay down as requirements for new allegories *simplicity*, *clarity*, and *grace*. He repeats most of what we have already heard; for after all, he knew the same books, and was particularly affected by his English readings: he greatly admired Addison, and had studied Spence carefully. But when Winckelmann comes to formulate his own new allegories, we find that he inhabits precisely that world of learning that he had apparently rejected, and that Spence, Addison, du Bos so despised. His sources are far from canonical. The post-classical texts and the commentaries, familiar from sixteenth-century mythographers, are all here again: Phurnutus, Hyginus, Eustathius, Macrobius and the rest. So are the ingenious readings. Theseus and Pirithoous are here as good neo-Classic exemplars of heroic friendship; but so are the lion and the hare, representing *antipathy*, or even less gracefully the elephant and the pig, the latter pair with Plutarch as authority. The tulip, which is beautiful but has no scent, signifies a man who is handsome but has no other merit; a man pouring the three Graces from a vase to the ground represents *ingratitude*. Clearly we are back in the world of Valeriano and Ripa. Of all Winckelmann's books this was the least well received. His contemporaries, more *modern* than he, complained of forced interpretations, absurdities, obscurities. But this was the other side of Winckelmann's nature, and he set great store by it.

VI

The last English Ripa, and perhaps the last of all, appeared in 1778, its author George Richardson, an architect. His long introduction rehearses doctrines about hieroglyphs and the sacred wisdom that might have come from any sixteenth- or seventeenth-century text. Invoking Winckelmann, he calls once again for a new iconology; but he gives us, after all, only Ripa classicised. Richardson published the book at his own expense; it was successful enough to be reprinted once, and no doubt had some influence somewhere on some neo-classical decorative scheme. Ripa had survived to be an elegant curiosity.

Ripa's fate in the eighteenth century is a history of cultural displacement. It involves the age's attitudes not only to a mode like allegory, but, far more strongly and significantly, to its own immediate past. And the classicising tendencies of the age conceal how very mixed those attitudes were—Winckelmann's startling apostasy springs, obviously, from sources very deep in his nature. For a different kind of example, we may return for a moment to Addison. In a note much better known than those passages I have cited from the *Dialogues*, Addison rejected the whole tradition of the allegorization and Christianising of Ovid. "I shall," he insisted, "only consider Ovid under the character of a Poet."[42] This has been taken to mark a decisive moment in critical history, and so it does. But the note relates to the two books Addison contributed to Sir Samuel Garth's collective translation of *The Metamorphoses*. Garth's Introduction expounds in detail the tradition of systematic allegorical interpretation, in which he fully believes; and Garth's Ovid, Introduction and all, went through thirteen editions between 1717 and 1826.

For Spence and Winckelmann, Ripa both was and was not a historical document. It was, in the sense that it illustrated the corruption of taste in modern art, the decline from Raphael. But it was not a historical resource, or instrument: as we have seen, it never occurred to Spence or anyone else to use Ripa to interpret the extravagant allegories of modern painting. Spence, du Bos, Winckelmann admitted only the two worlds of ancient and modern, and only the ancient was a proper object of historical investigation. Spenser and Rubens were not history. But at the same time, in Spence's England the sixteenth century was beginning to emerge as a historical realm; as we have seen, for Thomas Warton, Natalis Comes has almost acquired the status of a historical instrument for the interpretation of a Renaissance poet. In Warton's context, Spence and Winckelmann —and indeed, art history generally—are already reactionary. By the end of the eighteenth century, Ripa's *Iconology* had been consigned to the bibliophiles, who invariably placed it among the emblem books, quaint survivals of a playful past.

VII

We began with Mâle's question about how the attributes of Bernini's *Truth* are to be read. "What meaning lay hidden in them by Bernini, who had, we know, conceived this statue in a moment of deep melancholy?"[43] For all the iconographic detail supplied by Ripa, the question, in Mâle's account, remains unanswered. The statue was indeed a response to an emotionally charged situation, to what Wittkower calls the only frustrating experience of Bernini's brilliant career: the decision by the congregation of St. Peter's in 1646 to demolish the architect's tower there. Bernini ascribed great personal importance to the statue of *Truth*; he bequeathed it to his descendants as an inalienable possession, to remind them, as he explicitly said in his will, that Truth is the greatest virtue on earth. Mâle failed to see that in fact, Ripa could not tell him nearly enough; could not help him distinguish this statue of Truth from innumerable others.

In 1936 Fritz Saxl published a study of Bernini's *Truth* that contains two startling omissions: it mentions the names of neither Mâle nor Ripa.[44] The omissions are quite certainly deliberate, characteristic of Saxl's temperament, and indicative of a large impatience. One could not, he tacitly implied, simply consult Ripa under *Truth* and think that one had explained Bernini. To begin with, Mâle seems not to have realized that Bernini's statue is unfinished; what was the rest to have been? And Mâle pays no attention to that cloud of drapery; it is not in Ripa, and therefore it goes unnoticed. The figure of Truth is only part of a larger allegorical composition. Saxl recognised that Bernini's group was to have shown Truth being unveiled by Time; there are documents that substantiate this. Saxl's larger theme was *Veritas Filia Temporis*, Truth the daughter of Time, a humanist formula devised in the early sixteenth century, and applied with many transformations in a bewildering variety of contexts; and he was concerned to show precisely what Mâle had ignored, the individuality with which the great artist responds to a common theme. In bypassing both Mâle and Ripa, Saxl was, no doubt, a little mischievous. But he may serve to remind us thereby that first among the realities of art stands the object; that works of art are more than puzzles to be solved or riddles to be answered.

ESSAYS

Poet and Architect:
The Intellectual Setting of the Quarrel
between Ben Jonson and Inigo Jones

The Course of the Quarrel

What is known about the quarrel between Ben Jonson and Inigo Jones over their parts in the preparation of the court masques has been set out more than once; and there is agreement about the main lines of the story.[1] Jonson told Drummond of Hawthornden in the first weeks of 1619 how he had said to Prince Charles that when he wanted a word to express the greatest villain in the world he would call him an Inigo; and also that while he denied calling Inigo a fool he had certainly called him an arrant knave.[2] But Jonson had attacked Jones in public long before this, for we have an epigram, possibly written in 1612, or even earlier, in which he paints a bitter picture of "the town's honest man" and there is hardly room to doubt that he intended this time-server, flatterer and buffoon as a portrait of Jones.[3] His anger flashed out again in the last years of the old king's reign in a poem, and in a masque, intended to welcome Charles and Buckingham back from Spain but never performed. Nor did Jones's influence with the new king persuade Jonson to caution. Jones appears again in *The Staple of News* in 1626; and the famous quarrel in 1631 over the masque *Love's Triumph through Callipolis* which ended the long collaboration comes simply as the climax of this old story. When Jonson published the text of this masque he put his own name before Jones's on the title-page–"The Inuentors. Ben Ionson. Inigo Jones." Jones was angry. Jonson answered him with satirical invective and we get the most famous document of the long war, *An Expostulation with Inigo Jones*, with its companion pieces *To Inigo Marquess Would be. A Corollary* and *To a friend. An Epigram of him.*[4] Jones essayed a reply in kind but had stronger weapons than such halting lines. For after 1631 Jonson composed no more court masques, and when he wanted to bring Jones on the stage in *A*

Tale of a Tub, two years later, the passages attacking him were cut out by order of the Lord Chamberlain.[5] But outside London Jonson would still have his way, even in the presence of the king and queen, and so Jones turns up again in the shape of Colonel Iniquo Vitruvius in the last entertainment Jonson wrote, *Love's Welcome at Bolsover* (1634).

Of the origins of the quarrel we know nothing. But the collaboration, which began in 1605 with work on *The Masque of Blackness* and which lasted, with intervals, until 1631, offered, with the demands for closeness of working which it imposed, almost infinite opportunities for quarrelling if either man were disposed to take them. And indeed this quarrel has generally been considered as a manifestation of that endemic hostility between poet and *régisseur*. Jonson we know was aware of his dignity as poet and was hardly of a pacific disposition; and Jones was certainly ambitious and proud of his Italian culture and techniques. Judgment seems to have gone against Jonson. But if he appears the more quarrelsome that is, after all, partly because we have in print what he said about Jones. We do not know what Jones was saying about Jonson—or doing to him—through these years. The point is so elementary that to write it down may seem absurd, yet it has influenced opinion. Granted the characters of the two men—and we know practically nothing about Jones's personality—and the kind of work they had to do together, quarrels may have been inevitable, and the course they took may not seem to be of enormous interest. And if we consider the affair simply as a clash of personalities there is little to say about it that has not been said. Yet a fresh scrutiny of the documents can still yield interesting material. When Jonson insults Jones's character we have no means of knowing whether he was right or wrong: we do not know whether Jones was honest or dishonest, whether he was really a fool who would play any part to win notice, an ambitious pretentious man flaunting a culture patched together from bits and pieces picked up from "shop philosophy" and the works of his masters. These may simply be the insults of a jealous and angry man. But Jonson's insults are not all of this kind. His more considered insults presuppose a body of doctrine: a serious doctrine of what the masque is to the poet; a serious doctrine of what the practitioner of the visual arts and particularly the architect is and does. Jonson is criticizing not only a man but a theory. And Jones replies to him on the ground of theory—as well as with bad verse and court influence. We see architect and poet facing each other from well-prepared positions. The aim of this essay is to show what these positions were, to relate the quarrel to its proper intellectual context and observe how the personal situation finds ground and expression in terms common to European discussions of the fine arts. The method must largely be that of restoring to words their technical significances, for it is the terms used in this flyting that show us what its larger context was. The story of the quarrel moves from the world of gossip and personalities and illustrates a more important history.

The Poet

And I haue mett with those
That doe cry vp the Machine, and the Showes!

The majesty of Iuno in the Cloudes,
And peering forth of Iris in the Shrowdes!
Th'ascent of Lady Fame which none could spy
Not they that sided her, Dame Poetry,
Dame History, Dame Architecture too,
And Goody Sculpture, brought with much adoe
To hold her vp. O Showes! Showes! Mighty Showes!
The Eloquence of Masques! What need of prose
Or Verse, or Sense t'express Immortall you?
You are the Spectacles of State! Tis true
Court Hieroglyphicks! and all Artes affoord
In the mere perspectiue of an Inch board!
You aske noe more then certeyne politique Eyes,
Eyes that can pierce into the Misteryes
Of many Coulors! read them! and reueale
Mythology there painted on slit deale!
Oh, to make Boardes to speake! There is a taske
Painting and Carpentry are the Soule of Masque.[6]

The irony in the *Expostulation* is perhaps a little heavy, and there is perhaps a danger of seeing it as more heavy-handed than it is. Thus the word "soul" in the last line is not there simply to strengthen the irony in a rather palpable way. It has a sharp technical meaning. And full appreciation of the irony depends on our knowing this.

In considering Jonson's ideas about the masque—and though his references are not many they yield a clear statement—we should begin where he begins, with a distinction between body and soul. The fullest statement is in the prefatory lines to *Hymenaei* (1606); it is a much used passage but must be quoted again:

It is a noble and iust aduantage, that the things subiected to *vnderstanding* haue of those which are obiected to *sense*, that the one sort are but momentarie, and meerely taking; the other impressing, and lasting: Else the glorie of all these *solemnities* had perish'd like a blaze, and gone out, in the *beholders* eyes. So short-liu'd are the *bodies* of all things, in comparison of their *soules*. And, though *bodies* oft-times haue the ill luck to be sensually preferr'd, they find afterwards, the good fortune (when *soules* liue) to be vtterly forgotten. This it is hath made the most royall *Princes*, and greatest *persons* (who are commonly the *personaters* of these *actions*) not onely studious of riches, and magnificence in the outward celebration, or shew; (which rightly becomes them) but curious after the most high, and heartie *inuentions*, to furnish the inward parts: (and those grounded vpon *antiquitie*, and solide *learnings*) which, though their *voyce* be taught to sound to present occasions, their *sense*, or doth, or should alwayes lay hold on more remou'd *mysteries*.[7]

Jonson is asserting that the masque has two parts: one, which is addressed to the understanding, is the soul; the other, which is addressed to the senses, is the body. The body of the masque is the "outward celebration" or "shew." Jonson is making the same distinction two years later when he writes of the "carkasses" and "spirits" of the two masques he is publishing.[8] And the soul, the inward part, of the masque depends on "high and heartie" inventions. The soul is the more important, for the "shew" lasts only as long as sense experience itself. It is the soul, the invention which is the soul, that remains. Nor is the metaphor so banal as it may sound, for, as we shall see, it depends on a firm conception of the relationship between soul and body.

Jonson can distinguish between his share in a masque and Jones's in terms of this image. Thus, describing the décor of *Blackness* he writes: "So much for the bodily part, Which was of master Ynigo Iones his designe, and act."[9] But his key word in making the distinction is "invention" (which constitutes the soul). "Inuented by Ben. Jonson" appears on the title-page of *Blackness* and *Beauty* in 1608, and will reappear as a formula. In the references to his collaborators in the early masques the word is used in opposition to words indicating décor and construction:

> The deuice and act of the scene, M. YNIGO IONES his, with addition of the Trophæes. For the inuention of the whole and the verses, Assertor qui dicat esse meos, Imponet plagiario pudorem.[10]

Nor was Jonson's use of the word in this sense peculiar to himself. It was a technical term of the masque, and other masque writers use it in the same way.[11]

Before inquiring more closely into the meaning of "invention" we may consider the "body-soul" image a little further. The provenance of these terms is clear. They obviously come from the theoretical literature on the composition of *imprese* or emblems, where they have a precise connotation. The "body" is the visual image and the "soul" is the *mot*, the verse, the words that must accompany it. It was probably Paolo Giovio who first made them familiar by using them in his *Dialogo dell'Imprese Militari et Amorose*, published in 1555 and frequently reprinted through the century. They are repeated again and again and become stock terms. Giovio's precept that the perfect *impresa* must have both soul and body, words and image, has the same fortune.[12] We find this statement, for instance, in a disquisition on symbols prefixed to a famous edition of Alciati's emblems:

> Whoever wishes to make any symbol or emblem properly must first look to these things: that there be a just proportion between the soul and body. By 'soul' I mean the motto, expressed in one or two, or at most a few words; by the term 'body' I mean the image itself.[a]

But the point need not be laboured. Jonson himself was perfectly familiar with the technical usage. We can see him adopting it in a scene in *Poetaster* (1601) when Horace is accused of treason by the envious and ridiculous Lupus. Lupus' evidence is what he calls "a libell in picture." Horace explains to Augustus that Lupus has in fact found "the imperfect body in an *embleme*, Cæsar, I began for Mecœnas," and he proceeds to explain it:

> With reverence to great CÆSAR, worthy *Romans*,
> Obserue but this ridiculous commenter:
> The soule to my deuice was in this distich.

---

[a] qui symbolum aliquod vel schema commode volet effingere, spectanda haec primum proponuntur, vt iusta sit animi & corporis analogia (per animum, sententiam vno, altero, vel certe paucis comprehensam verbis intelligo: nomine corporis, symbolum ipsum designari placet).[13]

> *Thus, oft, the base and rauenous multitude*
> *Suruiue, to share the spoiles of fortitude.*
> Which in this body, I haue figur'd here,
> A VULTURE . . . [14]

What Jonson meant by "invention" comes out fairly clearly, though we should be on our guard against imposing too absolute a definition: the terms Elizabethan writers use in speaking about their work tend to float ambiguously. The "invention" is the fable itself and the theme it carries. It is close to the words "argument" and "device" and should be taken with them. When the fable is stated as a narrative it is the "argument," the plot-outline; but "argument" can also mean the subject, the theme illustrated by the fable. "Device" means plot-outline, fable or narrative. "Invention" is the most inclusive term.

> It was my first, and speciall reguard, to see that the Nobilyty of the Invention should be answerable to the dignity of theyr persons. For which reason, I chose the Argument to be, *A Celebration of honorable, & true Fame, bred out of Vertue.*[15]

"Invention" is here the whole dramatic fable carrying this given "argument" or theme. So it is in this sentence from the same text:

> The tweluth, and worthy *Soueraigne* of all I make *Bel-anna*, Royall *Queene* of the *Ocean*; of whose dignity, and person the whole *scope* of the *Inuention* doth speake throughout.[16]

We also possess a copy of the "summary description" of this same masque—*The Masque of Queens*—submitted to the court before performance. The editors rightly call it "The Argument of the Masque": it is an "argument" in the sense of plot-summary, such as masque writers sometimes printed as part of their text.[17] The running together of "device" and "argument" can be illustrated from *Neptune's Triumph*: in the anti-masque Cooke and Poet speak:

> COOKE I haue a suite.
> POET What is it?
> COOKE Your deuise.
> POET As you came in vpon me, I was then
>   Offring the argument, and this it is.[18]

What the cook wants to know is what the fable is; the poet is about to give a summary of the plot, and this he does. In *Chloridia* we hear of both "invention" and "argument" (and of "invention" meaning, as of course it must, not only the result of a process but the process itself):

> The King, and Queenes Maiesty, hauing giuen their command for the Inuention of a new argument, with the whole change of the *Scene* . . . It was agreed, it should be the celebration of some Rites, done to the Goddesse *Chloris*, who in a generall counsell of the Gods, was proclaim'd Goddesse of the flowers, according to that of *Ouid*, in the *Fasti*. *Arbitrium tu, Dea, floris habe.* And was to be stellified on Earth, by an absolut decree from *Iupiter*, who would haue the Earth to be adorn'd with starres, as well as the Heauen.
> Vpon this hinge, the whole Inuention moou'd.[19]

The whole invention is a fable carrying out this argument. When Jonson uses the word "invention" of Jones's share in an early masque–*The Masque of Queens*–he is crediting Jones with making a contribution to the development of the theme.[20] And it is important to note that "invention" is not synonymous with verbal statement. There is a distinction between "invention" and expression. As we can see from the passage already quoted where Jonson claims both the "invention" and the verses. Or as we can see in a later masque–when Jones was already encroaching on his sphere:

> For the expression of this, I must stand; The inuention was diuided betwixt Mr. Iones, and mee.[21]

"Invention" is ultimately a technical term from rhetoric. In the traditional five-fold division of the "parts" of rhetoric *inventio* comes first–"the finding out or selection of topics to be treated, or arguments to be used."[22] Long before the sixteenth century it had been taken over into poetics, and in the sixteenth century its use in discussions of poetic theory is a commonplace.[23] Jonson's use of it can be followed in the *Discoveries*, the note-book where he set down observations "made upon men and matter" drawn from his reading and experience. The exact sources or the originality of his reflections need not concern us: he is moving in the familiar world of humanist thought.

Invention is literally the finding of the subject of the poem. It is the first essential: without a fine invention there cannot be a fine poem.[24] Invention is also equated with the fable or fiction of the poem.[25] The central passage in the *Discoveries* is this, Jonson's definition of the poet:

> A *Poet* is that, which by the *Greeks* is call'd κατ' ἐξοχὴν, ὁ Ποιητὴς, a Maker or a fainer: His Art, an Art of imitation, or faining; expressing the life of man in fit measure, numbers and harmony, according to *Aristotle*: From the word ποιεῖν which signifies to make, or fayne.
> Hence, hee is call'd a *Poet*, not hee which writeth in measure only; but that fayneth and formeth a fable, and writes things like the Truth. For, the Fable and Fiction is (as it were) the forme and Soule of any Poetical worke, or *Poeme*.[26]

This fable and fiction which is the form and soul of the poem is the invention. It is the soul, and the words, the expression, are the body–just as the sense is the soul of the word, which is dead without it.[27]

We can return to the passage from which we began, the passage from *Hymenaei*. The masque is simply a poem. What comes first is the invention, the fable or soul of the work. Then comes the body, the scenic expression which can be compared to words that express sense and only live in so far as they do. It was noted earlier that the body-soul image is not used carelessly. Its meaning is given in the passage from *Discoveries*. The words used are "forme and soule": we are dealing with the traditional Aristotelian-Christian conception of the soul as form of the body, that in virtue of which the body has its proper and peculiar being.[28]

The masque then is a poem. Its preparation depends on the application of the poet's characteristic gift, the ability to find inventions; and of course also on his learning, for learning is needed to produce inventions.[29] And so Jonson is justified when in *Cynthia's*

Revels he shows the poet commanded to prepare a masque praying for inspiration in these exalted terms. He prays to Apollo and he prays for the faculty of inventing:

> PHOEBVS APOLLO: if with ancient rites,
> And due deuotions, I haue euer hung
> Elaborate pæans, on thy golden shrine,
> Or sung thy triumphs in a loftie straine,
> Fit for a theater of gods to heare:
> And thou, the other sonne of mighty IOVE,
> Cyllenian MERCVRY (sweet MAIA's ioy)
> If in the busi tumults of the mind,
> My path thou euer hast illumined,
> For which, thine altars, I haue oft perfum'd,
> And deckt thy statues with discolour'd flowres:
> Now thrive invention in this glorious court,
> That not of bountie only, but of right,
> CYNTHIA may grace, and giue it life by sight.[30]

And speaking in his own person as poet he can make the same prayer:

> Where are thou, *Genius*? I should use
> Thy present Aide: Arise Invention,
> Wake, and put on the wings of *Pindar*'s Muse,
> To towre with my intention. . . .[31]

So when Jonson writes that in this mechanical age "Painting and Carpentry are the Soule of Masque" he is stating, seriously, the reverse of the true situation. The places of body and soul have been inverted. The meaning of the masque now resides in mythology painted on slit deal. The visual has assumed primacy: the image no longer needs the words that should give it life. The image itself is the immortal soul.

> O Showes! Showes! Mighty Showes!
> The eloquence of Masques! What need of prose
> Or Verse, or Sense t'express Immortall you?

Renaissance theories of composition imply that finding the subject and expressing it are separate mental acts, and distinctions between invention and expression in the preparation of a masque have also this as background. But the invention is, other things being equal, the test of the poet's worth. If he is merely expressing another man's invention in verse then the poet is no longer fully a poet. With what reluctance Jonson must have written those lines that claim the "expression" only of the *Masque of Augurs* as wholly his and give Jones credit for sharing in the invention. And on the title-page of *Love's Triumph* he has to acknowledge Jones's part as "Inventor" and describe in the text how "Wee, the Inuentors" after some thought resolved on an argument . . .

> Whither? oh whither will this Tire-man growe?
> His name is Σκευοποιός wee all knowe,
> The maker of the Propertyes! in summe
> The Scene! the Engyne! . . .

Jones's job is to make the body:

> but he now is come
> To be the Musick Master! Fabler too!
> He is, or would be the mayne Dominus doe
> All in the Worke![32]

The climax of his arrogance is the claim to be the Fabler too. He would arrogate to himself the poet's part, the activity which is the heart and core of the poet's work and on which his very claim to call himself a poet rests.

To set beside the rapt poet praying for inspiration we have Jonson's version of how Jones set about devising a masque. This is in *A Tale of a Tub* where Jonson presents Jones as the rustic joiner In-and-In Medlay commissioned to prepare a masque for Squire Tub. The great writer D'oge Scriben is asked to do it but replies:

> Hee'll do't alone Sir, He will joyne with no man,
> Though he be a Joyner: in designe he cals it,
> He must be sole Inventer: *In-and-In*
> Drawes with no other in's project, hee'll tell you,
> It cannot else be feazeable, or conduce:
> Those are his ruling words . . . .

The story is to be the tale of a tub, Squire Tub's own story. Asked if he can "express" a tub Medlay replies with assurance:

> If it conduce
> To the designe, what'ere is feazable:
> I can expresse a Wash-house (if need be)
> With a whole pedigree of Tubs.

He asks to be shown the place where the masque is to be given:

> for all Invention, Sir,
> Comes by degrees, and on the view of nature;
> A world of things, concurre to the designe,
> Which make it feazible, if Art conduce.[33]

Some time later Medlay reports progress and we have his invention:

> What ha' you done?
> MEDLAY   Survey'd the place Sir, and design'd the ground,
> Or stand-still of the work: And this it is.
> First, I haue fixed in the earth, a *Tub*;
> And an old *Tub*, like a Salt-Peeter Tub,
> Preluding by your Fathers name Sir *Peeter*,
> And the antiquity of your house, and family,
> Originall from Salt-Peeter.
> TUB   Good y'faith,
> You ha' shewne reading, and antiquity here, Sir.

Medlay preens himself:

> I have a little knowledge in designe,
> Which I can varie Sir to *Infinito*.

Designer and patron however almost disagree. Tub insists that the tale is his, *he* is Tub, the *subjectum fabulae*. And Medlay is advised not to quarrel with the man who is going to pay. . . . But he gets everything into his hands:

> Give me the briefe o' your subject. Leave the whole
> State of the thing to me.[34]

The masque turns out to be a rendering of the absurd plot of the play in a series of "motions"—a shadow show cast on the transparent paper with which the top of the tub has been covered. All accompanied by wretched doggerel verses apparently composed by Medlay himself.

This is Dominus Do All in action then. His masque is a series of images illustrating a ridiculous plot conveyed in illiterate verses, his great invention a Tub—based on "reading and antiquity." Years ago Gascoigne had written "what Theame soeuer you do take in hande, if you do handle it but *tanquam in oratione perpetua*, and neuer studie for some depth of deuise in the Inuention, and some figures also in the handlyng thereof, it will appeare to the skilfull Reader but a tale of a tubbe."[35] So Jonson shows.

The Architect

Omnicompetence may have been Jones's foible. But Jonson well knew that the architect's claims to competence in all the arts had a long history and classical sanction. These claims he burlesques in the anti-masque of *Neptune's Triumph* (1624) when he puts them into the mouth of the master cook who disputes with the poet.

The cook claims that he and the poet are brothers because their arts stand on the same level: "Eithers Art is the wisdome of the Mind."[36] The art of cookery satisfies the senses, but also the understanding which rejoices in the experiences of the senses. And, angry with the poet, the cook goes further:

> Seduced *Poet*, I doe say to thee,—
> A Boyler, Range, and Dresser were the fountaines
> Of all the knowledge, in the *Vniuerse*,
> And that's the Kitchin. Where, a *Master-Cooke*—
> Thou do'st not know the man! nor canst thou know him!
> Til thou hast seru'd some yeares in that deep school,
> That's both the Nource, and Mother of the *Arts*,
> And hear'st him read, interpret, and demonstrate.
> A *Master-Cooke*! why, he is the man of men,
> For a Professor. He designes, he drawes,

He paints, he carues, he builds, he fortifies,
Makes *Citadels* of curious foule, and fish,
Some he dry-ditches, some motes round with broths;
Mounts marrow-bones; cuts fifty-angled custards;
Reares bulwarke pies; and, for his outer workes,
He raiseth ramparts of immortall crust;
And teacheth all the *tacticks* at one dinner:
What rankes, what files, to put his dishes in;
The whole *Art Militarie*! Then he knowes
The influence of the starres, vpon his meates;
And all their seasons, tempers, qualities,
And so, to fit his relishes, and sauces!
He'has *Nature* in a pot! 'boue all the *Chemists*,
Or bare-breechd brethren of the *Rosie-Crosse*!
He is an *Architect*, an *Inginer*,
A *Souldier*, a *Physitian*, a *Philosopher*;
A generall *Mathematician*![37]

Jonson had in mind the most famous of all descriptions of the architect. In his own copy of Vitruvius' *De Architectura* he had read and studied thoroughly at least the first chapter, *Quid sit Architectura, et de Architectis instituendis*.[38] It is this chapter that has provided the cook's description of his art. In one place Vitruvius explains—a passage which Jonson marked—that the architect must be:

> naturally talented ... and willing to be taught (for neither talent without training nor training without talent can produce the perfect craftsman), and he should be well-read, skilled in drawing, excellent at geometry, not ignorant of optics, a trained mathematician; he should know the results of new research, listen diligently to philosophers, be interested in music, learned in the law, and understand astrology and astronomy.[b]

This passage, with the elaborations it underwent, was a *locus classicus* in the development of that theory of architecture and the architect on which Jones took his stand.

For Jones had a position and could and did make his own claims. In 1632 he produced two masques at court with the collaboration of a minor poet, Aurelian Townshend.[40] These were the first masques since the quarrel over *Love's Triumph* and the bitter poems of a year before. It is when writing of Townshend's appearance as a masque-writer that a gossip writer tells us the story of that quarrel—"Ben Jonson being for this time discarded by reason of the predominant power of his antagonist, Inigo Jones, who this time twelvemonth, was angry with him for putting his own name before his in the title-page."[41] The events of last year must have been fresh in the minds of poet and designer too. And the triumphant architect retorts in his own medium to Jonson's attacks.

---

[b] ingeniosum ... & ad disciplinam docilem (neque enim ingenium sine disciplina, aut disciplina sine ingenio, perfectum artificem potest efficere) & vt literatus sit, peritus graphidos, eruditus Geometria, & optices non ignarus, instructus Arithmetica, historias complures nouerit, Philosophos diligenter audiuerit, Musicam non sit ignarus, responsa Iurisconsultorum nouerit, Astrologiam caelique rationes cognitas habeat ...[39]

The first of these masques was the king's, *Albion's Triumph*. It shows the king as heir to the glories of a Roman emperor and his union with the goddess Alba. It is notable for the splendour and variety of its architectural settings. We see first a Roman atrium, then a forum, then a temple showing in a grove, then a landscape with views of London and the palace of Whitehall.[42] The drawing for the richly decorated proscenium arch survives (Figure 57) and corresponds to the description:

57. Inigo Jones, drawing for the proscenium arch of *Albion's Triumph*, 1632. The figure of Theory is at the left, Practice at the right. (Devonshire Collection, Chatsworth.)

at the foot of the pillasters, on each side, stood two Women, the one young, in a watchet Robe looking vpwards, and on her head, a paire of Compasses of gold, the poynts standing towards Heaven: the other more ancient, and of a venerable aspect, apparreled in tawney, looking downewards; in the one hand a long ruler, and in the other, a great paire of iron Compasses, one poynt whereof, stood on the ground, and the other touched part of the ruler. Above their heads, were fixt, compertiments of a new composition, and in that over the first was written *Theorica*, and over the second *Practica*, shewing that by these two, all works of Architecture, and Ingining have their perfection.[43]

Details of Theory and Practice

Now these figures have no relevance to the special glorification of the king and queen which is the burden of the masque. But perhaps they have another relevance, they and the architectural settings of the masque. The triumphs of Roman architecture which lead up to the palace of Whitehall (and one would like to know whether the view showed the Banqueting House, or perhaps part of the projected palace), do they not celebrate the glory of the architect as well as of the king? In the *Expostulation* Jonson had compared Jones very unfavourably with the great ancient architects, and in his *To Inigo Marquess Would Be* had rudely suggested that far from being capable of designing cities or temples or palaces or forums Inigo reached his limit with scenery and "shows". And the basis of these marvels of the architect's art which we see is, we are told by the figures on the proscenium, the union of theory and practice.

The proscenium of the second masque, the queen's, *Tempe Restor'd*, which was given a few weeks later, is also relevant. Here is the description, which Townshend's editor suspects was written by Jones himself:

In the vpper part of the border serving for ornament to the Scene, was painted a faire compartment of scrowles and quadratures, in which was written *Tempe Restavratvm*. On each side of this, lay a figure bigger then the life, the one a woman with wings on her head like *Mercvrie* and a pen in her hand: the other a man looking downe in a booke lying open before him, and a torch lighted in his hand: that figur'd Invention; this Knowledge. Neere to these were children holding ougly Maskes before their faces in action as if they would afright them; others riding on tame beasts and some blowing such wrethen Trumps as make confused noyse, in the corners sat other Children hardning of darts in Lamps. But Invention & Knowledge seeme not to be diverted from their study by these childish bugbears. In the midst of the two sides of this border in short neeces sat two ougly figures, the one a woman with a forked tongue, and snaky lockes, and the vnderpart of a Satyre, this Hagge held in her hand a smiling vizard corwn'd with Roses, and was figured for Envie, vnder the Maske of friendship. On the other side was sitting as horrid a man Satyre with a wreath of poppy on his head, and a Frog sitting on the fore part thereof; and aboue a Batt flying, this represented curious *Ignorance*. The rest of the Border was fild vp with severall fancies, which lest I should be too long in the description of the frame, I will goe to the picture it selfe, and indeed these showes are nothing else but pictures with Light and Motion.[44]

This is certainly in part at least an allegorical statement of the theme of the masque, which was taken from Baltasar de Beaujoyeulx's *Ballet comique de la reine*:

That these Intemperate Beastes of *Circe*'s Court, should for a time possesse *Tempe*. The happie retreat of the Muses and their followers, is meant, the inchantments of vitious impostures, that by false meanes, seeke to extirpate the true louers of *Science* and *Vertue*, to whom of right only that place belongs.[45]

Yet Invention was not a particularly appropriate figure to choose. And I would suggest that when Jones chose it in this place and at this time he had Jonson in mind as well as the requirements of the masque. He is claiming the power that Jonson denied him. And that phrase "these showes are nothing else but pictures with Light and Motion" comes too pat as a retort to the *Expostulation* to be here by accident: and there was no need for the phrase here at all—it is dragged in.

We have four allegorical figures, then, Theory, Practice, Knowledge and Invention. To this list let us add Design—a word to which Jones attached much importance, if there is any truth under Jonson's exaggerations—as is most likely, for otherwise his attacks would have lost in point. In the *Expostulation* he refers contemptuously to what Jones does under the plea of design:

> To plant the Musick where noe eare can reach!
> Attyre the Persons as noe thought can teach
> Sense, what they are! which by a specious fyne
> Terme of the Architects is called Designe!
> But in the practisd truth Destruction is
> Of any Art, besyde what he calls his!

and

> that vnbounded lyne
> Aymd at in thy omnipotent Designe.

And later, as we have seen, the word echoes through Medlay's speeches in *A Tale of a Tub*: he prides himself on his skill in design, and to his design all else must "conduce" and be "feasible."

These words take us to theories about the visual arts which had been developed in the course of the sixteenth century, and particularly to theories developed in the world of full Mannerist art theory—which was the world of Inigo Jones. Emphases differ in the theoretical writings, and terminology differs, and metaphysical positions may differ slightly; yet there is fundamental agreement about common positions: an agreement which we can understand if we observe how certain theoretical positions were originally developed to meet a certain challenge; and that the need for this defence was still felt at the beginning of the seventeenth century. Jonson himself tells us what this challenge was. In the *Discoveries* he takes over—and thereby endorses these opinions—a passage from Vives on the distinction between the liberal and the mechanical arts:

> *Arts* that respect the mind were ever reputed nobler, then those that serve the body: though wee lesse can bee without them. As *Tillage, Spinning, Weaving, Building,* &c. without which, wee could scarse sustaine life a day. But these were the workes of every hand; the other of the braine only, and those the most generous, and exalted wits, and spirits that cannot rest, or *acquiesce . . . .*[46]

What Jones is doing in fact is to assert that architecture is a liberal and not a mechanical art. And he is using the language evolved by the theorists to meet those who included the visual arts with the mechanical arts, adopting such arguments as Jonson quotes from Vives. The passage from Vives dates from the early sixteenth century; and by now the controversy was an old one. From Alberti and Leonardo on, arguments in defence of the visual arts had been brought forward and their claims had been by tacit consent, at any rate, admitted. Yet the issue was not yet dead in Jones's time. Theorists like Scamozzi and Lomazzo still apparently find it necessary to defend their claims. They were defending themselves against the charge that Jonson liked to bring against Jones: that he is a craftsman only—a joiner in this case. And it had been of considerable importance to do so, for till well on in the sixteenth century the legal position of the artist had been that of member of a craft guild.[47]

When Jonson made his cook say to his poet "Eithers Art is the wisdome of the Mind" he showed precise knowledge of the architect's defence. This is the ground the defenders of the arts took. To the charge that they were craftsmen they replied that their arts were intellectual in origin, and that craftsmanship and manual skills came second only. The theorists have this at least in common: they agree that the mental act, the conceiving has primacy, and they sever this sharply from the act of expressing, of giving visual form to the concept.

This is emblematized by Jones's figures of Theory and Practice. The principles he was implying can be conveniently studied in a book whose title-page comes so close to the proscenium that there can be little doubt that he was deliberately imitating it. This book is

58. Vincenzo Scamozzi,
Architettura, 1615: title-page.

the enormous treatise on architecture by the inheritor of Palladio's mantle, Vincenzo Scamozzi, whom Jones had met in Italy, by whose work he was influenced, and whose book he possessed.[48] Scamozzi puts on his title-page (Figure 58) a portico carrying the inscription *Nemo huc liberalium artium expers ingrediatur*. On the plinths of the columns stand two allegorical figures, one *Theorica* who gazes upwards and carries a book in her left hand, the other *Experientia* who looks downwards and points to the ground with a pair of compasses. These figures correspond to Jones's, though he has taken the attributes of his from Ripa's *Iconologia* (Figures 59 and 60); and the meaning he gives to them—"by these two, all works of Architecture and Ingining have their perfection"—is the meaning that Scamozzi's design has.

59. Ripa, Theory.
(*Iconologia*, 1625.)

60. Ripa, Practice.
(*Iconologia*, 1625.)

All the arts depend on the union of theory and practice—which is a mode of procedure depending on experience, acquired through memory and judgment. All the arts in fact have their origin in experience. And practice is always needed to translate them into fact. But without theory no art can reach its full stature; and without theory no man has really the right to call himself an artist. The man who has practice but no theory is the craftsman who works in the dark, empirically. The true artist has both. This position is common to the treatises Jones knew—to Scamozzi's book, and to Barbaro's commentaries on Vitruvius and to Lomazzo's treatises on the arts.[49] Theory is knowledge of principles. It can be called knowledge itself; for theory has to do with the realm of the intelligible, as opposed to practice which has to do with the realm of the sensible. The realm of the intelligible and universal is the realm of the liberal arts. It is the realm of architecture too, for—as Barbaro and Scamozzi argue—architecture depends on mathematics, and mathematics is without doubt one of the bases of the liberal arts: four out of the seven, Arithmetic, Geometry, Music and Astrology, are mathematical disciplines; and had not Plato held that of all the disciplines mathematics is the highest, for only through it do we come to pure knowledge, verifiable truth, universally valid principles? Architecture then is, like the liberal arts, a *scientia*, a body of knowledge; it is also, so far as it is concerned with material constructions, an art.[50]

The allegorical figures on the title-page and proscenium bring out these ideas. Ripa explains the situation quite clearly:

> Theory is concerned with reason and the operations of the intellect; Practice with the operations and movements of the senses . . . the former contemplates highest causes, the latter investigates lowest effects. So that the one is the summit and the other the foundation of the whole fabric of human discourse.[51]

Theory (Figure 59) wears blue, the colour of the sky, because just as the sky is the limit of our sight, so God, whose seat is the sky, is the limit of our intellect. She gazes upwards to show that the intellect is finally concerned with heavenly and eternal things and with God. The compass with points turned upwards indicates this same concern with the sublime. The compass indicates the function of the intellect, which is to measure the discover the proportions of things.[52] She is young because youth is the age of ardour, promptitude, vitality, hope and happiness, gifts that should go with the mastery of theory. Practice follows ancient usages, is easily deceived, doubtful, suspicious, careless of principles: evils opposed to the light that Theory brings. She looks down because she is concerned with sensible experience only. And for this reason she wears the dark earth-coloured garment. She is supported by compass and rule. Reason, which is the compass, supports every human activity; but the compasses are pointed downwards because while reason works from the universal to the particular, practice seeks to work from the particular to the universal. The rule that touches the compass is intended to show that while theory draws its rules from eternal things, practice is rooted to earth and earthly things, which are subject to change and corruption, and require to have some measure of order imposed on them by man.

There can be little doubt that "Goody Architecture" who had figured in *Chloridia* appeared more or less as Ripa describes her: a woman of mature age with bare arms, holding in one hand a plumb-line, square and compasses, and in the other a sheet of paper with the plan of a palace surrounded by figures. The numbers and measuring instruments show that architecture is concerned with mathematics and is therefore *scientia*, while the bare arms signify that concern with action and the material, which is the reason why architecture must also be called an art.[53]

Knowledge and Invention embody other notions current in the theory of the arts; and come home to Jonson because the ideas they convey are shared by the theory of poetry. The painter or the architect has as valid a right to claim knowledge and invention as the poet has. Knowledge—with his easily intelligible attribute of book and lamp, the traditional lamp of knowledge which stands for the light of the intellect—is essential for the architect.[54] Scamozzi had put on his frontispiece the warning that no one unskilled in the liberal arts might have to do with architecture. And not only because architecture itself is a liberal art but because the proper practice of architecture requires—as Vitruvius had long ago insisted—a knowledge of all the arts. Scamozzi requires the architect to be familiar with grammar, history and poetry, with logic, mathematics and music, and with moral and natural philosophy.[55] Indeed the architect is master of all the arts and employs them for his purposes. The cook knew what he was talking about. Knowledge is also the knowledge necessary for invention. Parallel to the ideal figure of the learned poet who draws on all human knowledge for his inventions was the figure of the learned artist who requires the same basis for his.[56]

"Invention" had long ago been taken over by the theorists of the arts from rhetoric and poetics and made into a fundamental term, especially by the theorists of painting. Thus Dolce and Vasari had used this word to denote the first part of painting and of the arts in general:

>Invention always was and always will be considered the true mother of architecture, painting and poetry, indeed of all the higher arts and of every wonderful thing accomplished by man.[57]

In painting it had meant *historia* or subject or fable, and it was for the sake of finding the fable that the painter had to be well seen in the stories of the poets. But the meaning of the word is gradually refined. The wings which Jones's figure of Invention has—and which he has taken over from Ripa—indicate the nature of this refinement.[58] They represent the elevation of the intellect: it is through the intellect that inventions are found. Stress is thrown on the process rather than on the result. And the process belongs to the intellect. Invention belongs to the world of knowledge, the world of the intelligible, the same world as *Theoria*. (By emphasizing this concept and defining it in this way, the artist is also separating himself from the craftsman.) So it does when Scamozzi uses the word of the architect and his works. It is basic for his conception of the architect and an essential part in the defence of architecture as a liberal art. What is the business of the architect? He must, says Scamozzi, first invent and design the form of the edifice and dispose and distribute the parts in due correspondence and order so that beauty and decorum may be achieved both in the whole and in the parts; then he must see that the edifice is excellently constructed. All this, as it affects the whole and the parts, he will first of all have considered in his Idea.[59]

First comes the intellectual illumination, the Idea, the conception; from this comes the invention—or the form (the words seem to be almost equivalent for Scamozzi), which is the explication of the Idea. But the Idea is the source; and it proceeds from knowledge which comes from reason. This is the true beginning of architecture; and that which distinguishes the true architect from the craftsman. The centre of his activity has been removed altogether from the physical and has been placed firmly in the mind. All the work of building and construction is simply the realizing—the bringing in act—of the forms that existed potentially in the architect's mind; the artificers are simply the instruments through which this is achieved.[60] This is also the point of view taken about the arts by Lomazzo, whose treatises were known to Jones, and to an earlier generation of English artists and amateurs of the arts.[61] For him the Idea conceived in the artist's mind has absolute primacy: all else depends on this. And though his Idea may have a fully developed metaphysical meaning that we do not find in Scamozzi, yet in asserting the primacy of the conception, the mental act, they are at one.

It is in this same context of theory that we must read the word "design"—that "Omnipotent Design" which Jonson mocks, to which everything must "conduce." As Jonson uses it here, this word has obviously a special technical sense; and Jonson says it is an architect's term. And indeed the word "design" had important connotations in Mannerist art theory, from which Jones took it. An importance which derived, again, from the continued effort to place the source of the work of art in the realm of the mind. Design could have, of course, a simple meaning, and had been used by theorists in this sense: as the form, made by a system of lines, which the painter gives to what he is imitating; the form he gives to his invention. So Dolce, for example, had defined it. Vasari had conceived of the artistic process as the giving of visible expression or form to a mental "concetto." Vasari was anticipating the full Mannerist treatises.[62] This "concetto" is the Idea-Invention of Scamozzi. In Scamozzi "disegno" seems to be used in Vasari's sense: the lines which express the mental conception. So the designer may well take the design to be omnipotent. It is the expression of the conception, and if all does not "conduce" then the conception is not adequately realized. And if Jones—as is likely—knew not only Lomazzo's work but also the other great theoretical treatise of mannerist art,

61. Ripa, Design. (*Iconologia*, 1625.)

Zuccari's *Idea*, then he would have all the more reason for holding that design was omnipotent.[63] For Zuccari, design—"disegno"—is all. What Zuccari does is, in fact, fairly simple. He denies that *disegno* is simply the shape given by lines—and sharply criticizes the inadequacies of Vasari's definition.[64] This is only part of design, it is the body and visible substance, or *disegno esterno*. But *disegno esterno* is entirely subordinate to the conception, to *disegno interno*. What for Scamozzi or Lomazzo had been the Idea, is for Zuccari *disegno interno*. Their metaphysical views may vary, but the place assigned by these theorists to the Idea or the *disegno interno* in the artistic process is the same. Design, then, could mean the expression of the Idea, or conception, or invention; and it could even mean the Idea, or conception, or invention, itself; and could even be regarded, as Zuccari regarded it, as the sign, the stamp of God in man.[65] Certainly this line is unbounded, for it contains everything. And if Jonson and Jones consulted that handbook of crystallized commonplaces which they both knew so well, they would find design defined there as a "knowledge according to their proportions of all things that are visible and of determined size, together with the power to put this in use," and figured as a young man holding a pair of compasses (Figure 61) to show that design is based on measures, which are beautiful in so far as they correspond to right proportions, and a mirror, to show that design is the act of an interior faculty of the soul.[66]

There could be no way out of the quarrel. For of course everything depended on whose "design" came first: the poet's or the architect's, who was employing in these cases all the arts of design. The verbal or the visual—if the issue is forced one or other must take precedence. In any dispute the issues inevitably became personal. Theoretically, poet and architect were standing on the same grounds. The theory of the visual arts began, like Renaissance poetics, from the terms of rhetoric. And still, in these Mannerist treatises, Scamozzi and Zuccari set out, point by point, comparisons between architect, painter, sculptor and orator in terms of the five parts of oratory.[67] And Jonson's conception of the mental act issuing in invention, the soul of the poem, and followed by expression according to true order and decorum is essentially that of the artist whose mental act, *concetto*, *Idea*, or *disegno interno* is completed by execution which is the work of the hands. And both Jonson and Jones probably knew it. But Jonson could not or would not admit the claims of the architect. His last words on the subject are his best. He could not maintain the claims of the poet against the architect. But he could set him against a more powerful opponent. Set against the justified claims of royalty the architect's pretensions are ridiculous. This is the theme of the last of all Jonson's royal entertainments, *Love's Welcome at Bolsover*.

The True Harmony

Love's Welcome at Bolsover[68] is one of the most accomplished of Jonson's court entertainments. Brief and apparently slight, its scheme is completely unified and most deftly contrived to carry, with the utmost grace and ease, a theme rich in resonances; and grace and ease and deftness are shown, too, in the accommodation of the theme to the moment, and in the tone of the writing which is always that of the courtier, yet remains light, and witty: a model of urbanity. References to Jones and to the place of the poet at court have lost any touch of bitterness, and participate in this urbanity; and are the more effective for it.

The entertainment consists of a song sung by a chorus while the king and queen are banqueting, of a comic speech and dance given after the banquet by Coronell Vitruvius and his men, and of a dialogue between Eros and Anteros, and is concluded by a speech from Philalethes given after a second banquet.

The theme is mutual love and its nature. The examples are Charles and Henrietta Maria. The Neo-Platonic note is struck in the first lines:

> If Love be call'd a lifting of the Sense
> To knowledge of that pure intelligence,
> Wherein the Soule hath rest, and residence:

The question comes:

> When were the Senses in such order plac'd?
> The Sight, the Hearing, Smelling, Touching, Taste,
> All at one Banquet?

The answer is that Love has set forth this banquet. And to what end? The answer comes again: Love—"Love will feast Love!"

The banquet is a banquet of the senses, not apparently a Platonic symposium. Yet there is no contradiction between perfect love, which is finally a mode of knowledge, and this feast of the senses. The feast has been made by love, and love has ordered the senses—they are named in the right Ficinian order—in a descending scale.[69] Love works through the senses, orders them and transcends them. "Where Love is mutuall, still All things in order move." Love feasts Love. The king feasts the queen. And the food of love is love. Love is given and received. This mutual exchange is the food of love, the strength of love, and the reality of love. Only mutual love, a giving out and a taking in, is real love.

To "Love will feast Love" an objection comes:

> You make of Love, a riddle, or a chaine,
> A circle, a mere knott, untie't again.

The answer takes up the objections:

> Love is a Circle, both the first, and last
> Of all our Actions, and his knott's too fast.
> A true-love Knot, will hardly be unti'd,
> And if it could, who would this Payre divide?
>
> God made them such, and Love.—Who is a ring,
> The likest to the year of anything,
> And runs into it selfe.—Then let us sing.
> And run into one sound.

The perfect union of the voices images the perfect union of Love. The singers take up again the theme of the five senses—

> Could we put on the beautie of all Creatures,
> Sing in the Aire, and notes of Nightingales,
> Exhale the sweets of Earth, and all her features,
> And tell you softer than in Silke, these tales—

and end:

At every reall banquet to the Sense,
Welcome, true Welcome fill the Complements.

The real feast of the sense is the feast that love makes for love.

62. Cartari, Eros and Anteros.

Concepts and imagery are strictly Neo-Platonic. Love lifts the sense to a knowledge of the divine, when the soul has its rest. The nature of love can best be expressed by the circle—the familiar image of perfection—which has neither beginning nor end; and is like the year, in this, that there is no intermission in the movement of one year into another. Mutual love is this perfect circle. Love too as it relates to the divine is a circle, "The first, and last of all our Actions." In love God created the universe, in love we desire to return to him where only is the full satisfaction of love. This was the circle of love which Ficino had conceived as uniting God and creature.[70] Ficino had also argued strongly that only mutual or reciprocal love is good; indeed the lover who is not loved in return is dead. For he is already dead to himself, his life is in the other's. And if the other does not love him then his life is lost. But if the love is returned then each lover, though he has lost his life, lives twice: his life in his lover's and his lover's in his. This is the miracle of love and the food that love lives and thrives on.[71]

The brief action of Eros and Anteros (Figure 62) and their struggle for the palm is a rendering of this theme in mythological terms. The story as Jonson receives it from his sources, and as he had shown in an earlier use of it, is an apologue on mutual love.[72] The story, brought out in the dialogue, is this. Venus gave birth to Eros, who, however, failed to grow and thrive and fulfil his early promise. Not knowing what to do, Venus and the Graces, who were the nurses of Eros, sought the advice of the oracle, Themis (for this was before the days of Apollo). Themis replied that they had not understood the nature of the child. Love could be born alone but could not grow alone. Venus must bring forth another child—Anteros, "Love in return"—to keep her first child company. This Venus did; and, as soon as he saw his brother, Eros throve, he shook out his feathers, and grew in size. Since then both have flourished—but only when in each other's company:

> For, Love, by Love, increaseth mutually.

And the struggle for the palm is the struggle to see who can love more, the struggle that ends with division of the palm: the harmony of mutual love. Their home is the court of the king and queen: one represents the king's love, the other the queen's.

ANTEROS	And by this sweet Contention for the *Palme*,
	Unite our appetites, and make them calme.
EROS	To will, and nill one thing.
ANTEROS	And so to move
	Affection in our Wills, as in our Love.
EROS	It is the place, sure breeds it, where wee are,
ANTEROS	The King, and Queenes Court, which is circular,
	And perfect.
EROS	The pure schoole that we live in,
	And is of purer Love, the Discipline.[73]

Philalethes makes up the theme in his concluding speech, in words mock-serious and serious, when he adjures the two boys to:

> admire the Miracles you serve, this excellent *King*, and his unparallel'd *Queene*, who are the Canons, the Decretals, and whole Schoole-Divinite of Love. Contemplate, and studie them. Here you shall read *Hymen*, having lighted two Torches, either of which enflame mutually, but waste not. One Love by the others aspect increasing, and both in the right lines of aspiring.

This comes before he passes on to his final image of the king and queen, when he sees them, as in an allegorical portrait, trampling down Fortune and Time, with the Fates spinning only the whitest, finest threads for them.

Between the song and the dialogue of Eros and Anteros comes the comic episode: the speech of Coronell Iniquo Vitruvius and the dance of his men, which stands to the rest of the entertainment rather as anti-masque stands to masque. Coronell Vitruvius appears— misusing Latin tags—as "Surveyor" arranging and exhorting his minions. He sets his Vulcan, Captain Smith, with his assistants, or Cyclopes, to beat out the music on an anvil with their hammers (Vulcan was the artificer). Then come the Carver, the Freemason, the Carpenter and his man, and a second group of the Plumber, the Glazier, the Plasterer and the Mortar-man. The groups dance to Vitruvius' garrulous encouragement. The palpable burlesque, however, states a theme too.

In key sentences which Jonson gives to Vitruvius he touches a strong nerve in Renaissance architectural theory. "*Time*, and *Measure*, are the Father, and Mother of Musique, you know," he says to his smiths, and to the dancers, later:

> Well done, my Musicall, Arithmeticall, Geometricall Gamesters! or rather my true Mathematicall Boyes! It is carried, in number, weight and measure, as if the Aires were all Harmonie, and the Figures a well-tim'd Proportion . . .

Fundamental for architectural theory was the view that the building must reproduce the proportions of microcosm and macrocosm. The universe—and behind these views of course are Pythagoras and Plato—was created as a harmony. This harmony can be stated as a system of mathematical ratios which determines the proportions of architecture. These are also proportions of music. Coronell Vitruvius' ridiculous lines are intended to recall these profoundly serious doctrines, with which Jones was certainly familiar. Palladio held them. Barbaro and Scamozzi wrote about them.[74] And we know that Jones had sufficient curiosity to seek some information about their classical sources. In his copy of the *Republic*—an Italian translation—the section he marked most carefully was Book III, which deals with the place of music in education; he marked heavily that part of the translator's *argument* containing this explanation:

> because the soul according to Plato is a certain divine harmony, and was formerly familiar with the harmony of the spheres, and the body is harmoniously compounded, as is the spirit also.[c]

And in his copy of Plutarch's *Moralia*—again an Italian translation—he paid particular attention to the essay *Della creatione dell'anima nel Timeo di Platone*, and even more to the essay *Della Musica*, in which the whole theory of ancient music is discussed with particular attention to Pythagoras and Plato, and technical expositions of the musical proportions are given. He annotated very fully the page where Plutarch says:

> But the power of those proportions and those numbers of which the creator makes use is to achieve the corresponding harmony and pleasant concord of the soul within itself, by means of which the heavens are filled with infinite goodness, and on earth the succession and change of seasons are regulated and governed most excellently and felicitously for the generation and preservation of created things.[d]

The harmony achieved by the architect, image and instance of the cosmic harmony, is figured in dance—as the harmony of the royal love had been figured in song. But the dance is comic. The would-be creators of this harmony are the absurd vainglorious Inigo Jones and his clumsy louts of workmen. The architect's most ambitious claims are turned into burlesque.

How ridiculous they are when compared to the achievement of the royal love! The court is, says Philalethes, mockingly:

> An Academie, or Court, where all the true lessons of Love are throughly read, and taught; the Reasons, the Proportions, and Harmonie, drawne forth in analytick Tables, and made demonstrable to the *Senses*.

[c] percioche l'anima secondo Platone è una certa harmonia, et gia alla celeste harmonia assuefatto, & con harmonia è Composto il corpo, & lo spirito similmente.[75]

[d] Nondimeno l' ufficio di quelle proportioni, & di quei numeri, de' quali il creatore si valse, di esser attribuito all'harmonia corrispondente, & gratiosa dell'anima fra se stessa conconde; del quale ella adornata non solamente ha riempiuto il cielo di beni infiniti; ma etiandio quello, che pertiene alla terra misurando le successioni de' tempi, & dei mutamenti, eccellentissimamente, & leggiadrissimamente alla generatione, & conseruatione di tutte le cose, che nascessero, adornato & distinto.[76]

A joke about the shallow cult of Platonic love at the queen's court is certainly intended —though we are not, on this account, to take less seriously the presentation of Platonic love here—but Jonson is also saying: How ridiculous for an Inigo to think he can reduce to a set of mathematical tables the secrets of the universal harmony![77] Love is beyond such demonstration. And the true harmony is that shown in the mutual love of king and queen, which transcends sense and reaches the divine. This it is that is circular and perfect, image and instance of the link that runs from God to the creatures, of the bond that ties the universe together, of the true and sacred harmony. Compared with the living perfection before our eyes how ridiculous the claims of an Inigo to create it! The architect may have defeated the poet; when he would entrench on the claims of royalty how easy to show that he is a fool.

The Renaissance Poet as Classicist:
Chapman's *Hero and Leander*

I. The Classical World

It is probably as dangerous to have too simple ideas about what the 'kinds' were for the Renaissance poet as it is to forget them and their requirements. Now, perhaps, we are more likely to run into the first danger than the second. Certainly "Ovid" and "Ovidian" have been used in too simple ways about Elizabethan poems. The *Amores*, the *Heroides* and the *Metamorphoses* were not read in the same way by an Elizabethan poet: we have known this, and have known that the *Metamorphoses* was read allegorically for a long enough time by now; yet we still tend to assume that "Ovidian" meant for such a poet a straightforward prescription to be simple, sensuous, and passionate; and to refer all "Ovidian" poems to the type of *Venus and Adonis*.[1] Chapman's *Sestiads* of Hero and Leander have, traditionally, suffered from being read in this way.[2] Yet Chapman was interested, here, in another Ovid—as was Drayton in his *Endimion and Phoebe*—in Ovid the allegorical poet of the *Metamorphoses*. And Chapman has suffered because we prefer reading Marlowe, and because we seem to see an incongruity in aims and intentions between Marlowe and Chapman. Yet it is not so certain that Marlowe's aims were quite so simply sensuous; and Chapman certainly thought he was giving the poem an appropriate ending. Further, Chapman was thinking not only of the allegorical mythological tale but of the epic or heroic. He gives to the poem an epic title: it is really the *Sestiads*—the epic of Sestos—it was he who called the six books *Sestiads*: the model being Homer, whose whole poem is the *Iliads*, each separate book being an *Iliad*.[3] He had tradition behind him. For Musæus, with Orpheus and Linus, was bard and sage, philosopher and lawgiver, one of the bards who first brought wisdom and civility to the barbarous peoples. And it was to this Musæus that

Hero and Leander was still attributed; and scholars numbered it among the heroic poems.[4] Chapman's poem, then, combines two kinds, the epic and the metamorphosis: both kinds designed to instruct through exemplary human situations and symbolical figures and actions.

Such a poem on such a theme was an "imitation" of classical antiquity; and this "imitation" meant for the Renaissance poet a labour of amplification and re-creation. It meant such an amplification as Marlowe had begun with his account of Hero's dress, the temple of Venus, the nurse, the tower, the wooing. Chapman gives us the goddess Ceremony, Hero's sacrifice, the apparition of Venus and her creation of Eronusis, her talkative swan, Leucote, the marriage rites conducted by Hero, with the apparition of the nymph Teras and her tale of Hymen's love. And the principle of *decorum* prescribed that all such amplifications must be classical. Here, with Chapman, another difficulty has arisen. Venus, and even her swan Leucote, are recognizable enough as classical and easily acceptable; but how can such figures as Ceremony, Eronusis and Teras be called classical —and how can Chapman ever have thought they were? His poem has been condemned—it is one of the standard judgements—as quite "unclassical." An examination of the way in which Chapman found his amplifications and arrived at such figures will, however, show in what sense they are classical; and illustrate what "invention" and "imitation" meant for such a poet.

The tale of Hymen and Eucharis, which the nymph Teras tells in the fifth *Sestiad*, provides a good point of departure. This story of how the young Athenian wooed and won his beloved after disguising himself as a girl to be with her and vanquishing the kidnappers who seize them, with a group of Athenian girls, had been told in various sources that Chapman knew.[5] Chapman continues this story with an account of the marriage rites celebrated for the lovers: such a passage was important for the structure of his poem. This description F. L. Schoell thought Chapman had borrowed from Plutarch's *Moralia*. However I have shown elsewhere that in fact Chapman's account is textually dependent not on Plutarch but on the similar account given in Vincenzo Cartari's widely known manual of mythology, *Le Imagini de i Dei de gli Antichi*.[6] Chapman certainly knew Plutarch's text, for the *Moralia* was one of his favourite books (and Cartari refers here to Plutarch as one of his sources), but when writing the fifth *Sestiad* he remembered Cartari's actual wording. This makes it certain that he knew Cartari's version of the story of Hymen;[7] for Cartari tells it in immediate relation to his account of the classical marriage ritual. Both occur in his chapter on Juno and in connexion with Juno as patroness of marriage. I also pointed out that two incidental bits of mythology found in the same pages reappear in Chapman: a reference to the goddess Pudor,[8] and a reference to the lily that sprang from drops of Juno's milk.

Requiring, then, an episode connected with love that issues in marriage and the proper celebration of marriage rites, Chapman has gone to Cartari's chapter on Juno. We see him taking over and combining elements—the tale of Hymen and the account of marriage ritual; and taking over a detail like the story of the origin of the lily and inserting it into a little myth of his own—that of the origin of love—which is a quite new development of the Hymen story.

Other instances can be added of how Chapman would take a detail from Cartari and use it to build up his own image. Chapman represents Hero carrying as part of her attire as priestess of Venus

> a siluer wand,
> On whose bright top *Peristera* did stand,
> Who was a Nymph, but now transformd a Doue,
> And in her life was deare in *Venus* loue:
> And for her sake she euer since that time,
> Chusde Doues to draw her Coach through heauens blew clime.
>
> (IV, 19–24)

The idea of the bird-topped sceptre—for which no source has been found—may well have been suggested by Cartari's description (taken from Pausanias) of Juno carrying a sceptre crowned with a cuckoo: Chapman could hardly miss the illustration of this in his copy of Cartari.[9] The story of the nymph Peristera whom Venus loved—"già molto amata da lei"—is told by Cartari.[10] The car of Venus is drawn by both doves and swans. The poets whom Chapman knew tell that it was by doves or by swans, and the handbooks record this. The only source so far discovered where the car is drawn by both birds at once is an illustration to Cartari's chapter on Venus (Figure 63); even in his text Cartari keeps them separate.[11] And it is in this passage that Cartari mentions Peristera. Chapman names two

63. Cartari, the chariot of Venus drawn by swans and doves.

doves and two swans (this is the number shown in the Cartari illustration). No source has been found for this, or for the role that Chapman gives to the swan Leucote: it seems probable that Chapman simply invented names symbolic of qualities of Venus: pleasure, goodness, brightness, bounty.[12] Proof that Chapman remembered details from the illustrations as well as in the text of Cartari is afforded in one striking case: this is in the description of the four winds in *Sestiad* VI (see Figure 50). Eurus, Notus, Zephyrus and Boreas were familiar figures, and Chapman would hardly need Cartari to remind him of the texts in Ovid and Virgil on which their descriptions are based. It is also possible that Chapman might have arrived at Boreas "tossing of his rauisht loue" without looking at the illustration to Cartari's text—but when he comes to Notus

> leaning with his armes in folds
> Vpon a rock, his white hayre full of showres
> (VI, 41–2)

then it is the visual image he is remembering: for this detail is not in Cartari's text nor in the sources he quotes.[13]

It seems that Cartari may also be invoked to show how Chapman arrived at a figure of another kind: a personification, an entirely schematic allegorical figure. This is the complicated figure of Eronusis or Dissimulation, whom Venus creates from Hero's rejected sacrifice, from scraps of her robe and hair. Her body is girdled with painted snakes, her "down parts" are a scorpion's tail, spotted with many colours; and such colours shine in the wings at her shoulders:

> Cloth had neuer die,
> Nor sweeter colours neuer viewed eie,
> In scorching *Turkie, Cares, Tartarie,*
> Than shinde about this spirit notorious;
> Nor was *Arachnes* web so glorious.
> (IV, 298–302)

Jean Jacquot pointed out that this image must go back to Dante's representation of *Fraude* in the *Inferno*:[14] or rather his description of the monster Geryon whom he takes to personify Fraud. It would indeed be interesting to know that Chapman read Dante; but it is not necessary to suppose that he did. This figure seems to have enjoyed a special fame. Boccaccio and Giraldi report Dante's description in their mythologies, as does Ripa in his book of images.[15] Yet these versions would not account for Chapman's figure, as they fail to report details that Chapman knows. But Cartari quotes the whole passage, except for the lines, coming later, that describe Geryon's scorpion tail; and this point Cartari reports.[16] The process of modification, however, is repeated here. Geryon is male; Chapman needed a female figure—because it is Hero's dissimulation that produces this monster; and if he needed any justification, Cartari had just noted that Apelles drew Fraud as a woman.[17] Chapman takes over Dante's

> Lo dosso, il petto, & ambedue le coste
> Dipinte haueua di nodi, e di rotelle[18]

[his back, his breast, and both his sides were adorned with knots and little wheels], but has elaborated this to emphasise the variety and strength of Dissimulation's traps:

> Her armes were all with golden pincers drest,
> And twentie fashiond knots, pullies, and brakes. . . .

And, beginning from this same notion of the trap, he has given Eronusis one quite new and striking attribute:

> her tresses were of wire,
> Knit like a net, where harts all set on fire,
> Strugled in pants and could not get release.
> (IV, 290–92)

The conceit of the mistress' hair as wire was sufficiently familiar: witness Spenser,

> Her long loose yellow locks lyke golden wyre,
> Sprinckled with perle,[19]

or Shakespeare,

> If haires be wiers, black wiers grow on her head . . . .[20]

And the passage from wire to trap is as easy as the passage from hair to *net* in the sense of trap: so Donne writes,

> He call'd her beauty limetwigs, her haire net . . . .[21]

So far, then, we have seen Chapman basing his amplifications and 'inventions' on a popular manual of mythology—selecting details that struck him, but reserving freedom to combine and vary according to the needs of his context. We may now analyse some instances where Chapman is working, it seems, without the aid of such a source.

Chapman has two bird metamorphoses. There is Adolesche who becomes the parrot, and there are Hero and Leander who after death become acanthides or "Thistle-warps". These latter are gold-finches; and Chapman's description of their colours seems to be accurate, except that there is no blue on them (and by this Chapman may have intended—or an authority may have intended—a reference to blue sheen on black). No source has however been found for his description of their habits, except for their feeding on thistles: that they avoid the sea and that they always fly in couples do not appear and may well have been details invented by Chapman for their emblematic appropriateness; they are the only details—apart from that of diet—that he gives. This metamorphosis of the lovers is Chapman's invention. He probably began from the association of the gold-finch with the thistle, which he makes emblematic of their sorrows:

> And feede on Thistle tops to testifie
> The hardness of their first life in their last.
> (IV, 279–80)

The Greek name for this bird is ἀκανθίς or ἀκανθυλλίς,[22] from which Chapman derives his acanthides. And there is one myth of how Acanthis or Acanthyllis, daughter of Antonoos and Hippodamia, was turned into a bird of that name when the Gods turned her and the rest of her family into birds out of pity for their violent grief over the death of their son and brother.[23] This must be the basis of Chapman's myth. For the origin of the parrot no myth has been recorded—strangely enough, perhaps. There was however a very well known story of how that other talkative bird also capable of imitating the human voice came into existence: Ovid's story of the Pierides who rashly challenged the Muses in a contest and were turned into magpies as a punishment.[24]

A much more striking case, however, is that of the nymph Teras, the strange figure who appears at the nuptials in *Sestiad* V to tell the tale of Hymen and sing the wedding song.

> To these quick Nuptials entred suddenly
> Admired *Teras* with the Ebon Thye,
> A Nymph that haunted the greene *Sestyan* groues,
> And would consort soft virgins in their loues,
> At gaysome Triumphs, and on solemne dayes,
> Singing prophetike Elegies and Layes:
> And fingring of a siluer Lute she tide,
> With black and purple skarfs by her left side.
> *Apollo* gaue it, and her skill withall,
> And she was term'd his Dwarfe she was so small.
> Yet great in vertue, for his beames enclosde
> His vertues in her: neuer was proposde
> Riddle to her or Augurie, strange or new,
> But she resolu'd it: neuer sleight tale flew
> From her charmd lips without important sence,
> Shewne in some graue succeeding consequence.
> This little Siluane with her songs and tales,
> Gaue such estate to feasts and Nuptiales,
> That though oft times she forewent Tragedies,
> Yet for her stragenes still she pleasde their eyes,
> And for her smalnes they admir'd her so,
> They thought her perfect borne and could not grow.
>
> (V, 61–82)

And here is Teras when she departs:

> Herewith the amorous spirit that was so kinde
> To *Teras* haire, and combd it downe with winde,
> Still as it Comet-like brake from her braine,
> Would needes haue *Teras* gone, and did refraine
> To blow it downe: which staring vp, dismaid
> The timorous feast, and she no longer staid:
> But bowing to the Bridegrome and the Bride,
> Did like a shooting exhalation glide
> Out of their sights: the turning of her back
> Made them all shreike, it lookt so ghastly black.
>
> (V, 481–90)

Chapman's lexicon informed him that τέρας meant *signum, ostentium, portentum, prodigium, monstruum*: "peculiariter autem signum quo Deus nobis aliquid portendit, praedicit, monstrat, ostendit." Teras, that is, is applied to signs in the heavens portending good or evil; and it is also used of the comet that portends evil.[25] Items in Chapman's description explicitly recall the comet: Teras' hair breaks comet-like from her brain; she vanishes like a shooting exhalation; she often comes as forerunner of disaster. And some of what may seem her odder attributes are explained if we take into consideration contemporary discussions on comets. Chapman seems to have taken into account certain elements in the new disturbing theories about comets that mark this period. The new star of 1577 had produced a considerable body of observation and speculation on the nature of comets that was revolutionary in its bearings, and finally destructive of the Aristotelian conception of the heavens. In this movement English scientists had their place. Chapman was certainly in a position—if only through his friendship with Hariot—to be aware of these currents of opinion.[26] But indeed they were in general circulation. Thus some sentences from that widely known late sixteenth-century encyclopaedia, de la Primaudaye's *French Academy*, may be quoted for the light they throw on Teras. In his chapter on comets de la Primaudaye, with some hesitation, definitely comes down on the side of the new theories and against Aristotle. He quotes Aristotle's view, which had been the accepted one, that comets are "made of an hotte exhalation which attaineth to the supreame region of the aire, where it is inflamed by the element of fire". The essential revolutionary proposal of the new theories was a denial that comets were engendered beneath the moon, and the assertion that on the contrary they appeared in the heavens far above the moon: that they were either engendered there, or were stars which had always been there but which only became visible at certain times. And the light of comets is the sun's light. "Moreover the comet doth most usually accompany the Sunne and appeareth not but at eventide, and at the shutting vp of the day. Which giveth vs to understand, that a comet is a globe placed in heauen, which being enlightened by the Sunne doth plainely appeare."[27] This exactly suits Teras who appears in the evening, and when she leaves it is night; and who though small is great in virtue, for Apollo's beams enclose his virtues in her. Her back is black because it does not receive his rays. The dependence of the comet on the sun may also explain the image of Teras as Apollo's dwarf. The image is that of the dwarf attendant on his master, and we now know that our knowledge of the comet's presence depends on the presence of the sun's light; and, certainly, comets are diminutive in comparison with the sun. But Teras' smallness and her being "perfect borne and could not grow" probably need further explanation.

It is through the *coma*, the κομή, the comet's flying tresses of hair—the tail—that Chapman can link the heavenly phenomenon, the creature of Apollo that foretells doom, with the prophetess who delivers his oracles on earth. At the end of her tale Teras' hair "stares up" and dismays the guests. This must remind us of the accounts of Pythia—or of Virgil's Sibyl—their hair starting up when the presence of the god is felt:

> ventum erat ad limen, cum virgo 'poscere fata
> tempus' ait; 'deus ecce deus!' cui talia fanti

ante fores subito non vultus, non color unus,
non comptae mansere comae . . . .[28]

[They had come to the threshold, when the maiden said, "it is time to ask the oracles: the god,
behold the god!"; and as she spoke thus, before the doors, suddenly neither her face nor her
colour was the same, and her hair was unkempt.]

Why Chapman should have chosen to make his nymph a wood-nymph is perhaps difficult
to say. But he would find in his lexicon that κομὴ and κομήτης could be used of the
foliage of trees.[29] This may well be the link. And this may have led him to think of another
of Apollo's servants—a tree-haunter, the crow, which is certainly a "little Silvan". The crow
was "minister and servant" of Apollo (the words are Cartari's),[30] who indeed had once
transformed himself into a crow. It was a prophetic bird, for auguries could be read in its
voice.[31] Teras has an ebony thigh (if "ebon" is to be taken as ebony, here) and her black
and purple scarfs may well be the colours of the crow as well as colours emblematic of
mourning—the purple being the sheen on glossy feathers, as it is in the description of the
gold-finches at the end of the poem.

Eronusis is clearly an allegorical image in a sense that Teras is not. Teras interests us
first as a character: she is there, first, for her dramatic qualities. Eronusis is a defining image:
her main purport is the definition of dissimulation; we are required, immediately, to
interpret her attributes which state the general proposition: "Dissimulation, especially in
women, is like this . . . ." The great example in the poem of this sort of image is, however,
the goddess Ceremony. This figure is so complex and her role so crucial that analysis must
be reserved for the moment. Yet, it will be seen, the method Chapman is employing for
Ceremony is precisely this method of adaptation and combination: a difference being that
for Ceremony he had no received image to work on as he had in the case of Eronusis.
Doubt whether fresh sources for this imagery may not still be found does not affect the
general issue of the method in use, which is the same for the representation of familiar
deities as it is for the construction of allegorical figures that did not exist in the classical
pantheon. Nor is Chapman isolated or peculiar in his way of working. It is exactly by
adapting and combining that Ben Jonson, for example, creates figures in his masque (and
an excellent parallel to Chapman's Ceremony is Jonson's elaborate Truth, in the barriers
that follow his *Hymenaei*).[32] And the method would not seem strange at all if we were
more willing than we are to see the practice of such poets in connexion with Spenser's.

Two further points are to be made. We should not be too quick to say that such
figures as Teras or Eronusis or Ceremony are quite unclassical. We are still—in spite of the
labours of the anthropologists—too apt to be hypnotized by plaster-cast ideas of the twelve
Olympians. But this was not the pantheon as the sixteenth century knew it. The elaborate
abstractions of late antiquity were far more familiar to sixteenth-century writers than they
are to us. The syncretism of Plutarch in his *Isis and Osiris* and the mixture of Greek and
Egyptian cults in Diodorus Siculus were as present to their minds as the marbles of the
Olympians or the personifications on the coins they studied. A glance through the pages
of Cartari or at the illustrations to his text is enough to show how wild, how "unclassical"
in a romantic sense, this pantheon was: aniconic cult objects, hermaphroditic and beast

headed deities are there beside Olympian Zeus and Apollo Musagetes. It is one world. In this world, and in Chapman's poem, a description by Dante of Geryon as image of Fraud can find its place as authentic and classical.[33]

The second point is this: the idea that "imitation" of the classics could involve the creation of new classical figures arrived at by adapting and combining elements found in classical sources is not new at the end of the sixteenth century: it is present from the beginning. Chapman himself furnishes us with a neat illustration. Chapman's *Epicede or Funerall Song*, written for the death of Prince Henry, is largely based on a personification of Fever, who is incited to attack the prince by the jealous Nemesis. This goddess Fever has no direct classical prototype. Nor did Chapman invent her. This whole section of his poem is based (with modifications) on Angelo Poliziano's elegy *In Albieram Albitiam puellam formosissimam morientem*, (written presumably in 1473, when the girl in question died). It was Politian who invented the goddess *Febris* on the basis of a few references to *Febris* and her cult scattered in classical authors. His goddess is produced—as a recent study has admirably shown—by adapting and conflating descriptions of the Furies, of Cybele, of personifications of Evil and of demons, and of various accounts of illness and plagues.[34] Immensely laborious and complicated, then, is the process that lies behind a figure made by Chapman or Jonson. But the process is the same as Politian's, and the justification the same. These are figures that might have been created by the classical writers.

II. The Goddess Ceremony

As Leander lies in bed, on his return from Hero, the goddess Ceremony appears to him in a vision.

> The Goddesse *Ceremonie*, with a Crowne
> Of all the stars, and heauen with her descended,
> Her flaming haire to her bright feete extended,
> By which hung all the bench of Deities;
> And in a chaine, compact of eares and eies,
> She led Religion; all her bodie was
> Cleere and transparent as the purest glasse:
> For she was all presented to the sence;
> Deuotion, Order, State, and Reuerence
> Her shadowes were; Societie, Memorie;
> All which her sight made liue; her absence die.
> A rich disparent Pentackle she weares,
> Drawne full of circles and strange characters:
> Her face was changeable to euerie eie;
> One way lookt ill, another graciouslie;
> Which while men viewd, they cheerfull were & holy:
> But looking off, vicious and melancholy:
> The snakie paths to each obserued law,

Did *Policie* in her broad bosome draw:
One hand a Mathematique Christall swayes,
Which gathering in one line a thousand rayes
From her bright eyes, *Confusion* burnes to death,
And all estates of men distinguisheth.
By it *Morallitie* and *Comelinesse*
Themselues in all their sightly figures dresse.
Her other hand a lawrell rod applies,
To beate back *Barbarisme*, and *Auarice*,
That followd eating earth and excrement
And humane lims; and would make proud ascent
To seates of Gods, were *Ceremonie* slaine;
The *Howrs* and *Graces* bore her glorious traine,
And all the sweetes of our societie
Were Spherde, and treasurde in her bountious eie.
                    (III, 112–44)

Ceremony is a concept of which it is singularly difficult to find discussions in Renaissance literature; and the question arises whether in fact a general theory of ceremony existed; the reason being, presumably, that meanings included in the word were subsumed in discussions of topics of overriding importance – of social and cosmic order and the practice of devotion; and that it was not felt necessary to disengage them and erect a general theory. Yet we can catch sight of the grounds on which a general theory could be erected: such a theory as Chapman presents in his figure of the goddess and in the conduct of his fable.

There is a helpful passage in the *Ecclesiastical Polity* where Hooker does say something about the nature, place and purpose of ceremony:

The end which is aimed at in setting down the outward form of all religious actions is the edification of the Church. Now men are edified, when either their understanding is taught somewhat wherof in such actions it behoveth all men to consider, or when their hearts are moved with any affection suitable thereunto; when their minds are in any sort stirred up unto that reverence, devotion, attention, and due regard, which in those cases seemeth requisite. Because therefore unto this purpose not only speech but sundry sensible means besides have always been thought necessary, and especially those means which being object to the eye, the liveliest and the most apprehensive sense of all other, have in that respect seemed the fittest to make a deep and a strong impression: from hence have risen not only a number of prayers, readings, questionings, exhortations, but even of visible signs also; which being used in performance of holy actions, are undoubtedly most effectual to open such matter, as men when they know and remember carefully, must needs be a great deal the better informed to what effect such duties serve. We must not think but that there is some ground of reason even in nature, whereby it cometh to pass that no nation under heaven either doth or ever did suffer public actions which are of weight, whether they be civil and temporal or else spiritual and sacred, to pass without some visible solemnity: the very strangeness whereof and difference from that which is common, doth cause popular eyes to observe and to mark the same. Words, both because they are common, and do not so strongly move the fancy of man, are for the most part but slightly heard: and therefore with singular wisdom it hath been provided, that the deeds of men which are made in the presence of witnesses should pass not only with words, but also with certain sensible actions, the memory whereof is far more easy and durable than the memory of speech can be.[35]

Discussion of the full relevance of this passage must be postponed for the moment; but it is already clear why Chapman's goddess leads religion in a chain "compact of eares and eies," bizarre though the detail may seem; and also why Devotion, Order, State, and Reverence were her shadows.

On the plane of social intercourse ceremony might also be discussed in terms of *decorum*. Just how all embracing this concept was can be seen, to take an English example, from George Puttenham's long and important discussion of it in his *The Arte of English Poesie*, where we find that decorum controls not only the art of writing but the conduct of social intercourse in all its aspects of dress, speech, action and creation. The connexion could be made outright through considering Chapman's order, state, and reverence, and, especially, this:

> By it Morallitie and Comelinesse
> Themselves in all their sightly figures dresse.

The word *comely* is of marked importance. For here is Puttenham's definition of decorum:

> In all things to vse decencie, is it onely that giueth euery thing his good grace & without which nothing in mans speach could seeme good or gracious. . . . But herein resteth the difficultie, to know what this good grace is, & wherein it consisteth, for peraduenture it be easier to conceaue then to expresse, we wil therfore examine it to the bottome & say: that euery thing which pleaseth the mind or sences, & the mind by the sences as by means instrumentall, doth it for some amiable point or qualitie that is in it, which draweth them to a good liking and contentment with their proper obiects . . . . The Greekes call this good grace of euery thing in his kinde, τò πρεπον the Latines [*decorum*] we in our vulgar call it by a scholasticall terme [decencie] our owne Saxon English terme is [seemelynesse] that is to say, for his good shape and vtter appearance well pleasing the eye, we call it also [comelynesse] for the delight it bringeth comming towardes vs, and to that purpose may be called [pleasant approche] so as euery way seeking to expresse this τò πρεπον of the Greekes and *decorum* of the Latines, we are faine in our vulgar toung to borrow the terme which our eye onely for his noble prerogatiue ouer all the rest of the sences doth vsurpe, and to apply the same to all good, comely, pleasant and honest things, euen to the spirituall obiectes of the mynde, which stand no lesse in the due proportion of reason and discourse than any other materiall thing doth in his sensible bewtie, proportion and comelynesse.[36]

Comeliness, "this good grace of euery thing in his kinde" belongs to Decorum, and to Ceremony. But Ceremony is also Law. Chapman also calls his goddess Thesme, devising the name certainly from ϑεσμós by adding the feminine ending. Here Chapman intends law in a special sense. For while ϑεσμós could be understood as meaning law, human or divine, in general, a special sense was admitted in the sixteenth-century lexicons. ϑεσμós could be taken to apply specifically to institution, custom or divine rites.[38] And it is clear that this is what Chapman had in mind, for he qualifies her name thus:

> Thesme the Deitie soueraigne
> Of Customes and religious rites.
>   (III, Argument, 4–5)

So Morality too takes her shape from Ceremony, by following her structure of ordinances. But Thesme is not only a particular sense of law; she is law in general manifesting herself in this particular shape. She is divine—with a crown of all the stars; and she brings heaven down with her. Her flaming hair reaching to her bright feet "By which hung all the bench of Deities" can only be a version of that golden chain which Homer's Zeus threatened to let down from heaven: challenging all the gods to attempt to drag him down by it and threatening, if they dared the attempt, to pull them up with it, and the whole world too.[39] It was a famous passage, this of the *catena aurea*, and Chapman would understand it as allegorical of the omnipotent irresistible power of the divine will, and also of the indissoluble and uninterrupted sequence in which God has placed the orders of existence, from lowest to highest: this latter was the interpretation of the *catena aurea* best known to Renaissance writers, who received it directly from Macrobius; and it is the way in which, for example, Ben Jonson read the image.[40] Briefly, then, Ceremony's flaming hair with the clinging deities is an allegory of what we have learned to call "the great chain of being". Her pentacle "Drawne full of circles and strenge characters" is also to be read in this context. It is the five-sided star used in magical operations. And the art of magic and the power of the magus depends on this unity of creation: it is by manipulating the correspondences that the magus works: "magicam operare non est aliud quam maritare mundum" was Pico della Mirandola's succinct definition.[41] Furthermore five, the number of the star's points, was the marriage number—as we shall see in more detail later—and the *nexus omnia ligans*.[42] Again, the role of the pentacle in magic was to protect us from evil and evil spirits and draw the good to us;[43] and this is Ceremony's saving power.[44] There was classical authority for this use of the figure; for the pentacle was the sign of the goddess Salus or Hygieia.[45]

After all that has been said in recent years about them there is no need here for an exposition of Elizabethan notions about "the great chain of being", about the "order" and "degree" that are the controlling principles of microcosm and macrocosm, of the structure of man, of his society, and of the universe: a divinely instituted harmony that can only be violated at the price of disaster. It could be seen and expressed, this embracing order, in various ways: in terms of music, for example (and Ceremony appears to Leander in a burst of divine music) or of love. Puttenham's *Decorum* is an expression of it in terms of a special case, the principles that must govern a man's bearing towards his fellows, in his society and his works, written or spoken. Hooker saw this order in terms of law, and personified this Law in a famous passage:

> . . . of Law there can be no less acknowledged, than that her seat is the bosom of God, her voice the harmony of the world: all things in heaven and earth do her homage, the very least as feeling her care, and the greatest as not exempted from her power, both Angels and men and creatures of what condition soever, though each in different sort and manner, yet all with uniform consent, admiring her as the mother of their peace and joy.[46]

Hooker would have recognized Chapman's Thesme. Chapman's is the same law, but seen under the special aspect of law as established by custom and use—which in human affairs corresponds to the unchangeable divine plan for the universe—and manifested in the performance of ritual acts.

Performance of such ritual acts is acknowledgement of the divine principle of order and enactment of the workings of it; and to enact the workings of the principle brings it into operation. Ceremony is rightly seen as the guardian of society, memory, order, as distinguishing the different estates of men whose union in difference makes the hierarchy of society, and as the enemy of confusion, barbarism and avarice, themselves the enemies of order.[47] The laurel rod which she uses to beat down these latter two is Apollo's laurel, the laurel of arts and science. The light from her eyes focussed in a "Mathematique Christall" distinguishes the degrees of society, gives light, and a mirror for morality and comeliness to dress themselves in, and destroys confusion.[48] For opposed to confusion are those Platonic mathematical harmonies on which the fabric of the universe was built. This burning light, too, associates Ceremony with Apollo, for the burning glass has this power—as Ficino explains—because it is an image of the sun.[49]

> The snakie paths to each obserued law,
> Did *Policie* in her broad bosome draw.

Policy—certainly not used here in its pejorative sense, but in the sense of prudence[50]—illustrates on her bosom the winding indirect ways that must be followed if the law is to be observed, if human affairs are to be well conducted: snaky because the snake was a familiar emblem of prudence (and appears as such on the arm of Queen Elizabeth on one of the Hatfield portraits).[51] Indeed Policy could only become Prudence—and the meaning of the word be rescued[52]—if its aim were to lead to the observance of law. Properly then can it be said, in summing up, that

> all the sweetes of our societie
> Were Spherde, and treasurde in her bountious eie;

and properly is she accompanied by the Hours and the Graces. For the Hours and the Graces always went together: they are beautiful goddesses that turn the season of the year and bring to man the fruits of the earth that sustain him, and those virtues that bind men together and make civil life possible and raise us from the level of the brutes.[53]

Ceremony rebukes Leander for consummating his love without waiting for marriage—for his "bluntnes in his violent love". He accepts the rebuke and his heart is pierced:

> With sence of his unceremonious part
> In which with plaine neglect of Nuptiall rites,
> He close and flatly fell to his delites.
> (III, 156–58)

Plans are made for carrying Hero off and for an immediate marriage; but, as we know, it is too late. The lovers are punished for their sinful violation of the law of ceremony; and in Hero's case for her violation of the vow of chastity she has sworn to Venus. The simple moral is clearly stated:

And now ye wanton loues, and young desires,
Pied vanitie, the mint of strange Attires;
Ye lisping Flatteries, and obsequious Glances,
Relentfull Musicks, and attractiue Dances,
And you detested Charmes constraining loue,
Shun loues stolne sports by that these Louers proue . . . .
The God of gold of purpose guilt his lims,
This this word guilt, including double sence,
The double guilt of his *Incontinence*,
Might be exprest, that had no stay t'employ
The treasure which the Loue-god let him ioy
In his deare *Hero*, with such sacred thrift,
As had besemed so sanctified a gift:
But like a greedie vulgar Prodigall
Would of the stock dispend, and rudely fall
Before his time, to that vnblessed blessing,
Which for lusts plague doth perish with possessing.
  Joy grauen in sence, like snow in water wasts;
  Without preserue of vertue nothing lasts.
        (III, 11–16, 24–36)

And the importance of marriage rites is insisted on, structurally, in the action of the fifth *Sestiad*: here Hero, as priestess, marries Alcmane and Mya, and the blessing of their love is intended to comment, ironically or tragically, on Hero's own situation:

She sends for two betrothed louers,
And marries them, that (with their crew,
Their sports and ceremonies due)
She couertly might celebrate,
With secret ioy her owne estate.
        (V, Argument, 6–10)

The splendid epithalamium is sung for them; but not for Hero. And still further weight is given to the motif by inserting into these celebrations Teras' tale of the love and marriage of Hymen; for here the classical ritual is described in full; and Hymen is marriage itself.

Refusal or violation of the rite of marriage could quite easily be treated as an instance or metaphor of violation of the sacred harmony of the universe; for union in marriage could easily be seen as type of the divine union. Precisely this was, a few years later, to be the theme of Jonson's great wedding masque, *Hymenæi*. Here Jonson introduces a Roman bride and bridegroom and all the apparatus of the classical ritual, with Hymen himself presiding; and then, issuing from a microcosm, the Humours and Affections, momentarily out of the control of Reason, who wildly seek to disturb the rites. The whole complicated argument of this masque, with its Platonic basis, is the need for maintaining order and harmony within the all-embracing divine union: the symbolical vehicle is the marriage rites which are the rites of Juno, who is also Unio, Unity, the One.[54]

The sin of Hero and Leander obviously implies such a wild violation of cosmic order as that threatened in *Hymenæi*; for, as we have seen, Chapman's goddess is a version of this order. Further, Ceremony is specifically related to marriage rites. The five of Ceremony's pentacle is repeated in the five of the five torches carried during the marriage of Hymen, and known, by both Chapman and Jonson, to be carried in the actual Roman ceremony. There were five torches because, as we have seen, five was the *nexus omnia ligans*, and the marriage number. Jonson, as well as Chapman, knew the reason why, with its Pythagorean and Platonic sources:

> For *fiue* the speciall *number* is,
> Whence hallow'd VNION claymes her blisse.
> As being all the summe, that growes
> From the vnited strengths, of those
> Which *male* and *female* numbers wee
> Doe style, and are *first two*, and *three*.
> Which, ioyned thus, you cannot seuer
> In equall parts, but one will euer
> Remaine as common; so we see
> The binding force of *Vnitie* . . . .[55]

III. The Argument

The terms of Hero and Leander's offence, however, can only be understood by making yet another attempt to define the concept of ceremony. We have until now largely ignored what is after all the first thing to say about ceremony: that ceremony is a visible action or show. Ceremony appeals to the eye; and it was on this, and on the traditional notion of the primacy of sight among the senses that Hooker based his argument for the usefulness and power of ceremony in moving and instructing.[56] We can arrive at a definition of the nature as well as the function of this show if we study the words used when it is discussed. For although the concept itself is not isolated and systematically treated, the words used when allusion to it is made belong to a familiar philosophic vocabulary, and show us the way in which Hooker, say, and Ben Jonson, thought of ceremony.

The passage from Hooker which we have already quoted follows this paragraph:

. . . we are to note, that in every grand or main public duty which God requireth at the hands of his Church, there is, besides that matter and form wherein the essence thereof consisteth, a certain outward fashion whereby the same is in decent sort administered. The substance of all religious actions is delivered from God himself in few words. For example's sake in the sacraments. "Unto the element let the word be added, and they both do make a sacrament", saith St. Augustine. Baptism is given by the element of water, and that prescript form of words which the Church of Christ doth use; the sacrament of the body and blood of Christ is administered in the elements of bread and wine, if those mystical words be added thereunto. But the due and decent form of administering those holy sacraments doth require a great deal more.[57]

Substance, that is (and *substance* is synonymous with *essence*), consists in the union of *matter* and *form*: in the union, in the case of a sacrament, of element and word—of the water and the "prescript form of words". But in addition there is the "outward fashion" of administering the rite; and it is this outward fashion which Hooker then proceeds to discuss as "ceremony" and to justify for its power of edification. When, in *Hymenæi*, the Humours and Affections leave their microcosm and threaten to disturb the rites of Hymen, Ben Jonson finds it necessary to explain what the allegorical meaning of the episode is. This is how he does it:

> First, as in *naturall bodies*, so likewise in *minds*, there is no disease, or distemperature, but is caused either by some abounding *humor*, or perverse *affection*; after the same manner, in *politick bodies* (where *Order, Ceremony, State, Reuerence, Deuotion*, are parts of the *Mind*) by the difference, or prædominant will of what we (*metaphorically*) call *Humors*, and *affections*, all things are troubled and confused. These therefore, were *tropically* brought in before *Marriage*, as disturbers of that *mysticall bodie*, and the *rites*, which were *soule* vnto it.[58]

To these passages a third may be added. It is, again, from Hooker, when he is discussing the sacraments and their proper celebration:

> Now even as the soul doth organize the body, and give unto every member thereof that substance, quantity, and shape, which nature seeth most expedient, so the inward grace of sacraments may teach what serveth best for their outward form.[59]

Now this vocabulary is perfectly familiar. It is quite clear that ceremony and rite are being discussed in terms of the Aristotelian ontology. Substance or essence is the ὀυσία which is constituted by the union of ὕλη and εἶδος, matter and form; and εἶδος, form, is the determining principle, that which makes a thing what it is, and is synonymous with soul; for the soul is the form of the body.[60] For Jonson the "rites" are, explicitly, the soul of the mystical body of marriage: as, in general, Order, State, Reverence, Devotion are parts of the mind (or soul) of the body politic. Hooker makes distinctions: the form of words added to the element of water are form and matter in the sacrament: the additional and desirable "certain outward fashion" is what he is here calling ceremony. Hooker's problem was, after all, a polemical one; he is concerned at such moments with the defence of the ritual of his church against the presbyterian innovators; and his problem is, precisely, to distinguish between what, in rite or ceremony, is matter and what form, what body and what soul, what the substance is, and what is accessory. For our purposes it is sufficient to know that this was the language he used in his discussions and the context of ideas in which he saw the problem.

This is certainly the context in which Chapman was moving. For him ceremony was form in its Aristotelian sense. Ceremony's rebuke to Leander is reported, and can only be understood by reference to this idea of form:

> Thus she appeard, and sharply did reproue
> *Leanders* bluntnes in his violent loue;
> Tolde him how poore was substance without rites,
> Like bils vnsignd, desires without delites;

> Like meates vnseasond; like ranke corne that growes
> On Cottages, that none or reapes or sowes:
> Not being with ciuill forms confirm'd and bounded,
> For humane dignities and comforts founded:
> But loose and secret all their glories hide,
> Feare fils the chamber, darknes decks the Bride.
>   (III, 145–54)

Form is not only the informing principle: the formal is also the efficient and the final cause; form is also *entelechy*, which is *perfectio*; and it is of the nature of each thing—natural or artificial—that it must seek to achieve its form, which is its perfection.[61] Ficino puts it thus:

> Everything has its particular end. The particular end of a thing is its particular cause. For there it is perfected; all things seek a natural perfection as their end.[a]

The parallel cases which Ceremony cites to show Leander exactly what his situation is are precisely cases where form has not been achieved—form defined teleologically. The bill that is not signed has no validity: it is not a bill at all; for the essence of a bill is that it should be valid. Desire without delight cannot be complete because it is of the essence of desire that delight—of some sort—should be anticipated in accomplishing it. Meats unseasoned do not fulfil their proper function of pleasing as well as nourishing. The true end of corn is to be cultivated and harvested for the use of man. Leander's case is that of love consummated without marriage; and substance is poor without rites because without them—without the civil forms that "confirm" and "bound" love, thus, by defining it, giving it a form—substance has not really been achieved: it is not perfect.

How strongly Chapman's mind was at this moment impressed by such ideas can be seen from their reappearance not many lines after Ceremony's speech—in a rather surprising context. Chapman reports very briefly how Leander accepts Ceremony's rebuke and plans, with his father's consent, to marry Hero; he then announces that he is going to tell us about Hero. But before he does this he inserts his well known and moving address to Marlowe—"thou most strangely-intellectuall fire"—in which these lines occur:

> Now (as swift as Time
> Doth follow Motion) finde th'eternall Clime
> Of his free soule, whose liuing subiect stood
> Vp to the chin in the Pyerean flood.
>   (III, 187–90)[63]

Some difficulty has been felt about interpreting these lines, but there need be none. "Subject" as used here is a technical Aristotelian term, and is used of the body as "subject" to the soul:

> the soul is neither subject (i.e. substance) nor matter, but is *in* subject. The body, however, is subject and matter, not in subject.[b]

---

[a] Vnaquaeque res in proprio sui fine quiescit. Proprius finis rei est eius causa propria. Ibi enim perficitur, perfectionem verò naturalem appetunt omnia tanquam finem.[62]

[b] anima non est subiectum seu materia, sed est in subiecto: corpus autem est subiectum & materia, non in subiecto.[64]

Ceremony standing to the event as form does to matter has taken Chapman into the realm of ontology. This problem, posed in these Aristotelian terms, carries with it a set of related notions. These are concerned with how forms are perceived, with sight, and with the image. There is an ambiguity in the word form: its meaning can shift—and does so almost imperceptibly—between "visible form" and "internal or organizing form";[65] and it is of course this that permits ceremony to be conceived of in the terms we have displayed. By stressing the first meaning so that form means appearance or outward manner and behaviour in the simplest sense, Chapman extends the range of his subject so that he can introduce the problem of the relation of "appearance" and "reality", considered particularly in its moral implications. It is on this nexus, this warp of ideas, that Chapman composes his version of what happened to Hero and Leander.

Before tracing these threads, one qualification should be made. The ontology with which Chapman is working has been described as Aristotelian and stated in Aristotelian terminology. This is certainly right: the fundamental texts for it were Aristotle's. But it is not only Aristotelian. The elements described also belong to the Christian Aristotle which the sixteenth century still received from St. Thomas: in Hooker's case it is perhaps as much a question of Aquinas as of Aristotle. And they had passed, too, into the thought of the Renaissance Platonists: these elements are as much Ficinian as Aristotelian.[66] The *De Anima*, as it was read by Chapman's contemporaries, and probably by Chapman himself, is perhaps the best guide to *Hero and Leander*: but that is because it is the fundamental source for this nexus of ontological and psychological ideas: the poem is not such that it can be elucidated by reference to one key text. There are passages which are specifically non-Aristotelian. For example, when Chapman writes:

> So when our firie soule, our bodies starre
> (That euer is in motion circulare)
>
> (III, 245–46)

he is using notions that are explicitly rejected by Aristotle in the *De Anima*, where the Platonic notion of the circular movement of the soul is criticized at length.[67] So nothing in our analysis is to be taken as intended to disturb the view now currently and, I believe, correctly held, of the dominance of Platonic and Ficinian ideas in Chapman's thought.

When Chapman turns to Hero, in this same *Sestiad*, he is concerned to analyse a complicated state of mind, or succession of states of mind. Hero's mind is all confusion, the confusion that has followed her rash and guilty act: "Her maidenhead, her vowes, *Leander* gone". The image developed is that of a rich and peaceful city invaded by a wild foreign army. Hero's first preoccupation—the point at which her thought grows coherent—is the problem of how

> she could looke vpon her Sire
> And not shew that without, that was intire.
>
> (III, 233–34)

The problem is immediately generalized, and is first stated in the language of the Aristotelian psychology, in terms of the soul which "conceives a forme". According to Aristotle, the soul knows only form and all thought is in terms of forms, received as images.[68] The form once conceived, Chapman continues, is "conveyed" through the eye and made visible. He has introduced this passage by the standard comparison of the eye to the mirror:

> For as a glasse is an inanimate eie,
> And outward formes imbraceth inwardlie:
> So is the eye an animate glasse that showes
> In-formes without vs.
>   (III, 235–38)[69]

Consideration of Chapman's use of the Aristotelian theory of vision had better be postponed till later; but meanwhile there could be no better commentary on this whole passage than this description by Hooker of the mind's activity and how it is revealed through the eye:

> The mind while we are in this present life, whether it contemplate, meditate, deliberate, or howsoever exercise itself, working nothing without continual recourse unto imagination, the only storehouse of wit and peculiar chair of memory. On this anvil it ceaseth not day and night to strike, by means whereof as the pulse declareth how the heart doth work, so the very thoughts and cogitations of man's mind be they good or bad do no where sooner bewray themselves, than through the crevices of that wall wherewith nature hath compassed the cells and closets of fancy.[70]

The authority Hooker cites for this account is the *De Anima*.[71] It is precisely the mind's ceaseless commerce with images, how the mind strikes day and night on the anvil of imagination, that Chapman is seeking to render throughout his whole presentation of Hero: this and the power of the image, the thing seen, as illustrated by the effect of Leander's image on Hero.

These lines on the soul's conception and display of forms are preliminary to the introduction of the topic of "dissimulation": the relation between outward form and inward reality. The possibility of creating a false relationship is one the innocent Hero can hardly imagine:

> For yet the world's stale cunning she resisted
> To beare foule thoughts, yet forge what lookes she listed.
>   (III, 253–54)

Her predicament serves as occasion for a generalized attack on this impudent art, "That makes the face a Pandar to the hart," which ends in paradoxes on the nature of the soul. The climax to this phase of confusion and despair is represented visually. Hero makes herself into an image emblematic of the confusion that has attacked her. She

> tooke a robe was nigh,
> Exceeding large, and of black Cypres made,
> In which she sate, hid from the day in shade,
> Euen ouer head and face downe to her feete;
> Her left hand made it at her bosome meete;
> Her right hand leand on her hart-bowing knee,

> Wrapt in vnshapefull foulds: twas death to see:
> Her knee stayd that, and that her falling face,
> Each limme helpt other to put on disgrace.
> No forme was seene, where forme held all her sight:
> But like an Embrion that saw neuer light:
> Or like a scorched statue made a cole
> With three-winged lightning: or a wretched soule
> Muffled with endles darknes, she did sit.
>   (III, 292–305)

Hyperbolically, the images state that Hero's desperate confusion has destroyed her form. The embryo that never sees light, the soul muffled with darkness are cases where form and therefore being is not achieved. The image of the statue, which is matter that the sculptor endows with form, is traditional in the philosophical context: it was Aristotle's favourite instance of how matter is united with form to constitute being. Ficino used the image in the same sense.[72] Chapman has reversed it to show the statue whose form has been destroyed as an image of the destruction of being.

Tears, distraction and a swoon mark the end of this period. But the confusion is succeeded by new stability. This is the effect of thinking about Leander–represented as the invasion of her mind by his image:

> And here Leander's beauties were imbarkt.
> He came in swimming painted all with ioyes,
> Such as might sweeten hell.
>   (III, 328–30)

This image of invasion recalls that earlier image of Leander invading Hero like a conquering destroying army and reducing her to confusion. Now he invades her again and his image is of such force that:

> his thought destroyes
> All her destroying thoughts . . . .
>   (III, 330–31)

But poor Hero's new stability is based on a structure of sophisms intended to justify her love and the breaking of her vow, and issuing in the decision to dissemble:

> Thus, her sharpe wit, her loue, her secrecie,
> Trouping together, made her wonder why
> She should not leaue her bed, and to the Temple?
> Her health said she must liue; her sex, dissemble.
>   (III, 397–400)

She has accepted as possible what she had rejected as absurd. She will wear a false form.

It is this decision and the theme of dissimulation that control the next, the fourth, *Sestiad*. Apart from the description of her attire and her emblematic scarf, emphasis falls on analysis of Hero's state of mind as she performs her sacrifice to Venus, on the apparition of Venus, her rejection of the sacrifice and her creation of the figure of Eronusis or

Dissimulation. The function of this piece of mythological invention is, of course, to generalize Hero's action. Her action becomes the mythical occasion for the emergence of the emblematic figure which effects the statement "Dissimulation is a general vice—a ruling principle of human life".

> Venus flew
> From *Heros* sight, and at her Chariot drew
> This wondrous creature to so steepe a height,
> That all the world she might command with sleight
> Of her gay wings: and then she bad her hast,
> Since *Hero* had dissembled, and disgrast
> Her rites so much, and euery breast infect
> With her deceits, she made her Architect
> Of all dissimulation, and since then
> Neuer was any trust in maides nor men.
> (IV, 305–14)

To effect this general statement, and to show the individual case in relation to the general situation is one of Chapman's main interests in the poem—this is why most of his attention is given to Hero. The creation of Eronusis, then, is the climax of this theme.

Hero's decision to perform the rites of sacrifice is a reiteration, a more emphatic, final acceptance of the conclusion she had come to at the end of the third *Sestiad*, when she had already decided to dissemble: her action is the decisive, irrevocable step. The pattern of her mental struggle repeats that of her earlier experience—with the difference that this time she knows what the solution is and deliberately invokes it. When the odours turn into stinking fumes, the flames burn downwards, and the candles burn red, Hero is frightened, but does not hesitate:

> Then Hero wept; but her affrighted eyes
> She quickly wrested from the sacrifice:
> Shut them, and inwards for *Leander* lookt
> Searcht her soft bosome, and from thence she pluckt
> His louely picture: which when she had viewd,
> Her beauties were with all loues ioyes renewd.
> The odors sweetned, and the fires burnd cleere,
> *Leanders* forme left no ill obiect there.
> (IV, 132–39)

Earlier she had discovered by accident the cure for her distress. She now seeks it deliberately; and Leander's image is as effective now as it was before.

Chapman now makes his strongest statement of the power of the image. He expands these lines about the power of Hero's mental image of Leander into a little myth about the power of Leander's pictured image. After Hero had told how effective the mere evocation of Leander's image had been to convert into good the evil omens of this sacrifice, pictured images of him became the object of a cult and were cherished for their potency. For such images held all the power of Hero's mental image. They were sovereign against witchcraft, disease and madness, against the fear of thunder and death, against marital discord and mischief in general; they could both raise love and quench it; they could make the avaricious generous and the barbarous pitiful; and held in a prince's hand such an image could extinguish the most dreadful comet.[73]

The image, mental or pictured, has such power because:

> Such was his beautie that the force of light,
> Whose knowledge teacheth wonders infinite,
> The strength of number and proportion,
> Nature had plaste in it to make it knowne
> Art was her daughter . . . .
>   (IV, 140–44)

To explain these lines and what follows about the force of the image we have to go to the Platonists. Chapman knew from his reading in Ficino's commentary on the *Symposium* that beauty lies in the concord of a certain set of proportions (and proportions are stated numerically); he also knew, from the same source, that beauty is the splendour of the divine countenance, a ray shining through created things;[74] this too goes with 'number and proportion', for the study of light—optics—is a mathematical science and leads to knowledge of the harmonies of God's intelligible world.[75] The stirring, soothing and healing effects of Leander's image are—like the magical effects of music—the effects of harmony and concord.

Further, if the brightness, numbers and proportion of Leander's beauty are divine, a manifestation of the divine Idea, then an image which accurately retains this brightness, these numbers and these proportions, will have the power of the object it represents. Hence Leander's image has the power of Leander's beauty, the power, that is, of the divine Idea. This is the argument on which Chapman's little myth rests; it is the argument of the Neo-Platonic theory of the image, as it is expounded, for example, by Ficino.[76] We may illustrate from Ficino's exposition of the power of the image in his *De Vita* with a passage that takes us very close to Chapman. The power of the figure or image, rests on the correspondences between the sublunar and the celestial worlds. Of all things in this sublunar world colour, number and figures are least tainted by matter and therefore closest to the celestial world, and best able to draw down the celestial powers:

> Of light indeed what shall I say? For it is an act or image of Intelligence. Colours are lights of a kind; therefore when the astrologers say that lights (that is, colours, figures and numbers) have so much power in preparing the materials of our world for celestial purposes, you ought not lightly to neglect them. For you are not unaware that musical harmony, through its numbers and proportions, has a marvelous power to stabilise, to move, and to influence the spirit, mind and body. Now proportions, made up of numbers, are like figures of a certain kind; or as if they were made up of points and lines, but in motion. Similarly, the celestial figures exert their influence by their motion; for these figures, by their harmonic rays and motions that penetrate everything, constantly affect the spirit secretly in the same way that powerful music is accustomed to affect it openly.[c]

---

[c] De lumine vero quid dicam? Est enim actus intelligentiæ vel imago. Colores autem sunt lumina quaedam. Quamobrem vbi lumina, id est colores, figurasque, et numeros Astrologi dicunt in materiis nostris

Structurally, it must be admitted, Chapman's myth does not fit very well. His desire to develop this theme of the power of the image has led him into difficulties. It is not explained when Hero had time or opportunity to talk about the marvelous change of the omens at her sacrifice; nor is it explained why people at large should have found this episode so convincing. For the point about the effect of the image on Hero and the sacrifice is that it is false. The fire may burn clear, but heaven is not appeased. And the effect on Hero is simply to give her false peace and to confirm her in her wrong decision to dissimulate:

> Yet singularitie she would vse no more,
> For she was singular too much before:
> But she would please the world with fayre pretext;
> (IV, 192–94)

and

> Thus would she still proceed in works diuine,
> And in her sacred state of priesthood shine,
> Handling the holy rites with hands as bold,
> As if therein she did *Ioues* thunder hold;
> And need not feare those menaces of error,
> Which she at others threw with greatest terror.
> (IV, 204–09)

Love teaches her that she is doing best when in fact she is doing worst.

The argument of the next *Sestiad* takes us back to ceremony. Hero dispenses her young priestess Mya from her vow of chastity and marries her to Alcmane. The whole of this action, as we have already seen, is a comment on Hero's own situation:

> She sends for two betrothed louers,
> And marries them, that (with their crew,
> Their sports and ceremonies due)
> She couertly might celebrate,
> With secret ioy her owne estate.
> (V, Argument, 6–10)

But the comment is double. For the tale told by the strange apparition Teras, Apollo's nymph, at these nuptials is the story of the love and marriage of Hymen—the tale of marriage itself; and the great weight and space given to the account of Hymen's rites reminds us that these are the rites that Hero and Leander have neglected: the specific ceremony they have not cared to wait for. And the particular insistence on the symbolism

---

ad coelestia præparandis posse quamplurimum, non temere, vt aiunt, debes ista negare. Non ignoras concentus per numeros proportionesque suas, vim habere mirabilem ad spiritum et animum & corpus sistendum, mouendum et afficiendum. Proportiones autem ex numeris constitutæ, quasi figuræ quædam sunt, vel vt ex punctis lineisque factæ, sed in motu. Similiter motu suo se habent ad agendum figuræ coelestes, hæ namque harmonicis, tum radiis tum motibus suis omnia penetrantibus spiritum indies ita clam afficiunt, vt Musica præpotens palam afficere consueuit.[77]

of the five torches carried in the wedding procession, is, as we have seen, intended to refer both to the perfect harmony of the marriage union and back to the goddess Ceremony and the number five associated with her: to the marriage union of the universe, with its divine order of which ceremony is sign and acknowledgement.

This figuring of marriage union by numerical proportion should also recall to us the definition of beauty and love as proportion that comes at the beginning of Hymen's story.

> For as proportion, white, and crimsine, meet
> In Beauties mixture, all right cleere, and sweet;
> The eye responsible, the golden haire,
> And none is held without the other, faire:
> All spring together, all together fade;
> Such intermixt affections should inuade
> Two perfect louers: which being yet vnseene,
> Their vertues and their comforts copied beene,
> In Beauties concord, subiect to the eie;
> And that, in *Hymen*, pleasde so matchleslie,
> That louers were esteemde in their full grace,
> Like forme and colour mixt in *Hymens* face;
> And such sweete concord was thought worthie then
> Of torches, musick, feasts, and greatest men.
>   (V, 99–112)

The notion that beauty of the body is concord is Neo-Platonic and Ficinian: Chapman would find it in a text he knew well—Ficino's commentary on the *Symposium*: *humani autem corporis pulchritudo in quadam concinnitate consistit.*[78] Thus beauty is related to the harmony of music: and we have Chapman's:

> but he must proue
> How his rare bewties musick would agree
> With maids in consort.
>   (V, 128–30)

The concord of visible beauty, then, is the sensible copy of the perfect concord in affection of perfect lovers, "yet vnseene" because not realized on earth: a copy of the Platonic idea or form of perfect lovers. But the concord of Hymen's beauty is such that he can be regarded as the form of true lovers. (The relationship between form and colour we shall examine in a moment).

Further, the crisis of Hymen's love is presented in a way that makes the passage crucial for us. This is the account of the genesis of Eucharis' love for Hymen. It is given in mythological terms—a piece of invention and adaptation by Chapman, which he has added to Cartari's version of Hymen's story—and, as usual, this has the effect of making his account into a generalization: as do the philosophical terms in which he analyses the event.

> And now came *Loue* with *Proteus*, who had long
> Inggl'd the little god with prayers and gifts,
> Ran through all shapes, and varied all his shifts,

> To win *Loues* stay with him, and make him loue him:
> And when he saw no strength of sleight could moue him
> To make him loue, or stay, he nimbly turnd
> Into *Loues* selfe, he so extreamely burnd.
> And thus came *Loue* with *Proteus* and his powre,
> T'encounter *Eucharis*: first like the flowre
> That *Junos* milke did spring, the siluer Lillie,
> He fell on Hymens hand, who straight did spie
> The bounteous Godhead, and with wondrous ioy
> Offred it *Eucharis*. She wondrous coy
> Drew back her hand: the subtle flowre did woo it,
> And drawing it neere, mixt so you could not know it.
> As two cleere Tapers mixe in one their light,
> So did the Lillie and the hand their white:
> She viewd it, and her view the forme bestowes
> Amongst her spirits: for as colour flowes
> From superficies of each thing we see,
> Euen so with colours formes emitted bee:
> And where Loues forme is, loue is, loue is forme;
> He entred at the eye, his sacred storme
> Rose from the hand, loues sweetest instrument.
>
> (V, 206–29)

Proteus is allegorically the *materia prima*, the prime matter, and the *informis rerum materia* (as Giraldi has it)[79] which, for both Aristotle and Ficino, is pure potentiality.[80] This achieves the form of love: and takes visible shape as the lily (whose origin Chapman derives from Cartari). Eucharis receives this form through the eye—and loves because this form is love: and love *is* form. Chapman is here adapting for his own purposes familiar elements of the Neo-Platonic cosmology. That love is form, in the sense that matter achieves form through love, is a familiar doctrine. Thus Ficino, in his *Commentary* on the *Symposium* explains how the three worlds emerge from their respective chaoses and achieve form through love; and his account of the creation of the Angelic Mind brings us very close to Chapman in this passage:

> But the conception of Ideas, which is perfect, because created by God, was preceded by the uniting of the mind with God, this by the kindling of its desire, this kindling by the infusion of light, this infusion by the first stirring of its desire; and before this stirring there was only the unformed essence of that mind. Further, we say that this essence when still formless is Chaos; its first turning toward God, the birth of love, the infusion of light, love's nourishment; the kindling which follows, love's growth; its approach to God, love's passion; its formation, love's perfection.[d]

---

[d] Sed eam idearum conceptionem à formante Deo perfectam præcessit illa mentis ad Deum appropinquatio. Hanc præcessit appetitus incendium, hoc infusio radij, hanc prima illa appetitus conuersio, hanc informis mentis essentia. Porrò essentiam istam nondum formatam chaos esse volumus. Primam ipsius in Deum conuersionem, amoris ortum: radij infusionem amoris pabulum: incendium sequens, amoris dicimus incrementum: appropinquationem, amoris impetum: formationem, amoris perfectionem.

And again in this:

> The mind thus turns toward God just as the eye turns toward the light of the sun. First it looks, then it sees the sun's light, and finally in that light sees the shapes and colours of things. It is because the eye was at first dark and, like Chaos, unformed, that it loves light as soon as it sees it; seeing it, it receives its illumination, and so perceives the shapes and colours of things.[e]

It is worth noting that Giraldi also says that Proteus can be interpreted as an allegory of the Angelic Mind.[82] It almost looks as though Chapman had connected Proteus with this passage in Ficino, and had then taken Ficino's comparison of the Angelic Mind receiving form with the eye receiving form when it receives the colours and shapes of things in the light, and made it into his statement about Eucharis; though it is clear that Chapman does not intend us to have the Angelic Mind specifically in view in his episode. Chapman is using ideas from this context to create a new myth. His lily—matter and form united in this particular entity—is Love itself. And these lines:

> for as colour flowes
> From superficies of each thing we see,
> Euen so with colours formes emitted bee
> (V, 224–26)

are perfectly congruous with the Aristotelian doctrine presupposed in the poem (and the Aristotelian theory of vision could also be found in Ficino)[83] that seeing is receiving, and that what we see are forms. What we see, says Aristotle, is colour, and this we see only in light, and this colour is in fact the coloured superficies of the object which is its visible form.[84]

The effect of the silver lily on Eucharis is stated in images of the stormy sea attacking the land and the conquering invader entering a citadel. The process shown is the domination of the mind by the form. This is another version of the descriptions of the effect of Leander's image on Hero's mind, and the images belong to the same range, for those were images of invasion and conquest too. But we are now dealing with the general, not with the particular instance: Hymen is the type of beauty, his marriage is to represent marriage itself. It is therefore appropriate that the form he offers to Eucharis' eyes should be the form of love itself.

In the sixth and last *Sestiad*, which tells of Leander's death and Hero's, these themes we have been discussing appear at three places. Of these two revert to the theme of the false form, the false appearance, and come as very extended similes, which may well seem to be irrelevant digressions unless we realize that they have the function of carrying on this theme. In the first the Fates, who accept Leucote's plea that they should stay the winds only in order to entice Leander to his death, are compared to a fleering parasite who is all exaggerated complaisance and obsequiousness in bearing and manner, and all

---

[e] Eodemque modo mens ad Deum, quo ad lumen solis dirigitur oculus. Hic enim aspicit primo, videt deinde solis lumen: tertio in solis lumine rerum colores figurasque comprehendit. Quare oculus obscurus primo, et chaos instar informis, lumen amat dum aspicit, irradiatur aspiciendo, radium accipiendo rerum coloribus figurisque formatur.[81]

falseness within (VI, 19–34). In the second Leander in his state of happy optimism about his love and marriage is compared to an "empty Gallant full of forme"–one of those metropolitan fools who were favourite butts of contemporary satirists, affected in their manners, self-styled arbiters of fashion and oracles of political wisdom: Leander's idea of himself is as far from the truth as is this fool's:

> And so short of himselfe in his high thought,
> Was our Leander in his fortunes brought.
> (VI, 133–34)

The satire in both portraits on elaborate and affected manners is still within the context of ceremony.

And, in a final passage of sophistry, Hero is shown misapplying the notions of form, cause, and entelechy. This is in Hero's meditations on her torch, the famous torch that she lights to guide Leander across the channel. The torch is dear to her because Leander is to see it; for this she loves it and grieves to see it burn; yet it is precisely because it burns and turns to nothing in guiding Leander that it is precious to her. Chapman makes this the occasion for reflections on the fate of the virtuous man in our society: he who does good is consumed thereby; but Hero at least loved and raised her torch! He proceeds:

> Yet Hero with these [*i.e. the following*] thoughts her Torch did spend.
> When Bees makes waxe, Nature doth not intend
> It shall be made a Torch: but we that know
> The proper vertue of it make it so,
> And when t'is made we light it: nor did Nature
> Propose one life to maids, but each such creature
> Makes by her soule the best of her free state,
> Which without loue is rude, disconsolate,
> And wants loues fire to make it milde and bright,
> Till when, maids are but Torches wanting light.
> (VI, 66–75)

We have met the argument before–it is the argument of Ceremony to Leander. Each thing achieves perfection when it achieves that form which is also its cause: wax when human hands make it a torch; woman when she achieves love. But Hero's argument is fallacious, her analogy false. That we are not intended to accept it is clear from Chapman's comment:

> Thus gainst our griefe, not cause of griefe we fight,
> The right of nought is gleande, but the delight.
> (VI, 76–7)

–it is not the rightness or wrongness of anything that we are concerned with, but the delight it brings us. Hero's argument is fallacious because the soul is not free in this respect and in this way: the form of love is achieved in the ceremony of marriage. How poor is substance without rites, had been Ceremony's words to Leander.

Yet a further point is to be made. Chapman invents a new ending for his tale. Hero and Leander are metamorphosed into a pair of birds–of "Thistle-warps": birds that will never fly near the sea, that always fly in couples, and whose colours are emblematic of the lovers' sorrows: blue for truth; yellow for Venus' jealousy; black and red for death and ruth. This is the second metamorphosis that Chapman has invented for his poem. In the fifth *Sestiad* we have the story of Adolesche, one of the Athenian girls who accompanied Eucharis, and the only one who will not promise to keep quiet about their kidnapping and rescue by Hymen, so that Hymen himself can bring the news to Athens and win the praise and credit himself, and thus be able most effectively to press his claims to Eucharis. Adolesche refuses because she loves talking and gossip. She runs on to be first with the news, but comes too late, swoons with mortification and is changed into a parrot. (The episode may seem an intrusion—but it has this much justification, that the theme of harmful gossip and talk is one that Chapman has raised earlier).[85] Now the point about metamorphosis is that the subject is changed into a creature that expresses its essence, that most fully expresses its fate: Philomela becomes the lamenting nightingale. Adolesche's essence is her talkativeness. The essence of Hero and Leander is their love and their suffering. In death they finally achieve the form that is perfectly expressive of their being. The mythological inventions are parables of the doctrine; the end of the lovers is dramatically appropriate to the poet's characterization of their actions.

IV. The Moral

We are now in a position to see how Chapman in fact "moralized" Marlowe, He rejected, as Marlowe had done, the current moralization of the story, which was still that of Fulgentius. Fulgentius had seen the story as a simple allegory of the dangers and the transitoriness of Love: the torch of love tempts to encounter with the perils signified by the sea; the death of the lovers is the death of desire that comes with the end of youth; and the sea is also the cold extinguishing humour of age. And such a simple application was made by Chapman's younger contemporary Caspar Barth, whose *Leandridos* appears to be the only rival to the English poems in extension and elaboration of treatment. This is Barth's conclusion:

> My intention is not by soft words to seduce young men, and the blind common herd, away from the paths of reverend virtues to the deep darkness of error . . . but rather to give an example, that the snares and darts of love, so deceitful in so many ways, must be fled. The man who is wise through the destruction of another will learn to beware the dark dangers, and will oppose his prudent mind to love when it confronts him.[f]

---

[f] Mens mihi non est molleis seducere Ephebos
A venerandarum virtutum semita in altas
Errorum tenebras, et cæcum lumine vulgas . . . .
Sed magis exemplum fugiendi ponere Amoris,
Insidias et tela, modis fallentia miris.
Qui sapit, exitio alterius, cauet atra pericla,
Adversoque animum sapientem opponit Amori.[88]

Chapman can also write:

> Shun loues stolne sports by that these Louers proue.
>
> (III, 16)

But what he means by this is, as we have seen, much more complicated than anything Fulgentius or Barth intended: and much more apposite than has, it appears, been realized.

Chapman's decision to treat his part of the story in a complex scheme involving the relation of form and matter and the implications of this relationship, personal and social, private and public, was neither casual nor irrelevant. Only by so doing could he in fact draw from Marlowe's treatment the conclusions that he thought must be drawn. Chapman clearly saw the decision of Hero and Leander to become lovers as the crucial point in the story. What follows follows on this. Here are some of the arguments that Marlowe gives Leander to persuade Hero to break her vows:

> Like vntun'd golden strings all women are,
> Which long time lie vntoucht, will harshly iarre.
> Vessels of Brasse oft handled, brightly shine,
> What difference betwixt the richest mine
> And barest mold, but vse? for both, not vs'de,
> Are of like worth. Then treasure is abus'de,
> When misers keepe it; being put to lone,
> In time it will returne vs two for one.
> Rich robes themselues and others do adorne,
> Neither themselues nor others, if not worne.
> Who builds a pallace and rams up the gate,
> Shall see it ruinous and desolate . . . .
> Base bouillion for the stampes sake we allow,
> Even so for mens impression do we you,
> By which alone, our reuerend fathers say,
> Women receaue perfection euery way
> This idoll which you terme *Virginitie*,
> Is neither essence subiect to the eie,
> No, nor to any one exterior sence,
> Nor hath it any place of residence,
> Nor is't of earth or mould celestiall,
> Or capable of any forme at all.
> Of that which hath no being doe not boast,
> Things that are not at all are neuer lost.
>
> (I, 199–294)

Leander's speech is a splendid elaboration of a great *topos*, which we may call the *persuasion to love*; a *topos* that well deserves study as it moves from the classical poets—Marlowe found elements of it in the speech Musæus gave Leander—through the poets of the Renaissance till, in England, it finds its richest handling in Milton's *Comus*.[89]

Of course we recognize, in these lines of Marlowe's, elements that appear again in Chapman's *Sestiads*: the arguments that Ceremony uses to Leander, and those that Hero uses to herself as she stands distraught on the tower. What Chapman has done is to draw out the implications of Leander's speech. He has taken the arguments seriously—the Aristotelian references were already there for him—and examined their bases. He has broken down the *topos* by referring these elements to their true philosophical context; and from this examination and its results he has made a new structure.[90] In Ceremony's mouth the arguments are valid; when poor Hero uses them she is deceiving herself, because, as the poem has shown us, she has neglected fundamental premises. We find it hard to believe that Marlowe would have been interested in Chapman's conclusions or in his way of stating them. Yet we are not justified in believing that Chapman, when he set about finishing the poem in this way, thought he was doing anything that would not have been acceptable to Marlowe. For Marlowe presents Leander as speaking "like a sharp bold sophister" (I, 197–98): he does not intend us to believe in the general validity of Leander's arguments.[91] This was Chapman's point of departure. Chapman developes the poem, then, as a refutation of Leander's speech.

In yet another way Chapman has sought to complete the moral of the tale. His condemnation of Hero and Leander is final and inevitable. Yet it is not the whole story. Hero's arguments are invalid, her trust in "the logick of Leanders beautie" unjustified and vain, her prayer, "O Goddesse pitie loue and pardon it" (III, 282), unavailing. But Chapman's pity for the lovers sounds beside his condemnation. And finally the gods themselves pity them and seek to avert the tragedy:

> And pittie did the hart of heauen confound.
> The Gods, the Graces, and the Muses came
> Downe to the Destinies, to stay the frame
> Of the true louers deaths, and all world's teares . . . .
>
> (V, 20–23)

Leander is better than so many who survive him:

> I must describe the hell of thy disease
> That heauen did mint: yet I needes must see
> Our painted fooles and cockhorse Peasantrie
> Still still vsurp, with long liues, loues, and lust,
> The seates of vertue . . . .
>
> (VI, 142–46)

Chapman's pity is expressed in terms of one of his major themes: false forms, and "dissimulation." Hero is not the only dissembler. She is not the only false priest:

> O louely *Hero*, nothing is thy sin,
> Wayd with those foule faults other Priests are in . . . .
>
> (IV, 210–11)

Venus' swan, the bright Leucote, accuses Venus herself of dissimulation and hypocrisy:

> Why may not amorous Hero seeme a mayd,
> Though she be none, as well as you suppresse
> In modest cheekes your inward wantonnesse?
>   (IV, 277–79)

Above all, the cruel Fates, who are the authors of the disaster, are themselves guilty of dissimulation. At first they seem to accept heaven's pleas for mercy. But this is only a pretence:

> The Fates consent, (aye me dissembling Fates)
> They shewd their fauours to conceale their hates,
> And draw *Leander* on, least Seas too hie
> Should stay his too obsequious destinie . . . .
>   (VI, 15–18)

So the winds are stilled until Leander sets out, then stirred up again, while the Destinies sit dancing on the waves.

What it all builds up to is the sense that though sin must be punished those who punish are as guilty as those they condemn: that the greater guilt may escape while the lesser suffers: that a capricious fate which knows nothing of pity rings round human actions. What remains is a tragic sense of helplessness. Neptune loves Leander and tries to save him, yet his embraces kill; when, angry and despairing, he throws his mace at the Fates it hits Lachesis in the hand and sunders Leander's thread. Anger does not help: "If any comfort liue, it is in peace" (VI, 233). The conclusion is:

> O theeuish Fates, to let Blood, Flesh, and Sence,
> Build two fayre Temples for their Excellence,
> To rob it with a poysoned influence.
> Though soules gifts starue, the bodies are held dear
> In vgliest things; Sence-sport preserues a Beare.
> But here nought serues our turnes; O heauen & earth,
> How most most wretched is our humane birth?
>   (VI, 234–40)

To understand the prominence given to the Fates we have to go back to Marlowe. Hero's attempts to deny her love and renew her vows of chastity are thwarted by Cupid, who enraged by her attempt strikes her with an arrow. Then, moved by her sorrow, Cupid tries to avert the lovers' destiny by going to the Fates and begging that Hero and Leander may "enjoy ech other, and be blest" (I, 380). But the Fates will not even answer him. They are angry with him because he made them fall in love with Mercury who wanted to persuade them to overthrow Jove and reinstate Saturn: this was Mercury's revenge for Jove's anger at his theft of nectar for the country maid with whom he was in love; and when he had got this from them, he abandoned them and

> did despise
> The loue of th'euerlasting Destinies.
>   (I, 461–62)

Chapman makes no allusion to this episode. But, I take it, he is here attempting to expand and carry out what he thought were Marlowe's intentions. Marlowe's poem is not quite so simply and casually amorous and pagan as the critics have maintained. Leander's arguments, we have seen, were not to be taken as valid. Nor is the fact of Hero's broken vow evaded. Leander is condemned for wearing Hero's purple ribbon and

> The sacred ring wherewith she was endow'd
> When first religious chastitie she vow'd
> (II, 109–10)

and so making his love public knowledge. The end of the lovers is stated from the beginning—"On *Hellespont* guiltie of True loues blood" (I, 1). Their rashness is set against the idea of an impelling and controlling Fate:

> It lies not in our power to loue, or hate,
> For will in vs is ouer-rul'd by fate.
> (I, 167–68)

Cupid's arrow masters Hero's resistence and her attempt to be faithful to her vows. This fate is seen as grotesque and capricious: the Fates—and the idea of the Fates in love is a deliberate stroke of the grotesque—are motivated simply by feminine anger at rejected love. When Chapman, then, both condemns and pities the lovers, and sees their story as an instance of the cruel and capricious workings of fate to which human lives are subject, he is drawing out themes already present in Marlowe's beginning. His aim was not to contradict, but to complete.

The Imagery of Ben Jonson's
Masques of Blacknesse and Beautie

Onely the enuie was, that it lasted not still, or (now it is
past) cannot by imagination, much lesse description, be
recouered to a part of that *spirit* it had in the gliding by.
                                        Ben Jonson, *Hymenaei*

I

The performance of *The Masque of Blacknesse* at Whitehall in 1605 marks the beginning of the collaboration of Ben Jonson and Inigo Jones in the production of court masques. *The Masque of Beautie*, produced three years later, is a sequel to the first masque and the two must be considered together. If to the English masque Inigo Jones brought all that Italy knew of staging and direction,[1] Ben Jonson brought to its devising not only the excellencies of his verse, its grace, urbanity and strength, but all the resources of the late humanist poet and scholar.

The court festivals of Italy set the mode for the French *ballet de cour* and the English court masque. And the range of literary aids on which the begetters of these festivals drew, the work of Italian humanists, was as well known to Jonson who was so justly proud of the extent of his erudition as to any of the *littérateurs* and *dilettanti* who devised *intermezzi* and *mascherate* for the court of Florence or *ballets* for the court of France.

In the 16th century the mythological knowledge of European humanism was summed up in Italy in three great manuals: Lilio Gregorio Giraldi's *De Deis gentium syntagmata*, Natale Conti's (or Comes') *Mythologiæ* and Vincenzo Cartari's *Imagini degli Dei*, which draw not only on the new knowledge of the classical texts themselves, but on the complex tradition by which knowledge of the gods of Greece and Rome had been transmitted from late antiquity through the Middle Ages to the Renaissance. These manuals were not only composed for the edification of the erudite but for the information of artists who wished to represent the figures of the gods, and of poets who wished to write about them. So Giraldi will interrupt his exposition to provide visual material that might be helpful to the painter or sculptor, while the special importance of Cartari's volume is that its avowed aim is to provide such material—as his title itself would indicate. And these works fulfilled this purpose: they were used not only by scholars but by poets, painters, and all those who wished to recreate the antique deities, verbally or visually—and not least by the devisers of court festivals, in which Olympus' faded hierarchy played a bright and overwhelmingly important part.[2]

These books were the common property of Europe, the everyday authorities on classical mythology, and Ben Jonson, like other Elizabethan writers, made use of them. I shall show that in *The Masque of Blacknesse* Jonson uses Conti, and that in *The Masque of Beautie* he uses all three.[3]

Towards the end of the 16th century there appeared in Italy an extraordinary book, of extraordinary importance: Cesare Ripa's *Iconologia* or *Descrittione di Diversi Imagini*. In this fantastic lexicon the material assembled by the mythographers, and the whole repertory of Renaissance symbolism is gathered together, assimilated and arranged alphabetically, with admirable indexes. The title-page describes it as being "Opera non meno vtile che necessaria a Poeti, Pittori, Scultori, & altri, per rappresentare le Virtu, Vitij, Affetti, & Passioni humane." And Ripa seems to have made good his boast. Those for whom his book was intended were not slow to take advantage of it; its influence on the visual arts is a commonplace for the art-historian. The composers of masques inevitably used the *Iconologia*, and among them Jonson, who sometimes acknowledges his debt to it.[4]

Court festivals were also influenced by the Renaissance passion for emblematic imagery, for emblems, hieroglyphs and *imprese*. I shall show that in these masques Jonson draws on the standard encyclopaedia of hieroglyphs, the Italian humanist Giovanni Pierio Valeriano's *Hieroglyphica*.[5]

Ben Jonson, however, did not only bring to the masque his virtues as a poet and his accomplishments as a humanist: he brought a theory as well. For Jonson the masque was something more than a mere sumptuous court show, one night's ephemeral entertainment. He set out his views very clearly in *Hymenæi* (1606):—

> It is a noble and iust aduantage, that the things subiected to *vnderstanding* haue of those which are obiected to *sense*, that the one sort are but momentarie, and meerely taking; the other impressing, and lasting: Else the glorie of all these *solemnities* had perish'd like a blaze, and gone out, in the *beholders* eyes. So short-liu'd are the *bodies* of all things, in comparison of their *soules* . . . . This it is hath made the most royall *Princes*, and greatest *persons* (who are commonly the *personaters* of these *actions*) not onely studious of riches, and magnificence in the outward celebration, or shew; (which rightly becomes them) but curious after the most high, and heartie *inuentions*, to furnish the inward parts: (and those grounded vpon *antiquitie*, and solide *learnings*) which, though their *voyce* be taught to sound to present occasions, their *sense*, or doth, or should alwayes lay hold on more remou'd *mysteries* . . . .[6]

This is at any rate what Jonson thought—whether it represents accurately the views of most royal princes and greatest persons is another matter.

It is my belief that Jonson carried his principles into practice, that the heart of these two masques is a removed mystery that is indeed grounded upon antiquity and "solide learnings." I hope to demonstrate that these masques are images, whose significance is to be apprehended in the light of the doctrines of Beauty and Love held by the Platonists of the Renaissance and expressed in Ficino's commentary on the *Symposium* and Pico della Mirandola's commentary on Benivieni's *Canzona de Amore*.[7] This is the mystery their sense lays hold of. That Jonson should have known these treatises and made use of them in this way is not particularly remarkable; he was above all a learned poet, and these treatises were among the most influential of all Renaissance philosophical writings—it is much more surprising to find Carew using Bruno's *Spaccio della Bestia Trionfante* for his masque, *Coelum Britannicum*; yet he does so.[8]

I assume that Jonson meant what he said, that he did not work casually or carelessly, but consciously and with complete awareness of what he was doing—an assumption that is justified by all that we know of Jonson.

II

The scheme of the *Masque of Blacknesse* is very simple. Oceanus, guardian of the realm of Albion, is approached by Niger, "in forme and colour of an *Æthiope*." Niger is followed by the twelve masquers, the queen and eleven other ladies, in the guise of his daughters, Æthiopian nymphs. The masquers enter in a great shell accompanied by their light-bearers, the Oceaniæ, seated on sea-monsters swimming round it. Niger explains to Oceanus why they have left their home. After reading what poets have written about foreign beauties his daughters became sadly dissatisfied with their dark skins; eventually they saw reflected in the lake, whence they took their birth, a face glowing with light and inscribed with the words of an oracle: to find a remedy the nymphs must seek a land the name of which, in its Greek form, ends in TANIA, and which is lit by another and greater light than that Sun which darkened their skins. It is in search of this land that they have come so far West. Niger appeals to Oceanus to reveal the name of this country they have now found. Oceanus does so, and suddenly Æthiopia, the moon, appears and tells Niger that the quest is over: it was her own face that his daughers saw reflected in the lake, and this is the land they have been seeking. This island has now recovered for herself the name BRITANIA, and is

> Rul'd by a SVNNE . . .
> Whose beames shine day, and night, and are of force
> To blanch an ÆTHIOPE, and reuiue a *Cor's*.
>   (ll, 253–5)

The masquers land from their shell and go through their dances. Æthiopia finally interrupts them, with the promise that if they fulfil certain rites which she prescribes, their complexions will become fair. The nymphs re-enter their great shell and it moves out to the sound of a song.

An "artificiall sea" forms the background to the masque. In front of it are six Tritons "in mouing, and sprightly actions, their vpper parts humane, saue that their haires were blue, as partaking of the sea-colour: their desinent parts, fish, mounted aboue their heads, and all varied in disposition. From their backs were borne out certaine light pieces of taffata, as if carryed by the winde, and their musique made out of wreathed shells" (ll. 30–36). To this Jonson adds:

> The forme of these *Tritons*, with their triumpets, you may read liuely describ'd in *Ouid. Metamor. l.* I. *Cæruleum Tritona vocat, &c.* and in *Virgil. Æneid. l.* 10 *Hunc vehit immanis Triton. & sequent.* (Note f.)

In Conti we read:

> Fuit autem Triton Oceani ac Neptuni buccinator & tubicen, vt testatur Ouid. lib. I. Metam. in his: vbi etiam formam ipsius buccinæ describit:
>> Cœruleum Tritona vocat . . .[9]

> [Triton was Oceanus' and Neptune's trumpeter, as Ovid affirms in *Metamorphoses* I, where he describes even the shape of the trumpet: "He summons sea-blue Triton . . . ."]

A little later Conti also cites the passage from Virgil to which Jonson refers.[10]

From this alone we should not be justified in inferring that Jonson is using Conti, were it not that in his description of Oceanus that follows he draws directly on the *Mythologiæ*. Jonson presents Oceanus as 'horned,' justifying himself by saying in a note that the ancients always gave Oceanus a bull's head and adding an explanation of this in Latin. He also quotes Euripides as calling Oceanus ταυρόκρανος, having the head of a bull, and lists several Latin sources in which the epithet is applied to rivers. Jonson's Latin is a quotation from Conti, who has also supplied the reference to Euripides.[11] In the song that opens the masque, Niger is hailed as "sonne to great OCEANVS," because, as Jonson explains in another note, the ancients believed that rivers and fountains have their origin in the vapours drawn up out of the ocean by the heat of the sun. Conti has also supplied the material for this note with its Latin phrases and references to Homer and the Orphic hymns.[12]

Conti has also influenced the plot of the masque. The nymphs set out on their journey because of the oracle they see inscribed on a glowing face in the lake. Æthiopia, the moon,[13] when she appears, explains:

> I was that bright face
> Reflected by the *Lake*, in which thy *Race*
> Read mysticke lines; (which skill PYTHAGORAS
> First taught to men, by a reuerberate glasse.)
> (ll. 234–7)

Whalley noted in his edition of this masque that this is an allusion to a comment by the scholiast on a passage in the *Clouds* of Aristophanes: Pythagoras discovered a way of writing with blood on a mirror so that if the mirror were held opposite the moon, the writing would be reflected and appear to be written on the moon's orb.

But all this is to be found in Conti. Conti is discussing the belief that the moon can be charmed from the sky, quoting two verses from the *Clouds* to illustrate the belief that the women of Thessaly were particularly skilled in this art, and goes on to tell this story about Pythagoras.[14]

The twelve Æthiopian nymphs advanced to the dance two by two, "*euery couple ... seuerally presenting their fans: in one of which were inscribed their mixt* Names, *in the other a mute* Hieroglyphick, *expressing their mixed qualities.*" "*Which manner of* Symbole," Jonson continues, "*I rather chose, then* Imprese, *as well for strangenesse, as relishing of antiquitie, and more applying to that originall doctrine of sculpture, which the* Ægyptians *are said, first, to haue brought from the* Æthiopians."

The nymphs, then, are arranged in pairs. Each pair is distinguished by a "Hieroglyphick": the mute image is represented (painted, presumably) on the fan held by one of the nymphs, while the names of both nymphs are inscribed on the fan held by the other.[15] These names are Greek and of Jonson's own invention (except in one case), and taken together they express the meaning of the "Hieroglyphick"; they give the mute image a tongue to tell us what each pair of nymphs symbolizes.

Several of the six "Hieroglyphicks" were taken from the most obvious source, Valeriano's *Hieroglyphica*. The second pair of nymphs present "The figure *Icosaedron* of crystall." Valeriano tells us that the isocaedrum, which is according to Euclid a solid figure contained by twenty equal equilateral triangles, signifies water, because of the extreme mobility and divisibility of this element.[16] The reading *Isocaedron* is that given in the 1608 quarto of the masque, and in the 1616 and 1640 folios. The Oxford editors adopt Gifford's (1816) reading: *Icosaedron*. This is certainly the correct Euclidean name. Valeriano was wrong—though the name is given correctly in the index—and if the reading given in the quarto and the folios represents correctly what Jonson wrote, then Jonson had been misled by his source.

These two nymphs are called *Diaphane* and *Eucampse*. Taken together these names express the qualities of water. *Diaphane* is derived from διαφανής, transparent or translucent; *Eucampse* has behind it εὐκαμψία, flexibility—strictly, flexibility of the body. The relation of this to the passage from Valeriano is clear. That the *Icosaedron* in question is of crystal reinforces the symbolism.

The third pair of nymphs, *Ocyte* and *Kathare* present on one fan "A payre of naked feet, in a riuer," an image, which Valeriano tells us, means "the purifier."[17] Valeriano also says that the image comes from Horus Apollo, for whom it means "the fuller," whose business was cleansing. So we can follow this image back beyond Valeriano to the pages of that strange book which the humanists found so exciting: the *Hieroglyphica* of Horus Apollo.[18] (Figure 64). That this is the meaning Jonson intended his "Hieroglyphick" to carry is borne out by the names of these nymphs: *Ocyte* from ὠκύς, quick, swift: *Kathare* from καθαρός, pure.

The nymphs *Notis* and *Psychrote* come next with "The Salamander simple." *Notis* is from νότος, the South Wind, a word associated with ideas of dampness and moisture: *Psychrote* from ψυχρός, cold. Valeriano when writing of the meanings of the Salamander,[19] gives one of these as *Amoris Nutrimentum*, in connection with which he says

64. "A payre of naked feet, in a riuer," from the *Hieroglyphica* of Horapollo, Paris 1551.

65. "A clowd full of raine, dropping," from Horapollo, Paris 1551.

that it is a creature so cold and damp that it can extinguish fire by touch.[20] And in speaking of the first meaning which he gives to this marvellous creature, the Salamander, Valeriano had said:

> . . . tantus enim illi rigor, vt ignes tactu extinguat, non alio modo, quam glacies.

Glycyte and *Malacia* follow with "A clowd full of raine, dropping." *Glycte* is from γλυκύς, sweet, or γλυκύτης, sweetness, pleasantness; *Malacia* from μαλακός, soft, gentle, mild. Valeriano took this image over from Horus Apollo (Figure 65), who gives it as dew falling, and heads it πῶς παιδειάν. Valeriano retains this meaning of education or instruction,[21] which he extends and elaborates. He distinguishes between profane learning (*Doctrina gentium*) which is like bitter waters that bring forth no fruit, and heavenly learning (*Doctrina coelestis*) which brings forth much fruit. It was prophesied, he says, that the Apostles should go through the earth changing the *bitter* waters into *sweet* waters. The dew and rain falling from heaven is a particularly suitable symbol of celestial wisdom fertilizing the soul, and is so used by Moses.[22] That Jonson uses the Greek words meaning "sweet" and "soft" in connection with the hieroglyph of the cloud dropping rain suggests that he may have had the meanings given by Valeriano in mind.

The last pair of nymphs, *Baryte* and *Periphere* present "an vrne, spheard with wine." *Baryte* is from βαρύς, heavy, or, βαρύτης, heaviness or weight: *Periphere* from περιφερής, rounded or curving, or, when applied to bodies, spherical or globular: taken together, the names suggest earth. The hieroglyph of the urn encircled by a vine[23] is not to be found in Valeriano and Jonson may have taken it from some other source. In Ripa, *Terra* is represented as:

> Donna a giacere in terra, meza nuda, come cosa stabile, con vn braccio appoggiato sopra d'vn vaso, dal quale esce vna vite . . . .[24]

[a lady half nude, recumbent, as if immobile, with one arm resting upon a vase out of which a vine grows.]

This gives a combination of "urn" and "vine" representing earth, but the image is not identical with the one used by Jonson, which cannot be regarded as fully explained. For the general connection with the preceding image Jonson might have had in mind Valeriano's treatment of "Fontes" which he describes as waters springing from earth as compared with waters descending from heaven as rain or dew.[25]

We now return to the first pair of nymphs, *Euphoris* and *Aglaia*, who present "A golden tree, laden with fruit." The queen herself impersonated one of these nymphs. *Euphoris* is derived from εὔφορος, fertile. In the case of *Aglaia*, Jonson has refrained from inventing a name and has used a direct mythological reference. Aglaia was the first of the three Graces, who are associated with fertility and the productiveness of the earth.[26] Giraldi interprets her name as

ἀγλαΐα una, quae nobis dici potest Maiestas, seu venustas, honestasve . . . .[27]

In Ficino's symbolism Aglaia represents "splendour" or beauty of the spirit.[28] Her appearance here, with *Euphoris*, might thus suggest a royal and spiritual beauty fertilizing the earth.

The meaning which the hieroglyph of the golden tree may have had for Jonson is suggested by his use of it in the dispute he wrote for the "Barriers" that followed his masque *Hymenaei*, where Truth says that:

> The golden tree of *marriage* began
> In *paradise*, and bore the fruit of *man* . . . .[29]

The golden tree is not to be found in Valeriano, though he gives the palm as the symbol of marriage. In the lines quoted above Jonson seems to equate the fruitful tree of gold with the Tree of Life in paradise. Such a meaning would connect it with the prevailing theme of the other hieroglyphs. The Water of Life springs near the roots of the Tree of Life and afterwards divides into the four rivers of paradise,[30] which, in one of their interpretations, represent the four elements. The icosaedron and the pair of feet in a river, which in Jonson's scheme follow the golden tree, symbolize water and its purifying qualities. Fire is alluded to through the salamander; air through the cloud; and earth in the last image. And if the waters are the waters of paradise, the connection of the water imagery with "celestial doctrine" becomes less difficult to understand. These are the cooling and cleansing waters in which the nymphs are to bathe and become fair.

The scheme is thus a highly recondite one, and there is much in it which awaits fuller explanation.[31] There is obviously also a local application to the watery character of England's situation, cool both in climate and in the temperament of its inhabitants. The hieroglyphs emphasize a tempering of heat by cold. Fire is tempered by the coldness and dampness of the salamander, and the symbol of air is introduced through the cloud suggesting cooling rain. The blackness of the nymphs has been caused by the fiery power of the Ethiopian sun. This blackness, due to an over-enthusiastic heat, is to be cured by the cooler, damper air of Britain where the "sunne is temperate and refines all things." It is possible that this is how these hieroglyphs stand in relation to the theme of the masque.

III

The *Masque of Beautie*, given at court in January, 1608, is a sequel to *The Masque of Blacknesse*. It was the queen's pleasure, Jonson writes, "that I should thinke on some fit presentment, which should answere the former, still keeping them the same persons, the daughters of NIGER, but their beauties varied, according to promise, and their time of absence excus'd, with foure more added to their number."[32]

The slight narrative satisfies the queen's wishes. January is placed in the middle of the hall, "to keepe the state of the Feast, and Season." Boreas comes blustering in and explains to January that he has been charged with a message from the daughters of Niger explaining why, although they have received the beauty promised them, they have failed to appear before the king in the last two years.[33] The twelve nymphs were on their way to Britain when they heard that four other sisters of theirs, determined to seek beauty in Britain too, had been imprisoned by the malice of Night in a floating island, whence they could be freed only by the sight of the transfigured faces of their more fortunate sisters. The twelve immediately set out to seek the island, and by so doing at once put themselves in the power of Night, who has since kept them wandering through the seas. They have given up all hope of ever reaching Britain, and have entrusted Boreas with their tale. But no sooner has Boreas related this sad story than a gentler wind, Vulturnus, enters with good news. The spells of Night have been broken by the moon, and the nymphs are even now approaching Britain accompanied by their four sisters, themselves transfigured now by the influence of the others' beauty. And it is in the floating island that they are coming—the island that has now become the land of Beauty, and in which the moon has raised for them a Throne of Beauty.[34]

A curtain on which is painted a figure representing Night is drawn back: the action symbolizes the breaking of Night's charms. The wonderful island appears floating as it were in a calm sea. The masquers descend from their places in the Throne of Beauty followed by the Cupids who are their torchbearers, and are welcomed to land by the river Thames "that lay along betweene the shores, leaning vpon his Vrne (that flow'd with water,) and crown'd with flowers" (ll. 294–6).[35] The Throne of Beauty is in fact a very elaborate car and, when contriving it, the designer's imagination had been stimulated by the cars which played such an important part in Italian festivals. We can best form an idea of what it looked like and see the fashion he was following by having before our eyes such a car as the car of Venus which Gualterotti designed for the Medici-Capello wedding festivities in Florence in 1579 (Figure 66).

The base of the throne is formed by six steps on which sit a multitude of Cupids who act as torch-bearers to the masquers and carry the traditional ensigns of love. Beside the throne are arbours for the musicians, and behind it is "a *Groue*, of growne trees laden with golden fruit, which other litle *Cupids* plucked, and threw each at other, whilst on the ground *Leuerets* pick'd vp the bruised apples, and left them halfe eaten." The ground-plan which links together the arbours and the trees is in the form of a maze. In the two foremost angles are fountains, that of Hebe or Youth and that of Hedone or Pleasure. In the centre of this platform, at the top of the flight of steps, rises the structure of the throne itself, of which we are given a description that is elaborate yet vague:

66. The chariot of Venus, a pageant car designed by Gualterotti for the wedding festivities of Francesco de' Medici and Bianca Cappello, Florence 1579. (From Raffaello Gualterotti, *Feste nelle Nozze . . . Medici . . . Cappello*, Florence 1579.)

In the middest thereof was a seate of state, call'd the throne of beautie, *erected: diuided into eight* squares, *and distinguish'd by so many* Ionick pilasters. *In these* Squares *the sixteene* Masquers *were plac'd by couples: behind them, in the center of the* Throne *was a* tralucent Pillar, *shining with seuerall-colour'd lights, that reflected on their backes. From the top of which* Pillar *went seuerall arches to the* Pilasters, *that sustained the roofe of the* Throne, *which was likewise adorn'd with lights, and gyrlonds; And betweene the* Pilasters, *in front, little* Cupids *in flying posture, wauing of wreathes, and lights, bore vp the* Coronice: *over which were placed eight* Figures, *representing the* Elements *of* Beauty; *which aduanced vpon the* Ionick, *and being* females, *had the* Corinthian *order.*

On the cornice, then, that is supported by the Ionic pilasters that frame the niches in which the masquers stand are eight figures—the number corresponds to the number of the pilasters—which represent the elements of beauty. These figures are: Splendor, Serenitas, Germinatio, Laetitia, Temperies, Venustas, Dignitas, Perfectio. Above them all, crowning the whole structure of the throne stands a ninth figure: Harmonia.

The base of the throne, the steps, has a circular movement, from left to right; the throne itself has also a circular movement in the opposite direction, from right to left.

This richly conceived car is a visual expression of the meaning of the masque; it is a complex image expressive of the "more remou'd mysteries" of which the "sense" of both masques lays hold. An analysis of the imagery of the car and its significance is now the main intention of this essay. But before proceeding to this analysis we must discover what the basic idea is on which both these masques are built.

The central idea of these two masques is clear and simple: the king's presence turns Blackness into Beauty. The king is the sun; his rays accomplish this startling transformation because he is a more powerful luminary than that Sol whose rays first scorched the delicate skins of the Æthiopian dames. Bright Sol neither sets nor rises in Britain:

> *But in his Iourney passeth by,*
> *And leaues that* Clymat *of the sky,*
> *To comfort of a greater* Light,
> *Who formes all beauty, with his sight.*
> (*Blacknesse*, ll. 192–5)

and

> This *sunne* is temperate, and refines
> All things, on which his radiance shines.
> (*Blacknesse*, ll. 264–5)

Beauty's throne is made peculiar to Britain alone

> by'impulsion of your destinies,
> And his attractiue beames, that lights these skies:
> Who (though with th'*Ocean* compass'd) neuer wets
> His hayre therein, nor weares a beame that sets.
> (*Beautie*, ll. 388–91)[36]

Compliments in this vein were, of course, quite in order. That the place of the king in the social system is analogous to the place of the sun among the stars was a commonplace of writers on political and social theory, and images drawn from this were part of the stock in trade of every eulogist. But more is involved here than the formal, stereotyped gesture of the panegyrist; we are dealing here with notions more "remou'd" than the everyday apotheosis of the crown. A grander apotheosis is adumbrated, in which James is given the position and function assigned to the sun in the theory of beauty held by the Florentine Platonists.

The relation of the sun to beauty is stated explicitly in philosophic terms in Niger's narrative in *The Masque of Blacknesse*:

> . . . in whose sparckling, and refulgent eyes,
> The glorious *Sunne* did still delight to rise;
> Though he (the best iudge, and most formall cause
> Of all dames beauties) in their firme hiewes, drawes
> Signes of his feruent'st loue; and thereby shewes
> That, in their black, the perfectst beauty growes. . . .
> (ll. 139–44)

The terminology—"most formall cause of all dames beauties"—is Platonic and takes us straight to Pico's *Commentary*, to the passage in which he is explaining the modes of being of Sensible Beauty. He has just defined "amore volgare" as being the desire of Sensible Beauty that comes through the sense of sight, "appetito di bellezza sensibile per il senso del viso." Sensible Beauty has three modes of being: Causal, Essential or Formal, and Participated.[37] Sensible Beauty, the beauty that can be perceived through the sense of sight finds its formal or essential cause in the colours given by the light of the visible sun: "Lo essere suo formale & essentiale è in essi colori dalla luce del sole visibile illuminati, cosi come sono illuminate le Idee dalla luce di quel primo inuisibile sole."[38] And here we have the justification of the plot of the two masques, the key to the meaning implicit in *The Masque of Blacknesse* and more fully worked out in *The Masque of Beautie*. This is the hinge on which the whole invention moves.[39]

In consonance with this the Throne of Beauty, which is the central image of the second masque, is a translation into visual terms of certain ideas about love and beauty held by Ficino and the Florentine Platonists. In my analysis of the details and the total significance of this image I shall begin with the Cupids who throng the steps leading up to the Throne and work up to the figure of "Harmonia" which dominates the whole. To show the meaning which the Cupids have for Jonson, I shall have to adduce material from the songs in the masque; this will have the additional advantage of making it clear beyond doubt that Jonson is working with notions that take their spring from the Florentine Academy.

"The inducing of many *Cupids*," adds Jonson, "wants not defence, with the best and most receiued of the *Ancients*, besides *Prop. Stat. Claud. Sido. Apoll.* especially *Phil. in Icon. Amor.* whom I haue particularly followed, in this description." The orchard scene, with the Cupids, the apples and the hares, certainly comes from the *Imagines* of Philostratus. But whether Jonson was drawing directly on this source, we may doubt. The list of authorities given by Jonson here is, with the exception of the reference to Sidonius Apollinaris, that given by Giraldi before he goes on to give a summary of Philostratus' description.[40] But when Jonson says that the hares "were notes of *Louelinesse* and sacred to *Venus*. See *Phil.* in that place, mentioned" (note m), he was probably using Valeriano who gives "Venustas," as well as "Foecunditas," as one of the meanings of "hares," and also refers to the Philostratus image.[41]

The songs throw more light on how Jonson is thinking about his Cupids and about love. After the second dance a song is sung that begins:

> If all these CVPIDS, now, were blind
> As is their wanton *brother* . . .
> (ll. 341–2)

Jonson annotates these lines thus:

> I make these different from him, which they fayne, *caecum cupidine* [cupidinem?], or *petulantem*, as I expresse beneath in the third song, these being chaste *Loues*, that attend a more diuine beautie, then that of *Loues* commune *parent*.

And from this it is quite beyond doubt that Jonson is working along Neo-Platonic lines.

Professor Panofsky has shown how in the 16th century the bandage came to be removed from Cupid's eyes by the influence of Neo-Platonic doctrines—a point admirably illustrated by Lucas Cranach's charming picture of Cupid taking his bandage off with his right hand while he stands on a volume entitled *Platonis Opera*.[42] Cupid had to see, because, according to the Platonists of the Renaissance, love is the desire to enjoy beauty, and beauty can only be apprehended by sight. There came, then, to be two Cupids: the "seeing" Cupid who was associated with the higher love, the blind Cupid who was associated with earthly, sensual love. The distinction corresponds with the distinction between *Venus Coelestis* and *Venus Vulgaris*. Jonson knows all this. His Cupids are neither blind, nor wanton. They do not attend "Loue's *commune* parent," that is, *Venus Vulgaris*, but a "more diuine beautie," that is, *Venus Coelestis*. The next song begins:

> Yes, were the *Loues* or false, or straying;
> Or *beauties* not their beautie waighing . . .
> (ll. 358–9)

The wanton Cupid is concerned with individual beauties, not with the Idea of Beauty that shines through them, higher and greater than any individual exemplar of it. But this is not so with Jonson's Cupids.

The songs are steeped in the mythological thought expressed by Plato in Agathon's oration, infused with new power by Ficino and Pico and reiterated incessantly in the 16th century.

> When *Loue*, at first, did mooue
> From out of *Chaos*, brightned
> So was the world, and lightned,
> As now![43]
> (ll. 282–5)

And his note on the line "It was for *Beauty* that the World was made" (l. 289) Jonson again reveals the Platonic elements in his thinking:

> An agreeing opinion, both with *Diuines* and *Philosophers*, that the great *Artificer* in loue with his owne *Idæa*, did, therefore, frame the world.

Ficino tells us what Jonson means:

> The desire to propagate its own perfection is a form of love. Now absolute perfection is in the highest power of God; the divine Intelligence contemplates it, and the divine will desires to diffuse it beyond itself; and it is from this love that wishes to propagate itself that everything is created. Therefore Dionysius says, "Divine Love does not allow the king of the universe to live in himself, without bearing fruit."[a]

---

[a] Cupiditatis perfectionis propriæ propagandæ amor quidam est. Absoluta perfectio, in summa Dei est potentia. Eam diuina intelligentia contemplatur, atque inde voluntas eadem cupit extra se propagare, ex quo propagandi amore creata ab eo sunt omnia. Idcirco Dionysius noster, Diuinus, inquit amor non permisit regem omnium sine germine in seipso manere.[44]

And the rest of this chapter of Ficino's is the aptest commentary on Jonson's

> So beautie on the waters stood,
> When *loue* had seuer'd earth, from flood!
> So when he parted ayre, from fire,
> He did with concord all inspire!
> (ll. 325–328)

and on his note:

> As, in the creation, he is said, by the *ancients*, to haue done.

These notions had become commonplaces. They had been expressed, for example, in Spenser's *Hymne in Honour of Love*, or Jonson could have found them in Conti.[45] But Ficino's account of how Love drew like to like, separated the opposing elements and inspired all with concord is closest to Jonson's words.[46]

At the top of the six steps thronged with these graceful loves who bear such a burden of significance, between the arbours where the musicians stand, the orchard, and the fountains of Youth and Pleasure,[47] rises the Throne of Beauty itself. On the cornice of the throne stand the eight female figures that personify the elements of beauty,[48] and whose sources and meaning I shall now indicate.

The first of the elements of beauty is SPLENDOR. "Pulchritudo autem," says Ficino, "splendor quidam est humanum ad se rapiens animum" [Beauty is a certain splendour, ravishing the human soul to itself].[49] And this splendour is the splendour of the Divine Countenance: for Ficino, beauty is, above everything else, the glorious reflection of the face of God. One of the chapters of his Commentary is headed: "Pulchritudo est splendor diuini vultus."[50] This figure appears

> In a robe of *flame* colour, naked brested; her bright hayre loose flowing: She was drawn in a circle of clouds, her face, and body breaking through; and in her hand a branch, with two *Roses*, a *white* and a *red*. (ll. 180–84.)

Jonson has used Ripa's *Bellezza*, a woman

> che habbia ascosa la testa fra le nuuole, & il resto sia poco visibile, per lo splendore, che la circonda, porga vna mano fuor dello splendore . . . .

> [who has her head hidden in the clouds, and the rest of her body barely visible for the splendour that surrounds her, and she extends one hand out of the splendour . . . .]

However, in this hand she has a lily, not roses, and she has other attributes which Jonson does not take over. This presentation itself is based ultimately on Ficino:

> Beauty is represented with her head hidden in the clouds because there is nothing more difficult to talk about with mortal tongue, and which can less be known by the human intellect, than beauty, which alone of all created things is nothing else, metaphysically speaking, than a splendour deriving from the light of the face of God.[b]

---

[b] Si dipinge la Bellezza con la testa ascosa fra le nuuole, perche non è cosa, della quale più difficilmente si possa parlare con mortal lingua, & che meno si possa conoscere con l'intelletto humano, quanto la bellezza, la

67. Giorgio Vasari, the figure of Beauty in the *Mascherata della Genealogia degli Dei* presented in Florence, 1565. (Florence, Uffizi.)

Jonson's figure is just such as might have appeared in an Italian festival, as we can see if we compare his description with a drawing of *Bellezza*, "naked brested" and carrying a branch of flowers, done by Vasari for the *Mascherata della Genealogia degli Dei* given in Florence in 1565 (Figure 67).

The second of the elements is SERENITAS,

> In a garment of bright *skie*-colour, a long tresse, and waued with a vaile of diuers colours, such as the golden skie sometimes shewes: vpon her head a cleare, and faire *Sunne* shining, with rayes of gold striking downe to the feet of the figure. In her hand a *Christall*, cut with seuerall angles, and shadow'd with diuers colours, as caused by refraction. (ll. 186–92.)

And we have this gloss on "Christall":

> As this of *Serenity*, applying to the *Opticks* reason of the *Rainbow*, & the *Mythologists* making her the Daughter of *Electra*.

At first sight this may seem rather puzzling. But first of all it is necessary to remember that the meanings of *serenus*, *serenitas*, *serene* and *serenity* primarily had reference to the air, the sky, the weather. This figure is a representation of the serenity of the sky: Ripa's *Serenità del Giorno* is the source:

> A young girl in the habit of a nymph, yellow in colour, with long blond hair adorned with pearls and with veils of several colours; on her head rests a brilliant and beautiful sun, from

quale, nelle cose create, non è altro, metafisicamente parlando, che vn splendore, che deriua dalla luce della faccia di Dio . . .[51]

beneath which hangs a veil of gold falling gracefully over the shoulders of the figure . . . the colour of the garment deep blue . . . .[c]

Furthermore, Jonson's figure is a representation of Iris, in her function as precursor of fine weather. The crystal, we are told, is the hieroglyph of Serenity "applying to the *Opticks* reason of the *Rainbow*, & the *Mythologists* making her the daughter of *Electra*"–a crabbed sentence. The mythologists certainly made "her"–the rainbow, that is, Iris–the daughter of Electra. Conti tells us this in the first sentence of his article on Iris, and he also tells us that Electra is the daughter of the Sky or the Sun, and that her name means Serenity.[53] Jonson had already found this passage useful; he had quoted from it in his *Part of the King's Entertainment in passing to his Coronation*.[54] Iris can, then, be associated with Serenity; there was also authority for regarding the rainbow as a harbinger of serene skies. From his inexhaustible stores Conti again provides us–as he provided Jonson–with the information. The ancients, he says, feigned that Iris was the messenger of Juno and the sister of the Harpies, or winds, and adds that Virgil numbered the rainbow among the signs of coming rain, and that Valerius Flaccus in the first book of the *Argonautica* says the rainbow is a portent of fine weather, *indicem serenitatis*.[55] He then quotes the verses which Jonson had quoted in *Part of the King's Entertainment* (note e) after remarking casually that "*Val. Flac. Argonaut*. I. makes the rainbow *indicem serenitatis*."[56]

Jonson, however, does not give his Serenity the rainbow that might have been expected. He gives her a much more esoteric *Hieroglyphick*, in the shape of the cut crystal, "shadow'd with diuers colours, as caused by refraction." And in spite of what Jonson says,[57] I have not found this symbol elsewhere. The source of the invention is clear, and is again to be found in Conti's invaluable article. Conti has a long dissertation on the origin of the rainbow, in which he cites the opinions of various authorities, for indeed, as he remarks–perhaps wearily–"At enim de Iridis causa dissentiunt plurimum inter se sapientes" [most scholars disagree about the cause of the rainbow]. He begins by giving Aristotle's opinion:

> Aristotelis totam Iridis obseruationem ac naturam ad opticam rationem perduxit, nihilque esse re ipsa, neque alicubi illos colores consistere existimauit.[58]

> [Aristotle ascribed the entire appearance and nature of the rainbow to optics, and thought that the thing itself was nonexistent, and that its colours existed nowhere.]

We need go no further. This sentence, with Conti's sentence to the effect that Iris "è refractione radiorum scilicet" is enough to account for Jonson's crystal. Surely the clumsiness of Jonson's phrase "applying to the *Opticks* reason of the *Rainbow*" springs from his taking over Conti's "totam Iridis obseruationem ac naturam ad opticam rationem perduxit."

The reason why a figure representing the serene sky forms part of an image of Beauty is apparent in the passage from Pico on *Bellezza Sensibile* which I have already quoted: *La*

---

[c] Vna giovanetta in habita di Ninfa, di colore giallo, con bionde, & longe treccie ornate di perle, & di veli di più colori, sopra alla chioma poserà vn Sole chiaro & bellissimo, à piè del quale penderà vn velo d'oro, & con bella gratia caderà sopra le spalle di detta figura . . . . Il colore del vestimento sarà torchino . . . .[52]

Causa sua e il Cielo . . . And in Ficino's mythological thinking, *Venus Vulgaris* is the daughter of Jove. In the universe of which God is the end, the spring, the centre, there are, according to Ficino, four realms of being: *Mens Angelica*; *Anima Mundi*; *Natura* and *Materia*.[59] In the *Mens Angelica* are present the Ideas, the Forms of all things: forms and movement are transmitted to the realm of Nature by the *Anima Mundi*. The three powers, the three modes, of the *Anima Mundi* are called, in terms of myth: *Saturn*, in so far as the *Anima Mundi* directs itself upwards with understanding, *prout suprema intelligit: Jove, prout coelestia mouet*, in so far as it moves the world of the heavens, through which movement is transmitted to the sublunar world of Nature: *Venus, vt inferiora generat*, in as much as the *Anima Mundi* gives life and form to the world of Nature.[60]

We can now see, then, not only why Jonson introduces a figure representing the serene sky, but also why he follows it up with a figure representing GERMINATIO—his next, and third figure. GERMINATIO is

> In greene; with a *Zone* of gold about her Wast, crowned with *Myrtle*, her haire likewise flowing, but not of so bright a colour: In her hand, a branch of *Myrtle*. Her sockes of greene, and gold. (ll. 194–7.)

She carries myrtle because:

> So *Hor. lib.* I *Od.* 4 makes it the ensigne of the *Spring. Nunc decet aut viridi nitidum caput impedire myrto, aut flore, terræ quem ferunt solutæ, &c.*

We have here one of those graceful nymph-like figures, not over-burdened with attributes, who appear so often in painting, masque and festival. She is clothed in green, the colour of spring and growing things, and is crowned with myrtle like Ripa's *Primauera*, and for the same reason:

> Gli si dà la ghirlanda di mortella, percioche Horatio nel libro primo ode 4 cosi dice . . . ,[61]

and the same two verses are quoted.

The fourth figure is LÆTITIA. For Ficino, Lætitia or Euphrosyne, the third of the three Graces represents the joy caused by beauty of sound. Beauty of the spirit (symbolized in Aglaia or Splendor); beauty of visible forms seen through the eye (symbolized in Thalia or Viridity); and beauty which reaches the soul through the ear in the form of musical sounds (symbolized in Joy or Euphrosyne) are the three cardinal classifications of beauty for Ficino.[62] It seems not unlikely that Jonson may have remembered the Ficinian meanings of these figures. There is, however, no allusion to music in Jonson's figure of Lætitia which is a simple representation of Gladness:

> In a vesture of diuers colours, and all sorts of flowers embroidered thereon. Her sockes so fitted. A *Gyrland* of flowers in her hand; her eyes turning vp, and smiling, her haire flowing, and stuck with flowers. (ll. 199–202.)

The flowers are:

> euery where the tokens of gladnesse, at all feasts, sports.

Again we have a very simple figure, in the style of Ripa's presentations of "Allegrezza,"

which are variations on a few themes: "Giouane vestita con diuersità di colori piaceu-
oli . . ." "Giouanetta . . . vestita di bianco, & detto vestimento dipinto di verdi fronde, &
fiori rossi, e gialli, con vna ghirlanda in capo di varij fiori . . ." We have young girls because
"li fanciulli stanno sempre allegri," flowers because "i fiori significano per se stessi
allegrezza," garlands because "nelle feste publiche antiche tutti si coronauono, e loro, e le
porte delle loro case, e tempij, & animali . . ."[63]

Ripa has furnished dress and attributes for the next, the fifth figure, TEMPERIES. She is
dressed "in a garment of *Gold, Siluer*, and colours weaued." Ripa's "Temperanza" (the
fourth image) is "vestita di tela d'argento, con Clamidetta d'oro . . ." She carries in one
hand "a burning *Steele*" and in the other "an *Vrne* with water" which is "the signe of
temperature." So Ripa's fifth image of "Temperanza" has in her right hand "vna tenaglia
con vn ferro infocato" and in her left "vn vaso di acqua, nel quale tempera quel ferro
ardente . . ."[64] *Temperies* is the right mixture of elements, each present in its right
proportion, which is for Ficino a prerequisite of sensible beauty. Love is the desire for
beauty which is a certain grace:

> quæ vt plurimum in concinnitate plurium maxime nascitur.

Moreover:

> si amor erga hominem pulchritudinem ipsam desiderat: humani autem corporis pulchritudo
> in quadam concinnitate consistit: concinnitas temperantia est: sola quæ temperata, modesta,
> decora sunt, exigit amor.[65]

> [which in most cases is born of the harmonious blending of several elements . . . . If the love
> which has man for its object desires beauty in him, the beauty of the human body consist-
> ing in a certain harmony, and harmony in proportion, it follows that love can desire only
> that which is temperate, modest, decorous.]

And later, after discussing the conditions which the body must satisfy before the light of
beauty can shine from it, conditions as to *ordo*, or *partium interualla, modus*, or *quantitas*,
and *species*, or *lineamenta et colores*, and arguing that these are ultimately incorporeal in
nature, Ficino concludes that the basis for the satisfaction of these conditions is the right
mixture of the four elements.[66]

Beauty is not, however, inevitably produced by right proportion and apt disposition
of parts, for we know from experience that the presence of these qualities does not
invariably arouse love.[67] To harmonious proportion must be added that certain grace,
gratia quædam, in which beauty ultimately resides, and this grace is of the spirit.[68]

Pico echoes Ficino, insisting that the name Venus or beauty is properly to be given to
"vna certa qualità che per piu proprio nome che di gratia non si puo chiamare" [a certain
quality which we cannot call by a more appropriate name than grace], which does not
depend on the material disposition of the body.[69] And Ripa wrote in explanation of the
pearls which his figure of *Gratia* wears that they

> risplendono, & piacciono, per singulare, & occulto dono della natura, come la gratia, che è ne
> gli huomini vna certa venustà particolare, che muoue, & rapisce gl'animi all' amore, & genera
> occultamente obligo, & beneuolenza.[70]

[shine and delight by a singular and mysterious gift of nature, like grace, which is in men a certain special beauty, which moves, and ravishes the soul toward love, and strangely generates devotion and good will.]

Jonson's sixth element VENUSTAS is then Ficino's *gratia*, and appropriately follows TEMPERIES. This figure is dressed in silver and is enveloped in a delicate veil. At her neck and forehead she has pearls, and her socks are embroidered with them. She carries lilies. She wears pearls because:

> *Pearles*, with the *ancients*, were the speciall *Hieroglyphicks* of *louelinesse, in quibus nitor tantum & læuor expetebantur.* (Note f.)

And lilies because:

> So was the *Lillie*, of which the most delicate Citie of the *Persians* was called *Susæ*: signifying that kind of flower, in their tongue. (Note g.)

Except for the pearls, Jonson's image is not Ripa's, and Jonson justifies his pearls with a reminiscence of Valeriano.[71] His note on the lily is from the same source.[72]

The seventh element is DIGNITAS, a figure:

> In a dressing of state, the haire bound vp with fillets of golde, the garments rich, and set with iewels, and gold; likewise her buskins, and in her hand a *Golden rod*. (ll. 215–17.)

The golden rod is "The signe of *honor*, and dignitie." Jonson has aimed here at presenting a regal figure. Gold, jewels, the sceptre—these are the traditional attributes of awe and majesty. The sceptre is the sign not only of honour, but of power.[73] Such a figure might well have been suggested by a reading of Ficino and Pico, for the whole burden of the two commentaries is the honour, dignity and power of Beauty and of Love, Beauty's child. Beauty is the splendour of the face of God; *Venus Vulgaris* is the *vis generandi* endowing the world of Nature with life and form: Venus is the Mistress of the Fates.[74]

Eighth comes PERFECTIO. Ficino had said:

68. Perfettione, from Ripa, *Iconologia*, Padua 1625.

Est autem perfectio interior quaedam, est & exterior. interiorum, bonitatem, exteriorem, pulchritudinem dicimus.[75]

[There is, moreover, an inner and an outer perfection. The inner we call goodness, the outer, beauty.]

Jonson's figure of PERFECTIO is:

In a Vesture of pure *Golde*, a wreath of *Gold* vpon her head. About her bodie the *Zodiacke*, with the *Signes*: in her hand a *Compasse* of golde, drawing a *circle*. (ll. 220–22.)

She has the Zodiac because:

Both that, & the *Compasse* are known ensignes of *perfection*.

Ripa's "Perfettione" is the source (Figure 68):

Donna vestita d'oro, mostri le mammelle, & tutto il petto scoperto, starà dentro il cerchio del Zodiaco, disegnando col compasso nella sinistra mano vn circolo, il quale si scolpisca quasi finito.

[A lady dressed in gold, showing her breasts, and her whole bosom uncovered, stands in the circle of the Zodiac, with the compass in her right hand describing a circle, which is depicted as if completed.]

The dress is of gold, because gold is the most perfect of metals. The circle is the perfect mathematical figure, and the circle of the Zodiac "è simbolo della ragione, & è debita, & conueneuole misura dell'attioni perfette."[76]

There is a ninth figure standing on top of the throne ("as being made out of all these"). This is HARMONIA,

A Personage, whose dressing had something of all the others, and had her robe painted full of *Figures*. Her head was compass'd with a crowne of *Gold*, hauing in it seuen iewels equally set. In her hand a *Lyra*, whereon she rested.
(ll. 226–30.)

Ficino had written of *concinnitas*, and Pico tells us that when an object is constituted by the properly proportioned synthesis of several diverse elements, the word beauty is commonly applied to the propriety, harmony and measure that distinguish this synthesis.[77] Pico points out that as every created thing is composed in this way—so far as its nature permits—then every created thing can be called beautiful in this sense. In this large sense beauty is equivalent to harmony, "onde si dice Dio con musico & Harmoniaco temperamento hauere composto tutto il mondo."[78] The figure of Harmony, in which the image of beauty is summed up, emphasizes how the whole conception of the masque is based on that Pythagoro-Platonic tradition which the Renaissance inherited from the Middle Ages, and particularly from Macrobius, and which underlies the philosophy and the symbolism of both Pico and Ficino.

For his figure of Harmony, Jonson tells us that he had looked at Ripa's "Harmonia," and from Ripa he has taken the lyre and the crown with the seven jewels (Figure 69).[79]

69. Armonia, from Ripa: Jonson's details, however, come from Ripa's description; the illustrator has omitted the seven jewels in the crown and turned the lyre into a viola da gamba.

Ripa, however, does not explain the significance of these seven jewels, but Jonson does, correctly. They are seven in number because of "*Pythagoras* his comment, with *Mac. lib. 2. Som. Sci.* of the seuen *Planets* and their *Spheares*." And we read in Macrobius that "Concentum quendam effici motu cœlestium corporum, & quo modo ratio eius concentus à Pythagora sit deprehensa . . ." [a certain harmony is made by the motions of the celestial bodies, and how Pythagoras understood the manner of this harmony].[80] Harmony is "the *worlds soule*" (l. 374): "The *Platonicks* opinion. See also *Mac. lib. 1.* and *2. Som. Scip.*" And the robe of the figure is "painted full of *Figures*," for as Macrobius had written, Plato, following Pythagoras, held that God the Artificer in his ineffable providence created the "anima mundi" which gives movement to the visible body of the universe out of numbers which stood in a musical relationship to one another.[81]

The figure of Harmony is the apex of a machine the very movements of which are significant. The throne "had a circular motion of it owne, imitating that which we call *Motum Mundi*, from the *East* to the *West*, or the right to the left side. For so *Hom. Ilia. M.* vnderstands by δεξιὰ, *Orientalia mundi*: by ἀριστερὰ, *Occidentalia*." The movement of the throne, that is, imitates the movement of the *Primum Mobile* which sweeps the world round from east to west. Jonson's erudition has come into play again: Spondanus' commentary on the *Iliad* gave him authority to say that the movement is from the right to the left. Commenting on Book XII, lines 237–40, Spondanus writes, in refutation of those who believe that δεξιὰ is to be taken as *meridies* and ἀριστερὰ as *septentrio*, "Quod tamen Homeri sententiæ, vt ego iudico, repugnat. Illud enim τὸ δεξιὰ hoc *το* ἀριστερὰ explicat, vt dextra pars sit oriens, sinistra verò occidens" [which nevertheless I think is repugnant to Homer's meaning; for 'right' and 'left' he uses so that the right side is the east, and the left, the west]. This is the opinion of the most eminent authorities, continues Spondanus, citing Hadrianus Junius:

In siderum cursu, inquit, orientem nominari dextram coeli partem, occiduam verò plagam laeuam sinistramve . . . .

[In the courses of the stars, he says, the east is called the right section of the sky, the west is the unlucky or left quarter.]

And an array of supporting evidence is adduced.[82] The six steps which form the base of the throne and on which the Cupids sit have also a movement of their own, "a motion contrary, with *Analogy*, *ad motum Planetarum*, from the *West* to the *East*":

> Quas ideò veteres errare dixerunt, quia & cursu suo feruntur, & contra sphaeræ maxime (id est ipsius cœli) impetum contrario motu ad Orientem ab Occidente voluntar.[83]

> [The errant planets were so named by the ancients because they are borne along in their own courses, moving from west to east, in a direction contrary to that of the greatest or celestial sphere.]

This floating island then, the whole machine, is an image of the turning world, presided over by Harmony, with Beauty set in the wheeling heaven which is its cause, and attended by Love moving like the planets—

> And who to *Heauens* consent can better moue,
> Then those that are so like it, *Beautie* and *Loue*?
> (ll. 135–6)

Above the whole scene rides the Moon "in a *Siluer* Chariot, drawne by *Virgins*" and with "the *Signe Scorpio*, and the *Character*, plac'd before her." The tradition that is being followed here is not classical: it is in fact not literary at all but purely iconographical. The

70. Diana, the moon, from Hyginus, *Poeticon Astronomicon*, Paris 1578.

representation of Diana in a car drawn by two female figures is an invention which can be traced to a Florentine engraving of the late 15th century,[84] an adaptation of a relief by Donatello in the Palazzo Medici. This was the first of many such representations.[85] The type can be seen in an illustration which Jonson may well have known: the illustration of the moon in contemporary editions of Hyginus' *Poeticon Astronomicon*, a work with which Jonson was familiar (Figure 70).[86]

IV

What one would of course really like to know is just how far the "remou'd mysteries" of these two masques were appreciated by the spectators. The ribald and forthright Dudley Carleton, say, or that unfortunate correspondent of the *Mercure de France* who so sadly misinterpreted Campion's *Lords Masque*, mistaking Entheus for Mercury and Prometheus for Jove[87]—how far would they gather the Neo-Platonic significances which that brilliant and harmonious image *The Masque of Beautie* carries to eye, ear and understanding, *quæ per rationem, visum, auditum, animos nostros mouet atque delectat?*

One of the grounds on which Jonson attacked Inigo Jones after their quarrel was the unintelligibility of his conceptions:

> You are the Spectacles of state! Tis true
> Court Hiero-gly-phicks! and all Arts afford,
>   In the mere perspective of an inch bord!
> You aske no more then certaine politique eyes!
>   Eyes, that can pierce into the mysteries
> Of many colours! read them! and reveale
>   Mythologie, there, painted on slit-deale!
> O to make bords to speake! There is a taske!
>   Painting, and Carpentry, are the soule of Masque!
> Pack with your pedling Poetry, to the Stage,
>   This is the Money-gett, Mechanick age!
> To plant the Musique, where no eare cann reach!
>   Attire the persons, as no thought can teach
> Sense, what they are! Which by a specious, fine
>   Terme of you Architects, is call'd DESIGNE![88]

Charges of obscurity brought against Jonson's own work would only have drawn a retort about the levity of the spectators. It is in tones of some exasperation that he explains the allegory of the microcosm in *Hymenæi*, a mystery evidently too removed for some of the audience:

> And, for the *Allegorie*, though here it be very cleare, and such as might well escape a candle, yet because there are some, must complaine of darknesse, that haue but thicke eyes, I am contented to hold them this Light . . . .[89]

Jonson's masques as well as his plays were written for the judicious. When he contrived the 'devices' for the triumphal arch that stood at Fenchurch for James' procession through the city he aimed, he tells us, at making them such that

> as vpon the view, they might, without cloud, or obscuritie, declare themselues to the sharpe and learned: And for the multitude, no doubt but that their grounded iudgements did gaze, said it was fine, and were satisfied.[90]

Jonson was consistent in his views and aims. The rout of courtiers meant as little to him as the rabble of citizens. He had as little respect for the opinions of one group as for those of the other. No doubt the significances of *The Masque of Beautie* declared themselves to the sharp and learned among the audience at Whitehall—while the multitude gazed, said it was fine, and were satisfied. Jonson would have rested content with this. And, after all, he demanded as much from the writer as from the reader or spectator.

Hymenæi:
Ben Jonson's Masque of Union

Rich Minerals are digged out of the bowels of the earth,
not found in the superficies and dust of it; charms made
of unlearned characters are not consecrate by the Muses,
which are divine artists . . . .

George Chapman.

these dead rites
Are long since buryed, and new power excites
More high and heartie flames.

Ben Jonson.

I. The Occasion

On the fifth of January 1606 the young Earl of Essex was married to Frances Howard, the
even younger daughter of the Earl of Suffolk. That night a masque was given in Whitehall
to celebrate the wedding, a masque with all the magnificence required by the importance
of the occasion. And the occasion was very important. This marriage was dynastic. It was
calculated to tie together the political and family interests of great powers, to effect a new
grouping of great houses, to give added force and added security to manœuvres in which it
would be hard to disentangle the claims of the state from the claims of the family. No one
could forget the young man's legendary father—and there was the question whether he
would forget his father's enemies. Suffolk was one of the many Howards, whose influence
was as widespread as their lands. Another of his daughters was to marry the son and heir of
Robert Cecil, on whom the king still leaned. James himself may have made the match in an
effort to promote harmony among his mighty subjects. Or Cecil himself may have
contrived it, as the acute Venetian observer thought. He had been the chief architect of
Essex' ruin and may have hoped that this marriage would safeguard his son against
inheriting the debt of hatred owed to the Cecils by Essex' heir.[1] We cannot know how far
they understood the implications of the masque, called *Hymenæi* and given in their honour
but intended, as we shall see, for other ears than theirs.

Ben Jonson wrote the libretto and Inigo Jones was responsible for the décor;
Alphonso Ferrabosco was in charge of the songs and Thomas Giles invented and directed
the dances.[2] The result was the most sumptuous and intricate masque yet seen at court.

II. Removed Mysteries: the Union of the Universe

The plot of the masque is based on the celebration of a Roman marriage and culminates in the singing of an epithalamium. The ritual of the Roman wedding is the framework which encloses the rest of the action. Starting from this ritual Jonson can develop a number of related themes, and within this as framework they can be contained.

What first meets the eyes of the audience is an altar with this inscription in gold:

> Ioni. Oimae. Mimae.
> [Iunoni Optimae Maximae]
> VNIONI
> SACR.

And it is through playing on the meanings of this word *Unio* that the themes of the masque are developed.

The first application of the word is simple. The inscription on the altar, we are told, mystically implies "that both it, the *place*, and all the succeeding *ceremonies* were sacred to *marriage*, or *Vnion*; ouer which *Iuno* was President."[3] Altar, place and ritual, then, are dedicated to the celebration of marriage union; this is the first meaning of *Unio*, and this is the encircling theme within which other applications and extensions of the word are to be explored.

The bridegroom's procession approaches the altar; he is dressed in purple and white, his short hair bound with gold twist and parti-coloured ribbons; five pages all in white walk before him, each carrying a waxen taper. From the other side comes Hymen in saffron and white, crowned with roses and marjoram, a veil of yellow silk on his left arm and a pine torch in his right hand. After him comes a youth in white, carrying a wicker basket and a torch of white thorn. Then two boys appear, again in white, one with a distaff and the other with a spindle. Between them is the bride in a white dress, with a girdle of white wool tied with the knot of Hercules; down her back hangs a fleece of wool; her hair is loose, flowing and dressed with grey; on her head is a turret-shaped crown of roses. The *auspices* follow, then two singers, one carrying fire, the other water. And last of all come the musicians, crowned with roses.

The action opens with a song bidding the profane depart:

> For VNION, *Mistris* of these *rites*,
> Will be obseru'd with eyes,
> As simple as her nights.
> (ll. 73–75)

Hymen then addresses the king and queen:

> What more then vsuall light
>   (throughout the place extended).

Makes Ivno's *fane* so bright!
Is there some greater *deitie* descended?

   Or raigne, on earth, those *powers*
So rich, as with their beames
   Grace VNION more than our's;
And bound her *influence* in their happier streames?
             (ll. 83–90)

Already we can see Jonson's themes opening out: Union is not only the state of marriage union; she is a goddess, Juno the patroness of marriage whose "great name" ("IVNO") we hear later "Is VNIO, in the anagram." By equating Juno with Unio and Union Jonson will be able to extend the scope of his masque very considerably. And yet another sense of Union is given in this same song:

   O you, whose better blisses
Haue proou'd the strict embrace
   Of Vnion, with chast kisses
And seene it flow so in your happie *race:*

   That know how well it binds
The fighting *seedes of things,*
   Winnes *natures, sexes, minds,*
And eu'rie discord in true musique brings:
           (ll. 95–102)

The happy, fruitful marriage of James and Anne typifies the ideal marriage union. But, not content with this, Jonson goes on to make the marriage union they know but a particular instance of a more general union: the union wrought in the world by the power of love; a union which includes both man and the elements in an order figured by the concord of music.[4]

The general theme of the masque has been stated: in symbolic action Jonson will display the marriage he is glorifying as an instance of this universal union.

Jonson begins with man. Union's gracious rites are suddenly disturbed. Behind the altar hung a "Microcosme, or Globe," *"figuring Man"* and "filled with *Countreys,* and those gilded; where the *Sea* was exprest, heightned with siluer waues." This globe turns round showing itself to be hollow and from it comes the first masque, of eight men. These men represent the four humours and the four affections; their descent from the microcosm is accompanied "with a kind of contentious Musique"; they dance out on the stage, draw their swords and offer to surround the altar and disturb the rites. Man is in chaos, a chaos symbolized by the contentious music. That man's physical and mental well-being depends on the properly balanced mixture of the four humours, Melancholy, Phlegm, Blood and Choler, is an idea so commonplace that it hardly requires illustration. To round out his presentation of man Jonson has added to these constituents of his make-up four faculties of his soul: the four affections or passions. "Which Affections", says Stephen Batman, "bee foure, that is to say, Joy, Hope, Dreade and Sorrowe." The three major powers of the soul are the Rational, the Concupiscible and the Irascible, and from the last two powers spring the affections: "the first two come of Concupiscibili, for of the thing that we couet and desire, we haue ioy, and in ioying we hope. The other two dread and sorrowe, come of the Irascibili. For of things that we hate we haue sorrowe, and in sorrowing we dread." And further, "These foure affections be the matter of all manner vices and vertues."[5] And de la Primaudaye notes that "All perturbations are contained under these foure heads, Desire, Ioy, Feare, Griefe"; he goes on, following Cicero:

> through ignorance and basenes of minde, they proceed onely of the opinion of good or euill, either present or to come, which we imagine to be in the vnperfect and transitorie things of the world, and which are accompanied vnseparably either with good or euill. In respect of good things, we are carried away with a vehement desire or coueting of them, besides an immoderate ioy in them: in regard of euill things, we are oppressed with feare and sorrow. And these are the foure springs of all vices and sinnes wherein men plunge themselues during this life, and vnder which all perturbations are comprehended, which fill the soule with endlesse trouble and disquietnes.[6]

Well-being depends on the right ordering of the affections as well as on the right balance of the humours; and one is connected with the other.[7]

Who can tame these unruly and discordant humours and affections and reduce man to tranquillity and peace? Only a higher power of the human soul: reason. It is for reason to direct the passions or affections towards the proper objects. "Now because reason ought to be the Gouernesse and mistresse of the affections, it is necessary they should agree together. For as reason guideth before, the affections will followe after. Therefore wee may alwayes iudge of reason by the affections which it ought to gouerne, as of the gouernment of a good Prince by the estate of his subiects, and of a good father of a family by those of his household."[8] It is then Reason whom Hymen summons from the microcosm to control her riotous subjects:

> If there be
> A power, like REASON, left in that huge Bodie,
> Or little *world of Man*, from whence these came,
> Look forth, and with thy bright and numerous flame
> Instruct their darknesse, make them know, and see,
> In wronging these, they haue rebell'd gainst thee.
> (ll. 123–8)

And it is right that Reason should descend from the top of the globe, where she has been seated "as in the braine, or *highest part* of Man." For reason being the higher and nobler faculty has its seat in the highest part of the human body, while the affections, being less noble, and subject to reason, have their seat lower down, in the heart.[9]

Jonson's Reason is a venerable woman, with white hair which suggests the wisdom and dignity of age. She is "*crowned with lights, her garments blue, and semined with starres, girded vnto her with a white bend, fill'd with* Arithmeticall *figures, in one hand bearing a Lampe, in the other a bright Sword*" (ll. 131–4). Except for the lamp, these details are from Ripa's

Iconologia, that invaluable and ubiquitous encyclopædia of imagery which Jonson, like so many others, knew and used.[10] In his second design for Reason Ripa makes her carry a sword "to keep the field of the virtues free from the vices which prey on the good of the soul," and girds her with a white belt painted over with arithmetical figures "because it is by the use of such figures that Arithmetic provides proof of the reality of things, just as Reason which lodges in our soul tests and recognizes all that pertains to our good." In his third design Reason has a helmet crested with a flame because "the flame shows that it is the property of Reason to mount towards Heaven and seek to resemble God." And in his first design Ripa explains that the appropriate dress for Reason is celestial blue because Reason must always conform to heaven and be bright and splendid.[11] The lamp is easily enough understood: we hear in de la Primaudaye of the light of reason and of reason as the guide given us by God; Ripa's Wisdom carries a lighted lamp representing that light of the intellect which by God's particular gift burns in our soul and is never consumed or diminished.[12]

Reason responds to Hymen's call and with a speech on Union rebukes the Humours and Affections; they sheathe their swords and stand aside while the ceremonies go on under Hymen's care. They hear of the significance of the ceremonies, of the dresses and of the ritual objects, from Reason, who now acts as chorus, commentator and director. The first of these speeches is of immense importance, and if we do not understand it fully we cannot see the full range of the masque's meaning. But before approaching this speech we must take into account some further implications of the globe and its wild inhabitants—that is, of Jonson's presentation of man.

We have seen man composed of the humours and affections and have seen the disorder that ensues when reason is not master. And Jonson is also representing "the little *world of Man*": man as microcosm. The concept is a familiar one, as is its consequence: order or disorder in man will correspond to order or disorder in the state, the political organization of men. The man-state state-man correspondence is everywhere in Elizabethan writing; the images press on our memory and need not be recalled. The health of man has a correspondence with the health of the state: "Wherefore a sound body of a good constitution is like the body of a whole people and societie, that hath the members agreeing well together, so that euery one keepeth his ranke, not hurting one another. But a sick and diseased body is like to the body of a mutenous and seditious people, that breaketh the order it ought to keepe, and goeth beyond the appointed bounds."[13] And the rebellion of the affections or passions against reason is an image of civil insurrection: the moralists will not allow us to forget it.

Jonson's microcosm, and these Humours and Affections who riot in ignorance of Reason may seem to us an image that is only too commonplace. But not everyone who saw *Hymenæi* on that January night understood so easily. Jonson certainly thought such people were stupid, but when he printed *Hymenæi* he added, rather petulantly and with an ill grace, a footnote explaining for their benefit the allegory he intended:

And, for the Allegorie, though here it be very cleare, and such as might well escape a candle, yet because there are some, must complaine of darknesse, that haue but thick eyes, I am contented to hold them this Light. First, as in *naturall bodies,* so likewise in *minds,* there is no disease or distemperature, but is caused either by some abounding *humor*, or peruerse *affection*; after the same manner in *politick bodies* (where *Order, Ceremony, State, Reuerence, Deuotion*, are parts of the *Mind*) by the difference, or praedominant will of what we (*Metaphorically*) call *Humors*, and *Affections*, all things are troubled confused. These therefore, were *tropically* brought in, before *Marriage*, as disturbers of that *mysticall bodie*, and the *rites*, which were *soule* vnto it; that afterwards, in *Marriage*, being dutifully tempered by her *power*, they might more fully celebrate the happinesse of such as liue in that sweet *vnion*, to the harmonious lawes of Nature and Reason. (l. 112, note a)

Unrest in body and mind caused by the wrong mixture of humours and the wrong ordering of affections, unrest in the body politic caused—metaphorically—by the wrong mixture and wrong ordering of humours and affections: this is the situation Jonson presents by showing humours and affections turbulent and threatening to disturb the rites of marriage. For marriage, the mystical body,[14] the perfect union of two in one, figures harmonious union or health in the natural body, in the mind, and in the body politic. Moreover the rites with which marriage is celebrated give the appropriate form and shape to that union, that mystical body, just as the soul gives the appropriate form and shape to the body of man,[15] and as order, ceremony, state, reverence, devotion give the appropriate form and shape to the body politic. Disorder, then, is represented in man and in the state. Order and union will be achieved in these two realms when humours and affections bow to reason and instead of disturbing the marriage rites take part in their celebration. More, indeed, will be achieved; for we shall see that more than the harmonious man and the harmonious state are figured in the mystical body of marriage, in that sweet union.

Here is Reason's praise of Union which so subdues the jarring Humours and their companions:

> Forbeare your rude attempt; what ignorance
> Could yeeld you so prophane, as to aduance
> One thought in act, against these *mysteries*?
> Are VNION's *orgies* of so slender price?
> She that makes *soules*, with *bodies*, mixe in loue,
> Contracts the *world* in one, and therein IOVE;
> Is *spring*, and *end* of all things: yet, most strange!
> Her selfe nor suffers *spring*, nor *end*, nor *change*.
>
> (ll. 137–44)

Now the observant spectator or reader will have been prepared for the content of these lines by two things: by the girdle covered with arithmetical figures which Reason wears, and by these lines of Hymen's when he summons her:

> Looke forth, and with thy bright and numerous flame
> Instruct their darknesse, make them know, and see,
> In wronging these, they haue rebell'd 'gainst thee.
>
> (ll. 126–8)

The girdle associates Reason with number: the association is re-enforced by the adjective *numerous*, the significance of which is explained in a footnote which Jonson added to his text:

Alluding to that opinion of *Pythagoras*; who held, all *Reason*, all *Knowledge*, all *Discourse* of the *Soule* to be meere *Number*.

And he gives as his source that compilation of Plutarch's known as the *De Placitis Philosophorum*, which was included in the *Moralia*, a work extremely popular with Renaissance writers. The passage Jonson has in mind is certainly this, from the third chapter of the first book:

> Pythagoras . . . held that the principle of all things were Numbers, and their symmetries, that is to say, the proportions that they have in their correspondency one unto another; which hee calleth otherwise Harmonies: & these elements that be composed of them both, are tearmed by him Geometricall . . .

and later:

> And our soule (as he saith) doth consist of the quaternary number; for there is in it, understanding, science, opinion, and sense; from whence proceedeth all manner of art and knowledge . . .[16]

The association of reason with number and the explicit reference to Pythagoras show the way in which Jonson is thinking. He is thinking—as in *The Masque of Blacknesse* and *The Masque of Beautie*—in terms of the Pythagorean-Platonic tradition, powerful down the centuries, revivified and reinterpreted by Ficino and the Platonists of Florence, whence it was diffused through Europe. And Reason's lines on Union, vital for our understanding of *Hymenæi*, are only to be understood in reference to this tradition and to specific elements within it. Indeed the vision of the universe projected by this masque springs from Renaissance Platonism.

Union is *Unio*, that is Juno, goddess of marriage who "makes *soules*, with *bodies*, mixe in loue": marriage union unites two people, in body and in soul. Bolder claims follow. Union:

> Contracts the *world* in one, and therein IOVE;
> Is *spring*, and *end* of all things: yet most strange!
> Her selfe nor suffers *spring*, nor *end*, nor *change*.

The key to these lines is in a shift Jonson has made in the meaning of the word Union. Again his references guide us. Here the reader is told to turn to the *In Somnium Scipionis* of Macrobius; and in Reason's next speech, when she explains the import of the five candles that are carried in the marriage procession, Jonson refers us to Martianus Capella's *De Nuptiis Philologiae et Mercurii* as his authority on numbers. Now these, and especially the Macrobius, are cardinal texts in the tradition that Ficino inherited, and the revival of interest in them in the sixteenth century was certainly due to the general revival of interest in Platonism. Moreover, these two works were particularly important for the accounts they gave of Pythagorean and Platonic mathematics and number symbolism. It is this that at the moment interests Jonson. For the further meaning he has given to Union is this: as well as being *Unio*—Juno—Union is Unity, the state of being united, of being one. Union is *Unitas*, the number one. This is the *monas* of Macrobius, at once male and female, at once even and odd, not itself a number, but the source and origin of number, the beginning and the end of all things, itself knowing neither a beginning nor an end.[17] And further, this is the ineffable One of the Neo-platonists, that One (*unitas*) which must lie above the many and be the source of all number.[18] One represents, says Macrobius in the passage Jonson cites, the supreme God. And too, in the first book of the *De Placitis Philosophorum*, in the passage to which he has already referred us, Jonson would discover that Pythagoras "reckeneth among Principles, unitie (*unitatem*) and Twaine indefinit; of which, the one tendeth and hasteneth to an efficient and specificall cause, to wit, a Minde, and the same in God."[19] It was a daring innovation of Jonson's to equate *Unitas* with Juno. He may have been led to it by reading in Macrobius that one combines the male and the female; from this he may have reasoned that marriage too effects such a combination, and that so does Juno, who is the patroness of marriage.

Unity contracts the world in one; the world is One and has its source in the One. And this unity, this oneness of the universe is a union effected by love and a union in love. The existence of anything depends on the union of the parts that go to make it; if they are scattered, it perishes. It is on their love for one another that the union of these parts depends.[20] The concord of the elements and the humours makes the world and our bodies; if that is destroyed, they are destroyed. And in this union Jove himself is contracted because it was in love that God made the world—"The great *Artificer* in loue with his owne *Idæa*, did, therefore, frame the world."[21] In love each creature seeks to return to him:

> . . . the first motion, whereupon all the rest depend, is the loue of God, which proceedeth from his bounty, which he would not keepe shut vp nor enclosed in himself, but would manifest and communicate it with his creatures . . . loue and amitie is the good, by which all creatures haue an accord and agreement, first with God their creator, and then one with another: and . . . vpon the same cause their conuersation and perfection both depend. Wherefore loue must be the bond and vnion of all the world, which is an vniversall peace and concord betweene God and all his creatures. For the diuine prouidence hath so disposed all the order of them, that they all be conioined one with another by such loue and amitie, that euen they which seeme to be clean contrary, are allied, reconciled and vnited together by those, which haue more correspondencie between them. In such sort as we may therein behold, a very pleasant and perfect harmonie . . . like as in musicke . . . .[22]

So when the Humours and Affections participate in the celebration of these marriage rites at the command of Reason, this action will symbolize not only the achievement of harmonious unity on the plane of man and human society, but also the harmonious unity of the universe, and the union in love that marries the creatures with one another and with God himself.

From the profane to the sacred the transition has been made. The rites of Juno-*Unio* are the rites of God. The mimic marriage refers to the true ceremony performed that day, is a secular parable of its meaning. And, startling though it may seem, here, at this moment when the sacred meaning of the masque has been disclosed, another reference is intended, another correspondence has been set up. These wedding rites honour not only God but King James. The modern reader may perhaps be forgiven for feeling that we have been wrenched violently back from the sacred to the profane; but such a transition was neither blasphemous nor difficult if you believed with James that kings were sacred—the breathing images of God upon earth, little gods who sit upon his throne and rule over other men;[23] and James was not alone in his belief. In terms of the symbolism of this masque such a reference is natural. In Hymen's first verses he had hailed the king and queen as deities greater than Juno-Union, whose influence is bounded in their happier streames (ll. 89–90); he had hailed James as "The *king,* and *priest of peace!*" (l. 92). Priest of Peace—Prince of Peace? It is bold enough. When we come to Union-*Unitas* the association with James is inevitable. There was, said Martianus, one God, one world, one sun, one moon:[24] it was easy to add to the list one phœnix, one queen among the bees, one leader in the flock;[25] and how easy to add one king in the kingdom—especially when he was the first king of Britain. "Just in the same sort is hee called and chosen of God (without any doubt) the sixt of *Scotland,* to be the first, not onely of *Great Brittaine,* but also euerie where. Because in this *Vnitie,* the Veritie is founde, who is but *Onely One,* and as *Mercurius Trismegistus* saith, *The beginning and the rocke of All.*" So, a few years later, a pamphleteer states the correspondence exactly, and very publicly.[26]

The symbolic themes of the masque have now been stated, but they have not yet been worked out dramatically: this has yet to come. While Hymen arranges the persons and the ceremonies Reason explains the symbolism of dress and object to the now quiescent Humours and Affections. It is with the praise of Unity in terms of number symbolism that this speech ends: five candles are carried in the procession because five is the number sacred to Union. The number five is made up of three and two, which are female and male numbers; nor can five be divided into two equal parts—two plus one plus two is the nearest you can get:

> so we see
> The binding force of *Vnitie:*
> For which alone, the peaceful *gods*
> In number, alwaies, loue the oddes;
> And euen parts as much despise,
> Since out of them all discords rise.
> (ll. 206–11)

Now comes the most dramatic moment of the masque, when Juno herself appears. Behind the altar, on either side of the microcosm, stood statues, one representing Atlas and the other Hercules (who once bore Atlas' burden). These figures supported natural seeming clouds; above these clouds, stretching right to the roof of the hall, was a curtain on which clouds were painted. Suddenly as Reason ends her speech, this curtain opens to reveal the three regions of air. In the highest is Juno like a queen, enthroned on gold and encircled with comets and fiery meteors. Above her whirls the regions of fire and above that stands a statue of Jupiter Tonans who represents the heavens.

The relation of microcosm to macrocosm is now visible. So far we have seen the Humours and Affections, discord and the promise of harmony on the plane of man and of society. But through the humours, whose children they are,[27] man is related to the elements: to the elements that make the lands and seas shown on the surface of the globe, earth and water; to the elements that make the regions above the earth, air and fire.

We move from the humours and affections to the globe, to the lowest region of air, home of the rainbow, to the middle region, home of rain and hail and watery meteors, to the highest region, home of comets and fiery meteors and hottest and driest of the three regions because it is closest to the region of fire, thence to the region of fire itself, and finally with the figure of Jove we reach the heaven.[28] The picture is complete; the all embracing union of which Reason has spoken can now be celebrated and its consummation presented in terms of symbolic action. And it is through his use of Juno that Jonson effects the smooth transition from microcosm to macrocosm. For Juno is not only the patroness of marriage but, according to the mythographers, is also air. And Jove, her brother and her husband, is the heaven.

The consummation of the grand union is symbolized by the union in the dance of the eight men who represent the Humours and Affections and the eight women who descend from the regions of air and who represent the eight powers or functions of Juno as goddess of marriage. The dancers are led into position by Order the servant of Reason "*who was, there, rather a Person of* Ceremony, *than Vse*," and has these instructions from his mistress:

> Conuey them, ORDER, to their places,
> And ranke them so, in seuerall traces,
> As they may set their mixed *Powers*
> Vnto the Musique of the *Howers*;
> And THESE, by ioyning with them, know
> In better temper how to flow . . .
> (ll. 280–5)

Order's dress and attributes emphasize his relation to Reason and the Pythagorean-Platonic notions of the masque; thus he has blue in his dress and an upper garment painted with arithmetical and geometrical figures, and his age is venerable. A star on his forehead corresponds to the flame in Reason's crown and expresses the light of reason, the affinity of reason and order with the divine, and perhaps too the order kept by the stars. He carries a "geometricall staffe" for determining the right relationships of things.[29] Order is rightly the servant of Reason, for order is the due disposition of all things and, in man, comes from following the dictates of reason and, in the universe, springs from the Divine Mind. According to the tradition Jonson was following, as another glance at Plutarch's passage on Pythagoras will show, the nature of this order was mathematical and geometrical. When the dancers have been led into position by Order and have begun their dance, a song is sung that has a chorus proclaiming the consummation of the rites of Union:

> Whilst all this *Roofe* doth ring,
> And each discording string,
> With euery varied voyce,
> In VNION doth reioyce.
> (ll. 306–9)

With the consummation of the grand union the dramatic development of the masque has reached its climax. What now remains is the statement of this union in fresh and powerful symbols. And, to begin with, that the consummation should be reached in dance is itself significant, for the unity, the coherence, the consent of the universe was often expressed in terms of the dance.[30] More precisely significant however is the final movement of this dance. It ended with the dancers, their hands linked, placed in the shape of a chain; and this is Reason's comment:

> Such was the *Golden Chaine* let downe from *Heauen*;
>   And not those linkes more euen,
> Then these: so sweetly temper'd, so combin'd
>   By VNION, and refin'd.
>   (ll. 320–23)

This chain, is indeed another symbol of the grand union, a symbol at once familiar and emphatic. This "*Golden chaine* let downe from *Heauen*" is the golden chain which Zeus in the *Iliad* lets down from heaven to earth and of which, as Jonson tells us, the commentators offered various allegorical explanations. For Plato, in the *Theætetus*, the chain was the sun, because as long as the sun "circles the world in his course, all things are safe and preserued." But Jonson prefers the explanation given by Macrobius and quotes at length from *In Somnium Scipionis*, where Macrobius presents the view—Platonic strained through Alexandria—that from God comes the divine Intelligence, and from the divine Intelligence the soul of the world, which makes and fills all things with life; that Being stretches down in an endless chain embracing all and uniting all in its mutual and indissoluble links; and this, he says, is Homer's golden chain which God let down from heaven to earth.[31] Here, then, in this dance Jonson is giving visual expression to one of the most masterful and enduring concepts in European thought: the concept of the great chain of being which stretches from the hand of God down to the lowest form of inanimate nature, a chain in which no link is missing and in which each link, each order of creation, is related to that above and that below, through which the lowest is connected with the highest, and all with God. How pervasive this concept is in Elizabethan thinking and writing we already know. Indeed it had long ago reached the status of an assumption.[32] It was one way of envisaging the grand union.

The masque is now drawing to its close. The dancers are reminded that night is falling, the impatiently awaited night of the bridal bed. Bride and bridegroom must be led to the nuptial bower and over them the Epithalamium must be sung. Clouds cover the whole scene. In front the dancers fall into their final dance and at last are still, disposed in "a faire orbe, or circle," halted by Reason's words who stands in the midst of them and speaks:

> Here stay, and let your sports be crown'd:
> The perfect'st *figure* is the *round*.
> Nor fell you in it by aduenter,
> When REASON was your guide, and *center*.
>   (ll. 403–406)

The circle which—like *Unitas*—shows neither a beginning nor an end was commonly held to be the most perfect of figures. It was a favoured symbol and the interpreters gave it many meanings, among them God, eternity or perfection. And some of these meanings are shared by the orb or sphere, which can stand for eternity, or the sky, or the globe.[33] Reason equates the circle with the girdle of Venus:

> This, this that beauteous CESTON is
> Of *louers* many-colour'd blisse,

and bids Hymen lead the actors of the marriage rites into the circle to form an inner ring. So we now have Reason at the centre surrounded by this inner ring of the bride, bridegroom and their attendants, and an outer ring of the Humours and Affections linked by the Powers of Juno. This is the final grouping of the masquers, the final statement of the theme, the perfection of the grand union. The union of marriage consummated in love typifies the harmonious ordering of man's nature and man's society that follows when reason is obeyed: this is perfection. Nor can man and the elements that go to make him be separated from the world of nature, man from the globe, the *orbis terrarum*, microcosm from macrocosm. In both microcosm and macrocosm right order has been established by the Divine Reason, and perfection, right order, is achieved and maintained when the dispositions of reason, human and divine, are admitted and accepted. The circle is eternity, perfection, God. The orb is globe and sky and eternity. The circle is also the girdle of Venus: marriage that is a bond of union through love. And Venus is not only the power of love that ties the creatures together and sees to their reproduction, Venus is also that power of the *Anima Mundi* which under Divine Reason gives life and shape and unity to created things.[34] The union in order that links the creatures and their creator is also a bond of love.

III. "Present Occasions": the King, the Union and the Divines

As the masquers depart the masque's grand theme is brought down to the place and the time, to Whitehall on the night of the fifth of January, 1606. Reason speaks:

> And as, in *circle*, you depart
> Link'd *hand in hand*; So, *heart in heart*,
> May all those *bodies* still remayne
> Whom he (with so much sacred payne)
> No less hath bound within his realmes
> Then they are with the OCEANS streames.
> Long may his VNION find increase
> As he, to ours, hath deign'd his peace.
> (ll. 423–30)

"Sacred payne," "deign'd his peace"—the words might seem better suited to a holier labour and a holier blessing; but Jonson again chooses to shed the aura of divinity over the king. James, the one king, and the first of the two kingdoms, could as we saw be related to Unity itself, and that without blasphemy. Reason's words certainly carry a double reference, to the fruitful marriage union of James and Anne and to the union of the crowns effected in the king's own person. We are to think too of another union springing out of this: the full political union of the two realms that was one of the king's dearest projects. Praise of union in a piece of court writing during these years when the king was urging this project in every way could not but be taken in this sense. The audience probably found this the easiest to grasp of all the masque's significances.

> The concert or soul of the Mask was Hymen bringing in a bride, and Juno Pronuba's priest a bridegroom, proclaiming that these two should be sacrificed to Nuptial Union. And here the Poet made an apostrophe to the Union of the Kingdoms.

So one purveyor of news, John Pory, wrote to a client.[35] On January twenty-first, little more than a fortnight after the production of *Hymenæi*, Parliament—which had been prorogued since the preceding November—was to meet again; and it was expected that the question of the union would be discussed on the basis of proposals made by the commissioners representing both countries who had in 1604 been charged with this duty.

The 'topicality' of *Hymenæi*, however, does not lie merely in verbal references to important contemporary happenings. It is more intrinsic, and more striking. To see it fully we must look beyond the connection Pory saw between the nuptial union and the union of the kingdoms, though indeed this is the basic image relating the themes of the masque to the union, and the basic theme from which Jonson evolved the rest. The comparison between the union and marriage was a very obvious one, and came easily to the king's lips. In his opening speech to his first Parliament, when he introduced the idea of the union, James said "What God hath conioyned then, let no man separate. I am the Husband, and all the whole Isle is my lawfull Wife."[36] The image is also applied frequently to the relationship between the two countries. In the November following *Hymenæi* James talks to Parliament of the union being necessary as a contract is to marriage; and in his admirable address given the next March he declares roundly that "Union is a Marriage."[37] In 1604 an anonymous writer looking for the king's favour wound up the peroration of his discourse in praise of the union with an elaboration of the image:

> ... as at this marriage if you will daunce, you make the contract sure, and till death depart [*sic*]: For though they and you lye in one another of your houses; nay should they and you lye with one another of your wives and daughters; beleeue me *non concubitus sed consensus facit Matrimoniam*, say the Ciuilians; Marry then and make the bond holy and vnuiolable, or expect no securitie that the grandchildren in time to come shall alwaies proue comfortable to the old folkes.

And as an agreeable and apt conclusion he quotes first the tag from Catullus, *Hymen ô Hymenæe*, and then this from Sidney:

> God Hymen long your coupled ioyes maintaine.[38]

Sir William Cornwallis speaks to the same effect:

> Beholde how we are joyned, God, Nature, & Time, haue broght vs together, and so miraculously if wee obserue the reuolutions of time, as me thinketh the very words after the consummation of a marriage, shal not be vnproperly vsed, *Those whom God hath ioyned together, let no man seperate.*[39]

We shall see this marriage image recurring in other significant contexts.

Jonson takes his marriage, which is the marriage of the kingdoms, as type and instance of universal union. He could do this because in the world imaged in his masque every thing and every event has not only its fixed limits but its widest extension; this scheme of the world both limits and extends, fixes the bounds appropriate to event and thing and at the same time places event and thing, through a chain of correspondences, in a context that spreads till it includes the universe. Nor is this world a poetic fiction–though in our period it is on the verge of being so considered; its analogies are correspondences in nature and in fact. This order in which limits are tight and relationships infinite is categorical and compelling. It is categorical and compelling because it has its ground and sanction in the nature of the divine. Thus it is not only possible but necessary to see the marriage of man and woman as both type and instance of universal union. And so with any and every event; and so with the king's project. It is in the perspectives revealed by *Hymenæi* that those close to the king or seeking his favour set the proposed union. In terms of this compelling order they seek to defend the union in treatises aimed at convincing the sceptical and suspicious Commons of its desirability; in the consonance of the union with the order dear to God they find a main argument.

Thus when Sir John Hayward the historian (in an attempt, no doubt, to win from James the favour he had lost with Elizabeth) published in 1604 *A Treatise of Union of the two Realmes of England and Scotland*,[40] in which the arguments are mostly historical and political, he nevertheless felt it necessary to introduce his work with a chapter containing "a commendation of Union in generall." Union here has the *Unitas*-One meaning, and Hayward begins by citing Augustine's view that union not only represents the singleness of the soul, but is

> the very image of God, who both perfectly containeth, and infinitely exceedeth the excellencies and perfections of all creatures; who being the only true one, loueth this similitude of himself in all his creatures;

and he supports this from Macrobius, who

> referreth perfect vnion onely vnto God, terming it the beginning and end of all things, being altogether free from beginning, chaunge or end.

He also refers to the "more ancient" philosophers, including Pythagoras, who called "vnitie" μονας.[41]

Hymenæi, however, has a more intimate connection with two other tracts that come straight from the king's own circle. They were provoked by the first great crisis in the dispute about the union, the question of the king's style. From the beginning James wanted to call himself King of Great Britain. The first disagreement with the Commons came in the spring of 1604 when this suggestion was made. James held that union in name should come before union in fact; the Commons were not so sure, and disliked the new name anyhow. Eventually James agreed to let the matter drop, but he did not forget it and on the twentieth of October he issued a proclamation announcing his assumption of the style "Kinge of Great Brittaine."[42] This was immediately followed by another proclamation announcing the issue of new coins bearing appropriate emblems and mottoes. In the text of the proclamation of style the enemies of the union had been accused of endeavouring "to separate that whiche God hathe put together"; and one of the new coins, a silver piece worth twelve shillings and sixpence, was to carry this "word": *Quae Deus conjunxit nemo separet*. The marriage image has been given official status.[43]

On October twenty-eighth, a week after the adoption of the new style, a sermon was preached at Whitehall by a divine whom James particularly favoured.[44] This was John Gordon. A Scot, educated in France, he had returned to this country as a servant of Mary, the king's mother; in the last sad time he had left her household and gone back to France where he had since remained. In spite of these associations he was a violent Protestant, and had disputed with the great du Perron.[45] On James's accession he had written a panegyric in French which was thought so well of here that it was immediately translated into English by Grimestone and was issued three times in the years 1603 and 1604, under three different titles.[46] Gordon was recalled from France by the king, and in this same month of October he became Dean of Salisbury. It is not surprising that his sermon should be a defence of the union and of the king's new style.

One part of this sermon is especially important for *Hymenæi*. Gordon preached on the text "Euery Kingdome diuided against it selfe (or in the selfe) shall be brought to nought (or desolate); and euerie citie or house diuided against it selfe (or in it selfe) shall not stand." (Matthew xii. 25.) These three words, Kingdom, City, House, he argues, cover all men and all human society: the foundation is the union of man and woman in marriage, signified by the word 'house,' and on this foundation the rest is built. Having reduced everything to the individual man he proceeds to present an "image of a kingdome both in the *outward* and *inward man*," man being a microcosm. In the kingdom of the outward man the head is king and the other parts of the body his subjects who owe him obedience: so the whole island owes obedience to James. The image is scarcely new. More relevant is Gordon's picture of the kingdom of the inward man. Here reason is king; his duty is to keep his subjects "*Ira, Metus, Cupido*, anger, feare, couetousnesse" in due order. The application of the image to the immediate occasion is clear:

> Let vs drawe this example of the image of the kingdome, in the *inward man* to our selues, in this vnion of great Britannie, which great worke is now in hand, for euen as *Mens* or *Ratio* is the king, who ruleth, and keepeth in order his subiects, to wit, *Ira, metus, cupido*, euen so the king and head of this Iland must keep his subiects in the *South* and in the *North*, that are as diuers of nature as *Ira, metus, cupido*, in good order & temperature, least that not being ruled, and ouerruled by their King, they fall into a lamentable diuision, whereupon will follow according to Christs words in this text, a most miserable desolation (from the which I pray the Lord deliuer vs). So that I conclude if we be vnited vnder one head and one king, we must be vnited amongst our selues, or els be disobedient to *Reason* our *King*.[47]

Gordon develops his theme. Enough however has been given to show that Jonson's dramatic image of reason subduing the passions of the mind who rebel against union had already been applied to James and those who opposed the union he sought, and that on an important public occasion. And the relationship between the political event and the nature of man has already been stated.

More deeply involved in the defence of the union was John Thornborough, who at the time of the accession was Bishop of Limerick and holder of preferments in Yorkshire.[48] Royal approval came quickly, and in August 1603 Thornborough was installed as Bishop of Bristol. His enthusiasm for the union soon got him into trouble. On April twenty-seventh, 1604, Bacon read to the Commons a report prepared by a committee of the House summarizing the objections raised to the proposed change of style as they had come up in a conference between the two Houses.[49] Shortly afterwards an anonymous pamphlet appeared replying to these objections, reprinting in its preamble the very words of the report Bacon had read. The Commons soon knew of this pamphlet and that the author was the Bishop of Bristol himself. Trouble followed; for the Commons held that such a publication constituted a breach of privilege. Complaints were carried to the Lords, and after various goings and comings the Bishop went through the form of making an apology and the matter was dropped.[50] It probably could not be pushed too far—or as far as some members of the Commons wanted—because, as appears from the dedication to the king, the pamphlet was published with his knowledge and approval.[51] Here the contents of the pamphlet are not so important as the knowledge that the Bishop of Bristol was so close to the king. But we may note that Thornborough does use the familiar echo of the marriage service: "what God hath so ioyned together, let no man put asunder."[52]

Some time after the proclamation of the new style, soon after, probably, Thornborough, under his own name, published another piece of propaganda, *The Ioieful and Blessed Revniting the two mighty and famous kingdomes, England and Scotland into their ancient name of great Brittaine*.[53] With this work, I am convinced, *Hymenæi* has a close connection. It is a discursive, ill arranged treatise (the king himself pleaded more cogently than his supporters) assembling a variety of arguments in defence of the union and the style. Here the kind of argument I have indicated in Hayward's and Gordon's tracts is worked out much more fully; the perspectives in which Thornborough sets the union are very near to those revealed in Jonson's masque of union.

Union is a divine mystery. 'One' creates innumerable forms of things, yet remains one—just as Britain is one but contains kingdoms, counties, rivers, islands and people. This is but one instance of the divine power,

> compassing & passing through the whole world, making things either simple, or coniunct, but one; subsisting by, & vnder the divine essence, which is one; and consisting in all his members, & parts vnited, but one; where each, & every part of this vniversall world, respecteth the whole, otherwise innumerable, but brought by vnion to a number, without number, even beginning of numbers, which is but one.

Drawn together by this power the world is one:

> everie particuler being knit togither with the whole vniversality & diversity of things, & wrapt vp in one round orbe togither, that as partes of this worlde, they may dwell in one Center, or Circle togither.

This is what Jonson is stating when in the last dance the masquers fall "into a faire orbe, or circle." How this works out is shown in Britain, where all are part of one and subject to one: the king. As the excellent workmanship of union shows itself "in the mightie Masse, and fabricke of the whole worlde, so much more particulerly, and plainely doth it appeare in a modelle of the same, even in the name, and honour of great Brittaine." Caught in the bonds of neighbourhood and society man ceases to be absolutely one yet remains himself. In a healthy society "Where sacred vnitie is guide, and director" all sorts and conditions of men are united as one under one sovereign, as though they were one body.[54] A little later Thornborough explains the distinction between *vnitas*, the principle of good, and *Binarius numerus*, two, the principle of division, discord, and evil. This is the Pythagorean notion found in the sources with which Jonson was working. Exception is only made when two people persist in union, "as it is written, *they shall be two in one flesh.*"[55] Finally we are given an elaborate presentation of union which is so important for *Hymenæi* that it must be given at length in Thornborough's own words:

> All blessings, and graces, may be thought attendants, and companions to vnion, who alone knoweth, how to order al things in government: and is a princely commander of Subiects obedience, and subduer of gainsaiers, ordering vnrulie affections, bridling vntamed lustes, restraining swelling pride, composing rebellious appetites, determining al doubts, & rights, within the compasse of her iudgement, and yet giving to euerie one, his due, by her discretion: And therefore is like the Sunne in the middest of heauen, among the Stars; and as the Stars take light of the Sun, so al blessings of Weale publique proceede from this sacred, & thrice happy vnion into the name of great Brittaine, whose glorious light shineth to all, and euery one hath comfort thereby. It is also not vnlike the Soule in the body of man; for in the whole common Weale, it is wholly, and in every part thereof, whether it be of English, or Scottish entire. *Tota in toto, et tota in qualibet parte.* As a shining light, it sheweth a way for common good, and as a reasonable soule, giveth vnderstanding to the blindest body, to see the full fruition of al worldly happinesse . . . .
>
> If I could expresse the image of this vnion in liuely colours, I would surely make her a Goddes, faire, and beautiful, having a garland, & crowne, of al blessings vpon her head, & sitting in a Chaire of State, with al good fortunes, vertues and graces attending her, and as a Goddes in triumphant chariot going into the capitol, or temple of mighty Iupiter: where also the Poets haue found her, but called by another name, even Pallas, who is also named *Monas*, that is, vnitie: because having one only parent, shee resideth in Iupiters braine, even in the chiefe seate of his wisedome; where al the Muses are her companions, so called *Musæ*, quasi ὁμοιονσαι, that is altogither in one; where al the Graces go hand in hand, congratulating to vnion their mutual societie; where al vertue, and knowledge, are neere of affinitie, but Iustice, and government of consanguinity to her, her selfe stil holding primacy over al . . .[56]

Change Pallas into Juno, give her the appropriate attendants, make reason into a separate personage, and we have Jonson's figures, the parts they play and the meaning of them.

What Jonson did is now abundantly clear. He took as his basic image that marriage image which played such a part in the defence of the union and the style. He also found the union defended in terms of this theological, philosophical vision of the universe. He personified union as Juno because Juno who is anyhow goddess of marriage could by a lucky anagram be construed as *Unio*, and would then make a dramatic link between the ceremony of marriage and that union of the universe of which the king's union is type and instance.[57] The world picture offered by the divines, and the authorities on which it was grounded, were as well known to Jonson as to them, and he went independently to the sources. But in effect *Hymenæi* is not only a formal wedding masque; *Hymenæi* is a dramatic and symbolic representation of the Union of the Kingdoms as it was conceived in the propaganda issued by men who had the approval of the king himself. How close this propaganda and *Hymenæi* were to the king's own ideas can be seen from the summary we have of the peroration of the speech he made to his recalcitrant Parliament on the eighteenth of November in this same year:

> that sithence Union was the very Essence of Divinity, and the Staff of all States; was the Bond of Marriage, the Strength of Families, the Increase of Kingdoms and the Kiss of Enemies; let us all embrace it, that we may all enjoy it . . . .[58]

To relate present occasions to sublime and removed mysteries,[59] to link Whitehall, the marriage of the Earl of Essex with Frances Howard, James and his cherished plan to the union of man, the universe and God: this for Jonson was the art of the masque. Rarely has it been so ingeniously exemplified as in *Hymenæi*, where the altar that meets the curious eyes of the spectators becomes the nodal point on which the lines that connect the universe converge.

IV. Antiquity and solid learnings: the classical past as history and symbol

The applications of *Hymenæi* are both timeless and topical. But the vehicle chosen to carry these applications belongs to a particular age, and one that is not Jonson's. The altar and the marriage ceremonies are not English but Roman. Jonson's attempt is to combine in an imaginative unity the forms of classical life and worship, a world picture that is both Christian and classical, and the significance of a given event in the terms in which it was seen by a group of contemporaries. The nature and success of this attempt are now to be examined.[60]

It was as a scholar that Jonson came to devise the presentation of the marriage ceremony and the figure of the goddess. Every detail had to be impeccably accurate, based on the classical texts and on the findings of recent scholarship.[61]

For his information about mythology Jonson again relies, as we have already seen him do in *The Masque of Blacknesse* and *The Masque of Beautie*, on the great handbooks, on Giraldi, on Conti, and, in all probability, on Cartari.[62] A scrutiny of the image of Juno will show how Jonson built up his picture from details supplied by these books, and by the invaluable Ripa.[63] This is what the spectators see:

> IVNO, sitting in a Throne, supported by two beautifull Peacockes; her attyre rich, and like a Queene, a white Diademe on her head, from whence descended a Veyle, and that bound with a Fascia, of seuerall-coloured silkes, set with all sorts of iewels, and raysed in the top with Lillies and Roses; in her right hand she held a Scepter, in the other a timbrell, at her golden feete the hide of a lyon was placed . . . . (ll. 215–221)

Behind this lie three descriptions of Juno: Martianus' description of her in *De Nuptiis*, Apuleius' in book ten of *The Golden Ass*, and an account of a statue at Argos. Of these Martianus is the most important, for his Juno is an allegory of air, and it is as air that Jonson is mostly thinking of Juno here. Martianus' description is repeated by Cartari and by Ripa, who uses it as an image of air; and Jonson certainly had Ripa in mind. The different coloured silks and jewels signify the varying colours of the air; the peacocks, as Conti explains, have an "airy temperament," and Ripa has supplied the quotation from the *De Arte Amandi* with which Jonson introduces them. The timbrel indicates the noises of wind, tempest and thunder which have their origins in the region of air. So Martianus, Ripa and Cartari; and Conti gives the quotation from Virgil with which Jonson justifies himself for connecting these phenomena with Juno. The golden feet come from Giraldi who cites Hesiod and other poets. Juno as a queen with the sceptre and white diadem comes from Apuleius through Cartari or Giraldi. However the roses on the head-dress were perhaps really a mistake. The lily was peculiar to Juno and Jonson perhaps misread or did not properly remember a line in Giraldi: *Coronabatur interdum lilio: Iunonis enim flos lilium. & rosa Iunonia uocabatur*; the lily is called the rose of Juno. It sprang from the milk that dropped from Juno's breast when the infant Hercules was snatched away by Jupiter, who had put him there while Juno slept; Jonson could have read the story in either Conti or Cartari. The lion's skin at her feet is from the account of the statue of Juno at Argos as given by both Giraldi and Cartari, but Jonson is probably following Giraldi. Juno is trampling the skin underfoot to show her hatred of her stepchildren Hercules and Bacchus, with each of whom the lion's skin was associated. From such a tissue of details was this picture of Juno created.

And out of just such a tissue, such a conflation of sources, has Jonson built up his picture of the marriage procession. He has done as a scholar should do and has gone to the most comprehensive and the newest works of research for his information. He had read Catullus in a variorum edition of the Latin elegists published a few years previously by the learned French printer Claud Morel, where a useful commentary by Costanzo Landi on the epithalamium for Manlius and Julia was printed.[64] Then there were the works of the French and Italian jurists who in the sixteenth century were drawn to the study of Roman antiquities through their professional concern with the acclimatization of Roman law in their own countries. Jonson knew the *Genialium Dierum*, the famous discursive encyclo- pædia written by the Neapolitan Alexander ab Alexandro, and, I am certain, knew it in the fine new edition brought out in 1594 by the German jurist Christopher Coler. André Tiraqueau (or Tiraquelli), a French jurist, of an earlier generation, had prepared elaborate notes on Alexander's book, and these had been published along with Alexander's text in 1586. Coler reprints this work adding further notes by himself and by another French jurist, Dionysius Gothofredus (Denys Godefroy), famous as professor at Heidelberg.[65] Then there were two other small but very useful treatises produced by still other French students of Roman law; Barnabé Brisson's *De Ritu Nuptiarum*[66] and Antoine Hotman's *De Veteri Ritu Nuptiarum*.[67] Most of Jonson's knowledge of the Roman marriage comes from these books.[68]

From them he learns that the bridegroom's hair must be cut short, while the bride's is long and dressed with grey—grey hair which shows that she is about to enter a more responsible state; that she must be swathed in a fleece to show—this is the explanation he chooses—that she is capable of woman's work; that for the same reason a spindle and a distaff must be carried in the procession; that she is to be crowned with roses. From them he learns about the attendants, the *patrimi* and *maximi*, and their functions. From them he learns what kind of torches are to be used—a matter of grave dispute, depending on the correct reading of a line in Catullus: is it pine tree or white thorn? When Jonson makes Hymen carry a torch of pine and the Camillus (on whom he is particularly well informed) one of white thorn, he is allowing each view its place. And so a learned controversy between students of Catullus and of Roman antiquities affects the dressing of actors in this masque: an eminent example of the way in which Jonson came to prepare his scene.

The nature of Jonson's approach to the classical past, exemplified in his treatment of ritual and worship, can be further elucidated if we consider the treatment of these subjects in a contemporary play written rather later than *Hymenæi. The Two Noble Kinsmen*, by Fletcher and Shakespeare, is based on Chaucer's *Knight's Tale* with its story of the deadly rivalry of Palamon and Arcite for the hand of Emily, sister to Hippolita the bride of Theseus.[69] Chaucer's tale was itself based on Boccaccio's epic *La Teseida*. And the play is not only an instance of the survival of a mediaeval story but of the survival of mediaeval, or early Renaissance, attitudes to classical antiquity. Even when the dramatists have introduced a new episode of ritual, or have modified their source, they preserve Chaucer's—and Boccaccio's—feeling for these things.[70]

The play opens with an episode that is freshly conceived, the appearance of Hippolita's wedding procession:

> Enter Hymen with a Torch burning: a Boy, in a white Robe before singing, and strewing Flowres: After Hymen, a Nimph, encompast in her Tresses, bearing a wheaten Garland. Then Theseus betweene two other Nimphs with wheaten Chaplets on their heades. Then Hipolita the Bride, lead by Pirithous, and another holding a Garland over her head (her Tresses likewise hanging).[71]

Hymen certainly appears, with a torch—but there is no question about what kind of torch he should carry. Here there is no attempt at precise detail, nothing of *patrimi* and *maximi*, of the ritual objects. What is wanted is a pageant, an effective opening, strange and impressive, that will introduce the spectators to a world that is not theirs. New again are the details of the sacrifice Emilia makes to Diana before the tournament that is to settle her own fate and that of Palamon and Arcite. On the altar is set a silver hind containing incense and perfumes which are then lit. When Emilia has finished praying the hind suddenly vanishes and on the altar appears a rose tree bearing a single flower. This she takes to be a sign that

> I, a virgin flowre
> Must grow alone unpluck'd.

But the rose falls, the tree disappears, and Emilia accepts her fate:

The floure is falne, the Tree descends: O, Mistris,
Thou here dischargest me: I shall be gather'd:
I thinke so . . . .[72]

This is romance and mystery, fascinating and strange. The world of *The Two Noble Kinsmen* is a world whose appeal lies in strangeness and remoteness, a remoteness that has nothing to do with the precise location in time of ancient Greece. The desired effect could be produced equally well by a plot set in China or Peru. For these dramatists, as for Chaucer, location in time and location in space, history and geography, are on a level, apprehended in the same way, serve the same purposes. What happened then, what happens there —either will do to make a romantic world.[73]

The epiphany of Juno is as strange as the appearance of Diana's rose tree. But her figure is realized, Jonson hopes, as a Roman would have realized it. His archæological reconstruction, his search for detail and authority, come from and presuppose an awareness of the 'historical distance' of the classical world: an awareness of the pastness of this world, of its existence as a world that is not his, with a life, ritual and gods of its own whose forms and meanings must be laboriously rediscovered.[74] It is the attitude of a Renaissance scholar, but it was long in coming to England.

Aware in this way of the 'historical distance' of the forms of Roman ritual and worship, Jonson chose to translate the current image of the marriage of the kingdoms into terms of a Roman marriage, and make its interrupted but triumphant celebration, crowned by the epiphany of the goddess and her participation in the rites through the action of her powers, into a symbolic representation of the union the king so greatly wanted. This choice implies an attempt to make spectators, and readers, see the union in a new way. It implies the apprehension of a relationship between the union and these classical forms, historically conceived: a relationship which, once it is seized by the audience, will make them see the union in a fresh light. And it is here that *Hymenæi* fails, in the relationship it states between the classical forms and the political event, between past and present. The effect of failure is produced by the very cleverness with which Jonson has worked out the relationship. He did it, as we have seen, through the figure of Juno, whose name could be read, anagrammatically, as *Unio*. This was very clever. Too clever indeed, for his Juno is a cryptogram and never a potent symbol. The relationship between Juno and her rites and the king's union is an intricate riddle—no more than this. The historical conception of the Roman forms does not enter into the situation, does not modify or recreate the union, setting it in a new light. These historical forms remain apart; the historical approach produces only an interest in history, in the accurate reconstruction of the past: a pure archæological interest. History has not become symbol.

Any conscious recreation of the classical past draws what life it has, and what interest, apart from the purely archæological, from the life of the creator: this is inescapable. Its life will come from the creator's awareness, conscious or unconscious, of a relationship, direct or indirect, implicit or explicit, between this past and his own present. This is the new element that realization of 'historical distance' brings in: this is why Jonson cannot treat classical antiquity as the authors of *The Two Noble Kinsmen* could. The relationship of

Juno to Jonson's present occasions was little more than verbal: the lucky anagram. The device of Juno enables him to link Rome to Whitehall and to present a currently accepted world picture through an ingenious allegory. But though Jonson could use the language, it is questionable whether he was much interested in the Platonic Christian mysteries. He does not passionately grasp the sublimities deployed in *Hymenæi*. The whole body of his work shows that his real interests were not in theology or metaphysics, but in morals. This is why history in *Hymenæi* remains history and does not become symbol.

At least once in his works it did, and the contrast with *Hymenæi* is important. This happens in the Roman tragedy of *Catiline*, the first two acts of which, at least, must be put with his finest works. Jonson made full use of the classical texts and of relevant works by Renaissance scholars; the approach is that of *Hymenæi*, but the upshot is different. Jonson may not have been very deeply interested in the sublimer mysteries revealed in *Hymenæi*; but with the preservation of order under reason in the life of society he was most passionately concerned. This hierarchical order, this system of 'degree' he saw threatened all around him; he saw this with horror and disgust. It is out of this view of the corruption of contemporary society, of the modern overthrow of established values, that he makes the great satires *Volpone* and *The Alchemist*. And it is as agents of a similar threat to the fabric of Roman society that he sees Catiline and his fellows. Spawned by the corruption of society, like a Volpone or an Alchemist, they are at once symptoms and agents of its ruin. It would always have been easier for Jonson to see this relationship between present and past in terms of political and moral life; and he was helped by the belief in the constancy of human nature which permitted scholars to see the relevance of ancient experience in that field. Present fears, then, have entered into these early scenes in *Catiline* and have given special power to the verse of Catiline, which dominates them. The first great climax comes when Catiline, having roused the other conspirators to a frenzy of ambition and hate, administers to them a sacrament in the blood of a sacrificed slave to seal their compact:

> Goe you, and bid
> The Priest, he kill the slaue I mark'd last night;
> And bring me of his bloud, when I shall call him.
> I'haue kill'd a slaue,
> And of his bloud caus'd to be mixt with wine.
> Fill euery man his bowle. There cannot be
> A fitter drinke, to make this *sanction* in.
> Here, I beginne the sacrament to all.
> O, for a clap of thunder, now, as loud,
> As to be heard through-out the vniuerse,
> To tell the world the fact, and to applaud it.
> Be firme, my hand; not shed a drop: but powre
> Fiercenesse into me, with it, and fell thirst
> Of more, and more, till *Rome* be left as bloud-lesse,
> As euer her feares made her, or the sword.

> And, when I leaue to wish this to thee, step-dame,
> Or stop, to effect it, with my powers fainting;
> So may my bloud be drawne, and so drunke vp
> As is this slaues.[75]

The verse has been rising in energy and intensity until the horror of the scene finds its climax and fitting expression in this perverted sacrament. Jonson has not consciously made the doings of these evil men a parable or allegory of the dangers threatening his own society. But so deeply has he felt the contemporary relevance of his theme that he has conquered 'historical distance'; and at this moment history passes into symbol. The historicity of the episode was guaranteed by the authors Jonson followed with a scholar's patience; but here Roman ritual and Christian are instantly assimilated. The blasphemous parody of Holy Communion is immediately felt. The ritual is a dramatic symbol of willed perversion, of evil completely and monstrously accepted.[76]

V. Truth and Opinion: a coda to *Hymenæi*

The tournament of chivalry had become the ceremonial 'barriers', part of the elaborate pageantry of the court, a display both of skill and of gorgeous trappings. These barriers were often set in a symbolic action which provided dramatic justification for the exercise of arms. Such a libretto Jonson was called on to provide for the barriers that were to take place on the night after the masque and provide a further celebration of the marriage. And Jonson chose to relate his barriers to his masque in topic and in symbolism, to provide a rehandling and recapitulation of certain themes that had exercised him there.

Jonson now stages a conflict between Truth and Opinion. A mist—"made of delicate perfumes"—appears at the bottom of the hall. Through it, to the accompaniment of music that imitates the noises of battle, break two figures, one representing Truth, the other Opinion. But which is which cannot be told from their appearance, for both are dressed in exactly the same way:

> The colour of their garments were blue, their socks white; they were crown'd with wreaths of Palme, & in their hands ech of them sustain'd a Palm-bough. (ll. 686–88)

Only Truth should wear this dress and carry the traditional palm, which, as Ripa explains, signifies the power of Truth; for the palm will always spring up again, no matter how much pressure is applied to it, and no power can ever finally suppress truth.[77] Truth's colours signify other attributes, the blue her affinity with heaven, the white her purity.[78] Each speaker claims to be Truth and neither will give way. However they agree to settle the question by a debate on whether the married or the virgin state is preferable; Truth will defend the married state, Opinion will take the other side, and whoever makes out the most convincing case will be proclaimed Truth. They debate at some length, and, among other arguments, Opinion stresses the nobility of oneness, using the familiar examples:

> we doe still heare nam'd
> One *god*, one *nature*, and but one *world* fram'd,
> One *sunne*, one *moone*, one element of *fire*,
> So, of the rest; one *king*, that doth inspire
> *Soule*, to all *bodies*, in this royall spheare:
>   (ll. 794–98)

Truth retorts that this concluding instance is one that really argues for marriage, because the relationships of soul and body, king and subjects, are marriages that result in unity. Jonson has also an opportunity to translate a lovely and famous passage from Catullus' second wedding song: the image of the flower that blooms in beauty when left alone but fades when gathered and thrown aside by a careless hand, contrasted with the picture of the fruitful union of vine and elm.[79] The debate however settles nothing, for neither Truth nor Opinion will admit defeat, and each summons champions to support her cause with arms. So the contest of the barriers begins. But before this happens Truth has gone out, saying

> . . . if this varied triall faile,
> To make my TRUTH in wedlockes praise preuaile,
> I will retire, and in more power appeare;
> To cease this strife, and make our question cleare.
>   (ll. 864–7)

And the fight is stopped by the entry of an angel who heralds the reappearance of Truth. Truth descends in glory; Opinion is discomfited; and after Truth has made a complimentary speech to the king the barriers ends.

Such is the slight action: a framework for the contest. Slight though the action may be, however, it is concerned with questions of some seriousness, and is more closely connected with the elaborate masque than might at first sight appear.

The debate between Truth and Opinion takes place in the human mind. The appearance of the two figures through the mist was accompanied by sounds as of battle; the symbolism is explained by Opinion:

> My name is Truth, who through these sounds of *warre*,
> (Which figure the wise minds discursiue fight)
> In mists by *nature* wrapt, salute the light.
>   (ll. 697–9)

Though Opinion's claim to be Truth is false, yet the rest of these words are to be trusted; and indeed the image of the mind wrapped by nature in mist or darkness is common enough; de la Primaudaye employs such images frequently. The battle music symbolizes the strife within the reasoning mind as it tries to decide what is truth and what is not. The conflict between Truth and Opinion, visually presented, is also to be taken on this plane; the actual contest of arms can be taken as a further dramatization of the process of judgment, of the mind's perpetual debate.

We must understand what opinion is and how it is related to the powers of the mind.

For here Jonson is still concerned with reason and the affections, just as he was in *Hymenæi* itself. Opinion is bound up with the affections or passions. "Thus you see the principall winds from whence arise the tempests of our *Soule*, and the pit whereout they rise is nothing else but the opinion (which commonly is false, wandring, uncertaine, contrary to nature, verity, reason, certainty) that a man hath, that the things that present themselves unto us, are either good or ill: for having conceived them to be such, wee either follow them, or with violence fly from them. And these are our passions."[80] Here Charron, the sceptic, insists on the uncertainty of opinion: this is one of the bases of his argument that man is not really capable of attaining true knowledge. But it was not only the professed sceptics who put little trust in opinion. De la Primaudaye, though he gives a technical and neutral definition of opinion as "a knowledge that moueth vs to incline rather on the one side, then on the other, in regard of the appearance and shew of reason that it hath: so that wee are not fully resolued therein,"[81] yet distrusts opinion, and in his use of it the word generally carries with it something of disapprobation. For Jonson opinion seems to be quite simply false opinion, the opposite of truth. This distrust is based on the instability of opinion which comes from its connection with the affections. Our affections are essentially our impulses to embrace what we think to be good and eschew what we think to be evil, and thus they depend on our opinions. A judgment of value is involved, and by judgment the affections ought to be guided. But, as de la Primaudaye says, the motions of the mind are so light and quick that it is difficult to say whether the affections are following judgment or are, instead, running before.[82] They ought certainly to come after and be controlled by judgment, which is itself a function of reason, the highest power of the mind:

> This facultie and vertue of the soule, so necessary in man, and which is able to iudge of things imagined and perceiued by the other senses . . . to know whether they be good or bad, and what is to be embraced or eschewed, is called, the *Iudging* or discoursing *facultie*, namely *Reason*, which is the principall part and vertue of the soule, and beareth rule among all the other sences.[83]

Opinion uncontrolled by reason is worthless. But unfortunately the affections are too often contented with a more superficial judgment than reason provides: that offered by 'Fantasie.' Fantasy, or imagination—for de la Primaudaye the terms seem to be interchangeable—is the power of the soul "that receiueth the images imprinted in the sences" and "doth as it were prepare and digest them, either by ioyning them together, or by separating them according as their natures require."[84] And fantasy is a dangerous and unreliable guide:

> fansie being very turbulent and skittish, and drawing to it selfe confusedly some shew and apparence of opinion and iudgement, whereby it deemeth that which is offered vnto it to be either good or bad, is the cause that wee liue in the middest of marueilous troubles in respect of our affections of feare, of desire, of sorrow, of ioy, and that one while we weepe, and sodainly wee laugh againe.[85]

Fancy never rests, is never still: "euen in the time of sleepe it hardly taketh any rest, but is alwaies occupied in dreaming and doting, yea euen about those things which neuer haue beene, shall be, or can be."[86] For this reason Truth here calls Opinion

> some illusiue spright;
> Whom to my likenesse, the black sorceresse *night*
> Hath of these drie, and empty fumes created.
>
> (ll. 701–3)

What Jonson gives us, then, is a picture of the human mind trying to discriminate between truth and opinion, between what is really truth and what only appears to be truth, bred of the affections when they are not controlled by reason. Again we see, as we saw in *Hymenæi*, how necessary it is that reason should dominate the affections.

The debate is inconclusive; neither Truth nor Opinion is clearly victorious. But Jonson does not bring on Reason in person to settle the question, to vindicate Truth and dismiss Opinion. He develops another line of thought. He brings on Truth herself, in great state. Truth, as she is personified here, has many attributes (indeed she is little more than an agglomeration of attributes):

> Vpon her head she weares a crowne of starres,
> Through which her orient hayre waues to her wast,
> By which beleeuing *mortalls* hold her fast,
> And in those golden chordes are carried euen,
> Till with her breath she blowes them vp to heauen.
> She weares a robe enchas'd with eagles eyes,
> To signifie her sight in *mysteries*;
> Vpon each shoulder sits a milke-white doue,
> And at her feet doe witty serpents moue:
> Her spacious armes doe reach from *East* to *West*,
> And you may see her heart shine through her brest.
> Her right hand holds a *sunne* with burning rayes,
> Her left a curious bunch of golden kayes,
> With which *heauen* gates she locketh, and displaces.
> A christall mirror hangeth at her brest,
> By which mens consciences are search'd, and drest:
> On her coach-wheeles *hypocrisie* lies rackt;
> And squint-eyd slander, with *vaine-glory* backt,
> Her bright eyes burne to dust: in which shines fate.
> An *angell* vshers her triumphant gate,
> Whilst with her fingers fans of starres shee twists,
> And with them beates back *Error*, clad in mists.
> Eternall *Vnitie* behind her shines,
> That *fire*, and *water*, *earth*, and *ayre* combines.
> Her voyce is like a trumpet lowd, and shrill,
> Which bids all sounds in *earth*, and *heav'n* be still.[87]
>
> (ll. 885–912)

One thing is certain. This Truth is not of human origin, she is divine. She is heralded by an angel; the crown of stars indicates her affinity with heaven; true believers clutch her golden hair and are eventually carried to heaven; she brings knowledge of mysteries; she carries doves in token of her purity, and serpents accompany her in token of the wisdom that knowledge of the Truth needs, and gives; her arms, like Truth's dominion, embrace the world; she shows her heart because Truth has nothing to conceal; she carries a sun to show that she is the ally of light, or rather is light herself, or to show that she is close to God—the sun—without whom there is no truth, and who himself is truth (*Ego sum via, veritas, et vita*); she carries the keys of power with which she unlocks the gates of heaven. Truth, says Ripa, lies in the agreement of the intellect with intelligible things. Truth is spotless, like light, and opposed to darkness—as Christ himself is called Light and Truth: this meaning will be carried by the splendour of her attire. For Jonson her mirror symbolizes the truth to which men's thoughts and deeds must be referred; Ripa explains the mirror by saying that as truth is perfect when the mind is in agreement with intelligible things, so the mirror is when its reflection of the objects in front of it is accurate.[88] And, finally, behind Truth shines "Eternall *Vnitie*" "'That *fire*, and *water*, *earth*, and *ayre* combines.'"

The problem that lies behind the *Barriers* is this: how can knowledge be attained of the eternal Unity which is the ground of the universe? Such knowledge is truth. Jonson stages an inconclusive debate because truth is ultimately beyond the reach of the unaided workings of the mind. Truth must descend from on high, ushered by an angel. Jonson knew, as we saw, that in the *Theaetetus* Homer's golden chain was said to symbolize the sun;[89] if he turned to the text of the dialogue itself he would find that Plato is there concerned with the problem of knowledge. He would find that there, the claims of perception, true judgment, and true judgment accompanied by an account or explanation[90]—*cognitio, opinio vera,* and *opinio vera cum ratione* in Ficino's version, which Jonson would certainly have used—to constitute knowledge are examined in turn and found unsatisfactory, so that at the end the problem remains unsolved, and we remain ignorant of what knowledge is. In Ficino's introduction to the dialogue he would not only find a discussion of fantasy, opinion and the discursive reason, but would discover why the problem of knowledge is not solved, and wherein, for Plato, true knowledge lies. There are two orders of things, says Ficino, the intelligible and the sensible, the one unchanging and incorporeal, the other changing and corporeal. And true knowledge lies only in the understanding of the intelligible, the divine order; only here lies certainty:

> There is therefore true knowledge, the sure comprehension of divine things by reason, a knowledge residing in the mind, flowing forth into reason, implanted in the mind by God, reduced to reason by the teacher of dialectic with God's help, directing reason to mind, and joining mind with the divinity.[a]

Such notions find their way through the century. The distinction between the intelligible and the sensible worlds persists, with its consequences for the theory of knowledge. Thus de la Primaudaye will write that "all things are either of this mutable and temporary nature or of the other which is immutable perpetual and aboue that nature" and will point out how strictly limited is the knowledge we can have concerning mutable and

---

[a] Est ergo scientia, diuinorum certa ratione compraehensio, in mente residens, in rationem profluens, Deo menti inserta, a dialectico praeceptore in rationem Deo aspirante reducta, rationem in mentem dirigens, mentem cum diuinitate coniungens.[91]

temporary things. True knowledge is concerned with things of the other order, and to attain this knowledge, fallen as our nature is, we need help:

> If the question be concerning immutable, perpetuall and supernaturall things, we haue neede of another light, that is greater and more agreeable to their nature, which is giuen to men by diuine inspiration. This light or knowledge is called *Sapience* or *Wisdome.*[92]

This drama of Jonson's, then, reminds us that truth cannot ultimately be found on earth, or by human means. Truth's home is in heaven; she must descend, ushered by an angel. For knowledge of truth, which is knowledge of the intelligible world and the eternal Unity, cannot be reached by the discourse of reason unless reason be aided by divine inspiration: only sapience or wisdom brings knowledge of truth. Such wisdom King James has—James who is the British Solomon. Such wisdom, and such knowledge are his to impart to his adoring subjects; and as a final magnificent, outrageous compliment Truth resigns her attributes to him:

> To whose right *sacred highnesse* I resigne
> Low, at his feet, this *starrie crowne* of mine,
> To shew, his rule, and iudgement is diuine;
> These *doues* to him I consecrate withall,
> To note his innocence, without spot, or gall;
> These *serpents*, for his wisedome: and these *rayes*,
> To shew his piercing splendor; those bright *keyes*,
> Designing power to ope the ported skyes,
> And speake their glories to his subiects eyes.
>> Lastly this *heart*, with which all hearts be true:
>> And TRVTH in him make *treason* euer rue.

Ben Jonson's *Haddington Masque:*
The Story and the Fable

I

The Viscount Haddington was one of those whom the king delighted to honour. He had saved the king's life—or so James said—in the notable affair of the Gowrie Conspiracy. Part of his reward was that he "got to his Bedfellow one of the prime *Beauties* of the Kingdom, daughter to *Robert* Earl of Sussex,"[1] the Lady Elizabeth Ratcliffe. Their marriage took place on Shrove Tuesday 1608 and was celebrated with proper magnificence; and the day was crowned by the performance of a masque devised by Ben Jonson and set by Inigo Jones, and attended by the king and the ambassadors.

II

The action of this masque is simple and nicely contrived to admit the necessary element of surprising spectacle; and in it Jonson first uses an 'anti-masque' to precede the masque proper, that is the entry of the masquers whose appearance constitutes the climax of the whole.

But first the setting, which Jones made appropriately simple. In the background is a high red cliff signifying, Jonson tells us, the "*height, greatnesse,* and *antiquitie*" of the bride's family, and also, by an obvious though dubious etymology, the origin of her name—Radcliffe.[2] In front of the cliff, on either side, stands a pilaster "chardg'd with spoiles and trophees, of loue, and his mother." These emblems are familiar enough—flaming hearts and so on; and among them we see "rocks and spindles," those ritual objects from the ceremonies of the Roman marriage with which Jonson after writing *Hymenaei* was so well acquainted.[3] Flying figures of Triumph and Victory join the pilaster to make an arch whose keystone is a garland of myrtle held between them. They are not described, but neither can have been far from the traditional representation of Victory: a winged female figure with a wreath of laurel or olive in one hand and sometimes a branch of palm in the other. Jones's figures, however, carry a wreath of myrtle, a plant that is peculiarly sacred to Venus.[4] It is the triumph and victory of Venus and Cupid that is celebrated here.

Behind the cliff are clouds which suddenly break open. From the clear sky thus revealed descends Venus, crowned with her star, in a chariot drawn by doves and swans. She is attended by the Graces. The action of the anti-masque begins.

For his anti-masque Jonson has chosen a dramatization of that poem by Moschus known to the Renaissance as *Amor Fugitivus*: a monologue in which Venus describes the person, attributes and powers of her runaway son Cupid, asks for help in finding him—offering a kiss as a reward—and warns of the dangers of harbouring him. It was a favourite poem and there were many adaptations before Jonson's.[5]

Venus tells her story and the Graces make formal proclamation, in alternate verses, of the loss, the reward and the description of Cupid. Suddenly, from behind one of the pilasters, Cupid himself appears surrounded by twelve boys representing "*the sports*, and *prettie lightnesses that accompanie* Loue." These boys fall into an amusing and fantastic dance which is the proper climax of the anti-masque. Cupid has been boasting of a feat

> That hath so much honor wonne,
> Vnto VENUS, and her *Sonne*,

but he refuses to tell his mother what it is and escapes from her, leaving the explanation to a new personage who now enters. This is Hymen, who comes with a rebuke to Venus for having left her star on the very night when it should have shone most brightly: the night of Cupid's triumph graced by the presence—and here he points to the king—of a new Aeneas.[6] Venus acknowledges that James deserves as much of her as ever her son Aeneas did and promises to cherish for his sake the man who saved his life. What is more, Hymen says, at this very moment Venus' own husband, Vulcan, is busy with his Cyclopes underneath the Red Cliff forging a "curious peece" to adorn the nuptials. No sooner has he spoken than Vulcan enters. At his word the cliff flies open to show a cavern in which stands an enormous celestial globe, eighteen feet in diameter, perpetually turning. On the globe, as well as "*the* Arctick *and* Antartick *circles, the* Tropicks, *the* Æquinoctiall, *the* Meridian, *and* Horizon," is the circle of the Zodiac, with the signs in gold. Under the Zodiac stand the masquers who represent the signs themselves. This globe, or sphere, signifies—so Vulcan tells Venus—"The *heauen of marriage*," while the twelve signs are the sacred powers that preside over marriage. Vulcan then explains the symbolism of the signs, ending thus:

> And thus hath VULCAN, for his VENUS, done,
> To grace the chaster triumph of her *sonne*.

And Venus replies:

> And for this gift, will I to heauen returne,
> And vowe, for euer, that my lampe shall burne
> With pure and chastest fire; or neuer shine,
> But when it mixeth with thy *spheare*, and mine.

So Venus and the Graces retire. Vulcan summons the priests of Hymen to sing, but is interrupted by Pyracmon, one of the Cyclopes, with the suggestion that the Signs should descend from the globe and dance. This they do at Vulcan's bidding, and the Cyclopes make music for them. Before each of their four dances Hymen's priests sing stanzas of the Epithalamium that ends the masque. With the appearance of the masquers and their dances the masque reaches its dramatic climax.

III

Jonson has, as usual, based his representations of the classical deities on the accounts given in the hand-books of mythology. Here, however, he seems to have used only Conti's *Mythologiae* and Cartari's *Imagini dei Dei degli Antichi*, which he knew in Verderius' Latin translation as the *Imagines Deorum*.[7]

Thus when Jonson describes the car of Venus as being drawn by both swans and doves (note on l. 44) and cites two passages from the *Metamorphoses* to justify his description he is following Conti's account of the car.[8] From the same chapter in Conti comes Jonson's note on Venus as *Nuptiis Praefecta* with the enumeration of the other deities who preside over marriage and the authorities quoted (note on l. 209); and in the same passage gives the quotation from Horace which Jonson gives to cover his introduction of the *Ioci* and *Risus* who attend Venus when she is acting in this capacity (note on l. 162).[9] The Cupid of Jonson and Moschus is common form; but for his wilder exploits—his power over the sun, Neptune, Jove, Minerva, Rhea and the rest—Jonson troubles to give his sources. Again he has turned to Conti, who provides the epigram by Philippus telling how Cupid despoiled the deities of their weapons, to which Jonson refers;[10] and here Jonson adds material he found in two of Lucian's dialogues.[11]

The case of Vulcan is more interesting. Indeed his role is crucial, but a full consideration of it must be deferred a little. Details of his appearance—and of some of his activities—Jonson owes to Cartari (though they could have been found elsewhere), whose influence is greater here than in any of the earlier masques. "The ancient *Poets*," we read, "whensoeuer they would intend any thing to be done, with great *Masterie*, or excellent Art, made *Vulcan* the artificer, as *Hom. Iliad* Σ in the forging of *Achilles* his armour: and *Virg.* for *Aeneas, Aenei.* 8." (note on l. 249). And at the end of the same note we have this reference: "For his description, read *Pausa. in Elia.*" Here Jonson is drawing on a passage in Cartari which tells how the Gods when they wanted arms for themselves or for anyone dear to them went to Vulcan, as Thetis did for Achilles' armour and Venus did for Aeneas, how "*Poetae, cum quidpiam magno cum artificio confectum, ac affabre factum describere volunt, id a Vulcano fabricatum dicunt,*" and how "*Ita is fuit in Cypseli arca exculptus, vt Pausanias in Eliacis prioribus refert, dicens, eum, qui Thetidi arma praeberet, claudum fuisse.*"[12] [The poets, when they wished to describe how anything was very artistically devised and skillfully done, said that it was made by Vulcan .... He was carved on the arch of Cypselus, as Pausanias reports in the chapter on ancient Elis, saying that he who supplied arms to Thetis was lame.] This lameness has passed into Jonson's description of Vulcan,

> attyr'd in a cassocke girt to him; with bare armes; his haire and beard rough; his hat of blue, and
> ending in a Cone ....
>   (ll. 255-7)

Other passages in this same chapter of Cartari have been pressed into service. Vulcan, we discover, is said to be lame, black, dirty, soot-stained—just like workers in iron—and should be so represented; some authorities describe him as naked, others as being half-clothed in rags and wearing a pointed cap (*pileus*); and elsewhere we are told that this cap is blue.[13]

Jonson of course based this episode of Vulcan and his Cyclopes forging a "curious peece" to adorn the nuptials on Virgil's account, in *Aeneid*, VIII, of how Vulcan makes arms for Aeneas—to this passage, specifically, we owe the presence of the three Cyclopes, Brontes, Steropes, and Pyracmon[14]—and on its original in *Iliad*, XVIII, where Vulcan forges Achilles's armour. And Jonson notes that the dance of the masquers, those supposed statues representing the signs of the Zodiac, was suggested by Homer's account of Vulcan's moving tripods or "stooles with golden wheeles" in this same episode. He adds that this "is in the *Poet* a most elegant place, and worthy the tenth reading" (note on l. 327).

But the story of Jonson's debt in this masque to his Homeric studies must be carried further. Jonson, like Chapman, read Homer in the edition by the French scholar Jean de Sponde—Spondanus—which contains a Latin translation and an elaborate commentary as well as the Greek text.[15] And if we read about the forging of Achilles's armour in this same edition we find suggestions which led Jonson to make his Vulcan forge a moving celestial sphere with animated signs of the Zodiac.

Here are the tripods which interested Jonson so much:

> She (Thetis) found him in a sweat
> About his bellows, and in haste had twenty tripods beat
> To set for stools about the sides of his well-builded hall,
> To whose feet little wheels of gold he put, to go withal,
> And enter his rich dining room alone, their motion free,
> And back again go out alone, miraculous to see.[16]

And here is what Spondanus says about them:

> Therefore this movement of the tripods is spontaneous, like that of the celestial sphere, of which the Milanese philosopher has made a model, which in our time may be seen moving itself with a strong and natural motion in either direction.[a]

---

[a] Fuit ergo motus hic tripodum spontaneus, qualis in sphaera illa coelesti, quae nostro tempore visa est vtroque motu se mouente, nimirum violento & naturali cuius artificium videtur exhibere Philosophus Mediolanensis de Rerum varietat. lib. 12.[17]

Here the tripods are compared to the modern revolving celestial sphere as described by the ingenious Cardan.[18] And if we read a little further we find that Vulcan was credited with having made a celestial sphere which–possibly–moved. The passage on the shield of Achilles was then as now one of the most admired 'places' in the *Iliad*. And it offered splendid opportunities for allegorical interpretation. The shield, Spondanus holds, is nothing less than an image of the universal orb, showing the moving heavens and stars, sea and land, cities at peace and in war, and the diverse occupations of man.[19] Spondanus takes these lines from the beginning of the description of the shield:

> And first he forg'd a strong and spacious shield
> Adorn'd with twenty several hues; about her verge he beat
> A ring, three-fold and radiant, and on the back he set
> A silver handle; five-fold were the equal lines he drew
> About the whole circumference.[20]

And makes this comment on them, following, he tells us, Eustathius:

> What he calls 'a ring, three-fold and radiant' he says is to be understood as the Zodiac, which is called triple on account of its width, through which the twelve signs move, and radiant because of the perpetual journey of the sun in that circle. By the silver handle he means the axis round which the heaven revolves. By the five folds, the five parallel or equidistant circles, that is to say, the northern, the summer solsticial, the equatorial, the winter solsticial, and the southern.[b]

Here are the features of the celestial sphere: the circle of the Zodiac and the other circles. And Spondanus has already recorded that in the view of some scholars all the features of the shield move spontaneously–"just like Vulcan's tripods."[22]

From these suggestions, then, come Jonson's revolving celestial sphere and animated signs. His interpretation of the signs as the powers governing marriage seems, however, to be an invention of his own.

IV

Venus and the Graces, Cupid, Hymen, Vulcan–these figures were familiar and recognizable. And to recognize Vulcan was to know him for the artificer. The Zodiac and its signs were part of the stock of common knowledge. And the story that links these figures is simple enough and self-explanatory: the hunt for the runaway Cupid, Vulcan forging the "curious peece" to adorn the nuptials; so far there is nothing but an elegant rendering of classical story ingeniously applied to the particular occasion but not over intricate or difficult to follow.

[b] Quod autem ἄντυγα τρίπλακα μαρμαρέην ('a ring, three-fold and radiant') appellat, ait intelligi Zodiacum, qui triplex dicatur propter eius latitudinem, per quem duodecim mouentur signa: et splendens, propter Solis perpetuum in illo circulo iter. Per ἀργύρεον τελαμῶνα ('A silver handle') axem intelligit, circa quem coelum voluitur. Per quinque plicas, quinque circulos parallelos vel aequidistantes: nimirum Septentrionalem, Solstitialem, Aequatorem, Brumalem, Antarticum, etc.[21]

But the association of these figures has its grounds in more than casual ingenuity. Venus and the Graces, Cupid and his Sports, Hymen and Vulcan and the Signs play necessary parts in conveying with strict accuracy a general truth which makes the masque more than the elegant celebration of a particular marriage, which turns the story into a fable: a fable about marriage, or, specifically, about procreation which is the fulfilment of marriage.

It is Vulcan who gives the key to the meaning of the fable. Vulcan wears, as we have already noted, a blue pointed cap. And Cartari, from whom Jonson took this detail, explains that Vulcan is the power of fire and that the blue cap symbolizes the heavens where pure fire is found. The fire we know on earth, nourished as it is by matter, has lost its purity; the flames we see on earth waver from side to side because their impurity prevents them from going straight up. The lameness of Vulcan symbolizes the wavering movement of these earth-bound flames.[23] There were three ways of interpreting the pagan myths: there was the moral interpretation, the historical interpretation and the interpretation according to natural philosophy. It is this last kind of interpretation that Cartari is giving here and that Jonson adopts throughout this masque—as, for example, Bacon was to adopt it in several of the chapters in his handbook of mythology, *De Sapientia Veterum, The Wisdom of the Ancients.* Conti's book was a prime source of this reading of the myths *ad physicam*, as he calls it, and it is Conti who gives the explanation of Jonson's fable.

In his note on Vulcan (l. 249, n. a) Jonson says that he "is also said to be the god of *fire* and *light*. Sometime taken for the purest beame: and by *Orph. in Hym.* celebrated for the *Sunne* and *Moone*." All these points are taken from Conti,[24] whom Jonson is still following in this important passage:

> But more specially, by *Eurip.* in *Troad.* he is made *facifer in nuptiis.* Which present office we giue him here, as being *calor naturae* and *praeses luminis.*[25]

Vulcan is not in fact torch-bearer at these nuptials; but Jonson associates him with marriage and knows and tells us what are the real grounds of this association that are symbolically expressed by making him torch-bearer. Vulcan is associated with marriage because he is light, and especially because he is heat: *calor naturae.* As Conti, whose words Jonson is giving us, explains:

> Since natural procreation cannot take place among mankind without the presence of heat, for this reason torches—which were thought to be in charge of Vulcan—were kindled at marriages.[26]

Vulcan is the heat without which procreation cannot take place; and—adopting the same mode of interpretation—Venus is nothing else than the hidden desire for copulation grafted in human nature in order that procreation may ensue.[27] For procreation, then, the conjunction of Vulcan and Venus is necessary. This is why they are represented as being man and wife, and why the influence of both is needed if a marriage is to be successful, and why their appearance in a wedding masque is so appropriate. It is as "Praefect of Mariage" that Venus appears;[28] and it is emphasized that this night of all nights her influence—exerted through her star—is required.

The "iocound sports" of the anti-masque have also their place in the fable. They "*accompanie* Loue, *vnder the titles of* IOCI *and* RISVS; *and are said to wait on* VENUS, *as she is* Praefect *of* Mariage" (ll. 160–2). To support this Jonson quotes a line from Horace:

Erycina ridens
Quam Iocus circumuolat, & Cupido.

Conti gives this quotation and later explains that Venus favours laughter for either of two reasons: because laughter favours love or because creatures are liveliest when ready to breed.[29] In this context Cupid too has his part to play. Jonson is careful to tell us that he is here "expressing" "*Cupid*, as he is *Veneris filius*"[30] (and not, for instance, the Platonic Cupid who is the child of Porus and Penia). As the son of Venus Cupid is the divine power which draws like to like and promotes their union.[31] So it is right that Cupid should appear. And it is equally right that his part should be confined to the anti-masque. When he has brought the pair together Cupid's part is done. He makes way for Hymen, the solemnization of the union through ritual, its social sanction, and for Venus and Vulcan who must effect its perfection. And just as Cupid, Vulcan and Venus see to the perpetuation of the human race, so do the Graces see to the perpetuation of human society; for they are the graces, that mutual exchange of goodwill through which cities flourish and civilized life is possible.[32]

V

The form of the masque demands that the appearance of the masquers and their dances should constitute the climax of both symbolic and dramatic action. The appearance and descent of the signs of the Zodiac, then, and their dances should clinch the meaning of Jonson's symbolic scheme. And this is the case.

The dances are accompanied by a wedding song with a clearly defined burden; it can be seen from these two stanzas, the first and the last:

Vp *youthes* and *virgins*, vp, and praise
   The *god*, whose nights out-shine his daies;
HYMEN, whose hallowed *rites*
Could neuer boast of brighter lights:
   Whose bands passe libertee.
Two of your troope, that, with the morne were free,
   Are, now, wag'd to his warre.
      And what they are,
   If you'll perfection see,
      Your selues must be.
Shine, HESPERVS, shine forth, thou wished *starre*.

That, ere the rosy-fingerd *morne*

> Behold nine moones, there may be borne
>   A babe, t'vphold the fame
> Of RADCLIFFES blood, and RAMSEY'S name:
>   That may, in his great seed,
> Weare the long honors of his *fathers* deed.
>   Such fruits of HYMENS warre
>   Most perfect are;
>   And all perfection, wee
>   Wish, you should see.
> Shine, HESPERVS, shine forth, thou wished *starre*.

'Perfection' is the burden of the song. Each stanza ends with the invocation to Hesperus —Venus' star—preceded by four lines introducing the idea of perfection: the perfection of marriage in general and of the Haddington marriage in particular. And that marriage is the perfection of life Jonson already knew: in *Hymenaei* he had quoted from a classical source this comment: "*Nuptialls are therefore calld τέλειοι because they effect Perfection of life, and do note that maturity which should be in Matrimony.*"[33]

The celestial globe and the signs of the Zodiac are visible and actual symbols of the perfection celebrated in the song.

Jonson calls his machine (including the Signs) the "heauen of marriage" and describes it thus:

> It is a *spheare*, I'haue formed round, and euen,
> In due proportion to the *spheare* of heauen,
> With all his *lines*, and *circles*; that compose
> The perfect'st forme, and aptly doe disclose
> The *heauen of marriage*: which I title it.
>   (ll. 276–80)

The sphere is of course the most perfect of all forms.[34] And it was a commonplace that the heavens were themselves perfect, being composed of a mixture of elements so truly proportioned that it undergoes neither change nor corruption. Their movements are circular, and the circle which has neither a beginning nor an end is also a perfect shape. The signs are the powers presiding over marriage, or, to translate, the characteristics, physical, moral and social, possessed by the bride and bridegroom which will ensure the success of the marriage. And only a few weeks before Jonson had introduced the Zodiac as part of a visual image of Perfection, borrowed from Ripa's *Iconologia*.[35] With this association in mind, and considering that the Zodiac is one of the circles "that compose the perfect'st forme" Jonson could easily justify his introduction of the signs as part of this new symbol of perfection in marriage.

It is particularly apt that the machine created by Vulcan, for the sake of Venus, to celebrate this wedding should take the shape of "the heauen of marriage." The perfection of the heavens depends on the absolute symmetry of that mixture of the elements of which they are made. The creatures can only reproduce their kind when they are in a state of vigorous health. This vigorous health depends on an *apta elementorum symmetria* produced by Vulcan, or heat—and this is one of the reasons why he is called the husband of Venus.[36] And it is the procreation of children that signalizes perfection in marriage:

> That, ere the rosy-fingerd *morne*
> > Behold nine moones, there may be borne
> > > A babe, t'vphold the fame
> > Of RADCLIFFES blood, and RAMSEY's name:
> > > That may, in his great seed,
> Weare the long honors of his *fathers* deed.
> > Such fruits of HYMENS warre
> > > Most perfect are;
> > And all perfection, wee
> > > Wish, you should see . . . .

This is the moral of the fable, and the last, best wish that can be offered.

Chapman's *Memorable Masque*

I

Chapman's only masque, or only surviving masque, was written for the Middle Temple and Lincoln's Inn as their contribution to the great festivities that celebrated the wedding of King James's only daughter Elizabeth to the Elector Palatine in February 1613. It was one of three, the others being Campion's *The Lords' Masque* and Beaumont's, written too for the Inns of Court and sponsored by Bacon, *The Masque of the Inner Temple and Gray's Inn*. Chapman's collaborator for setting and costumes was Inigo Jones.

This is a simple masque; but its simplicity is an elegant simplicity. And its elegance lies in the economy and ease with which it accomplishes its aim. Chapman prefixed to the printed text an indignant answer to critics who had objected to the length of the speeches. His defence consists in saying that the length of the speeches was made necessary by the nature of the masque form itself, and he defines the nature of masque in terms of its scope:

> as there is no poem nor oration so general, but hath this one particular proposition; nor no river so extravagantly ample, but hath his never-so-narrow fountain, worthy to be named; so all these courtly and honouring inventions (having poesy and oration in them, and a fountain to be expressed, from whence their rivers flow) should expressively arise out of places and persons for and by whom they are presented; without which limits they are luxurious and vain.[1]

Chapman's achievement lies in the economy and ingenuity with which he accomplishes this aim, in his variation and application of themes, so that the voice of his masque sounds to present occasions while the sense lays hold on more removed mysteries—to use Jonson's formulation of the proper aim of the masque writer: Jonson who said, you will remember, that apart from himself only Chapman could make a masque. And it is this success that makes Chapman's masque worth analysis, not simply because it is Chapman's, but as an example of the English masque in its most precise form. It is interesting to see, besides, how well a constricted, sharply defined form suited Chapman: his masque is very well written, both prose and verse—the songs are charming. The same is true of those comedies where the classical form acted as both discipline and release.

II

We may begin an analysis by quoting Chapman's own "Applicable Argument":

> Honour is so much respected and adored that she hath a temple erected to her like a goddess; a virgin priest consecrated to her (which is Eunomia, or Law, since none should dare access to Honour but by virtue, of which Law, being the rule, must needs be a chief), and a Herald (called Phemis or Fame) to proclaim her institutions and commandments. To amplify yet more the divine graces of this goddess, Plutus (or Riches) being by Aristophanes, Lucian, etc., presented naturally blind, deformed, and dull-witted, is here, by his love of Honour, made see, made sightly, made ingenious, made liberal, And all this converted and consecrate to the most worthy celebration of these sacred nuptials; all issuing (to conclude the necessary application) from an honourable temple, etc.

This Temple of Honour is placed on an eminence to one side of the central feature of the scene, a great rock rising almost to the roof. On the other side in the rocks, balancing the temple, is an enormous dead tree. The rock is veined with gold and at the summit is all of gold.

Plutus, who is formally the presenter of the piece, appears. Capriccio, a figure whose fantastic costume is derived from Ripa's *Iconologia*, suddenly enters the scene by bursting through the rock. (See Figure 42.) The dialogue between them ends in a dance of baboons; and this is the formal anti-masque. The rabble dismissed, the masque proper begins. Plutus calls Eunomia to appear from the Temple of Honour and begs her to grant access to Honour so that her appearance may grace these nuptials. Honour and Phemis join Plutus and Eunomia on the stage. Honour calls Phemis to summon the Virgin knights whom she has brought from Virginia for this occasion. The Phoebades, or priests of the sun enter and to the accompaniment of their song the summit of the mountain opens disclosing the Virginians seated in a mine of gold, their torchbearers before them, and behind them the sun setting in the sky. This is the hour when the Virginians perform their evening rites; and the Phoebades address a hymn of worship to the sun. This is countered by another hymn addressed to the true Phoebus, King James. Eunomia summons the princes to descend, renounce their false worship, and turn to the British Phoebus. The torchbearers come down, dance—and this is described as another 'anti-masque'—and are followed by their masters. Their dances constitute the climax or dénouement of the masque; and these past there is a hymn to Love and Beauty, after which the masquers dance again with the ladies. A final invocation to sleep and a short speech to the masquers by Honour bring the masque to an end – the masquers, led by Plutus, Honour and the rest, making their exit through the Temple of Honour.

III

The main proposition of this masque is the reconciliation of opposites, of warring, antagonistic forces. In the Temple of Honour, Honour and Virtue are reconciled. Chapman has brought Virtue – or a specific aspect of virtue – into Honour's temple as her priestess; but what he had in mind were the Roman temples of Honour and Virtue, which he knew through descriptions. These temples were placed so that one had to go through that of Virtue in order to enter the temple of Honour, "*vt ostenderetur, aditum non patere ad verum honorem consequendum, nisi per virtutem ipsam*" [in order to show that there is no approach to true honour except through virtue]. Chapman might have read of these temples in many places; but I have quoted the phrase which his own words echo from one of his favourite source-books, Vincenzo Cartari's *Imagini degli Dei*.[2] And the idea that true honour proceeds from virtue is a commonplace with the moralists of the sixteenth century who wrote on this topic: "the subiect and materiall cause of honour ys even vertue itself which shineth and glisteneth of yt self" – so wrote the Englishman Robert Ashley in his essay on honour.[3] But the topic is fundamental in such well known treatises, for example, as those by Stefano Guazzo and Annibale Romei.

In linking Honour with Virtue, then, Chapman was not doing anything out of the ordinary. As indeed he is not when he makes Fame appear as Honour's herald; for however attitudes might differ about the precise role or value of fame, or opinion – for opinion was a questionable affair – it was agreed that honour was essentially linked to public esteem. In choosing to make his Virtue assume the specific aspect of Eunomia or Law Chapman was, however, giving the topic a significant and very Chapmanesque twist. To understand what he is doing we must understand two things: first, what the evil correlative of honour is; and, second, the breadth of the meaning of Law.

There is a significant passage in Plutarch's *Praeceptae gerendae reipublicae* in the *Moralia*, which Chapman knew well:

> As for ambition, although it carrie with it a fairer shewe than avarice, yet neverthelesse it bringeth after it a traine of mischiefes and plagues, no lesse dangerous and pernitious unto the government of a common-wealth: for accompanied it is ordinarily with audatious rashnesse more than it; inasmuch as it useth not to breed in base mindes, or in natures feeble and idle, but principally in valiant, active, and vigorous spirits; and the voice of the people, who by their praises lift it up many times and drive it forward, maketh the violence thereof more hard to be restrained, managed, and ruled. Like as therefore *Plato* writeth, that we ought to accustom yong boies even from their verie infancie to have this sentence resounding in their eares: That it is not lawfull for them neither to carrie gold about their bodies as an outward ornament, nor so much as to have it in their purses, for that they have other golde as a proper coffer of their

owne, and the same incorporate in their hearts: giving us to understand by these ænigmaticall and covert speeches (as I take it) the vertue derived from their auncestors, by descent and continuation of their race; even so wee may in some sort cure and remedie this desire of glorie, by making remonstrance unto ambitious spirits, that they have in themselves gold, that cannot corrupt, bee wasted or contaminated by envie, no nor by *Momus* himselfe the reproover of the gods, to wit Honour, the which we alwaies encrease and augment, the more we discourse, consider, meditate, and thinke upon those things which have beene performed and accomplished by us in the government of the common-weale: and therefore they have no need of those other honours, which are either cast on moldes by founders, or cut and graven in brasse by mans hand, considering that all such glorie commeth from without foorth, and is rather in others than in them, for whom they were made.[4]

The evil correlative of honour is ambition−or ambition is the excess of the virtue of honour as pusillanimity is its defect, to use the Aristotelian terminology of writers who dwell on this point, like Robert Ashley or Amadis Jamyn, who pronounced before the Académie du Palais a discourse entitled *Discours de l'Honneur e de l'Ambition*. To be ambitious is to desire to move beyond one's proper place, to threaten the subversion of that order which is the fabric of society and the universe: the sin of Lucifer. The function of honours−the tribute paid to the personal honour that comes from virtue−is precisely to maintain this order. As Guazzo has it:

> Honours and high rank distinguish courageous and magnanimous men from the base and idle: honours worthily employed bestow universal benefits, by keeping the peace, maintaining justice, encouraging the good and punishing the wicked, observing divine and human laws. Honours are the most welcome and precious gift of princes, testimony of virtue, stairway to greatness, physic to poverty, antidote to injuries, well-spring of joy, sea of consolation, gateway to happiness, sustainer of life, triumph over death.[a]

The expression of this fundamental order is law. Honour therefore must come within the rule of Law.

Chapman had already written a tragedy dedicated to the exploration of these questions, of the relationship between honour and law, honour and ambition, honour and virtue. This was the double tragedy of the conspiracy and fall of *Charles, Duke of Byron* (1608).

> See in his revolt how honour's flood
> Ebbs into air, when men are great, not good,

declared the prologue.[6] Byron is the exemplar of the man whose honour-become-ambition turns into treason as he involves himself in conspiracy against the state−which indeed owes much to him, but to which he himself owes much. It is worth noting how the idea of

---

[a] Gli honori, & le dignità distinguono le persone valorose, & magnanime dalle vili, & inutili. Gli honori degnamente impiegati recano vniuersal beneficio per la conseruatione della pace, per lo mantenimento della giustitia, per fauor de'buoni, per castigo de'rei, per osseruanza delle diuine, & humane leggi. Gli honori sono gratissimo, & pretiosissimo dono de' Prencipi, testimonio delle virtù, scala della grandezza, medicina della pouertà, antidoto contra l'offese, fonte d'allegrezza, mare di consolationi, porto di felicità, sostenimento della vita, et trionfo della morte.[5]

law is emphasized in the tragedy: the king, Henry, refuses to condemn Byron until he has been found guilty by due process of law. And in another way this tragedy is important for our understanding of another reconciliation that Chapman proposes through his Temple of Honour. This is the reconciliation of Honour and Virtue with Fortune. The figure of Fortune does not appear, but her emblem does. Crowning the cupola of the temple the audience saw a round stone of silver with a pair of golden wings growing out of it:

> The round stone (when her feet trod it) ever affirmed to be rolling, figuring her inconstancy; the golden wings denoting those nimble powers that pompously bear her about the world; on that temple (erected to her daughter Honour and figuring this kingdom) put off by her and fixed, for assured sign that she would never forsake it.

The dispute between Fortune and Virtue, and about whether honour is achieved through one or the other, was a great topic in Renaissance discussion; it goes back to classical sources, of which the most important, the *locus classicus* of the argument, is another of Plutarch's essays, once again in the *Moralia*, his *De Alexandri Magni fortuna aut virtute*. Now it was shown long ago that Chapman had made extensive use of this essay in the Byron plays: and one scholar has recently and I think rightly seen this relationship as the key to Chapman's intentions, his Byron being an Alexander in reverse.[7] Alexander represented for Plutarch the triumph of virtue over fortune; this is how Byron is made to see himself. But the identification is wildly mistaken: Byron is claiming a virtue that is not his. His ambition is in fact the perversion of virtue, his tragedy lies in his rejection of virtue. It is the king, the great opposing figure, who is the true Alexander. And some words of the king's show how close the context of ideas in the masque lies to the tragedy: towards the culmination of his prayer for his new-born heir he says,

> Let him by virtue quite cut off from Fortune
> Her feathered shoulders and her winged shoes,
> And thrust from her light feet her turning stone
> That she may ever tarry by his throne.
> (I.i. 141–44)

In his masque Chapman did not seek to deny the role of Fortune—no one ever did: Honour is her daughter. But he asserts the reconciliation of Fortune, Honour and Virtue.

He also shows the reconciliation of Plutus or Wealth with Virtue or Honour. Behind this, I suspect, lie traces of the old dispute about true nobility, and the part played in it by wealth, a question which had rather vexed those concerned. But if wealth did not confer nobility, the true use of wealth was nevertheless an element in nobility: this was the virtue of liberality, as opposed to the excess, prodigality, and the defect, avarice. We are also to remember, certainly, that this was particularly true of the king. Liberality was an important kingly virtue—as James himself had emphasised in his *Basilicon Doron*. Love of Honour has transformed the ugly, blind, maimed Plutus of the classical writers; and it is such a purified use of wealth that must be in question. He is associated with Capriccio in the anti-masque because Capriccio stands for unprincipled wit (that Capriccio really possesses wit is not in question), working at the service of the highest bidder: the bellows, which in Ripa show willingness to praise virtue, here show that Capriccio can puff up with glory all who affect him, and the spur, which had indicated capacity to punish vice, has become an instrument for punishing those who will have nothing to do with him. To pay for the services of such a creature is to buy—the wrong use of wealth—false honour. (And there is presumably an oblique comparison intended between such unprincipled wits and the poet of the masque, who sings only of true honour). The baboons introduced by Capriccio are parodies—apes—of true honour. They are dressed like 'fantastical travellers' in foreign clothes: such travellers were familiar contemporary types of those aping false gentility; and they are trying to win honour by prodigal scattering of largesse, in this case *cockle-demois* instead of money.

How all these reconciliations have been effected we shall see; the important thing to remember is that the Temple of Honour, as Chapman tells us, figures England.

IV

Having discussed the presentation of the virtues and the anti-masque let us pass to the third movement, which contains the discovery of the masquers in their mine of gold, the rites done to the sun, and the invitation to the masquers to descend.

We now come to the pivotal image of the masque, that of King James as the sun. The Virginians are presented as sun-worshippers. Chapman is clearly not thinking of Virginia here at all: behind this lies some account of the religion of the Incas; but his version has perhaps this bit of factual support, that Harriot had described the Virginians as worshipping one God, who had created other gods as his instruments in the creation of government in the world, and then the sun, moon and stars as petty gods. From this account, worship of the sun could be deduced. But Chapman, as we shall see later, is not concerned, or is only concerned within certain limits, with the actual Virginians.

To the sun of the Virginians is opposed the British Phoebus. The priests sing an invocation to the setting sun; another set of singers hymns the rising sun—James—

> our dear Phoebus, whose true piety
> Enjoys from Heaven an earthly deity.

Honour summons them thus:

> of your fit devotions turn the events
> To this our Briton Phoebus, whose bright sky
> (Enlightened with a Christian piety)
> Is never subject to black Error's night . . . .

To understand what is happening here, and the full bearings of the sun image, we have, I think, to keep in mind such a range of ideas as is presented by another of Chapman's favourite authors, Marsilio Ficino, in his little treatise *De Sole*. To worship the sun was in some sense already to worship God. Ficino collects the evidence from the 'ancient theology' about the gentile worship of the sun, and its reasons; and he proceeds to elaborate a set of comparisons between God and the sun, incorporating, as usual, the pagan material within the Christian:

> *perspicuam Dei statuam in hoc templo mundano, ab ipso Deo positam, intuentibus ubique praeceteris admirandam* [the bright statue of God placed by God himself in this temple of the world, to be admired with wonder everywhere, before all else].[8]

This image of himself has been placed by God in the tabernacle of the world. The movement from the Virginians' sun to this sun is as easy as the movement from the Orphic sun to the Christian sun. It is a reconciliation rather than a violent conversion, a reconciliation facilitated by the fact that James *is* the sun: in certain senses he had always been that in England. He was the sun that had come to lighten the thickening darkness over England on the old queen's death, and was so hailed at his ceremonial procession through London on his accession. In the same pageant he had been hailed as Apollo, being himself a poet and protector of the muses, on the triumphal arch erected by the Italians, and elsewhere; and this image followed him. In the preface to the Authorized Version of the Bible, which was published two years before Chapman's masque, James was still being hailed as the "sun in his strength" who had "dispelled those supposed and surmised mists" and "thick and palpable clouds of darkness" that many thought would have overshadowed the land on Elizabeth's death. This image of the king as sun is too common to require further illustration; but James is also, here, explicitly, sun-as-God: his

> true piety
> Enjoys from Heaven an earthly deity—

"an earthly deity" because he is a king (and kings are divine, little gods, as James himself called them in *Basilicon Doron*), marked by his true piety. But what are the limits of the sense in which the Virginians are being called to worship James because in worshipping him they will be worshipping God, or what was the precise meaning of the divinity of the king asserted by James and others, it is perhaps better not to enquire too closely. We are dealing with a highly ambiguous area of meanings and feelings, as we are when we ask what precisely, in Ficino's mind, was the relationship between the image and the thing imaged, between the sun and God.

The last reconciliation that is to be accomplished is nothing less than the reconciliation of earth and heaven. This is presaged in the song calling the rock to open, which precedes the songs to the sun.

> Ope, Earth, thy womb of gold,
>   Show, Heaven, thy cope of stars.
> All glad aspects unfold,
>   Shine out and clear our cares;
> Kiss, Heaven and Earth, and so combine
>   In all mixed joy our nuptial twine.

The gold of Virginia has been reconciled with the true sun of Britain, as the earthy Plutus has been transformed through his reconciliation with the heavenly Honour. What remains to show is the reconciliation of heaven and earth through love, instanced in the marriage which now is being celebrated. "The bride and bridegroom were figured in Love and Beauty", Chapman tells us, and in a song sung to them, he invents a little myth about the origins of love and beauty. Love and Beauty are twins born of Panthaea (a deity who does not figure in the mythologies) and Eros:

> Bright Panthaea, born to Pan
> Of the noblest race of man,
> Her white hand to Eros giving,
> With a kiss joined heaven to earth
> And begot so fair a birth
> As yet never graced the living.

And this Briton Phoebus has this power because, and I return to Ficino, the sun is

Supereminens coeleste lumen, coelestia temperans, et mundana. Harmonicum mundi cursum ducens, sive trahens.[9]

[Most majestic heavenly light, ruling celestial and earthly things, guiding or leading the harmonious course of the world.]

Ficino is here paraphrasing the Orphic hymn to the sun. Or again,

Solem apud theologos veteres Apollinem arbitror nominatum, et harmoniae omnis authorem, ducemque Musarum, quoniam animos non tam manifestis quam occultis influxibus radiorum a confusa quadam turba resoluat, et harmonice moderetur, atque ad intelligentiam postremo perducat.[10]

[I believe that the sun was called by the ancient theologians Apollo, and the author of all harmony, the leader of the Muses, because he sets free minds from disorder and confusion, and regulates them by harmony, not so much with the visible as with the secret influence of his rays, and finally leads them to intelligence.]

V

We must, finally, turn to the political meanings of the masque. Something of this has been noted, but not, I think, the full implications. Virginia was obviously a topical subject. This was the period of the great concerted efforts to settle the colony on a large scale. In 1609 a new, second charter had been given to the company; and in 1612 a third. It was the period of the voyages which so profoundly influenced *The Tempest*, a play almost contemporary with the masque. The theme of the conversion of the Virginians to Christianity is central; for this was one of the main objects of the colonizers: this was asserted again and again by the preachers and pamphleteers who were busy defending and making propaganda for the enterprise, and was insisted on by the company itself. So much is palpably clear. But more oblique political references seem to be intended.

Chapman's American land is as much Guiana as it is Virginia; in fact there is more of Guiana in it. The worship of the sun, we have seen, is not really Virginian, but must come from some account of the sun-worshippers whom the Spaniards had met and conquered. The gold—the mountain of gold—is not Virginian at all. This comes from Guiana:

> Guiana where rich feet are mines of gelde,
> Whose forehead knockes against the roofe
> of Starres:

so Chapman had written in 1596 in the commendatory verses to Laurence Keymis' account of the second voyage to Guiana. And this of course brings us to Ralegh. It was Ralegh who discovered Guiana for the English; it was he who wrote the first account of it, and he who dreamt of its fabulous riches in gold and dreamt of finding El Dorado there. Nor did Ralegh forget his dream; from the Tower he had been attempting to revive interest in an expedition to Guiana, and in 1612 he had offered to send Keymis there again, offering to fit out vessels at his own expense. In 1616 he persuaded James to release him from the Tower and allow him to return to Guiana to find the great mine. We know of Chapman's connexions with the Ralegh circle, and I cannot doubt that the colonizing projects and the political ideas of the Ralegh circle are present in this masque. For this circle—and for a far wider one—colonizing expeditions in the Americas had from the beginning been also part of an anti-Spanish policy, a Protestant anti-Catholic policy. Now whatever reservations may have been in the king's mind, the marriage of his only daughter Elizabeth to the Elector Palatine was hailed in England as a Protestant stroke against Spain, a great Protestant match which would consolidate the forces of England and Germany. Indeed for some years relations between Spain and England had been steadily worsening, for reasons connected both with Europe and the colonies. Late in 1612 the Spanish government was indeed considering sending an expedition against Virginia, and when the marriage and the masque were performed Spanish feeling was still high. Indeed in the beginning of 1613 a Spanish invasion of England was feared and precautionary measures were taken. Set in this context, then, Chapman's masque takes on a quite sharp relevance to the marriage it celebrates and the political circumstances of the moment. Reminders of Virginia and Guiana, of the Christian duty of colonizing, of the fabulous wealth that lay at hand, had bearings that cannot have been missed by the king to whom they were directed, or by anyone else. And this too was proper in a masque which had to arise "expressively . . . out of the places and persons for and by whom it was presented."

Name and Fame:
Shakespeare's *Coriolanus* [1]

"estrangement between your name and you"
W. H. Auden

I

Name is fame, is honour, and is won by deeds; in Rome, by deeds in war.

> Now in those days, valliantnes [so North renders Plutarch] was honoured in Rome above all other vertues: which they called *Virtus*, by the name of vertue selfe, as including in that generall name all other speciall vertues besides. [2]

So Cominius the general in his formal encomium, his *laus* of Caius Marcius, begins:

> It is held
> That valour is the chiefest virtue and
> Most dignifies the haver. [3]

We are shown the deeds of Coriolanus, and their rewarding in the field: the garland, the horse, the name with the consenting acclamations. Cominius proclaims:

> Therefore be it known,
> . . . that Caius Marcius
> Wears this war's garland; in token of the which,
> My noble steed, known to the camp, I give him,
> With all his trim belongings; and from this time
> For what he did before Corioli call him
> With all th' applause and clamour of the host,
> Caius Marcius Coriolanus.
> Bear th' addition nobly ever! [4]

Drums and trumpets sound and the gathered army shouts, in formal acclamation:

Caius Marcius Coriolanus!

Coriolanus enters Rome wearing the wreath, and a herald proclaims:

> Know, Rome, that all alone Marcius did fight
> Within Corioli gates, where he hath won,
> With fame, a name to Caius Marcius; these
> In honour follows Coriolanus.
> Welcome to Rome, renowned Coriolanus![5]

And again there is formal acclamation by the city, people and patricians:

> Welcome to Rome, renowned Coriolanus.

And Volumnia says:

> My gentle Marcius, worthy Caius, and
> By deed achieving honour newly nam'd
> What is it, Coriolanus must I call thee?[6]

Those speeches Shakespeare did not find in North's Plutarch (in general it may be taken that what I am pointing to in Shakespeare is not in North: significant coincidences I shall indicate).

Honour as reward for virtue, as a motive for action, is taken for granted. So is our concern for self-perpetuation in futurity: it is to this that our procreation of children, our anxiety to continue our names, our practice of adoption, inscriptions on monuments, panegyrics, all testify—so Cicero says.[7] It is the name that endures. All this is so quietly assumed—Plutarch does so throughout—that it requires only formal statement: as by the women in their last appeal to Coriolanus to spare the city—and here Shakespeare has expanded and heightened his source—when his wife Virgilia speaks as one

> That brought you forth this boy to keep your name
> Living to time.[8]

And Volumnia recalls the existence and function of the historian:

> if thou conquer Rome, the benefit
> Which thou shalt thereby reap is such a name
> Whose repetition shall be dogg'd with curses;
> Whose chronicle thus writ: "The man was noble,
> But with his last attempt he wip'd it out,
> Destroy'd his country, and his name remains
> To th' ensuing age abhorr'd . . . ."[9]

Banished from Rome, Coriolanus makes his way to his and Rome's chief enemy, Aufidius the Volscian, enters his house in disguise, and with his head "muffled." This is from the source. But new is Coriolanus' dialogue with the servants, and with Aufidius when he is sent for:

Aufidius. . . . Thy name?
    Why speak'st not? Speak, man. What's thy name?
Coriolanus [*unmuffling*].   If, Tullus,
    Not yet thou know'st me, and seeing me, dost not
    Think me for the man I am, necessity
    Commands me name myself.
Aufidius. What is thy name?
Coriolanus. A name unmusical to the Volscians' ears,
    And harsh in sound to thine.
Aufidius. Say, what's thy name?
    Thou hast a grim appearance, and thy face
    Bears a command in't; though thy tackle's torn,
    Thou show'st a noble vessel. What's thy name?
Coriolanus. Prepare thy brow to frown—know'st thou me yet?
Aufidius. I know thee not. Thy name?[10]

This leads up to the disclosure of the name, in a speech that follows North closely:

  Coriolanus. My name is Caius Marcius, who hath done
     To thee particularly, and to all the Volsces,
     Great hurt and mischief; there to witness may
     My surname, Coriolanus. The painful service,
     The extreme dangers, and the drops of blood
     Shed for my thankless country, are requited
     But with that surname—a good memory
     And witness of the malice and displeasure
     Which thou shouldst bear me. Only that remains:
     The cruelty and envy of the people,
     Permitted by our dastard nobles, who
     Have all forsook me, hath devour'd the rest;
     And suffered me by th' voice of slaves to be
     Whoop'd out of Rome.[11]

In *Coriolanus*, as in the other two plays in which he is substantially concerned with the critique of honour, *Henry the Fourth*, Part I and *Troilus and Cressida*, Shakespeare takes honour won in war and sets it in relation to the civil life, seen as "the specialty of rule", which in all three plays is offered as "policy." Here its scope is within the city, Rome.

II

   . . . by the voice of slaves to be
   Whoop'd out of Rome.

In a passage where Shakespeare has wished to assimilate and preserve the recorded words of history so faithfully, the smallest departure from his text marks an act of significant choice. His transformation of North's "let me be banished by the people"[12] is radical. *Whooped* is a trivial word: a whoop is a phatic gesture expressing what its context requires. It is rare in Shakespeare, and only here does he use it as part of a transitive verb. This weight augments the sense of its triviality; it cheapens those who use it, and him it is used against. Itself meaningless, it is uttered by the voice of the people (that Shakespeare should make Coriolanus call them, here, slaves belongs to a story other than that I am telling now). What has made Shakespeare's play possible is the meaning of the word 'voice.'

Voice, *vox*, is what utters, and what is uttered, and also what is uttered in a special restricted and technical sense. This technical sense we translate as *vote*. It is what Hamlet means when he says of Fortinbras

> . . . I do prophesy the election lights
> On Fortinbras, he has my dying voice.[13]

In the procedure of election to the Elizabethan House of Commons the first and often the only method was that by voice; this means in the first instance literally what it says, by utterance. The election was held at the County Court, presided over by the sheriff. If there were more nominations than seats, then the electors shouted for their man, and the sheriff had to decide who had more voices. Coriolanus is elected consul by the voices of the people: the voices that whoop him have the technical meaning.

It is the word Shakespeare found in North; and North had it from Amyot's French, which he was following. Amyot uses *voix* to translate Plutarch's ψῆφος; or sometimes *voix et suffrages*. Amyot was accommodating the Roman to the French usage; and North[14] could take his word over because French *voix* and English *voice* coincided in their applications. Yet for the Englishman the meaning was more urgent: its immediate association with the turbulence of Elizabethan elections guaranteed that; and a curious point verifies the supposition. When it came to Coriolanus' final formal trial before the people, Plutarch describes how the Tribunes rigged the voting by arranging that it should be done not by centuries but by tribes, to guarantee a majority for the people. Amyot, thinking it necessary to explain how this worked, inserted a parenthesis in the text:

> à cause que les voix se comptaient par tête.[15]

North retained this and translated *tête* by *poll*:

> bicause their voyces were numbred by the polle.[16]

This is a highly technical phrase and brings Coriolanus right into the thick of a disputed English election. Numbering by the poll was the last resort—heads were counted as the qualified voters passed before the sheriff or his officer. At this point, says Sir John Neale—whose account of procedure I have been following—"the lists compiled during the canvassing seem to have come in useful both for marshalling the voters and recording their names and their votes."[17] And it is this procedure that Shakespeare envisages when, before

Coriolanus comes to face the people, he makes one of the tribunes say to an aedile – sheriff's officers, obviously –

> Have you a catalogue
> Of all the voices that we have procur'd,
> Set down by the poll?[18]

The word *voice*, then, in a flash, holds a past world and a present world together. Further, it is an active word, containing act, situation, what utters, the uttering as well as the significance of what is uttered. The degree of abstraction required to make it synonymous with vote, to separate that out from the act, is high and could, I believe, only be achieved in a strictly controlled context. What is likely to happen is shown in a sentence Neale quotes from a letter written in 1614 by an anxious parent to a son about to stand for Parliament: "Your friends must not be spare-voiced, but with their voices pronounce it (i.e. his name) roundly and fully."[19] The tribune's meaning, controlled as it is by "catalogue", "procur'd" and "set down", is clearly closer to the neutral sense given in, say, an election writ. But Hamlet's lines have in them as well as the formal vote the physical act we watch, a man speaking in anguish, in a death agony. Coriolanus' "by the voice of slaves" contains act and significance.

In act II scene iii Coriolanus, back from the wars in triumph, his surname formally pronounced, standing for the consulship, the final honour that the city can bestow, must, as the custom is, stand in the forum, wearing the napless vesture of humility, display his wounds, and ask the people for their voices. This word echoes through the scene. Formally, at the beginning: "if he do require our voices, we ought not to deny him," "Are you all resolv'd to give your voices?" With a sense of the act: "everyone of us has a single honour in giving him our own voices with our own tongues." On Coriolanus' lips, humiliated, frustrated, furious that he should come to this, the word is qualified mockingly: *good* voice, *sweet* voice, the *tune* of your voice, *worthy* voices – resentment at the power of what they say, of the uttering, and his need of it, expressed by the ironical assumption that it is the uttering itself that he is wooing and the people are their voices, personified voices. Here is the bitter climax of this episode:

> Here come moe voices.
> Your voices. For your voices I have fought;
> Watch'd for your voices; for your voices bear
> Of wounds two dozen odd; battles thrice six
> I have seen and heard of; for your voices have
> Done many things, some less, some more.
> Your voices?[20]

When the tribune speaks of "all the voices that we have procur'd," the use is quite technical and the abstraction is so complete that the sense of the act has quite gone; when Coriolanus says "Here come moe voices" we see the men; his synecdoche reduces their whole reality to this one function or attribute. This is supported by the assimilation of the people to the organs of speech. They are mouths, or tongues, in the heads that contain them, with a reference to the polls that are counted, and there are two inclusive references, to Hydra, the monster with many heads, and to the anthropomorphic image of the body politic established by Shakespeare—however equivocal his purposes may be—in the first scene of the play when he makes Menenius retail, from Plutarch, the famous apologue of the belly and the other members of the body. From voice there are further stages. When the tribunes pronounce the formal sentence of banishment Coriolanus turns on the people—the last time he speaks to them:

> You common cry of curs, whose breath I hate
> As reek o' the rotten fens . . . .[21]

From the human voice to the cry of animals. Not the cry of hounds, those noble and disciplined beasts, but of base-born and ill-conditioned curs. With those lines compare Cominius and Menenius to the crowd when the news of Coriolanus' approach on the city has come:

> *Com.*   Y'are goodly things, you voices!
> *Men.*   You have made
> Good work, you and your cry![22]

and, in the same scene, Menenius to the tribunes:

> . . . you that stood so much
> Upon the voice of occupation and
> The breath of garlic-eaters![23]

Voice and breath need not be paralleled; voice is subsumed in breath.

> Not all the water in the rough rude sea
> Can wash the balm off from an anointed king;
> The breath of worldly men cannot depose
> The deputy elected by the Lord.[24]

In those famous lines from *Richard II* the passage voice/breath is clear; and so is the significance of reducing voice/vote to what it uses or is made of. Coriolanus pleads that he be not forced to expose his wounds

> As if I had received them for the hire
> Of their breath only.[25]

And the power, existence, of the mob is located in its stinking breath:

> Nor showing, as the manner is, his wounds
> To th' people, beg their stinking breaths.[26]

These are prologues to the banishment and election scenes; and it is to this that Coriolanus and Menenius return. And further, voice like *vox* has a technical sense in grammar: a voice means *word*, what is uttered, and the voice, utterance, that Coriolanus is asking for, is his name.

III

Let us start again, this time from a passage in one of Seneca's letters. He is trying to convince Lucilius that to argue for the worth of posthumous renown (*claritas*) does not contradict the view that there is no such thing as an extrinsic good. It is the opposition's arguments, as Seneca presents them, that concern us:

> "Dicitis", inquit, "nullum bonum ex distantibus esse? Claritas autem ista bonorum virorum secunda opinio est. Nam quomodo fama non est unius sermo nec infamia unius mala existimatio, sic nec claritas uni bono placuisse. Consentire in hoc plures insignes et spectabiles viri debent, ut claritas sit" . . . . "Claritas", inquit, "laus est a bonis bono reddita; laus oratio, vox est aliquid significans; vox est autem, licet virorum sit bonorum, non bonum."

And, a moment later, he reiterates such objections:

> "Quid ergo", inquit, "et fama erit unius hominis existimatio et infamia unius malignus sermo?" "Gloriam quoque", inquit, "latius fusam intellego, consensum enim multorum exigit."

And again:

> "Ad gloriam aut famam non est satis unius opinio."

And:

> "Sed laus", inquit, "nihil aliud quam vox est, vox autem bonum non est."[27]

All this Shakespeare's contemporary, Thomas Lodge, in 1614 rendered:

> Thou wilt say, You other Stoicks maintaine that no good is composed of things distant. But this glorie whereof we entreat, is a fauourable opinion of good men. For as a good fame is not one man's words, neither infamy one mans misreport: so is it not praise to please one good man, many famous and worthy men must consent herein to make it glorie . . . . glorie (saith he) is a commendation given by good men to a good man: commendation is a speech, a speech is a voice that signifieth something. But the voice, although it be a good mans voice, is not goodnesse . . . .

and:

> What then (saith he) shal fame depend vpon the estimate of one man, and infamie be tied to the mis-report of another man? Glory also (saith he) as I understand, is spread more largely. For it requireth the consent of many men.

and:

> "The opinion of one man (saith he) sufficeth not to give glory and renowne vnto another."

and—the Latin being simply "laus nihil aliud quam vox est, vox autem bonum non est":

> But praise (saith he) is but a voice spread in the ayre, and that a word meriteth not the name of good.[28]

Claritas, for which Lodge takes *gloria* as synonym (justifiably, I think, at this point in that word's long eventful history); *fama*; *laus*; *existimatio*; *opinio*; *vox*; glory; fame; report; praise; opinion; voice. Let us add *honor* and *nomen*, honour and name. These are the words Shakespeare inherited.

It is a set of words describing certain relationships between a man and other men, all seen as together forming a group or community; relationships that will or may survive the death of that individual man, on the unvoiced assumption that the community will have a continuing existence.

Gloria is an intensification of honour; it is the relationships described by honour that come first. The most famous definition of *honor* is certainly Cicero's: "cum honos sit præmium virtutis iudicio studioque civium delatum ad aliquem, qui eum sententiis, qui suffragiis adeptus est, is mihi et honestus et honoratus videtur."[29] [Since honour is the reward for excellence given to someone by the judgment and enthusiasm of the citizens, he who has received it by their opinion and choice seems to me both honourable and honoured.] Here, in the opening clause, Cicero is, in fact, translating a phrase from Aristotle, in the *Nicomachean Ethics*. And these passages of Aristotle, with Cicero himself, and some passages from Stoic writers were to be the main sources for sixteenth-century discussion. Aristotle is concerned to show that τιμή—honour—is not the "good". It is the end of the political or public life, but it cannot be the final good because it is extrinsic to the subject: it is thought to depend on those who confer honour rather than on him who receives it.[30]

Later, we have honour—"the due of the gods and what is desired by the eminent and awarded as the meed of victory in the most glorious contests"—as "the greatest of external goods."[31] And in the *Rhetoric* he lists the marks of honour—a list that was to be repeated, brought up to date, commented on—in many a sixteenth-century discourse:

> sacrifices; commemoration, in verse or prose; privileges; grants of land; precedence; sepulchres; statues; pensions; among foreigners, obeisances and giving place; and such gifts as are among various bodies of men regarded as marks of honour.[32]

The marks of honour demonstrate the relationship an individual has with his community, and with the continuing city; but they follow a judgment made on him, a judgment of value. Honouring is an act of which he is the subject, proceeding from *existimatio*, estimation, issuing in *laus*.

Who judges and who praises? Ideally the whole community. This, we are told, was fundamental to the prime meaning of the Roman *gloria*. Even to ask the question was to question and modify the whole concept of *gloria* as stimulus and reward of action; and this happened, we are told, in the last century of the Republic, under the pressure of social and political changes, and found its formulations in the disquiet of Greek philosophers. The disquiet was about the basis of the judgment that issues in the marks of honour; and is focused on the word δόξα with its double sense of 'my opinion,' *opinio*, and 'the opinion others have of me.' What certainty does *opinio* hold? If it holds none, what then is the basis of fame, reputation, renown, what *is* opinion?—a question Cicero and Seneca received from the Stoics. A temporary way of answering it is to restrict the judgment and the verdict to those competent to make it: *bonorum virorum secunda opinio.*[33] With *gloria* or *honor* goes *fama*:

> Gloria est frequens de aliquo fama cum laude.[34]

Gloria and *honor* depend on *fama*, and *fama* comes from *opinio*. *Fama*, my fame, is what people say about me: it is the utterance of the judgment or opinion. One citizen says to another in the first scene of *Coriolanus*:

> Consider you what services he has done for his country[35]

and gets the answer

> Very well, and could be content to give him good report for't but that he pays himself with being proud.[36]

This good report is quite strictly the *fama* which is *praemium* for Coriolanus' services. But from the beginning *Fama*'s words are dangerously ambiguous; for *Fama* contains *Rumor*:

> With regard to rumour and common report, one party will call them the verdict of public opinion and the testimony of the world at large; the other will describe them as vague talk based on no sure authority, to which malignity has given birth and credulity increase.[a]

And it is of *Fama-Rumor* that Virgil and Ovid made their powerful and fortunate images. Ovid's House of Fame, we recall, is made of sounding brass:

> The whole place resounds with confused noises, repeats all words and doubles what it hears. There is no quiet, no silence anywhere within. And yet there is no loud clamour, but only the subdued murmur of voices, like the murmur of the waves of the sea if you listen afar off, or like the last rumblings of thunder when Jove has made the dark clouds crash together. Crowds fill the hall, shifting throngs come and go, and everywhere wander thousands of rumours, falsehoods mingled with truth, and confused reports flit about. Some of these fill their idle ears with talk . . . .[b]

Fame's connections with words, breath, air, wind, are established in the classical images. Her trumpet figures this connection. The first instance I have found of the metaphor is in Juvenal,[39] and the full development seems to be certainly post-classical, but Fama was *nuntia veri* in Virgil,[40] and very often indeed, in other writers, *nuntia*. And there are the

---

[a] famam atque rumores pars altera consensum civitatis et velut publicum testimonium vocat: altera sermonem sine ullo certo auctore dispersum, cui malignitas initium dederit, incrementum credulitas.[37]

[b] tota fremit vocesque refert iteratque quod audit;
nulla quies intus nullaque silentia parte . . .
atria turba tenet: veniunt, leve vulgus, euntque
mixtaque cum veris passim commenta vagantur
milia rumorum confusaque verba volutant;
e quibus hi vacuas inplent sermonibus aures . . . .[38]

potent Virgilian phrases: the *ventosa gloria*[41] of which the unlucky warrior speaks to Camilla, and the splendid line in his own prayer to the Muses:

et meministis enim, divae, et memorare potestis; ad nos vix tenuis famae perlabitur aura.[42]

[For you, goddesses, remember and can retell; some faint breath of fame scarcely wafts to us.]

Shakespeare knows the tradition. We hear in *Romeo and Juliet* of "Three civil brawls bred of an airy word"[43]; in *Troilus and Cressida* of "that breath fame blows" and of fame's trump and "Having his ear full of his airy fame".[44] But the whole image had been shown in *Henry IV*, Part II, where, as Induction, Rumour enters "painted full of tongues", making the wind her post-horse. The trumpet is no longer an attribute of *Fama-Rumor*: it *is Fama-Rumor*, and included in the metaphor is the mob:

> Rumour is a pipe
> Blown by surmises, jealousies, conjectures,
> And of so easy and so plain a stop
> That the blunt monster with uncounted heads,
> The still discordant wav'ring multitude,
> Can play upon it . . . .[45]

This is Ovid's mob. Or Cicero's, when in his Stoic vein, he rejects popular judgment: fame, he says—*famam popularem*—cannot be counted a good when it is called into being by the united judgment of fools and knaves (*stultorum inproborumque*), and if things like fine eyes or a good colour are to be so considered then the philosopher's seriousness is no better than the *vulgi opinione stultorumque turba*.[46] Or Montaigne's in his essay on Glory, when he rejects "honor and glory, which is nought but a favourable judgement that is made of us". "And the judgement of our inclinations and actions (the waightiest and hardest matter that is) we referre it to the idle breath of the vaine voice of the common sort and base raskalitie . . . . In this breathie confusion of bruites, and frothy Chaos of reports and of vulgar opinions, which still push us on, no good course can be established."[47] For honour, glory, and fame are not to be dissociated. They are all favourable judgments, and the expression of the judgment is in speech, words, voices, which are breath and air, or wind, because the voice that utters does so through the vehicles of breath and air. It is because of this complex I have tried to describe that Falstaff can be made to say

"What is honour? A word. What is in that word? Honour. What is that honour? Air."[48]

IV

Honour, Name and Fame are words, *voces*. They are voices because voice is both uttering and what is uttered; they are acts of judgment or opinion issuing in words. Their relationship to their subject is that of word to things. A word has two relationships: to him who utters it, and to its subject. Further, uttering happens in a community and establishes a relationship between the subject and that community; words are what the community says about him. They must be right, and the rightness of the relationship lies in its truth. It must be true between speaker and word, and true between word and thing. Language, what people say to each other about things, is constitutive of society, of the civil life. Working within the scheme I have outlined, exploiting and realizing its semantic possibilities as only Shakespeare in his full greatness could, Shakespeare offers a show of the civil life in terms of empty, perverted, destructive relationships between speaker and utterance, word and subject, which is between man and man and man and himself. In this play no one is innocent, except Virgilia who is silent: "My gracious silence."[49]

Honour and fame are words that go with the deed. The formal position—shown in the honouring of Coriolanus in the field—is simple. It posits a simple, direct act, involving recognition, between word and deed. Honour is naming the deed. They cannot be separated. In the city honour is not given, the deed is not named without request— "policy," which expresses the way of keeping society together, imposes this. The act of naming is expressed by voices.

Of all formulas connected with the word none is more ancient than that which, in various versions, states an opposition between word and deed. This formula is basic for the play. Deeds, blows, acts are consistently opposed to words—in simple ways like this:

> Has struck more blows for Rome
> Than thou hast spoken words[50]

or:

> When blows have made me stay, I fled from words.[51]

But the formula mutates into an opposition between deed, and word as *vox*; voice. It is the implied ground of that speech I have already quoted:

> Here come moe voices.
> Your voices. For your voices I have fought;
> Watch'd for your voices; for your voices bear
> Of wounds two dozen odd . . . .[52]

Voices, *voces* are the opposite of deeds or acts. They are devalued further through their definition as breath, light and empty; and stinking breath, offensive. Yet the mob's voices are intolerable because they are voices that are acts: acts of uttering that are acts of decision. Voice is deed and not deed in the same moment. Coriolanus' deeds, which must be named, fall into this nexus, the relationship between name and thing is disrupted: deed must be *honour*, its name, its *voice*. Deed, being named, passes into its opposite: voice.

In seeking the voices Coriolanus is a subject looking for his name: it is his name that will be uttered. But the search leads him into the gravest danger. He must ask.

"The price is to ask it kindly", says a citizen.[53] In Coriolanus' mind to ask is to beg. He sees himself as a beggar troubling the poor with begging, the napless vesture of humility as a disguise. When he takes it off, he says, he will know himself again.

> . . . It is a part
> That I shall blush in acting.[54]

The beggar is like the actor: he mimics what he is not and utters words that are not his. The danger for Coriolanus is that to get his voice he must seem what he is not and utter words that are false and have no right relationship to the speaker: analogous relationships of falsity. Still more is required of him: the trap springs a second time. Acting and speech again go together. Brought in to persuade her son that he must formally appear before the tribunes and the people, answer the charges brought against him and accept their verdict, their voice, for otherwise the city will be destroyed, Volumnia instructs Coriolanus that he must act a part and speak the words appropriate to his role of suppliant for mercy, and she seeks to convince him that to do so is consistent with his "honour." Coriolanus opposes to all this the idea of nature, disposition, truth, himself. Words and action must correspond directly to the nature which is a man's truth. This idea of his about words is reiterated through the play. It is recognized by friends and enemies alike:

> His heart's his mouth;
> What his breast forges, that his tongue must vent.[55]

Volumnia allows for it; he must speak to the people not

> . . . by th' matter which your heart prompts you,
> But with such words that are but roted in
> Your tongue, though but bastards and syllables
> Of no allowance to your bosom's truth.[56]

Coriolanus is persuaded. Then he is permitted a moment of illumination—he cannot stand by it because his mother, not arguing, but taunting, dominates him—when he knows that to accept the role will be to destroy himself:

> . . . I will not do't.
> Lest I surcease to honour mine own truth
> And by my body's action teach my mind
> A most inherent baseness.[57]

There is, he says, a truth; it must be named in honour by himself and no other. Honour is the name for it and he must give it. To do otherwise, to utter words that do not correspond or perform actions that contradict, is to alter his very being.

The relationship is between "I" and "myself." To trace the history that made possible this great leap, through Stoic and Christian—Montaigne in such a context quotes St. Paul: *Gloria nostra est testimonium conscientiæ nostræ*, and Montaigne in his quotation is following Augustine,[58] and through the critique of chivalry with which Shakespeare is explicitly and persistently concerned: the history of the interiorizing of honour, which is never quite complete—all this would be beyond my power. Shakespeare is using at this moment the language of the Schools. It is the only time in his whole *oeuvre* that he uses the word *inherent*; and I cannot believe that he did not fully know its technical use in connection with substance. What Coriolanus is being asked to do is to transform disgracefully his being.

In *Troilus and Cressida*, where honour and love are treated, conceptually, as cases of "estimation", and the question is specifically asked whether value is intrinsic or extrinsic, the doubleness of Cressida–Troilus's Cressida, Diomede's Cressida, every man's Cressida –becomes, with painful irony–for it was Troilus who had insisted that value lies only in estimation–proof that a thing can be itself and other than itself in the same moment; and this denies the principle of oneness, which guarantees being, which rests on the sacred and indivisible *unitas*:

> If there be rule in Unitie itself
> This is not she,[59]

he cries. Being is disrupted and the fabric of the universe torn.

In *Coriolanus* we are concerned only with the community or city, *civitas*, localized as Rome, the *urbs*, in danger of destruction. Questions of the self, its maintenance or destruction, rise within the social context and are limited to that. A name stands at the centre of the play; and it is in the name that these questions are focused.

The name is a voice, a word, one of the two fundamental parts of language, which the ancients distinguished, names or nouns and verbs. It is the vocable that belongs to a man:

> Nomen est quod uni cuique personae datur, quo suo quaeque proprio et certo vocabulo appellatur.[60]

It can go with Fame, in the Name and Fame formula, because a name is the word people use about me. It states both individuality and membership of family and group. It is the third name, the *cognomen*, Coriolanus, that most strictly marks the individual: no one else has this:

> The third, was some addition geven, either for some acte or notable service, or for some marke on their face, or of some shape of their bodie, or els for some speciall vertue they had.[61]

Giving the name "Coriolanus" to him is to give him fame, a name that will last, honour, a new individuality, like a baptism:

> By deed-achieving honour newly nam'd.[62]

It asserts his uniqueness, but a uniqueness that is an *assertion*, a uniqueness given in relationship to those who gave it. When he comes to Aufidius, muffled, disguised, and the question "What is your name" echoes, he answers, as we saw: "*Only that name remains.*"[63] All else is devoured. Cominius, on a fruitless embassy from Rome, later, reports

> . . . 'Coriolanus'
> He would not answer to; forbad all names;
> He was a kind of nothing, titleless
> Till he had forg'd himself a name i' th' fire
> Of burning Rome.[64]

In the scene that immediately follows, when Menenius goes to see Coriolanus, the theme is pointed, serio-comically, in his dialogue with the guards. He appears as Coriolanus' reporter: he is in estimation with him: he is Coriolanus' liar–so the forthright soldiers turn the phrase:

> The virtue of your name
> Is not here passable,[65]

they greet him with; and mockingly when he goes,

> *1 Watch.*   Now, sir, is your name Menenius?
> *2 Watch.*   'Tis a spell, you see, of much power![66]

What is the relationship that word or name holds with the thing named? Here we come to the old story of whether words or names relate to their objects by nature or convention. Shakespeare knew both accounts. His statement of one has become proverbial:

> 'Tis but thy name that is my enemy;
> Thou art thyself, though not a Montague.
> What's Montague? It is nor hand, nor foot.
> Nor arm, nor face, nor any other part
> Belonging to a man. O be some other name!
> What's in a name? That which we call a rose
> By any other name would smell as sweet;
> So Romeo would, were he not Romeo call'd,
> Retain that dear perfection which he owes
> Without that title. Romeo, doff thy name,
> And for thy name, which is no part of thee,
> Take all myself.[67]

It is a virtuoso handling of the argument. Put it beside the paragraph which introduces Montaigne's essay on *Glory* (he is working from Sebond):

> There is both name, and the thing: the name, is a voice which noteth, and signifieth the thing: the name is neither part of thing nor of substance: it is a stranger-piece joyned to the thing, and from it.[68]

But when Adam named the beasts he named them according to their natures: the connection was real, not conventional. Further, as Dr. Walker has said, in his discussion of this view in the sixteenth-century Neo-Platonic texts: "the word is not merely like a quality of the thing it designates . . . it is, or exactly represents, its essence or substance."[69] So it came about that the name has power, is magical; and so it can be said that the name Menenius carried to Coriolanus has virtue, is *a spell of power*. And on this view Juliet is wrong—and the play shows it—when she argues that Romeo's self can be disseevered from his name, which is indeed a part of him. Shakespeare does not always laugh, like the sceptical soldiers. It seems to me that the name, in his usages, hovers in an ambiguous zone, its status not quite determined, and the possibilities capable of powerful exploitation. Take that sinister little scene in *Julius Cæsar* when the mob, loosed by Antony, blind and frantic, encounters the poet Cinna. The answer to his scream

> I am not Cinna the conspirator,

is

> It is no matter, his name's Cinna; pluck but his name out of his heart . . .[70]

It is precisely the ambiguity that makes that so resonant. And it is, for instance, in such ambiguity, such doubt, that lie the tragedy and destruction of Richard II, who has to learn to ask what is the connection between his name and him.

> Is not the king's name twenty thousand names?
> Arm, arm my name! a puny subject strikes
> At thy great glory.[71]

In the abdication scene meditations on crown and self—"I must nothing be"—are followed by refusal of forms of address:

> ... I have no name, no title—
> No, not that name was given me at the font—
> But 'tis usurped ... ,[72]

and the call for a mirror. Name and mirror: guarantees of a continuing self. Meditations on either are dangerous, and subversive. And, at the end, in prison, Richard's recreation of himself through a sequence of images comes back to this:

> ... Then am I king'd again; and by and by
> Think that I am unking'd by Bolingbroke,
> And straight am nothing ... .[73]

Montaigne, whose essay so clearly demonstrates that the argument about Fame is an argument about Name, when he rejects honour, glory, fame, rejects his name. His surname is common to all his race; his Christian name belongs to anyone that wants it: "I have no name that is sufficiently mine." "As for me," he says, "I hold that I am but in my selfe; and of this other life of mine, which consisteth in the knowledge of my friends, being simply and barely considered in my selfe, well I wot, I neither feel fruite or jovissance of it, but by the vanity of fantasticall opinion."[74]

This way is not permitted to Coriolanus, for he is involved in the active life. He has a name that is sufficiently his, unique. Banished from Rome, it is all that remains to him. And this he rejects, as he has rejected the city: "I banish you."[75] Properly—the city gave it. He must forge a new name in the fires of Rome, as Herostratus—it is the example always used—perpetuated his name by burning down the great temple of Diana at Ephesus.[76] Without "Coriolanus" he is "a kind of nothing, titleless."[77] What is nameless is monstrous, "a deed without a name." It belongs to the realm that is not subjugated. "When he shall be able to call the creatures by their true names he shall again command them," wrote Bacon from his dream of knowledge that is power.[78] Naming gives identity to nothings. It is also the poet's function: his pen gives shapes to the forms of things unknown, products of the imagination, "to airy nothing a local habitation and a name ... ." Shakespeare is here using as a frame of reference a great argument of which he shows elsewhere—as in *The Tempest*—full knowledge.

The monstrous, the unsubjugated, the unknown, the nothing, are what is outside the frontier of language, or the frontier of the human. For language is vehicle and expression of *ratio*, of reason, of what makes man man. A Macbeth denies his humanity, and an idiot's gabble is the metaphor for the final nonsense to which he has reduced his world. The origins of language, if we follow those ancient writers who denied that it was given by a God or some nameless lawmaker, are inextricably connected with the joining together of men in groups—"in conversation with each other," with the origins of building and law.[79] Naming is within the family and the community: it asserts individuality through relationships. The community, the rational, human life, is defined by the walls of the city: it is the life of *conversazione civile*, civil intercourse, *civil conversation*—and our meaning for that word was separated out of the first: the earliest meaning of *conversation* is *living together*. The bond is language. The city of *Coriolanus* is certainly London, but first it is Rome, *Urbs*, *the* city: consciousness of the city is sustained throughout the play, in awe, question or doubt: often from the lips of the unimportant, the bystanders. Banished from the city, banishing the city, Coriolanus leaves the pale of humanity: he sees himself and is seen as a lonely dragon, one of those fabled or perhaps real monsters from which men, in story, sheltered themselves behind the city walls. When Aufidius' servant says:

> Where dwell'st thou?

he answers

> I' the city of kites and crows:[80]

a total reversal of meaning—scavenger birds that feed on carcases.

And, finally, he is titleless, a kind of nothing. To lose the *name* is to lose the self, and at that moment when the women come to intercede he asserts his singleness, his refusal of relationships: he will

> stand
> As if a man were author of himself
> And knew no other kin.[81]

He cannot sustain this, and breaks himself; and indeed in the Shakespearean world it is blasphemy. From the beginning Coriolanus had been accused of denying relationships in the city: of pride, of speaking of the people as though he were a God to punish, "not a man of their infirmity."[82] The basis is in North where Shakespeare read that Coriolanus was "churlishe, uncivill and altogether unfit for any mans conversation."[83] Consistently he equates "good words" to the people as false words: "flattery."

Finally he accepts again his relationships, with mother, wife and child; with the city in which his son will perpetuate his name, of whose history his name will be part. This identification brings accusation in Corioli: his last outbursts are reassertions of his name, his Romanness, of himself, his Fame—they go together:

> If you have writ your annals true, 'tis there,
> That, like an eagle in a dove-cote I
> Fluttered your Volscians in Corioli.
> Alone I did it.[84]

This great play, relentless, unremitting, misunderstood, offers us no easy comfort of confirmed anticipation or imagined identification. And not the liberating ritual comfort of tragedy. It is a show of the civil life. The city must stand and must continue, for outside it there is the monstrous, or the nothing. But within the walls absolutes turn out to be instrumental; the words that identify and bind become words that debase and destroy: whoops, or hoots, curses, lies, flatteries, voices, stinking breath. Words are torn from what they signify. They pass into their antonyms. Deeds are not—deeds. Names are not—names. The absoluteness of the self, the I, cannot be maintained; but the necessary relationship of the I with name or fame destroys. In this city to speak is to be guilty.

Veritas Filia Temporis:
Hadrianus Junius and Geoffrey Whitney

I

In his essay published in *Philosophy and History*[1] Fritz Saxl traced the various uses to which the motto "Veritas Filia Temporis" was put by English monarchs from Henry VIII to Elizabeth, showing how it was made to serve the causes of Protestantism and Catholicism in turn. I wish to indicate some uses of the motto in the same period which Saxl did not deal with.

There is a dramatic use of "Veritas Filia Temporis" centring round the figure of Mary Tudor, who had adopted the motto as her personal device, and representing the confluence of several streams of tradition.

In 1553 was published "a merye enterlude" called *Respublica*, "made in the first yeare of the moost prosperous Reigne of our moste gracious Soverainge, Quene Marye the first." The plot of the play is simple. The widow Respublica, who laments the plight into which she has fallen, is deceived by Avarice, Oppression, Adulation and Insolence, into taking them as her ministers. (They present themselves as Policie, Reformation, Honesty, and Authority.) Naturally things go from bad to worse, and People's state is worse than it had ever been. God sends Misericordia, Veritas, Iusticia and Pax to help Respublica; the villains are unveiled, and judged by Nemesis, who departs leaving Respublica under the tutelage of the four sisters. The application of the play is made clear by the Prologue, who ends:

> We children, to youe olde folke, bothe with harte and voyce

Maie Ioyne all togither to thanke god and Reioyce
That he hath sent Marye our Soveraigne and Quene
to reforme thabuses which hithertoo hath been.
And that yls whiche long tyme have reigned vncorrecte
shall nowe foreuer bee redressed with effecte.
She is our most wise and most worthie Nemesis,
Of whom our plaie Meneth, tamende that is amysse;
Which to bringe to passe, that she may have tyme and space,
Leat vs, booth yong and old, to Godde commend her grace.[2]

The first reference to Veritas is in the first part of the prologue:

veritee the daughter of sage old Father Tyme,
Shewith all as yt ys, bee it vertue or Cryme.

The second is in III, vi. Avarice is bidding his fellow conspirators make the most of their opportunities:

. . . Now tyme willnot tarye & therefore take good hede:
despache while tyme serveth and all your matiers spede.
Tyme hath no reine nor bridle/but renneth a pace . . . .
And tyme hath this one vngracious propertee
to blab at length & open all that he dothe see.
Than a daughter eke he hath, called Veritee,
As vnhappie a long-tounged girle as can be.
she bringeth all to light, some she bringeth to shame,
she careth not a grote what Manne hath thanke or blame.
yf men be praise worthie, she dothe so declare them,
And if otherwyse, in faithe, she dothe not spare them.

In V, ii Misericordia has arrived, and comforted Respublica with promises of help, and gone to fetch Veritee to diagnose the causes of Respublica's decay. Avarice enters just before she leaves and is disturbed by her arrival, although he pretends to welcome her. While he is talking with Respublica, Adulation enters to announce Veritee's arrival:

. . . I have certaine Newes / which are bothe brym & hotte,
there is newe sterte vp a ladye cald Veritee.

Avarice is vexed by the news and asks if Adulation is certain: is it the real Veritee?—

        . . . of whiche Veritee wast, trowe youe, that thaye spake ytt?
Adul: Of the generall Veritee, Olde tymes daughter. /
Avar: Feith, they were not our frendes that firste hither brought hir.
        Old tymes doughter? that shuttle brained tall, long man,
        That nere standeth still / but flyghth as fast as he canne,
        muche like as he swymmed or glided vppon yce?
Adul: yea.

Resp: for all that, of wise men, he is thought mooste wise.
Avar: I knowe hym; he carrieth a clocke on his heade,
         A sandglasse in his hande, a diall in his foreheade.
Resp: ye saie truthe, Policie, the same is veraye he.
Avar: Old tyme the evisdropper; I knowe hym, pardee.
         An Auncient turner of houses vpside downe,
         & a common consumer of Cytie and towne.
         Old tymes doughter (quod he)? I shrewe his naked harte;
         Manie of my frendes hathe he brought to paine & smarte.

When Veritee enters with Misericordia (V, iii) she tells Respublica the true names of her ministers. Pax and Iusticia enter (V, iv) and so the four sisters are reunited and take charge of Respublica. In V, ix the sisters meet the Vices. Avarice boldly asks their names. This is his dialogue with Veritee:

Ver: I am dame Veritee.
Avar: What, the daughter of Tyme?
Ver: yea.
Avar: I knowe my Mr. your father well afyne.
        welcome, faire Ladie, swete ladie, litle Ladye,
        plaine ladie, smoothe ladie, somtyme spittle ladye,
        Ladie longtong, ladye tell-all, ladye make-bate,
        & I beseche youe from whence are ye comme of Late?
Ver: I am sproong oute of the earth.
Avar: what, ye doo butt ieste.
Ver: The booke saieth *Veritas de terra orta est.*
Avar: happie is he which hathe that garden platte, I trowe,
         owte of which such faire blossomes doe springe & growe.[3]

Veritee then unveils Avarice for what he is.

   In this presentation of Truth there are three points to note. Truth is the daughter of time. This is not surprising in a play written to honour Mary Tudor. (Veritee delivers a laudation of Nemesis, i.e. Mary, in V, ix.) Time is described in a familiar way, by Avarice—who emphasises the notion of Time the destroyer. But Truth is not delivered from captivity by her father Time; she starts up out of the earth; she applies to herself the text "Veritas de terra orta est." Saxl has shown that as early as 1521 John Knoblouch of Strasbourg who printed works by Luther, Melanchthon and Erasmus, adopted an illustration of this same text as his printer's device.[4] It is a quotation from the Psalms (lxxxv, 12) and there refers to the coming of an age of peace in which Truth will blossom from the ground like a flower. For Knoblouch the text and its illustration indicated the coming triumph of Protestantism. In our interlude this text is united with the Humanist motto to celebrate the triumph of Catholicism. And, last, Truth is the daughter of Time, but she is associated with her "sisters" Mercy, Justice and Peace. These are the Four Daughters of God, according to mediaeval tradition.[5]

II

Two other occasions on which our motto appeared in England are connected with the figure of the Dutch humanist, Hadrianus Junius of Hoorn. The full, chequered story of Hadrianus' contacts with England has not yet been told, and cannot be told here, but I can give an outline against which to set his uses of this device.[6]

Hadrianus Junius was born at Hoorn in 1511, and was educated at Haarlem and at Louvain, where he studied medicine and philosophy. From Louvain he travelled in Germany and Italy, and became Doctor of Medicine and Philosophy of Bologna in 1540.[7] He then went to France, and from France he came to England, to one of the most distinguished and ill-fated of English households, that of the Duke of Norfolk and his eldest son, Henry Howard, Earl of Surrey, poet, soldier and either too much or too little a politician.

During the siege of Landrecy, Junius became acquainted with Bishop Bonner, who offered him many inducements to come to England, but upon his arrival there, Bonner failed to provide the promised patronage. He was, however, introduced to the Duke of Norfolk, who received him into his family "in the quality of a Physician," and towards the end of March, 1544, gave him lodgings at Lambeth, the duke's house in London. Meeting Junius frequently there, Surrey came to admire the learning of this erudite scholar, and before the first of the August following he had begged his services from his father to make Junius the tutor of his children.[8]

This was in 1544. But Hadrianus had by no means found a safe harborage. Whether Surrey was indeed "the most foolish proud boy in England" or whether, as Casady maintains, he was caught in the net of intrigues carefully spun by his enemies, of whom the most prominent was Seymour, later to become Duke of Somerset and Protector of the Kingdom,[9] he paid for his folly or his lack of guile, or both, with his head. He was executed on January nineteenth, 1547, a few days before Henry died. His father was imprisoned at the same time, and remained a prisoner till he was released by Mary in 1553.[10]

Hadrianus may have thought that his patron died "dolisque circumvento"[11] but that could not interfere with his search for patronage. Yet it is a little distressing to find him, in 1548, welcoming the rising power of Somerset so effusively. He had left England, but finding no means of support in Holland, had come back and found a temporary shelter. His Latin-Greek Lexicon was published at Basle in 1548, and this he dedicated to Edward VI, with the usual emblazonry of humanistic compliment.[12] Edward was ten years old when his father died, and Hadrianus' dedication is obviously not directed at him, but at Somerset, who held the power. For he spends pages congratulating Edward on his good fortune in having a Somerset to conquer Scotland for him, and on a description of Somerset's recent campaign against Scotland. It was this campaign that had culminated in the victory of Pinkie in October 1547. Did Hadrianus remember that the Duke of Norfolk had been in charge of the victorious campaign which ended at Solway Moss in 1542?

It is not displeasing to record that all Hadrianus' works were put on the Index because he had, unprophetically, dedicated this harmless dictionary to "*Eduardo, Angliæ regi, fidei defensori . . . .*" I have not found Hadrianus' name in any copy of the Index before that of Rome, 1559. Here we find that the list of authors whose names begin with H and whose "libri et scripta omnia prohibentur" begins with Hadrianus Junius. And in Pius IV's Index (Rome 1568) Hadrianus' name again is among the "Auctores Primae Classis"—that is, whose works are absolutely forbidden. But in 1570 Plantin published two editions of the Index "cum regulis confectis per patres a Tridentina synodo delectos, auctoritate Sanctiss. D. N. Pij. IIII, Pont. Max. comprobatus. Cum Appendice in Belgio, ex mandato Regiae Cathol. Maiestatis confecta" [with the rules composed by the fathers appointed by the Council of Trent, and approved by authority of our most holy lord Pope Pius IV, Pontifex Maximus. With an appendix in Flemish, compiled by the command of his royal Catholic majesty]. In the first part of this index, Hadrianus' name still occurs among those "Primae Classis." But in the appendix, in the "Secunda Classis," we find this:

> By Hadrianus Junius, physician, the dedication prefixed to the preface in many copies of his Greek-Latin Lexicon. That dedication excepted, the remainder of his works may be read, because they contain nothing contrary to sound doctrine and the author himself is firm in his profession of the Catholic faith.[a]

This appendix is prefaced thus:

> Preface to the subjoined appendix of the worshipful commissioners, to whom, by authority of his Catholic majesty Philip II, the responsibility for augmenting the catalogue was deputed by the Duke of Alba, at Brussels, September 1569.[b]

So it appears that the long letter which Hadrianus wrote in his defence, and which is published without date under the heading "Cardinalium consessui, aut Commissariis, vel caenobio," was written to this commission during its session and had the desired result.[14] His defence was that though reluctant to give this title to Edward, he had been persuaded to do so by his friend Franciscus Dilfus (van der Delft), the emperor's ambassador to London, "qui serio et vultu et animo contendit, non semel admonens." And also "capitalem in eo Regno noxam fuisse, edicto quoque sanctam in illos, qui illo ipso Regem titulo fraudarent"[15] [who pressed me with earnest look and intent, and frequently urged it . . . it was a capital offence in that kingdom, ratified by edict, for anyone to deprive the king of that title].

Hadrianus apparently did not think it wise to mention the episodes that had followed this unlucky dedication. He had left England between 1549 and 1551 but had met with little encouragement at either Haarlem or Hoorn. Edward died in 1553 and his sister and successor Mary married Philip of Spain that same year. Hadrianus decided to try his luck

---

[a] Hadriani Iunij nempe medici, titulus Praefationi praefixus in nonnullis exemplaribus Lexici Graecolatini. Eo titulo excepto, caetera eius opera legi possunt, quod nihil contra sanam doctrinam habeant, et auctorem ipsum constet catholicam fidam profiteri.[13]

[b] Praefatio in subiectam appendicem venerabilium Deputatorum, quibus a Duce Albano ex Philippo ij. Catholici Regis auctoritate, Catalogi augendi cura commissa fuit, Bruxellis, mense Septembri M.D.LXIX.

in England again and wrote an heroic poem for the wedding, the *Philippeis*.[16] The dedication to the poem is followed by this:

On the mottoes of the king and queen
Of Philip
Neither in hope nor fear.

Neither hope nor gnawing fear moves the intrepid, courageous king, lover of constancy, from righteousness.

Of Mary
Truth the daughter of Time.

Nothing lies in darkness, for Truth brings all to light, and Time is the divider of true from false.[c]

It must have been common knowledge—at any rate among those who had access to the Court—that Mary had taken the motto "Veritas filia temporis" to herself. Hadrianus came across to London to present his poem but was bitterly disappointed with his reward. He went back to Holland, and Scheltema[17] thinks he did not return to England. But here, I think, Scheltema is mistaken.

In 1556 Hadrianus, unwearied, dedicated his *Commentarius de Anno & Mensibus* to Mary:[18]

For after I had last year written—or rather poured on to paper—the *Philippeis*, the work of a month, for your most auspicious wedding, I took in hand a little work which was to contain histories delightful and pleasing in their variety. From this your majesty might learn in brief the mighty events and achievements, worthy of perpetual memory, of yourself and your ancestors—everything, whenever it was done or seen to be done.[d]

He goes on:

What I once offerred, written by my own hand as a little gift to your brother King Edward, it seems good that I now offer to your majesty in print, augmented by a third section of history and things worthy of record . . .[e]

And he ends:

So may almighty God preserve us and our studies long and happily; so that, all cause for strife

[c] In Regis & Reginae Symbola
Philippi
Nec spe, nec metu.
Intrepidum, fortemque virum, & constantiae amantem,
Nec spes a recto, nec metus acer agit.
Mariae
Veritatis Temporis Filia.
Nil latet abstrusum, Tempus luci omnia sistit,
Et veri aut falsi Tempus elenchus erit.

[d] Posteaquam enim Philippeida, menstruum poëmation, superiore anno in auspicatissimas vestras nuptias lusissem, aut effudissem verius, in manus sumpsi opusculum, quod historiarum cognitionem varietate delectabilem, atque jucundam contineret, ex quo fatales, et suos pariter et progenitorum suorum eventus aut res gestas aeterna memoria dignas, compendio T.M. cognosceret; omnia, certo quopiam die observata et facta.

[e] Quod quia olim xenioli loco fratri tuo Eduardo Regi, manu propria exaratum exhibueram, visum est idem, nunc tertia historiarum, rerumque memorabilium parte auctius typis excusum, T.M. offere . . .

being extinguished and the stormy waters of discord being stilled, the once flourishing realm of England may acknowledge, honour, and enjoy your rule in perfect peace.[f]

Ten years later, in 1568, Hadrianus is invoking blessings on Elizabeth's head in the "Epistola Dedicator. in Eunapium Sardianum."[19] This work was translated into English and published in 1579 as "The Lyves of Philosophers and Orators: Written in Greeke, by Eunapius, of the Cittie of Sardeis in Lydia. Brought into light, translated into Latine, and Dedicated to the Queenes most excellent Maiestie, our most gracious Princesse and Soveraigne, Queene Elizabeth. By the great learned man, Hadrianus Iunius Hornanus, 1568. And now set forth in English, at his request: and Dedicated to the right Honourable, the Lord Chancellour of England. 1579."[20]

The Epistle Dedicatory to the Lord Chancellor, Sir Thomas Bromley, says:

> This Booke laye hid in Hungarie, tyll Hadrianus Iunius, a great learned man, did cause it to be Printed in Greek, and Traunslated it into Latine: and a eleven yeares since, Dedicated it to the Queenes most excellent Maiestie, our Souveraigne Lady Elizabeth, and brought it over into England: where, hauing continued thus long, is now become English, and under the protection and authoritie of your Lordship, he sueth and beseecheth that it may be made of the English nation, And so being accepted, remaining also, a faithful member: he may, with feruent minde, pray to the Lord of Lords, for the longe preseruation of your Lordship, in continuance of Honour and good lyking, to the glory of God, the contentacion of the Prince, and commoditie of the Countrie.

Whether Hadrianus had anything to do with this second dedication or not,[21] he certainly in 1568 dedicated his book to Elizabeth in almost the same terms, with the same trailing flourishes of compliment, that he had used to address her sister Mary in 1558. He begins in both cases with a reference to Plato's opinion that the happiest states are those where philosophers are kings—which provides a good beginning for the obvious compliments to England and Mary, and / or Elizabeth. I doubt if either Mary or Elizabeth thought God could bless them both, and certainly few people in England did. He compliments Elizabeth on her gift of tongues—"ut doctissimi quique Regum Legati ea obstupescant & percellantur" [by which the most learned royal ambassadors are dumfounded and surpassed]. This dedication is followed by a set of acrostic verses to the queen.

In 1572 Hadrianus wrote to Cecil to introduce a Dutch embassy to him. He says he has been requested to do this

> so that I might open to them, in a country strange to them but once very familiar to me, some haven to acquaintance and friendship. This kind of service I could not deny to such distinguished friends, but I found myself in great want of those other friends of whom death and disaster have bereft me. You, Cecil, occurred to me as the one remaining person to whom I could address a few words of recommendation, because—as I know from report and from my own former experience—on you are heaped the praises of all humanity. I was the more eager in this, because through no one else could they have readier and easier access to the inner counsels

---

[f] Ita illam Deus Opt. Max. nobis et studiis diutissime felicissimeque longaevam conservet ut extinctis dissidiorum causis, sedatisque discordium opinionum aestuariis, florentissimum alias Angliae regnum, vestrum Imperium pacatissime agnoscat, revereatur, amet.

of Her Royal Majesty than through you, the most faithful Nestor, on whom the affairs of that mighty realm happily depend.[g]

Hadrianus' contacts with England had not indeed been very happy. He had been with the Norfolks and their fall had left him to scramble for patronage. He had never got as much support in England as he expected. The men to whom he wrote letters, and some of whom he called friend, were not noted for their tranquil lives. There are letters to Bishops Bonner and Gardiner, who paid for their opposition to rising Protestantism with imprisonment under Edward VI. (And Bonner was to acquire evil fame as a persecutor under Mary.) To Sir John Cheke, great Cambridge scholar, intransigent Protestant, opponent of Gardiner, tutor to Edward VI, who was imprisoned by Mary, released, kidnapped by Philip between Brussels and Antwerp and sent back to the Tower where he stayed till he was 'converted', and who died soon afterwards. To Nicholas Wotton, an able diplomatist, so valuable and so discreet that he served Henry, Edward, Mary and Elizabeth. To Walter Haddon, a younger Cambridge scholar, latinist and Reformer, University administrator, diplomatist (who worked with Wotton in the Netherlands, 1565-6). The younger Howards had as mixed and violent lives as their fathers. There is a letter of Hadrianus to Philip, eldest son of Thomas, the fourth duke, who was executed for treason in 1572 (the year of Hadrianus' letter to Cecil, which perhaps refers to this). Philip himself was to be tried and condemned for treason in 1586 and to die in prison nine years later. Even Martin Gregory, Philip's tutor, to whom Hadrianus had written in 1568, had a far from peaceful life. His life, to some extent, runs parallel to that of Edmund Campion, his contemporary and friend at Oxford. After his patron was sent to the Tower Gregory escaped to the new English College at Douai and he shared the vicissitudes of this house till he died in 1582.

In 1585 another of Hadrianus' works appeared in English: *The Nomenclator, or Remembrancer of Adrianus Iunius . . . now in English, by Iohn Higins.*[23]

In 1586 Geoffrey Whitney's "*A Choice of emblemes, and other Devises,*" the first English emblem book, was published.[24] The Victorian editor of Whitney's book, Henry Green, [25] traced twenty of his emblems to their sources in Hadrianus' "Emblemata," which had been published in 1565,[26] and among the twenty is "Veritas temporis filia." The same plate has been used in each book (Figures 71 and 72).

In the foreground of the illustration, to the right, we have Time, (or, in the Latin of Junius, Saturn) a naked, muscular old man, winged, with a scythe in his left hand, with his right hand raising Truth from the cave in which she has been lying. In the foreground, to the left, we have three female figures: Calumny holding a lighted torch in her raised left hand, and with her right grasping the hair of a male figure kneeling before her, his hands lifted together in petition; Envy stepping forward on her right foot, naked to the waist,

[g] ut in peregrina sibi, mihi vero notissima olim regione, portum aliquem amicitiae cotitiaeque, aperirem, quod officii genus quum denegare claris amicisque capitibus non possem, in magna amicorum quos vel mors, vel calamitatis mihi ademit, inopia, unus Cecilli occurristi reliquus, cui illos tribus verbis commendarem, quem humanitatis omnis laudibus cumulatissimum et compereram et fueram olim expertus, ac tanto quidem studiosius, quod per alium neminem quam per te (quo velut fidissimo Nestore potentissimi regni res feliciter innituntur) accessus proclivior paratiorque ad R. M. interiusue concilium patesceret.[22]

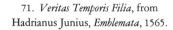

71. *Veritas Temporis Filia*, from
Hadrianus Junius, *Emblemata*, 1565.

holding her heart to her mouth with both hands (so that her breasts are covered by her arms), her head wreathed in snakes and her face very ugly; Discord, her head too adorned with snakes, pressing with her right foot on a bellows, the nozzle of which is directed to a fire of faggots behind her, and with her right hand holding a lighted torch to the ground. The background is of little hills, with trees and monuments.[27]

These three figures are not narratively connected within the terms of the design, with each other or with the action of Time in releasing Truth; each stands by herself displaying her attributes. Perhaps this is why Junius and Whitney can use the same picture to illustrate such divergent themes. The title of Junius' emblem is:

Veritas tempore revelatur, dissidio obruitur.

[Truth is revealed by time, and smothered by discord.]

Veritas temporis filia.

THREE furies fell, which turne the worlde to ruthe,
  Both Enuie, Strife, and Slaunder, heare appeare,
In dungeon darke they longe inclofed truthe,
But Time at lengthe, did loofe his daughter deare,
    And fetts alofte, that facred ladie brighte,
      Whoe things longe hidd, reueales, and bringes to lighte.

Thoughe ftrife make fier, thoughe Enuie eate hir harte,
The innocent though Slaunder rente, and fpoile:
Yet Time will comme, and take this ladies parte,
And breake her bandes, and bring her foes to foile.
    Difpaire not then, thoughe truthe be hidden ofte,
      Bycaufe at lengthe, fhee fhall bee fett alofte:

Diſſidia

72. *Veritas Temporis Filia*, from Geoffrey Whitney, *Choice of Emblemes*, 1586.

And his verse:

> Quid penniger Saturne in auras virginem nudam rapis?
> Quid feminarum cœtus aggesta obruit terra scrobem?
> Specu emicantem veritatem, temporis natam, triplex
> Obruere pestis apparat; Lis, Inuidia, Calumnia.

[Why, winged Saturn, do you snatch that naked maiden into the air? Why is that pack of women burying her in a ditch with heaps of earth? A threefold plague goes about overwhelming Truth, daughter of Time, as she emerges from the cave: Strife, Envy, Calumny.]

There is nothing of the apocalyptic here; no assertion that Time reveals Truth and Truth stands. The title is cryptic, its meaning is difficult to pin down, but is limited by the verse. Time may release Truth from her prison, but her enemies are waiting to overwhelm her.[28] The illustration does not assert this; it leaves the exact relationship between the figures undefined, asserting only that there is a relationship.

Whitney is positive, apocalyptic, optimistic. His motto is the traditional "Veritas temporis filia," and his verse:

> Three furies fell, which turn the world to ruthe,
> Both Enuie, Strife, and Slaunder, heare appeare,
> In dungeon darke they longe inclosed truthe,
> But Time at lengthe, did loose his daughter deare,
>   And setts alofte, that sacred ladie brighte,
>   Who things long hidd, reueales, and bringes to lighte.
>
> Thoughe strife make fier, thoughe Enuie eate hir harte,
> The innocent thoughe Slaunder rente and spoile:
> Yet Time will comme, and take this ladies parte,
> And breake her bandes, and bring her foes to foile.
>   Dispaire not then, thoughe truthe be hidden ofte,
>   Bycause at lengthe, shee shall bee sett alofte.

The motto is not, now, applied to any particular contemporary event, but has become a prophecy that Truth will prevail. Junius has ceased to think so. But the design can illustrate both texts because it makes no positive assertions, because it is neutral, because, in fact, it illustrates neither.

In 1553 Hadrianus had accepted the conventional use of the motto in applying it in compliment to the queen who had taken it to herself. In 1565 he had reshaped it pessimistically, refusing to give it an absolute meaning. In 1586, after Hadrianus' death, Whitney took his device, but interpreted it conventionally, and made it assert that "Time will prevail"–so unknowingly repeating the assertion that Hadrianus had already made in England, but had afterwards rejected.

III

Whether Whitney's emblem exercised any direct influence, I do not know. But Robert Greene, in 1588, looking for a moral to garnish his novel *Pandosto* and appease the consciences of his readers, chose "Veritas Filia Temporis." The title-page reads:

Pandosto. The Triumph of Time. Wherein is discovered by a pleasant Historie, that although by the meanes of sinister fortune Truth may be concealed, yet by Time in spight of fortune it is most manifestly revealed.—Pleasant for age to avoyde drowsie thoughtes, profitable for youth to eschue other wanton pastimes, and bringing to both a desired content.—*Temporis filia veritas*—By Robert Greene Maister of Artes in Cambridge.—Omne tulit punctum qui miscuit utile dulci.

The motto has no organic connection with the working out of the story. It is a convenient didactic pretext. When Shakespeare used *Pandosto* for the plot of *The Winter's Tale* (c. 1611) Greene's title-page certainly gave him the idea of bringing in Time to bridge the gap of sixteen years between Acts III and IV. Time introduces himself thus:

> I that please some, try all, both joy and terror
> Of good and bad, that makes and unfolds error,
> Now take upon me, in the name of Time,
> To use my wings.

Time is now both enemy and friend. The conception of Time as enemy, as the destroyer, is dominant in Shakespeare.

Chapman takes over the image and turns it in an interesting way. He, like Greene, uses it to refer to the clarifying of a plot. Rinaldo, the agent of the plot, is speaking to a friend about the progress of their intrigue:

> And therefore when he comes to learn the truth
> (As certainly, for all these sly disguises,
> Time will strip Truth into her nakedness)
> Thou hast good plea against him to confess . . . .
> (*All Fools*, 1598–9. IV.i. 210–13.)

The implication is that Truth is reluctant, but that Time will master her and make her reveal herself.

Chapman in the Epistle Dedicatory to his *Odyssey* (1614) says:

> Why then is fiction to this end so hateful to our true ignorants? or why should a poor chronicler of a Lord Mayor's naked Truth (that peradventure will last his year) include more worth with our modern vizards than Homer for his naked Ulysses clad in eternal fiction . . . .

He is sneering at popular taste through a reference to Thomas Middleton's pageant *The Triumphs of Truth* (1613).[29] At one point the new mayor is met by Truth's angel, escorted by Zeal, Truth's champion. The angel speaks, blessing the mayor as the friend of Truth, but telling him that the victory against Error is not yet won. Zeal also exhorts him:

> The trumpet then sounding, the Angel and Zeal rank themselves just before his Lordship, and conduct him to Paul's-Chain, where, in the south yard, Error in a chariot with his infernal ministers attend to assault him, his garment of ash-colour Silk, his head rolled in a cloud, over which stands an owl, a mole on one shoulder, a bat on the other, all symbols of blind ignorance and darkness, mists hanging at his eyes. Close before him rides Envy, his champion, eating of a human heart, mounted on a rhinoceros, attired in red silk, suitable to the bloodiness of her manners; her left pap bare, where a snake fastens; her arms half-naked; holding in her right hand a dart tincted in blood.

Error addresses his lordship, bids him join her and away with Truth. Zeal then attacks Error and Envy and drives them away. Truth appears in her chariot, equipped with the most elaborate attributes, which Zeal explains. His lordship passes on, escorted by Truth and her attendants and by Error and hers. A company of Moors appear, who adore Truth—this symbolises their conversion to the true religion by English merchants. Error flouts Truth,

> But Time sitting by the frame of Truth his daughter's chariot, attired agreeable to his condition with his hour-glass, wings and scythe, knowing best himself when it is fittest to speak, goes forward in this manner:
>
> > This Time has brought t'effect, for on thy day
> > Nothing but Truth and Virtue shall display
> > Their virgin ensigns; Infidelity,
> > Barbarism and guile, shall in deep darkness lie.

The pageant goes on for a considerable time yet, but enough has been said to indicate the use of our theme.[30] It is similar to the use made of the theme in Elizabeth's royal entry, as noted by Saxl. And we have the same linking of Truth with Religion (i.e. Protestantism). An investigation of the attributes given to the allegorical figures would take us far into the by-ways of Renaissance iconography. And to point to the immediate sources of inspiration for this pageant would, I imagine, be next to impossible. Let us be content to note that this presentation of Truth and her associates is in the same tradition that produced the illustration of "Veritas filia temporis" used by Hadrianus and Whitney.

Giannotti, Michelangelo and the Cult of Brutus

Vegga ancora con quante laude ei celebrano Bruto; talchè, non potendo biasimare quello [i.e. Caesar], *per la sua potenza, ei celebravano il nimico suo.*
[Again, see what praises they bestow upon Brutus: not daring to censure Caesar because of his power, they honour his enemy.]

Machiavelli, *Discorsi*, I. 10.

It was in 1539 that Michelangelo's friend Donato Giannotti, last Secretary of the Ten in Florence, went to Rome to enter the service of the great Cardinal Ridolfi. And it was some time after that, presumably, that he persuaded Michelangelo to begin work on a bust of Brutus for the Cardinal.[1] (Figure 73.) This magnificent prince of the church, famous for his love of learning and his generosity to scholars, was one of the leaders in the campaign of opposition to the Medici waged so long and so hopelessly by those Florentines whom the capitulation of the city and the return of Duke Alessandro in 1530 had spilled out into exile over Italy. It was long ago suggested, and the idea has been generally accepted, that this unfinished bust must be seen in connexion with the republican ideals of these exiles. But it seems worth while to attempt a fuller reconstruction of this environment than has been given.[2]

Ridolfi had gone to Florence with the other two Florentine cardinals, Salviati and Gaddi, in 1537, after the murder of Alessandro, to take part in the ill-managed and useless attempt to remove the newly installed Cosimo and restore the republic. In these muddled negotiations Giannotti too had had a brief part, emerging into public life again from the silence of seven years' exile given to his literary studies. But now, in 1539, all that was over. Two years earlier the last desperate effort of Filippo Strozzi, secular leader and banker of the *fuorusciti*, against Cosimo had met its miserable defeat at the battle of Montemurlo; Strozzi had endured his imprisonment and torture and, a year before, had killed himself. Giannotti never returned to Florence.

From 1537, it seems, Giannotti had been putting the final touches to his most important works, the *Della Repubblica de' Venezianii* and the *Della Repubblica Fiorentina*.

73. Michelangelo, *Brutus*. (Florence, Museo Nazionale.)

They were—or it could still be hoped they might be—of immediate relevance. For the first is concerned with the lessons Florence might learn from Venice; and the aim of the second is to draw up a constitution that would ensure the maintenance of liberty in Florence. And this he dedicates to the Cardinal Ridolfi with the brave words:

> Among all the undertakings, my lord Cardinal, which are entered upon for the general benefit of mankind, the liberation of cities from tyranny is for two reasons accounted great and splendid. The first is that, since so many share the profit of such an action, only a person on the highest *virtù* can undertake an enterprise which is so beneficial and advantageous to the people as a whole. Second, since the overthrow of a tyranny is a most dangerous act, it is universally agreed that a man who puts himself in such great and manifest peril must be armed with the greatest courage. This is why the highest praise is accorded to the man who takes such an initiative, and why those who bring tyrants to destruction remain glorious in every man's memory.[a]

This is the language of the classical republicans. Giannotti and the *fuorusciti* inherited it from earlier generations of enemies to the Medici. For, naturally, it was always round opposition to the Medici that republican ideas crystallised, and in these opposition circles that the classical heroes assumed new life as saints, heroes, exemplars: and sometimes, it would seem, as daemons. It is such a note, as of *possession*, that is struck, for example, by Paolo Boscoli, the young man condemned to death for his part in the anti-Medici conspiracy of 1513, who cried aloud to Luca della Robbia,

> Deh! Luca, cavatemi della testa Bruto acciò io faccia questo passo interamente da cristiano.[4]

[Ah! Luca, pluck Brutus from my mind, that I may pass from the world a perfect Christian.]

It was in this same conspiracy that Machiavelli was suspected of being involved; and it was now that after questioning under torture and brief imprisonment he retired to San Casciano where he began to write, as well as *The Prince*, the *Discourses of the First Decade of Livy*, that sustained and moving document of this classical republicanism. Writing of Rome Machiavelli was writing of his own Florence. The problems of the maintenance or death of freedom were his problems; and when the cool tone of the analyst yields to the passionate, magnificent indictment of Caesar, "E conoscerà allora benissimo quanti oblighi Roma, l'Italia, e il mondo abbia, con Cesare"[5] [and then it will be clearly seen under what obligation Rome, Italy, the whole world was to Caesar], it is because the passion is a living passion, and Caesar a symbol of every destroyer of freedom; the corruptions of civil life that followed him are the monstrous diseases that now feed on the

---

[a] Tra tutte le imprese, Monsignor mio, le quali per universale benefizio degli uomini si prendono, il liberare le città dalla tirannide è reputata, per due cagioni, grande, e maravigliosa. La prima è, perche essendo quelli assaissimi, che di tal benefizio partecipano, non par credibile che alcuno, senza grandissima virtù, possa una così fatta impresa pigliare, la quale insieme a molti sia utile e fruttuosa. Secondariamente, perche essendo il rovinare una tirannide azione pericolosissima, niuno è che non giudichi, colui essere di somma fortezza armato, il quale a tanto e sì manifesto pericolo si mette; e perche gli uomini celebrano con grandissima lode il nome di coloro, che tali imprese pigliano; perciocche quelli, che sono autori di rovinare le tirannidi, restano nella memoria di ciascuno gloriosi.[3]

body of Italy. It is worth remembering that the *Discourses* were first published in 1531.

When Lorenzino de' Medici horribly murdered his brutish cousin Duke Alessandro on that January night in 1537 he did more than present the *fuorusciti* with the chance they had been waiting for (and which they mishandled so badly). He offered them the classical situation. This was the tyrannicide: the classical gesture, the one thing wanting to seal their enterprises with the authority of the sacred tradition. They had seen themselves as classical-republican heroes. Lorenzino's deed authenticated the images.

For Lorenzino himself, his deed was a re-enactment of the sacred moment when the hero kills the tyrant. In the north of Italy he had a medal struck to commemorate the event (Figure 74). It carries a portrait, in Roman dress, and, on the reverse, the Phrygian cap—symbol of liberty—between two daggers. This is a replica of one of the coins of Brutus: the cap and the daggers commemorated the murder of Caesar.[6] In the famous *Apology*, which he wrote later, Lorenzino compared Alessandro to Nero, Caligula,

74. Lorenzino de' Medici's medal of himself as Brutus, struck to commemorate the assassination of Alessandro de' Medici; it is a replica of a coin of Brutus' commemorating the assassination of Caesar. The reverse shows a Phrygian or liberty cap between two daggers.

Phalaris, and himself to Timoleon; and he opens it with a declaration parallel to Giannotti's dedication:

> If I had to justify my actions before those who do not know what liberty and tyranny are, I should use all my powers to demonstrate, to give reasons (and they are many), why men should desire nothing beyond the civic life, that is to say, liberty. For a free polity is less frequently found and less lasting under all other kinds of government than a republican one. I should also show, since tyranny is contrary to true political existence, that men ought equally to hate it above all things; and that in former times the opinion prevailed that those who freed their country from tyranny were to be held worthy of honour second only those who had founded it.[b]

[b] Se io avessi a giustificare le mie azioni appresso di coloro i quali non sanno che cosa sia libertà o tirannide, io m'ingegnerei di dimostrare e provare con ragioni, che molte sono, come gli uomini non debbono

Finally convincing explanations of Lorenzino's personality and his motives elude us, as they eluded his contemporaries. We can, if we wish, and indeed we are impelled to, add darker and still more ambiguous colours taken from modern investigations in psychopathology; but anything of this sort must remain conjectural; and we can still do little better than Varchi's capital account.[8] Certainly the "desire for glory" was in him, a desire recognised as valid by his world–however we may choose to explain its roots in his particular personality–and one that could be satisfied in terms highly acceptable–perhaps those most highly acceptable–to his world through the emulation of a classical hero.[9] Yet a strange note is struck in this relationship of Lorenzino to his heroes. Long before the murder there was the curious episode which led to his banishment from Rome. One day the citizens of Rome woke to find that the heads had been struck from the figures of the emperors on the Arch of Constantine and from those of Apollo and the Muses on San Paolo fuori le Mura. After the murder this decapitation of the emperors could be seen as a prefiguration of the later blow struck for liberty. Yet surely what Lorenzino was doing was acting Alcibiades;[10] he in his turn was mutilating the sacred Herms, in this case images of empire and the arts. The figure of Alcibiades, and the affair of the Herms, are ambiguous enough; and it is difficult to guess what Lorenzino thought he was doing or what great action he thought he was preparing. And Anton Francesco Doni tells a story–it seems to have been overlooked by writers on Lorenzino–which throws a queer light on him. In 1550 Doni dedicated to Duke Cosimo a little account of the life of Caesar with a preface in which he compares Alessandro to Caesar, Lorenzino to Brutus and Cosimo to Augustus (it will be understood that it is Caesar and Augustus who are his heroes). Doni wishes to argue, in this preface, that ancient heroes can have their modern counterparts; and, without apparently feeling that he was being in any way tactless, he tells how Lorenzino was in the habit of making a close examination of the features of living men notable either for virtue or vice, and how he would then seek counterparts for such individuals on the portraits on ancient medals, and having found such a counterpart would study what was known about him; and in most cases would find that the physical resemblance meant also a resemblance in character and deeds.[11] This story has all the marks of truth–and Doni was telling it to those who would have known if it were false. And it seems to suggest that when Lorenzino acted the part of Alcibiades or Brutus he was perhaps doing more than model his behaviour, in an acceptable way, on that of classical heroes. He was doing more, in fact, than act a part; he behaved like Brutus, because in some real sense he was Brutus. This is the note of *possession* struck by Boscoli's cry, though that may seem purer, less mixed with turbid, ugly elements. We have reached the ambiguous frontiers between imitation of classical models and possession by them: the ambiguous frontiers between what a given society will admit as sane and admirable and what it will condemn as insane, and shut away.

desiderare cosa più del viver politico, et in libertà per conseguenza, trovandosi la politià più rara e manco durabile in ogni altra sorte di governo che nelle repubbliche; e dimostrerei ancora come, essendo la tirannide totalmente contraria al viver politico, che e'debbono parimente odiarla sopra tutte le cose, e com'egli è tanto più prevaluta altre volte questa oppenione, che quelli che hanno liberata la loro patria dalla tirannide sono stati reputati degni de' secondi onori, dopo gli edificatori di quella.[7]

Whatever their second thoughts may have been, the enemies of the Medici began by taking Lorenzino's act in the sense that he had intended. In these circles he was hailed as the "Bruto toscano."[12] "Mi raccomandi cento milla volte al giorno al glorioso Lorenzo de' Medici, il cui atto magnanimo avanza Bruto" [commend me a hundred thousand times a day to the glorious Lorenzo de' Medici, whose great-souled act surpasses that of Brutus]—so wrote one, and another, still more excited, and varying the reference, exulted "et iam erexit cornu salutis nobis in manu David pueri sui" ["and hath raised up an horn of salvation for us, in the house of his servant David" (Luke I.69)]: this in a letter to the Cardinal Ridolfi.[13] Benedetto Varchi, who was later to compose so cool, careful and subtle an analysis of the mystery of Lorenzino's motives, in a fit of enthusiasm wrote a suite of classical compositions in honour of the new liberator.[14] One is an inscription to be placed under the image of Lorenzino hung up in Florence in token of condemnation. He imagines Brutus in Elysium hearing of the deed:

> . . . Cum iuvenis destra iuvenem cecidisse Tyrannum
>   immitem audisset Brutus in Elysiis;
> et forte inciderat sermo de Caesare, victi
>   tot viri ab uno, inquit, iam sumus et puero . . . .

[When Brutus in Elysium heard that the young, cruel tyrant had fallen by a young man's hand, and when the talk had chanced to fall upon Caesar, he said, "Many that we are, now we are outdone by one man, and that a youth."]

Then there is an inscription for a statue of Lorenzino, QUOD LIBERTATEM PATRIAE, PATRIAMQUE TYRANNO / VI COESO, SOLUS RESTITUIT POPULO / LAVR / MEDICE / LIBERATORI [to Lorenzo de' Medici, the liberator, who slew the tyrant single-handed by force of arms, restoring liberty to his native city and the city to its people], with verses; and a Horatian ode to Lorenzino's mother, Maria Soderini:

> Sancta, cui sacrum peperisse Laurum
>   liberatorem simul, et parentem
>   patriae, indigni pereuntis alto
>   vulnere monstri.

[O sainted mother of the sainted Lorenzo, whom the deep death-wound of the infamous monster made the liberator and father of his country.]

It is to Varachi's credit that he did not later conceal the fact that he had so raised his voice in the chorus.[15]

Filippo Strozzi himself thought in the classical mode. We find him using it in a letter to the Cardinals Ridolfi and Salviati to sum up the situation in Florence now that Cosimo has been called to replace Alessandro:

> parmi che il benefizio del nostro Bruto riesca vano, come di quell' altro, succedendo Augusto in luogo di Cesare

> [it seems to me that the advantage conferred by our Brutus comes to nothing—as it did in the case of that other Brutus—since Augustus succeeds to Caesar's place].[16]

And, in the same period, his prudent Florentine friend Piero Vettori urging moderation shows an understandable impatience with what he obviously considers to be the jargon of the *fuorusciti*:

> Our most revered Salviati has lifted from us the burden of war which threatened from Perugia; do you also lift that which menaces from Romagna and the Bolognese; and do not depend upon Brutuses and Cassiuses, nor on restoring the city to the condition of a republic, because that is not possible.[c]

It may be that Strozzi was in some way not indisposed to listen to such advice. But he was carried on to the muddled and bloody anticlimax of Montemurlo, to imprisonment and torture of body and of mind, as the complicated manoeuvres on which his life depended were played out between Florence, Rome, France and the Imperial court. At last he cut the knot. On 18 December 1538 a guard left a sword in his cell – it is difficult to imagine that this can have happened by accident – and he killed himself. In this classical drama he would not play Caesar or Augustus, and could not play Brutus. But one part had still to be filled, and Strozzi could die as Cato. The magnificent letter he left behind him – it was so stained with his blood that his Spanish gaoler could only send a copy to the Emperor – is inscribed *Deo Liberatori*. His intention is declared in these words:

> I, Filippo Strozzi, have considered with myself in what manner, however dearly it may cost me in respect of my soul, I can put an end to my life with my own hands. I commend my soul to God and his great mercy, humbly praying that if he will grant me no other favour, he may at least place me with Cato of Utica and other like virtuous men who have made such an end.[d]

And these are his final words to Caesar, and his subscription:

> And you, Caesar, I beg with all reverence that you better inform yourself of the condition of the unhappy city of Florence and look to her good – if indeed it is not your intention to destroy her.
>
> Filippo Strozzi, now at the point of death: "There shall rise from my death another, the avenger of my blood."[e]

This is the most moving utterance of the classical republicanism of Florence, and the last: the voice of an earlier world; this, and Michelangelo's Brutus.

A bust of Brutus made at Giannotti's suggestion and intended for the Cardinal Ridolfi can only have been read in this classical republican context. Brutus and his fate had

---

[c] Il reverendissimo Salviati ci ha levata di dosso la guerra, che ci soprastava di verso Perugia: levateci voi quella che ci potesse venire di Romagna e del bolognese, nè stiamo sui Bruti e Cassi, nè sul voler ridurre la città a repubblica, perchè non è possibile . . .[17]

[d] io, Filippo Strozzi, mi son deliberato, in quel modo ch'io posso, quantunque duro, rispetto all'anima, mi paia, con le mie proprie mani finire la vita mia. L'anima mia a Dio, somma misericordia, raccomando, umilmente pregandolo, se altro darle di bene non vuole, le dia almeno quel luogo dove sono Catone Uticense ed altri simili virtuosi uomini che tal fine hanno fatto.

[e] E te, Cesare, prego con ogni riverenza t'informi meglio dei modi della povera città di Firenze, riguardando altrimenti al bene di quella, se già il fine tuo non è di rovinarla.

Philipus Strozza iam iam moriturus: "Exoriare aliquis, ex ossibus meis, mei sanguinis ultor."[18]

become, for this particular group, an image with meanings so fixed and definite that no version of it produced in this milieu could be divorced from these meanings.[19]

Giannotti himself shared the general feeling for Brutus. In the first years of his exile he had planned a tragedy on Brutus.[20] And, later, he showed himself and Michelangelo arguing about Brutus.

This is in the famous *Dialogues*, "De' Giorni che Dante consumo nel cercare l'Inferno e'l Purgatorio." The scene of these dialogues is in Rome, and they show Michelangelo talking to a group of friends about the chronology of Dante's journey through Hell and Purgatory: to Giannotti himself; to Luigi Riccio, another Florentine, an exile, established as a business agent; to Antonio Petreo, a Florentine in the service of the Cardinal Ridolfi, and a minor man of letters; to Francesco Priscianese, another republican and exile printer, and author of a celebrated Latin grammar, and associated, he too, with the hospitable household of the Cardinal.[21]

The *Dialogues* were not published until the nineteenth century, and we do not know for certain when Giannotti composed them.[22] And arguments about the date of composition became involved with the problem of the *historicity* of the content. Do the *Dialogues* represent an actual occasion and give us a factual account of what was said? If so, it is possible to fix limits for the date of composition by investigating the chronology of the lives of the interlocutors and finding when they can all have met in Rome. This is in great measure the position and method adopted by the latest editor. Giannotti makes Michelangelo declare that he is in his seventieth year: and this would fix the date of the conversations between 6 March 1545 and 6 March 1546; by studying the dates within this period when the interlocutors could have met and walked and talked in Rome, de Campos concludes that the conversations must have taken place between the last days of January and 6 March; and that the composition of the dialogues must have followed fairly soon.[23] This assumes, of course, that the dialogues record words actually spoken and arguments in fact used. De Campos holds that words and phrases are put into the mouth of Michelangelo which are so idiosyncratic that they cannot have been invented. About this I shall not dispute; but de Campos has a second argument which, as I shall show, cannot be sustained. De Campos admits that Giannotti's *Dialogues* are only one example of this literary form so favoured in the sixteenth century, and that they must be seen in relation to the conventions governing that form, which permits, as he says, many variations and degrees in its presentation of "what actually happened." Yet I cannot think that he allows enough for this. Giannotti would not have composed his *Dialogues* before Michelangelo was in fact in his seventieth year. But unless evidence of a different order is found we can only say that he may have written them at any time after that. It was enough that such occasions as this walk and this discussion should be conceivable; and that nothing should be put into the mouths of the speakers that was "out of character." We cannot put the case for their historicity—in the sense of being a direct record of events—more strongly than this. If there are phrases and modes of expression that are characteristic of Michelangelo, it was surely not beyond the power of a friend of his to introduce them; and it was highly desirable that he should, to give the note of dramatic appropriateness that he wished.

The discussion between Michelangelo and Giannotti about Dante's treatment of Brutus comes as a lively postscript to the disquisitions on the time scheme of the *Commedia* which were the main business of the *Dialogues*, and provides an entertaining change of tone; it is a recognisably human and domestic exchange, so that we seem to move, from being perhaps a little too close to the lecture room, to a less formal and restricted air.

When the master's exposition of the time-scheme of Dante's journey is complete, Riccio remarks that Giannotti has been silent all day. Giannotti answers that he has been better employed listening than talking, then turns to Michelangelo with a spirited protest against his idolatry of Dante. After all, he says, Dante was a man, and there is no need to suppose that he was always right. Michelangelo challenges him to find one instance of a clear mistake in the poet's works, and Giannotti immediately cites the case of Brutus and Cassius whom Dante has placed in the lowest pit of Hell, in two of the mouths of Satan. That, replies the master, is an old story and others have already justified Dante. This is not enough for Giannotti: unless Michelangelo can give a better answer than the others have done he will go on thinking that Dante was greatly at fault in so punishing the authors of Caesar's death. There is no way out of it, Giannotti continues, either Dante did not know that Caesar was a tyrant, or he would not have punished his murderers so ferociously; or he did not know that those who kill a tyrant to liberate their country are universally honoured, and he did not know how Greeks and Romans hated tyrants and honoured their destroyers. If he did know all this, and still judged Brutus and Cassius as he did, then so much the worse for him, and we have to charge him not with simple ignorance, but with grave and culpable error. Michelangelo replies rather sharply that when Giannotti confessed earlier in the day to not understanding Dante he was obviously telling the truth. "I understand this much," answers Giannotti, not in the least subdued, "that he has put Brutus and Cassius in the mouths of Lucifer, and I would put them in the most honoured seats in Paradise." Michelangelo explains why he refuses to be impaled on the horns of Giannotti's dilemma. Of course Dante knew perfectly well what tyrants are and how they are to be punished by God and man: Dante numbers them among those guilty of violence to their neighbour and places them in the seventh circle, in the hell of boiling blood threatened by the Centaur's arrows. Any who have shown some compensating virtue he shows in Purgatory painfully expiating their sin of tyranny among the proud. And of course Dante knew that Caesar was a tyrant, and that the act of Brutus and Cassius was justified—for certainly the laws of all the world reward the slayers of tyrants. They did no more than kill a man whom every Roman citizen was in duty bound to kill; and in fact it was not a man whom they slew but "a beast clothed in the image of a man." All this Dante knew; and how could anyone who remembers how he honours Cato in the first Canto of the *Purgatorio* imagine that the poet thought of his adversary as anything but a tyrant? Certainly, then, he knew that Brutus and Cassius were to be rewarded, not punished. This does not mean, however—as Giannotti wishes to demonstrate—that Dante was sinning against the light in punishing them. In the lowest circle of Hell Dante puts the greatest sinners, the traitors. These are of four kinds, those who betray their relatives, their country, their friends and the imperial and divine majesty. Those guilty of this last betrayal are the worst of all, and those are punished in the final zone, the Giudecca.

>And since he, in accord with Christian opinion, believes that by the special providence of God, the empire of the world was given into the power of the Romans and then of the Emperors, he holds that whoever betrays the majesty of the Roman Empire is to be punished in that same place and with those same pains as is the betrayer of the divine majesty,

that is, with Judas, who betrayed Christ, and is held in Satan's central mouth. As Dante, then, needed examples of those who have betrayed the Roman empire, he chose Brutus and Cassius who in the person of Caesar betrayed the empire. He chose them because of their eminence and fame. He did not mean to do them wrong, for he meant by them, not Brutus and Cassius, but "betrayers of the imperial majesty," which was signified by Caesar—and this did not exculpate Caesar for the crime of being a tyrant and reducing his country to slavery. Giannotti is by no means disposed to accept all this, and provokes the master exceedingly by asking the awkward question whether, when Dante puts Caesar in Limbo, he is there as Caesar or as "the imperial majesty"; and by reiterating that he understands Michelangelo's explanation completely and is prepared to believe it—but that Caesar should be in Limbo and Brutus and Cassius in Hell is too much for him. Michelangelo is now sufficiently irritated to begin questioning the rightness of Caesar's murder. Did it not lead only to disaster? What a line of emperors succeeded him! Would it not have been better to let him live—even if it had meant his becoming king? And how do we know what would have happened eventually? Is it not possible that like Sulla he would have restored his country's liberty? Is it not rashly presumptuous to murder the head of a government, unjust though he may be; when alive, something may be hoped for him—but we cannot know what will follow his death. Doing ill—murdering—is not the only way of bringing good about. Times change, and persons, and there is always the hope that good may come. There is always the case of Sulla and his achievement. If Caesar had done the same, how wrong anyone would have been who had planned to murder him—and perhaps Dante thought that Caesar would have followed Sulla's example, and that therefore Brutus and Cassius were wrong, and deserved to be punished.

>"Have you finished your sermon?" asks Giannotti, and brings the discussion to an end—"Let's go home. We are at the gate and it's evening already, so I don't want to make any other answer to your nonsense about Brutus and Cassius. Especially because I see the others laughing at us . . . ."

And he turns to the aged master with a gesture of affection.

De Campos' favourite argument for the actuality of the conversations reported is that Michelangelo's defence of Dante in this passage is so absurd that Giannotti would never have invented it, and that only a desire to record the *ipsissima verba* of the master could have led him to include it.[24] But this argument falls to the ground. Absurd the argument may be, but it was not invented either by Michelangelo or Giannotti. It comes from Landino's commentary on *Inferno*, xxxiv—the most obvious of all sources, for Landino's was the best-known commentary.

Landino's aim was to exculpate Dante from the accusation that Giannotti is still bringing against him. He points out that Dante chooses Brutus and Cassius because their deed was parallel to that of Judas: he betrayed the divine emperor, and they the human:

because by common consent of those who bear the name of Christians it is agreed that the Roman emperor is master of the temporal power in the entire state of Christendom, just as the pope is of the spiritual . . . .[f]

However Caesar is not here as Caesar, nor Brutus and Cassius as the individuals Brutus and Cassius:

Take Caesar in the first place not for Caesar, who, not being a just man, could not be a just emperor, but for the power of empire; and Brutus and Cassius, who slew him, not for Brutus and Cassius, but for anyone who slays the true monarch.[g]

For certainly it would have been wrong—and alien to Dante's beliefs—to impose eternal punishment on those who

for the most passionate love committed themselves to death to rid their country of the yoke of servitude—for which, had they been Christians, they would have been allotted a place of honour in heaven.[h]

For Caesar, in spite of his many gifts, was the enemy of his country:

And indeed, what virtue can be greater than to avenge the wounds of one's country, in whose service every good citizen is bound not to spare his property, his children, even his life? O best of men, and fully worthy of Rome, their fatherland! The memory of these will endure forever.[i]

We may note further that when Giannotti makes Michelangelo say,

it may truly be said that he who kills a tyrant kills not a man but a beast in human form, because, since all tyrants are devoid of the love that each man ought naturally to bear toward his neighbour, they lack human affections, and are therefore men no longer, but beasts,[j]

he is using the classical definitions of the nature of the tyrant as expounded at great length by Landino in his commentary on *Inferno* XII:

The way by which we enter upon violence is pride and wrath, by which we are made forgetful of our humanity and grow bestial in our cruelty . . . . Divine justice decrees that he who rejoices in blood shall be punished by blood . . . . Violence is a great force for harm: it is born of

---

[f] perche di comune consenso del nome christiano è instituito, che il Romano Imperadore ha cosi capo dell' amministratione temporale di tutta la christiana Repubblica, come il Papa nell' amministratione spirituale . . .[25]

[g] pone Cesare primo non per Cesare, il quale non essendo giusto, non potea esser giusto Imperatore: ma per l'Imperio, & Bruto, & Cassio, i quali l'uccisero non pone per Bruto & Cassio: ma per chi uccide il uero Monarca.

[h] per ardentissima carità, si misero alla morte, per liberare la patria dal giogo della seruitù, per la quale se fussero stati christiani haurebbono honoratissima sedia nel supremo cielo aquistato.

[i] Et certamente qual puo essere maggior uirtù, che uendicare le ingiurie della patria, per la quale ogni buon cittadino è tenuto di non perdonare alla roba, non a' figliuoli, non alla propria uita. O huomini eccellenti, & al tutto degni, a' quali Roma fosse patria. Et de' quali resterà sempre eterna memoria.

[j] egli si può probabilmente dire che chi ammazza un tiranno non ammazza un huomo, ma una bestia in forma d'huomo; perchè, essendo tutti i tiranni spogliati dell' amore che naturalmente ciascuno debbe portare al prossimo, conviene che manchino degli affetti humani, et conseguentemente non siano più huomini, ma bestie . . .[26]

greed, which has its root in pride . . . . The tyrant wants his wish to have the force of divine command, his avarice that of just law. Cruelty accords with his nature. He rejoices in tormenting the righteous, and finds happiness in the shedding of innocent blood. Thus he is not only not royal, but not human; for he is devoid of all humanity, endowed with all ferocity—the most pernicious of men.[k]

Giannotti's editor is hardly to be blamed for not being able to take Michelangelo's arguments seriously: certainly Giannotti did not. However, they were not invented by either Michelangelo or Giannotti. The discussion on the chronology of the poet's journey through Hell and Purgatory is, explicitly, a refutation of Landino's conclusions on that matter;[28] and the discussion on Brutus has the same bearing: it is a version of Landino's defence of the poet put forward so that Giannotti can dismiss it.

Early commentators had known—as Landino did—why Dante put Brutus and Cassius with Judas in Satan's mouths. Judas betrayed the highest spiritual power, and the two Romans betrayed the highest temporal power, in the person of Caesar, head of the divinely instituted Roman empire.[29] As early as 1400 the Dante passage was considered a crucial text in discussions of tyranny: Coluccio Salutati dealt with it his his *De Tyranno*, and justified Dante's judgment in the familiar terms:

> It was a reasonable idea to plunge Judas, Cassius and Brutus into the same place to which the prince of demons, who through pride had rebelled against God his maker, was relegated in the plan of the poem. For Judas betrayed the God-man, and Cassius and Brutus treacherously slew Caesar, the image, as it were, of divinity in the rightfulness of his rule and in the multitude of favours which he had abundantly heaped upon them, thus destroying the Republic and bereaving the Fatherland.[30]

Salutati's discussion of Brutus is incidental to his discussion of Caesar. This is what happens to Brutus, too, in the great polemic about the character of Caesar waged between Poggio Bracciolini, Guarino Veronese and Ciriaco d'Ancona in the late fourteen-thirties. It was such discussions and the humanist concern for the principles of "tyranny" and "liberty" in the fifteenth century that eventually, by the end of the century, made the classical names live and have power in direct political action, in the world of the conspiracies against the new tyrants—the world from which we have heard Boscoli's voice. The fate of the Dante passage echoes and illustrates the main theme. Thus one commentator, writing towards 1474 what is little more than a version of a comment produced a century earlier, feels impelled to add to what his authority had said of Brutus and Cassius this clause:

> nec est verum quod ipsum occiderint propter liberare patriam.[31]

> [nor is it true that they killed him to free their country.]

---

[k] il passo, donde entriamo nella uiolentia, è superbia accompagnata da l'ira, per la quale dimentichiamo l'humanità, & diuentiamo fiere per crudeltà . . . chi s'è dilettato del sangue, permette la diuina giustitia, che sia punito nel sangue . . . Violentia è forza uasta a danno, & nasce da cupidità: la quale ha origine da superbia . . . . Vuol [i.e. the tyrant] che la sua libidine sia come un diuin precetto, la sua auaritia sia per giusta legge, la crudeltà gli si conuenga, godono de' tormenti de giusti, rallegransi di sparger il sangue de gli innocenti; la onde non solamente non sono Re: ma non son huomini: ma spogliati d'ogni humanità & uestiti d'ogni ferità sono somma pernitie de gli huomini.[27]

Seven years later Landino publishes his comment—on the other side.

It was a hopeless attempt to save the appearances. The author of the most important of the sixteenth-century comments—Velutello, whose comment was published in 1544, and was known to and condemned by Michelangelo[32]—was more faithful to Dante's intentions when he defended him by writing a spirited eulogy of Caesar. Landino's method, here, was not valid. It was not possible to have Brutus the classical republican hero, and Dante's Brutus at the same time. When Landino's Dante was published in 1481 it was illustrated with drawings by Botticelli. Botticelli's illustration of the Brutus scene shows a monstrous Gothic Satan crushing three minute and ridiculous figures in his mouths, following faithfully in the tradition of the illustrators of the manuscripts of the *Comedy*, who were themselves following the iconographical tradition of the representations of the punishment of the damned. Botticelli illustrates Dante; it would be difficult to say that he illustrates Landino's interpretation of Dante—or how that could be illustrated. Nor does Michelangelo's bust illustrate Dante's Brutus; and if he ever thought it did, he was in error. This noble *gravitas*, image of resolution and magnanimity, speaks to us of a different world. That it is a world that never was realised, nor ever could be, is another matter.

75. Stage façade of the Teatro Olimpico, Vicenza, by Palladio and Scamozzi.
(Engraving by V. Brunello, 1824.)

Academicians Build a Theatre
and Give a Play: The Accademia Olimpica

I

It may well be that a general study of the Italian academies of the sixteenth century is an impossible notion, simply because there were too many of them, in too many places. Yet it is a pity that historians have not devoted more time to a study of their role in the diffusion of ideas, agents as they were, in varying degrees, in different places, and in various fields, of conservation and innovation, popularisation and controversy; and also to their roles as groups in the society of their places. Their relationship to school and university studies should be investigated; their relationship to government, secular and ecclesiastical; what models of social organisation they initiated or created; and—and this would be fundamental—what sort of people participated in their activities, what were their origins, occupations, and status, and what kind of nexus of interest tied them together.[1]

This study aims at no more than telling, more fully than has yet been attempted, on the basis of some contemporary documents that have not hitherto been used, and some, unfortunately of later origin, that have long been known, although haphazardly, part of the story of the most memorable action of one academy. It was a small academy in a small town, Vicenza, which had produced one writer and theorist of international influence and an architect of great genius: Giangiorgio Trissino and Andrea Palladio. Our story is of an academy at work, making decisions.[2]

These decisions resulted in the building of Palladio's Teatro Olimpico, a building largely irrelevant to the course that the modern stage was to take, but a great work by a noble and humane genius, and calculated, more than any other modern theatre, to ennoble and aggrandize the human body in certain stances; and in that inaugural production of the *Oedipus Rex*, which caught and blended in one dazzling manifold image so many ideas and prepossessions and inventions and achievements. With an account of theatre and production, with the general activities and ambience of the academy we are not here concerned: only with the day to day provisions as our documents allow us to see them, that finally achieved these results.[3] Our story—the nature of the documents is such—shows the academicians at their worst: their proceedings are disordered, often trivial, often—watched from our safe distance—tiresome and absurd, yet at the same time very serious in endeavour and purpose. And even this partial chronicle has implications about the composition and functioning of social groups that would contribute to, even as they could only be fully understood in the light of, the unwritten social and ideological history of this part of Italy at that time.

Founded in 1555, five years after the death of Giangiorgio Trissino, the Accademia Olimpica of Vicenza certainly inherited and saw itself as inheriting the kind of culture and educational activities associated with his name in that city.[4] From the first the academy, like many another, interested itself in the production of plays; and the most striking episode of its early days was the production, in 1562, for the first time, of Trissino's exemplary tragedy, the *Sofonisba*, on a stage designed by Trissino's protégé, Andrea Palladio. It was the memory of this that, seventeen years later, started the academicians on the course that was to lead to the Olimpico and the Sophocles.

II

When members met in council on August 10th, 1579, they recorded in a formal resolution that fear of not being able to equal the great success of that production had ever since prevented them from attempting any other. However, the minute goes on, this fear should no longer be allowed to deter them from attempting another play:

> Certainly our academy has behind it a series of learned occasions, and the experience of many years gives it the right to expect that any of its activities will at least be worthy of itself and of the city, if not the equals of those past. It ought not, therefore, by setting itself too severe a standard, allow itself to be deflected from such a praiseworthy intention, when prompted by its inclination, its *virtuoso* impulse, its obligation to its profession, its own disposition, and the expectations of others.[a]

So the academicians decide—the twenty or so who were present—that a public performance of a play should be given in the house of the academy during the next carnival season. The play, furthermore, is to be a pastoral, "cosa nuoua et non più fatta fin'hora da

---

[a] Ma certamente essendo l'Academia nostra fondata sopra i continui essercitij uirtuosi et dall'esperienza di molti anni essendo gia conosciuta tale, che puo sperare sempre d'operare se non cose eguali, almeno degne di se medesima et della Patria, Non deue da questo troppo seuero rispetto lasciarsi impedir quel si lodeuol corso, a cui dal genio suo, dallo stimolo uirtuoso, dal debito della professione, dal desiderio, et dall'aspettatione altrui si sente eccitata.[5]

quest'Academia,"[6] and it is to be produced as cheaply as is compatible with the dignity of the academy. A committee of four is appointed to prepare the ground.

This is how it all began; and right away the changes of mind that bedevilled the conduct of business in the academy appear. At the next meeting, in October, the committee is instructed to decide on where the play is to be given—perhaps doubts had already arisen about whether the academy's house was suitable. But we find in November that nothing can be done in time for next year's carnival and that the whole project must be dropped and taken up again at a better moment. Then, on January 3rd, 1580, the academy decides that, after all, the production cannot be postponed beyond the spring. A committee of four is elected to choose the play, consisting of Paolo Chiappino, the Cavaliere Barbarano, A. M. Angiolello and Fabio Pace; and nine days later a further committee is set up to take charge of the *intermedii* for it: Silla Palladio, the architect's son, was proposed for this committee but not elected. Early in February the prince and other officers are confirmed in office until such time as the play shall be given.

The academy is busy now. It meets once a week in this February of 1580, and it is at the next meeting, on February 15th, that the crucial step is taken. Once committed to producing a play, the academy is committed to finding a place to produce it in. Doubts may have already arisen, as we have seen, about whether the accommodation in the house where the academy normally met at this time was suitable. But it is one thing to have doubts of this kind, and quite another thing to decide to build a theatre. Yet that is what we now find the academy deciding to do. There were twenty-nine members present, and no adverse vote is recorded. Here is the text of the resolution, and the beginning of Palladio's theatre:

> It has occurred to our lord prince and to many academicians that it would be possible to provide the stage for the presentation of our pastoral on the site of the old prison, under a roof, with much less expense, and to the greater satisfaction of the whole academy, than anywhere else. Therefore application must be made in the academy's name to the worshipful magistrates of the commune, in whatever manner shall seem most appropriate and convenient, to be pleased to allow the said place to be used for this purpose and for all others conducive to the eternal glory of this city and of our academy.[b]

On February 24th there is another meeting. The application to the magistrates has been successful, and it is the business of this meeting to ensure that certain terms laid down by the magistrates should be binding on all academicians present and future. It is resolved that these pledges be entered in the book containing the laws of the academy.

Whether it was thought that a theatre could be ready by spring we do not know. But at any rate preparations go ahead. On February 28th two committees are elected, one to be responsible for actors, and the second for the invention of costumes. And on March 23rd

[b] Essendo uenuto in pensiero al Signore Principe nostro et à molti Academici che il poter fare l'apparato per rapresentar la nostra pastorale nel loco delle pregion uecchie al coperto seria et con minor spesa assai, et con maggior sodisfatione di tutta l'Academia che in alcun' altro loco, pero l'andarà parte che a nome dell'Academia si debba suplicar alla Magnifica comunità con il modo parerà più à proposito, et conueniente; che uoglia conceder il detto loco per poter ualersene in questa attione, et in ogn' altra à eterna gloria di questa città, et dell'Academia nostra.[7]

Angelo Ingegneri is elected academician, an election which has probably, as later events indicate, some direct connection with the promised production.

However, we hear no more about a play in 1580. What we hear about, and are going to go on hearing about for many a day to come, is money. How is the academy to pay for its theatre? It appears to have had no regular fixed income, academicians not paying, it seems, an annual subscription, but contributing according to their discretion. And now, when the academy has just embarked on this ambitious enterprise, it is clearly not well off. In 1579 it had been difficult to get contributions; and in March of this very year 1580 there is the awkward case of a *lettore* who, on the failure of the academy to pay him his full stipend, has complained to the *Podestà*, an incident which had to be settled, as it hardly suited the academy's dignity to be taken to court. At any rate the business of financing the theatre seems to have come up seriously for the first time on May 23rd. Contributions from the members must be assured

> . . . as this whole council knows, the building having been begun on the site of the old prison, where the academy, together with its theatre, is to be located. This will also serve for public performances, and for the functions of the academy in perpetuity.[c]

And that same day the academy adopts a scheme for raising money from its members which probably seemed extremely ingenious when first proposed, but which in the event gave nothing but trouble. The scheme is this. In return for his contribution, each member is to have the right to have a statue of himself with his name and his *impresa* placed in one of the niches or on the pedestal of one of the columns of the *apparato*; all the statues are to be of the same size and the same cost. Academicians of longest standing shall have precedence in having their statues made and placed. It may have been a moment of realism that was responsible for altering this resolution at the meeting on June 2nd, when it was decided that the best places shall be allotted to those members who subscribe most—"essendo molto più conueneuole et utile all'Academia"—in cash or promissory notes. Everyone is to be given a fresh opportunity to subscribe, and if many members give the same, then the places they shall have are to be decided by lot once the *apparato* is ready.

The name of Andrea Palladio has not so far appeared in the records of these transactions. We do not even hear of him preparing the plans, let alone whether, as is highly probable, he was directly or indirectly responsible for that sudden decision to build a theatre. When his name does come up on August 25th, 1580—shortly after his death—it is in the shape of a *pro forma* resolution declaring that what the officers of the academy have done in connection with his funeral is approved of: because of the shortness of time the prince had had to act on his own initiative. We first hear of Palladio's plans for the theatre—to anticipate our story a little—some months later, while Silla Palladio gets the permission of the academy, on January 27th, 1581, to include them in a new edition of the *Architettura*. The academy even votes a grant towards the expenses of engraving these drawings, but this, like another project of August 25th, for publishing the compositions

---

[c] Essendosi dato principio come sà tutto questo consiglio alla fabrica nel loco delle pregion uecchie, oue ha da esser l'habitatione de la Academia et insieme teatro, et sera per publici spettacoli à perpetua conseruatione et ad esercitio di essa Academia.[8]

in verse and prose prepared by the academicians on Palladio's death, came to nothing.

In November, 1580, we learn that the theatre is almost ready and that only a little more money is needed, and needed urgently, to roof it. Delay would be dangerous. It is proposed and decided to authorize one member to borrow up to five thousand ducats in the name of the academy.

We do not know whether the academy was successful in negotiating this loan, but certainly by January of the new year, 1581, the financial position is so urgent that on the 19th the Council feels it necessary to pass a resolution recording in full gravity the responsibilities that the academy has undertaken:

> On 14 December 1579 a document was drawn up to which almost all the academicians subscribed, each binding himself to pay as much as was necessary for the production of a pastoral, upon execution of which, preparations for the pastoral were begun. And matters have gone further, the academy having conceived the noble idea of building this theatre, for which expenses already incurred amount not only to the sum which has been collected, but to much more. There is, moreover, need to spend still more for the completion of these works, and also for the production of our pastoral.[d]

A drastic step is taken at this meeting. It is resolved that the original subscribers be required to pay as much again as they had put themselves down for, either in cash or in promissory notes to fall due at Easter; those who wish to avail themselves of this latter alternative are given a short time limit within which they must come into the scheme. It is not really surprising to find that there was a reaction to this, or that a week later a new resolution is passed recording the disapproval felt by many of the academicians.

It is obviously felt that the original subscribers are being penalised for the mere fact of having signed the original subscription, and are in a worse position than members elected since the original subscription-list was drawn up or than members who should be elected in the future. The new resolution, clearly a compromise, or a "once only but never again" motion, provides that the original subscribers shall, this once, double their subscriptions. New members and future members shall not be obliged to sign the subscription-list and shall be free to pay what they think fit. And if at any future time it should be necessary to raise new subscriptions, everyone shall be compelled to pledge himself afresh.

Resolutions may be passed; but the Olympians are quite capable of ignoring them. By March 20th it is obvious that unpleasant steps will have to be taken. The *bidello* has been going round the academicians, trying to get them to produce their subscriptions, but in some cases he is being put off from day to day. A committee of three is chosen now (it must have been ungrateful) to get the subscriptions in from their recalcitrant fellows and see that they pledge themselves to the new terms as well. If these three gentlemen should

---

[d]Sotto di 14 Decb. 1579 fu fatto un scritto al quale quasi tutti gl' Academici si sono sotto scritti obligandosi pagar ogn'uno quel tanto che l'tornaua accompto per causa di rappresentar una pastorale in essecutione di che si cominciò à tratar di far detta pastorale, et si passò più inanzi essendo uenuto alla Academia un si bel pensiero di fabricar questo teatro in che si hà speso fin ora non solamente quella quantità di denari che si hanno riscossi ma molto maggiore, et bisognando spender ancora molto si per finire le dette opere, come anco per rappresentare la pastorale.[9]

formally, in full council, name an academician for having refused to pay his dues, then unless the dues are paid within eight days the member named will be expelled from the academy. It was, after all, a grave enough threat, for in a small town like Vicenza this sort of expulsion would surely have had some undesirable social consequences, and the council may well have thought that this was the final sanction it could apply. The resolution is carried unanimously.

The progress of the building can be judged by the urgency the question of providing and placing the statues on the *proscenio* assumes in this spring of 1581. We can perhaps also judge of the success of the council's threats—it probably never dared put them into effect—by the terms of a resolution of April 1st to the effect that everyone intending to increase his subscription on the terms laid down on June 2nd, 1580, must now do so within ten days "facendo bisogno di cominciar subito a lauorar in dette statue"[10] [it being necessary to begin at once on the said statues]. After this date has passed the placing of the statues will be decided according to the order in which members have subscribed. At the same meeting it is decided to put the arms of the magistrates of the city over the main door of the theatre, in gratitude for the liberality of the city towards the academy. Measures —and what measures!—are taken to make up for the lack of an overseer to supervise the workmen who are busy on the building every day. It seems that an experiment tried the previous year of having a paid overseer had not been successful. So the council decides that every academician shall be required to serve as overseer for one day or to send a substitute in his place, on pain of a fine if he does neither (the order to be decided by drawing lots). Academic democracy has perhaps, we may feel, been carried to excess.

Meetings come fast: the building of the *proscenio* is in crisis. On April 14th it is decided to extend the time allowed members to increase their subscriptions towards the making of their statues. Cash or promissory notes must be in hand before a statue can be begun. The proposed extension is for eight days: after that the positions of the statues will be allocated by lot; and after that there will be no further opportunity to commission a statue. At the next meeting, the term of grace having expired, positions are ballotted for: and the minute gives a list of names and positions.[11] On April 17th there is a curious and unexplained note: the city has empowered the academy to create twelve citizens. It seems safe to infer that this was an attempt to help the academy out by giving them an honour to dispose of in some helpful or profitable way.[12] On April 18th Silla Palladio is appointed paid overseer of the work—so much for the idea of academicians doing this in turn for nothing. On the 24th it is decided—not surprisingly, and rather late in the day—that the academy wants to see the accounts for the building, and a special committee is created to take charge of them until the building is completed. On April 26th, apparently, the city is asked for still more land, which will be needed to accommodate the stage perspectives.[13]

The series of resolutions passed on April 27th shows just how dire the financial position had become. The academy, it is recorded, has two major responsibilities: the first is the building of the theatre, and to abandon this would be "di estrema nostra uergogna" [to our extreme shame]; the second is the payment of its debts, and to leave this undone would be "di uituperio, et infamia alla nostra Academia"[14] [insult and infamy for our academy]. Members who have outstanding obligations must pay one third in May, one third in June, and the rest on the last date agreed on for the promissory notes. Defaulters will be expelled. And in future every newly-elected member must pay down one half of his subscription in cash on election, and the rest within a month. Those who have been elected since the placing of the statues had been decided on shall be allowed to choose a place according to the order of their election; and this rule is to hold for the future. In June it is decided to take shares for the academy in the Venetian lottery; but the records do not tell us whether this was actually done—or with what success. In view of all this, it is rather surprising to find the academy deciding, two months later, on August 17th, that it must have a house beside the threatre, and resolving, as it would not be possible to build a suitable place at short notice, that the city should be asked to hand over a house that is already occupied, and that the academy will make the present occupant a suitable allowance until he can find fitting accommodation.

After the rather frenetic activity of early summer there is a lull. The business of the end of the year is the election of new officers. But in February 1582 we return to the *proscenio* and the statues.

The academicians are being as dilatory as usual. The completion of the theatre is being held up because only a very few of the members are actually having their statues made: although the academy has taken great pains to see that sculptors are available and to inform the members of the places allotted to them. The *bidello* is to be sent round again (on one of his thankless errands) to warn defaulters that if the work is not begun within eight days (or twenty if the member concerned should happen to be in the country) they will lose their places, which can then be assigned to someone else. Disapproval of the academy's choice of sculptors, the resolution adds quite firmly, will not be accepted as an excuse for delay: any academician who does disapprove is at perfect liberty to find a sculptor for himself. It is however added that no academician is to be expelled for failing to comply with this resolution.

But all this is merely an eddy in the financial storm. In March the situation is still more urgent, naturally enough because the root cause is the same. The academicians will not pay their dues. It is now an absolute necessity—so an elaborate resolution of March 10th goes—that payment should be enforced, under pain of expulsion. Money is owed to merchants and to workmen. Work on the building goes ahead quickly, but the workmen have to be paid every day, and if this cannot be done the work must stop. And all this could be provided for from the money owed by members. In view of this it is resolved that a separate claim for payment be made to each debtor; and if he fails to pay within the time limit prescribed he is automatically expelled from the society and can never be readmitted. Nor will any plea for special treatment be admitted unless it receives five-sixths of the votes of the council. So far so good. It is the usual story of warnings and threats of expulsion—the sharpest sanction the academy could invoke. (And in spite of all the threats there is no evidence in the minutes that any member was actually ever expelled). But now comes a further threat, and this is a step that can only have been taken with great reluctance, for if carried out it would have meant exposing the troubles of the academy to public notice. Defaulters are threatened not only with expulsion but with legal proceedings. Furthermore, anyone who has not yet put his name down for a subscription in the *libro ordinario* is instructed to do so within a prescribed limit of time, under pain of expulsion. And other measures of the same order are proposed. The hard-worked *bidello* is to announce these resolutions to everyone as soon as may be; and he is to make to the secretary a *giuridica relatione* that warning has been given "affine che alcuno non habbia occasione di dolersi"[15] [so that no one will have cause for complaint]. At this crucial meeting only fifteen were present.

From the large discretion apparently left to individual members, it might have been foreseen that there would be dissatisfaction about the arrangements for the statues. The academy is now driven, on April 1st, to appoint a committee to take charge of the whole business so that nothing shall be done which would offend the *decoro et ornamento* of the building.[16] In cases of difficulty the committee's decision is to be final. However, the academy's method of coping with its difficulties is, as so often, rather peculiar. The committee is to consist of the prince and six members. These six members are subdivided into three groups, each group being responsible for one of the three orders of the *proscenio*,–"quello delli dieci tabernacoli", "quello delli nicchi, et quariselli", and "l'ordine superiore." Each group has executive power, and power to take advice; but any decision taken by the group must be approved by at least one member from each of the two other groups.[17] A week later, on April 7th, the prince reports in the name of this committee on their decisions, and on previous decisions which the academy has taken with regard to the statues. The committee has decided–and this is a record of some importance for the history of the theatre as it passed from Palladio's project to the building we now know–that every academician must have his statue made in the shape of a man "uestito, ouero armato all'antica," and his statue may if he chooses be a portrait of himself. Such statues as have already been made in the shape of female figures must be altered to conform with this decision. And although it appears from the resolution of June 2nd, 1580, that each academician has the right to put at the foot of his statue his name, surname, arms and *impresa*, he must limit himself to name, surname and father's name, without the addition of any title or any other word. Any arms or *impresa* already executed must be removed. Name and surname are to be in the Latin form. The inscription to be made for the present prince is offered as an example: "JVLIO POIANA LVD. F." showing how the word "son" is to be rendered by the initial only, and the father's name in as few letters as possible. The inscription is to be placed on the base of the statue, in Roman letters, black and of uniform size, and is to be cut in living white stone. These stones, which must be uniform and of the size thought best by the committee, are to be bought and placed by the academicians in the appropriate places and in the way decided by the committee. The arms and *impresa* provided for in the earlier resolution are to be placed elsewhere in the theatre as may seem most suitable, subject to this proviso, that in the centre of them, and done on a large scale, is to be the academy's own *impresa* supported on the right by the *impresa* of the first academician, and on the left by that of the second; the rest of the *imprese* are to follow in the order in which their owners come in the book recording the allocation of places for the statues. The shape and ornament of the *imprese* are to be uniform; each member will have his own and his arms coloured as he thinks fit. Only his academic name is to be given, but he may put the initial letters of his name and surname beside his arms. The *imprese* are to be of stucco and not to be moveable. Above the central arch of the *proscenio* a general inscription is to be placed in the name of the academy, recording in suitable words that the academy has erected these statues to the academicians as founders of the theatre. Some such formula at any rate is to be used.[18]

It was sensible, and clearly necessary, for the academy to appoint, also on April 7th, a paid and permanent secretary.[19]

It is not long before the drastic resolution of March 10th is smoothed away. By April 24th the time limit set up by that resolution has already been passed; but it is agreed that more time is to be allowed before proceeding to the expulsion of those academicians who are now subject to it: the grounds for this relaxation are that the required announcement had not in fact been made to everyone. So another period of grace is allowed. At this same meeting it is resolved that a statue of Palladio should be placed in the third order of the *proscenio* with an appropriate inscription. And it is at this meeting too that the academy begins, to put it brutally, to sell membership: a new academician is elected on his promise to pay on his election forty ducats towards the expenses of building. This was one of the more obvious ways of raising money, and it is one which in the future the academy is to practise. In June, September, December, and in January of the following year (1583) new members are elected under the same conditions. A member elected in December began by offering twenty *scudi* as a special contribution, and was not elected; he then offered twenty-five *scudi*, and was elected.

In May, July and December repeated consideration has to be given to this problem of money. Draconian measures were never successful, for the academy, when it came to the point, was never willing to impose the threatened penalties. In May still another concession is made. More time is given to the defaulters, with the proviso that no further postponements are to be allowed. On July 29th a new impost is proposed which will involve every academician inscribed in the *libro ordinario* in paying two ducats for every one ducat he is down for, the payment to be made in two instalments and completed by the end of August. But in December this proposal is abandoned as being undesirable. Some other solution must be sought.

In the middle of these troubles the academy was honoured by a state visit from the Duke of Mantua. Being in the city in August, the duke expressed a desire to see the Teatro Olimpico (and this seems to be the first time the name appears officially) and was received there on August 22nd, when Angiolello made a speech of welcome, poems by Maganza were read, and a concert was given. The duke was so impressed that he created Angiolello cavaliere on the spot and gave him a gold chain worth a hundred *scudi*.

On December 9th the prince presents a formal statement to the council about the financial position. He declares that each academician must in the present crisis be willing to make a special contribution to the academy's funds. He has found an interest-free loan of five hundred ducats to be repaid by the end of May 1583. Security, however, must be offered, and he proposes that this loan be taken up and that those academicians who may be willing to guarantee it should in the event of the academy failing to repay the loan in the required time be empowered to dispose of their guarantees in any way that is convenient to them and at any cost to the academy and without regard to the interests of the academy. This proposal is accepted. There is something slightly touching–or perhaps bitter–about the prelude to a further resolution passed later this month:

> Cities, republics and kingdoms preserve themselves not so much by good and virtuous ordinances, but even more by money, the chief sinew of all our actions. By their example our academy should be governed and maintained. So it must be that everyone, in one particular respect, show himself to desire the advancement of the academy (which God in his mercy aid and render ever fortunate), in order that money may be forthcoming to preserve the reputation of the academy and its credit, which depend upon the satisfaction of the many important and pressing expenses incurred.[c]

The text goes on to repeat those familiar threats of expulsion and of legal proceedings to be brought against any academician who has not paid his debt by the end of the month; and to state that the prince and the principal officers of the academy have the right to claim the support of any academician in any action they should think fit to take, and to threaten with expulsion any academician who fails when called on to give this support.

Perhaps more important for the new year than such proceedings was the election of Leonardo Valmarana, a rather splendid figure, as prince: later (April 19th, 1583) he is to be confirmed in this position until the play is carried through.[21]

III

In 1583 we come eventually to discussions about what play is to be given at the inauguration of the theatre, a question that had apparently been allowed to drop. The original intention had been, as we have seen, to produce a pastoral, and Fabio Pace had then written his *Eugenio* specifically for the occasion.[22] Two years ago Angelo Ingegneri had offered his pastoral *La Limonata* to the academy. But it had been rejected owing, it seems, to the opposition of Pace and Livio Pagello;[23] and in the same year, 1581, Pagello had proposed that the academy should present works by Vicentine authors; and some had moved for the production of Pace's work.[24]

These names are important. They figure in the complicated troubles that now come to afflict the academy. For the discussions about the choice of play provoked–as might have been expected–jealousies and intrigues and bitter disappointments. Our documents unfortunately in part fail us at this interesting point. But enough remains to enable us to construct at least in outline the story of what happened. And it is easy enough to see through the notes and formal records something of the personal situations that had arisen.

---

[c] Non tanto le città, le Republiche, et i Regni si conseruano lungamente con li buoni, et santi ordini loro, ma pur' anco co'l denaro neruo prencipalissimo di tutte le attioni nostre. Ad essempio dunque loro cosi si deue governare, et mantenere l'Academia nostra. L'andarà però parte à fine che tutti in un punto solo si mostrino amatori de i progressi di essa nostra Academia (che iddio per sua misericordia l'auti, et faccia sempre felice) et co'l mezo del denaro sia conseruata la riputatione et credito di essa, il quale dipende dal sodisfar' à molte urgenti et importanti spese fatte.[20]

We must keep our eyes on Fabio Pace. He was a doctor with literary pretensions. At this time his career was still young and his greatest fame was still to come. Of Vicentine birth, he had graduated in 1575 at Padua, where he had studied logic, philosophy, Latin, Greek and Hebrew, in addition to the medicine he had learned as a pupil of his uncle, the eminent Alessandro Massaria. From Padua he had returned to Vicenza where he set up a school of philosophy and medicine and an anatomical theatre. He practised with great success in Venice for a time, but returned to Vicenza permanently in 1590. However, he was an active member of the academy and is said to have read to them his translation of the first book of the *Iliad*. It was Pace's literary aspirations that gave trouble, and the great question before the academy in these months could probably be reduced to this: whether to produce the pastoral Pace had prepared or not.[25] There was a local rival in the field in the person of Livio Pagello, but he seems to have given less bother; he probably did not have so many supporters.[26]

In January or February, then, the academy heard a reading of Pace's pastoral.[27] We do not know whether this came before or after a meeting on February 7th, 1583, when the question of whether a tragedy or a pastoral should be performed was formally put to the academy. That day's resolution proposes that the prince and other officers be instructed to take advice about this choice from persons they think best qualified to give it, from within the city or outside it. The hope is that such a verdict will be accepted as dispassionate and disinterested; and that those academicians who do not agree with it will nevertheless accept it and not refuse to co-operate in the carrying out of the decision. A discussion follows, and the resolution is carried by twenty votes to nine.

On February 19th the prince reports to an assembly rather larger than usual—thirty-two members are present—that the advice received has been in favour of a pastoral. This, it might be supposed, should have closed the matter. Far from it. A very invidious motion is put to this same meeting—and a conflict of parties is clearly visible. It is now proposed that the academy shall decide whether to produce *alla Pasca delle Pentecoste* next (1584, that is) Fabio Pace's pastoral, provided that it meets with the approval of the academy's censors, (and apart from any earlier resolution taken by the academy about the production of a pastoral), or a tragedy, composed by one of themselves or by an outsider . . . . Votes are taken and run thus: for a pastoral 15, with 17 against; for a tragedy 20, with 12 against. It is therefore resolved that a tragedy be produced.

But the game is not over. Only two days later—on February 21st—we find another meeting being held. This is remarkable enough. Even more remarkable is the number of people who attended: no fewer than 44—which is the largest attendance recorded in these years. The meeting is called to consider a new resolution. This has been made necessary, the wording tells us, by objections that have been raised to the validity of the last. It has been objected, apparently, that that resolution did not get the two-thirds majority required by the constitution. However others have maintained that the resolution was perfectly valid: or, if it were not, that the matter is one to be handled by the intervention of the *Conservator delle leggi*. In view of these disagreements the prince and his associates have decided to bring forward a new motion that the academy should produce, first a tragedy, written by a member or by an outsider, and second, Pace's pastoral (provided always that censors elected by the council should approve of it). The compromise is all too patent. There was a party for Pace and a party against. The constitutional objections must have been raised by his supporters (and one wonders about the startling increase in attendance, too), who have been at any rate in part successful.

Pace himself took the next step. Two days later, on February 23rd, a meeting is called to hear a letter of Pace's read. It had been sent that very day, to Giulio Poggiana, who had immediately brought it to the prince. It is neither very clear in its phraseology, nor, perhaps, particularly convincing: Pace asks Poggiana to speak for him to the academy, in the event of a meeting being held which he cannot attend; he asks that his pastoral should not be performed—a request made in that same spirit of desire to serve the academy that had led him to compose his play; he is perfectly satisfied, for two reasons. He has seen the goodwill that the academy bears him; and he will not be compelled to give his work to the public, which he would have been reluctant to do; his friends too must be satisfied; they have got what they wanted; he had yielded to their pressing appeals; and now they must pardon him for taking this step; finally, those who did not want to see a pastoral produced will now be satisfied too. Pace offers some explanations about why he did not make this statement earlier, before the resolution had been passed, but they are distinctly vague. Clearly to get the resolution passed was enough to save his face. The struggle cannot have flattered his vanity, and this was a way out. The letter was accepted and read into that day's minutes. But although Pace had insisted on his willingness to contribute to the expenses of producing the tragedy he, or his friends, may have been responsible for further awkwardness.

The next firm date is May 8th, 1583, when we find that the academy is still concerned with how to choose a tragedy. At that meeting a committee is set up to do this: it is to consist of the prince, four censors, and six academicians. A majority decision is to be allowed, provided that the play in question receives not less than six votes in its favour. But this has to be fitted into a complicated story that was going on: and may have been an effort to cut a knot.

Between early in 1583 and May 1584 there was much discussion.[28] A list of the plays considered survives and has been transmitted: Muzio Manfredi's *La Semiramide*, Livio Pagello's *L'Eraclea*, Tasso's *Aminta*, Massaria's *L'Alessandro*, Maffio Venier's *L'Idalba*, Luigi Valmarana's *La Placidia*, Girolamo Vida's *L'Alessio* (and a pastoral of his) and a Latin tragedy by Antonio Loschi.[29] Pastoral is here, and the mention of Losco, that distinguished Vicentine diplomatist and humanist of the fifteenth century would seem to show that someone had remembered his *Achilles* and seen in him a figure comparable to Trissino, who might well be celebrated by the academy that had given the *Sofonisba*.[30] Of Massaria's play nothing is known.[31] Maffio Venier was Archbishop of Corfu and his *L'Idalba* was published in Venice in 1596. Luigi Valmarana's *Placidia* is a mystery, and perhaps a ghost.[32] Girolamo Vida is known as the author of *Filliria. Favola Boschareccia, fatta rappresentare per la prima volta dall'autore in Capodistria a' 27 Gennaio 1585* (Padua 1585)—and this might well be relevant; but there is no trace of a *L'Alessio* by him; and anyhow, as we shall see, it looks as though the *L'Alessio* in question may well have been by someone else. Many plays, of course, existed in manuscript that were never published and may have been lost; but the surprising uncertainty of the Valmarana reference, and the obvious confusion about *L'Alessio* must cast some doubts on the list as a whole.

There were certainly comings and goings. Livio Pagello's ambitions were now in the forefront. Ambitions, doubts and dissensions, however, resulted in a text of remarkable interest for the light it throws on the climate of critical opinion in which the academicians prepared and launched their play: and indeed on the importance of opinion; the play chosen had to be theoretically right. The academy sought advice from high quarters. Again, unfortunately, the documentation is not quite final, but what we have is substantial. Some years after the whole affair was over, in 1589, Muzio Manfredi got hold of written opinions sent to the academy about the *L'Alessio* and *L'Eraclea* and about his own *Semiramide*, and copied some of them down: Angelo Ingegneri on *L'Alessio*—which Muzio attributes to Vincenzo Giusti, a minor dramatist, among whose published works it does not, however, appear; Ingegneri again on *L'Eraclea*, and a second essay, on that same unfortunate play, almost certainly by Antonio Riccoboni, the Paduan Aristotelian, whose huge commentary on the *Poetics* was shortly to appear; and still another on *L'Eraclea* by no less person than Guarini: all unfavorable.[33]

Pagello even revised his tragedy—either before or after this ordeal—but Pace was firm in opposing it. Pagello even wanted to go with a party sent to Padua to discuss—with Riccoboni, perhaps, among others—the plays, so that he could defend his own in person. At some point in all this turmoil the *Oedipus Rex* must have been suggested and discussed: and the motion, wherever it came from, must have seemed a happy inspiration. What could have been more unexceptionable than the tragedy that had been made a sacred text by Aristotle's discussion of it? Pagello was asked to translate it, but refused; and he managed to get a letter approving his tragedy from the old humanist Marc Antoine Muret;[34] and the academy, with relief perhaps, turned to a Venetian *littérateur*, Orsatto Giustiniano, who had a translation ready.[35] It is not until May 28th 1584, however, that official mention is made in the minutes of the *Oedipus*, when a resolution is passed electing Giustiniano academician in view of the courtesy with which he has put his translation at the academy's disposal.[36]

By May 1584, in fact, the crucial decisions had been made and the problems of organising the production had been thought out. At the meeting of May 6th, three weeks before Giustiniano's election, a series of committees is set up to manage the production; the fault, as usual, is over-elaboration and bad definition of terms of reference.

First, there is a committee of six, with the prince, charged with finding actors, assigning them their parts, making them learn their parts, and rehearsing them. It has authority to spend what may be necessary on travelling to find suitable actors outside the city. It is also empowered to appoint "una persona sopra intendente" at such a fee as is thought proper. This person is to be in charge of the actors and of the *stabilimento* of the production—that is, presumably, of all the apparatus connected with it. He is also to decide whether vocal or instrumental music is to be used with the choruses, so that they serve as *intermedii*; or whether the choruses are to be left *interi* and the tragedy *continuata* (that is given as a continuous production); and whether another way is to be found of introducing music (that is, an alternative to the introduction of *intermedii*). But the special committee for the choruses is also to have a say in this. The position of the producer (if we may call him that) is obviously going to be extremely awkward. To what extent it was anticipated that he should share responsibility with his committee for training the actors is left doubtful; and he has to make important decisions about music and the conduct of the chorus, but is subjected at this point to the authority of still another committee.

Second, there is a committee of six charged with obtaining from the state the piece of ground girt with walls adjoining the theatre, with having a door made there and what other work is necessary. This committee indeed could be described as a works committee. Its terms of reference include the final stages of the theatre. It is instructed

> to have the proscenium erected, and the scenes, both of relieve and painted, with the perspectives, and to provide for the orchestra, the curtains, draperies, and the heaven or ceiling above the theatre;[f]

and also to see to the installation of lights both within and without the *scena*; and to see to the instruments of war that will be needed at the moment when the *scena* is disclosed (that is, to produce the clash of warlike noises that is to signalise this moment). This committee has power to spend money and to summon, if need be, experts from outside the city. Its functions seem rather badly defined; clearly it must deal with matters that call for the intervention of the producer, as well as with major structural matters.

A third committee is set up for music and the choruses. It has to commission the composition of music *sopra li cori con accomodata imitatione*, and is empowered to employ "foreign" musicians, to arrange fees and incur travelling expenses. A fourth, which includes the prince, and the *sopra intendente*, is to be responsible for costumes, including both design and materials. This committee too has authority to spend and incur travelling expenses.

Three separate committees are put in charge of arrangements for entrance and seating: one specifically for controlling all the entrances to the theatre; one to see to the seating of men; and another to the seating of the ladies in the *orchestra*.

We now hear no more about the production until the end of the year.

IV

The academy, however, was not free from other preoccupations during this period. The fabric of the theatre had to be completed, and paid for. And still more money had to be raised to pay for the expenses of the production. We shall go back a little to pick up these threads.

---

[f] di far dirizzare il proscenio, la scena di rileuo, et di pittura con le prospettiue, di far accommodar la orchestra, cortine, et tende, cielo ouero soffitto sopra il Teatro.[37] [Scenes of relieve were cut-out settings arranged in rows at the rear of the stage, which gave an illusion of great depth.]

At that same meeting on May 8th, 1583, when a committee was set up to choose a tragedy, it was also given authority to have a suitable inscription put up above the arch *del fronte della scena*—that is above the *porta regia*, where we can still see it. And the same committee is to remain as a standing committee to assist the prince in managing the financial side of the production. The play is to be paid for by special subscription from the academicians. A resolution is immediately added that all those academicians who have not already subscribed must do so before the end of the month, on penalty of becoming ineligible for election to any office connected with the production. The minutes record no further meetings until December.

On January 1st, 1584, a supper was held *á simbolo* in the new room, now ready, adjoining the theatre. On March 5th, we find that academicians must have their *imprese* placed *nella stanza nostra ordinaria*. They have, as usual, been dilatory. Some have indeed decided on their *imprese*; but they have not been carried out. Every academician must have found his *impresa* by the end of August and had it executed in paint and stucco. Then everyone has to contribute to the *fregio* to be made in this room: a frieze of which the *imprese* are to be part. The contribution is assessed at one *scudo*, or more if necessary. If any member has not been able to find a suitable *impresa* by the time prescribed he must at least have had the ornamental frame in which it is to be set executed. The penalty for failure to comply is ineligibility for office for the space of two years.

The affair of the statues is still giving endless trouble in 1584 to the office-bearers of the academy. Not all the diligence of the present prince or his predecessors in reminding members of what they still have to do, we learn from this same meeting, has been sufficient to get the statues completed. Vacant and unfinished places are there on the *proscenio*, which brings shame to the academy. Severe penalties are threatened if the same work is not finished by the end of April. This, however, as experience might have shown, was not the way to get anything done. The knot has obviously been cut in May when the prince, still Leonardo Valmarana, and three colleagues who are in charge of the fabric make an agreement with two sculptors to do all the work necessary to complete the statues. The sculptors were Ruggero Brascape and Domenico Fontana. They undertake to supply the statues that are wanting, and the inscriptions; to put in order any that are defective; to cover the nudes and put a male head on any statue that still has a female one; to repair all the cornices on the *proscenio*, to repair and complete where necessary the *Historia*—the reliefs, that is, of the labours of Hercules.[38] However, on November 14th, the academy is still talking about the statues. Apparently a number of members had been summoned by name to attend a special discussion: a number have failed to attend—of whom our friends Livio Pagello and Fabio Pace are two. There seem to have been differences of opinion about the inscriptions. The perspectives, however, must be well advanced, because it is laid down, at the same meeting, that from now on no member is to bring anyone—"native" or "foreign"—to see them; members when they come are even to leave their servants outside. Only the "theatre" (as distinct from the *scena*) is shown to "foreigners."

In connection with the progress of the *proscenio* we may note that some time this same year, 1584, following the resolution of May 8th, the inscription was placed above the *porta regia.* The Modena humanist, Paolo Teggia, sent the academy a paper of suggestions for it.[39] The problem he had been given was, it is clear, to prepare an inscription which recorded not only the founding of the theatre by the academicians but that the statues are the memorials of those academicians whose liberality made the theatre possible. There were perhaps good reasons why this second feature should have been cut out of the inscription. Apparently objections were raised even to Teggia's formula *Virtuti ac genio,* and even to the inclusion of Palladio's name: these however remain.[40]

In the second part of the year there is a great deal of activity, not all of which we can follow. Paolo Teggia sends a discourse on the production; he, Muzio Manfredi, and Camillo Camilli are elected to the academy. Speron Speroni sends some advice, in his own hand. Montagna, of Ferrara, sends a paper on lighting. Guarini writes from Ferrara about il Verato, the actor, who should take the part of Tiresias; and he also recommends as an expert in lighting the Duke of Ferrara's engineer, Pasi da Carpi. Francesco Bembo writes about the perspectives, choruses and actors; and so does Giustiniano. There are letters from Filippo Monte about the music, from Scamozzi, letters to Verato. Luigi Groto, the famous *cieco d'Hadria,* is invited to act, first Tiresias, then Oedipus. Maganza, Chiappino and Groto are invited to submit prologues for the tragedy; but opinion is so divided about them it is decided to use none.[41]

In the last days of the year, when the play is so well on its way new crises threaten. A meeting on December 23rd is very well attended—there were forty present—and the reason why is fairly clear. Still another important resolution on finance was to be brought forward. A financial crisis affects not only the extraordinary expenses for the theatre and the production, but the ordinary activities of the academy. We learn from this record about the ordinary annual expenditure to which the academy is pledged: the fixed salaries of the *bidello* and his two sisters; the rent of the house; about the need to appoint at least two good lecturers. Voluntary subscriptions cover hardly a third of these ordinary expenses. Appeals to the goodwill of the academicians have proved useless. Many members are openly unsatisfied, complaining that although they are carrying almost the whole weight of the academy's expenses, others who contribute little or nothing have an equal voice, and sometimes a majority in the academy's deliberations. Nor is it fair that the prince, in addition to the other calls made on him, should also be responsible for substantial expenditure on the production. Unless something is really done the production cannot go ahead. In these circumstances it is proposed that—without prejudice to any existing subscriptions or obligations—every academician who wishes to be eligible to vote or to be voted for in the council must, within a given term of days, pledge himself to an annual subscription of 12 *scudi d'oro*: a sum which, at the very least, is paid to every other academy in the country. Those academicians who refuse are not to be expelled, but are to be declared ineligible for office and are excluded from the business of the council. This resolution is never to be altered, revoked or annulled, unless by five sixths of the votes of those who, by its provisions, are eligible to vote. The resolution was passed by twenty-seven votes to twelve. There may have been some results: at any rate some salaries were raised and a grant was made to the poet-in-ordinary, Maganza. But at a meeting on

January 6th, 1585, Pace got himself included in the small list of those who were specifically excepted from the provisions of the resolution.

A second crisis is more mysterious. We find that the *Podestà* has refused to allow the production to take place—even though Mercuriale, Guilandrini, and Zabarella have been removed from the cast. These were distinguished visitors, professors at Padua, who clearly wanted to take part; why the *Podestà* should have objected does not emerge. Nor do his further objections to the production. In any case an appeal is made to Venice, and on January 1st the necessary permission comes through.[42]

Ingegneri had arrived in Vicenza in December, and at the beginning of the year the chief participants were in town, Pasi, the lighting expert; Groto, the Oedipus, Verato and his wife (Guarini himself had brought him, with Pasi, from Ferrara), Tiresias and Jocasta; that other professor, Riccoboni, whose comments are to be so sour.[43]

On January 30th there is a resolution in council that tells us something about the progress of the stage. Referring to the earlier resolution (November 14th, 1584) governing access to theatre and stage, the text goes on:

> at that time outsiders were not denied access to the theatre as a whole, but only to the stage, which was under construction. It was shut off, and those who were admitted freely into the theatre could not see it. Now that the stage is completed, ready for use and open to view, the prohibition ought to be extended to a total ban on entry to the theatre. For it is tiresome that visitors are shown into the auditorium every day, to the hindrance of those who are seeing to matters necessary for the presentation of our tragedy. It is therefore proposed that, from now on, no one of whatever rank, citizen or foreigner, may, under any pretext, be brought into the theatre, and still less be allowed to inspect the stage.[g]

To give effect to this every academician is to be liable, at the prince's request, to give a day to mounting guard at the doors of the theatre; and is to refuse admission to everyone except workmen or those who in the prince's opinion are genuinely concerned with the production. And on February 9th plans are made for seating and protocol. Academicians are to have a special place in the *orchestra*; and one or two *gradi* are to be provided for their wives, also in the *orchestra*; but the first of the *gradi* is to be reserved for the wife of the Capitano and other Venetian or "foreign" ladies of note. Wives are to proceed to the theatre in the company of the prince's wife and be there to welcome the Capitano's wife and the other ladies on their arrival: the Capitano's wife is to be the first woman to enter the theatre. Unmarried academicians may bring as guests ladies related to them who are to be treated as wives. "Foreign" ladies staying with the academicians as guests may

[g] si, come alhora non doueua prohibir l'adito al Teatro massimamente a persone forestiere, ma solamente la scena, che si facceua. La quale scena a quelli che fossero uenuti nel Teatro facilmente per se stessa, essendo chiusa, non si uedeua; Cosi hora che detta scena è finita est conuien esser essercitata et scoperta, deue esser' aumentata con una totale prohibitione anco di esso Teatro; poi che ogni giorno importunamente uengono introdotte persone sobra i Gradi con disturbo di coloro che attendono del continuo alle cose necessarie nella rappresentatione della Tragedia. Però si propone . . . che da qui inanzi niuno sia di qual siuoglia conditione ò terriero ò forestiere possa esser introdotto nel teatro, et tanto meno à ueder la scena sotto qualsiuoglia pretesto imaginabile.[44]

accompany the ladies of the house, but are to be seated elsewhere. It is expressly laid down that no masked or disguised persons are to be admitted to the *orchestra* or to any other part of the theatre. There is also concern about whether the theatre is big enough to hold the numbers of "foreigners" who are said to be coming; and a small committee is appointed to try to find out how many are to be expected and to arrange seating for them.

Still, at this point, when things had gone so far, and only about a fortnight before production, there was not the money to pay for it. On February 16th there is a meeting attended by as many as 38 members, which is not surprising in view of the situation. Every attempt to get the necessary money together has failed. New ways must be tried out (but, in effect they are the same old ways which had never worked). Every academician is within eight days at most to deposit a promissory note for all that he owes the academy in the way of ordinary and extraordinary subscriptions; this is to fall due on April 1st next, and the time is not to be extended. The penalty for failure to comply is automatic expulsion, not to be revoked except by a unanimous vote. (A vote of February 17th adds that letters of notification were indeed sent to eight—named—academicians.) This was the last meeting, it seems, before the production.

On February 27th there is a rehearsal and Pace took the opportunity to make it clear that he was glad that it was not his work that was being given. Guards are placed round the theatre.[45] Sunday, March 3rd, 1585, is the day of the first performance. [46] There are, it is said, about two thousand visitors, lodged in the town, and the streets are full of carriages, horses, ladies, "foreigners." The audience begins to enter the theatre between ten in the morning and two in the afternoon.[47] Among the first are Mercuriale, Massaria, and Riccoboni.[48] No one, we are told, grew bored with waiting; there were refreshments of wine and fruit and every provision for the comfort of the audience. And then there was the arrival of the ladies to watch, and how they were conducted to their seats in the *orchestra*: one spectator says there were four hundred of them. The same witness—Filippo Pigafetta—says that finally the audience numbered more than 3,000, figures it is hardly possible to believe, though we can well believe that the theatre was crammed full. There was the Capitano, Alvise Mocenigo; there was the Ambassador of France to the Serenissima and his wife; and a whole concourse of the distinguished.[49] But the *Podestà* did not attend. At long last the time comes for the performance to begin. The odour of perfumes reaches the audience: the perfume strewn in Thebes to placate the angry gods. At half-past seven the curtain falls. To the sound of trumpet and the music of war, in the twinkling of an eye, the stage stands revealed. For about four hours the audience listens to the *Oedipus*: the performance ends some time after eleven—when some visitors had spent eleven hours or so in the theatre. We hear only of excitement and pleasure and of admiration for the magnificence of theatre and play—but Mercuriale had faults to find, and Riccoboni threatened to write about the mistakes that he had noted, and indeed carried out his threat.[50]

For these last days of Carnival, life in Vicenza is sumptuous and splendid. Solemn masses alternate with concerts of music and receptions. Alvise Mocenigo entertains the academy formally. There is a great ball in the *Palazzo della Ragione* with five hundred ladies present. There is another performance of *Oedipus*, March 5th, the last day of Carnival.[51]

V

We may end this story on a less elevated plane, and on a not unexpected note. The business before a meeting of May 5th, 1585, tells us how the *Oedipus* was really financed. The prince, Leonardo Valmarana, paid for it. At the last moment, seeing that the money was not forthcoming from the academicians, he borrowed it himself: 1000 ducats from the *Monte di pietà* of Verona; 1400 from the Signora Claudia Piovene; and smaller sums from other individuals. He has had to pay interest; he has had to raise money on his own property; and for the last year he has had to incur extraordinary expenses in connexion with the production. In short, the academy has a debt to him personally of 1633 ducats, 4 *troni*, 3 *marchetti*. This debt must be paid off; and, so the resolution runs, the academy must

> hold in perpetual remembrance the fact that its own ardent spirit, its own diligence, the expenditure of its own resources and what was owed to the academy, were the principal reasons for this most momentous undertaking's being brought to a conclusion.[h]

The academy has settled the rest of its debts, and arrangements are proposed for repaying this personal debt within eight years, interest of six per cent being paid meanwhile; and the formal agreement is entered in the minutes. But the academy was incapable of settling such matters; and the whole question of the Valmarana debt and how to pay it is dragging on in meetings in December, involved with the old questions about whether there should be a fixed annual subscription or not. We do not know whether Valmarana ever got his money back or not: that he ever got it all back we may doubt. And we may record our conviction that it was he who was finally responsible not only for finding most of the money for the production, but for seeing through the completion of the theatre and the preparations for the play during the two years when he was prince. During that period there must have been some force at work strong enough to overcome the dilatoriness of the academicians and their reluctance—or was it after all, inability?—to pay for their ambitions: not to mention their jealousies and intrigues. That force was most likely Valmarana.

[h] tener perpetua memoria, che il suo ardor d'animo, la sua diligentia, lo spendere il suo proprio, et obligarlo inuece dell'Academia sono stati principal cagione che questa importantissima attione sia stata condotta à fine.[52]

APPENDICES

Appendix I:
Poet and Architect

Notes on the Terms used by Other Writers of
Masques and Pageants

The purpose of these notes is simply to provide a survey of the practice of other writers for comparison with Jonson's. Certain rough generalizations emerge. "Invented and written" is probably the full and accurate formula to be used when the poet has both found the subject and written the words. A distinction is frequently made between the invention— which is the subject or fable—and the writing. The separation of functions was by no means abnormal. When a poet claims only to have "written" the masque it cannot be stated without further evidence whether he invented it or not. Invention can include both finding and expressing.

I. Masques

Tethys Festival (1610) was "devis'd by Samuel Daniel," according to the title-page.[a] The text contains the well-known passage obviously aimed at Jonson:

> But in these things wherein the onely life consists in shew; the arte and invention of the Architect giues the greatest grace, and is of most importance: ours, the least part and of least

[a] A summary view of title-pages can be got from W. W. Greg, *A List of Masques, Pageants*, etc. (London, The Bibliographical Society, 1902).

note in the time of the performance thereof; and therefore haue I inserted the description of the artificiall part, which only speakes M. Inigo Iones.

Samuel Daniel, *The Complete Works*,

ed. Grosart (London, 1883), III, p. 307.

The "Maske . . . in honour of the Lord Hayes" (1607) was "*Inuented and set forth by Thoma. Campion Doctor of Phisicke.*" His *Lords' Maske* (1613) and his *Somerset Masque* (1614) are both described as *Written by Thomas Campion.* It is perhaps not very surprising that Chapman's language should be difficult to interpret—he was given to gnarled and knotty phrases. He describes his *Masque of the Middle Temple and Lincoln's Inn* (1613) as: *Invented, and fashioned, with the ground, and speciall structure of the whole worke: By our Kingedomes most Artfull and Ingenious Architect Innigo Jones. Supplied, Applied, Digested, and written, by Geo. Chapman.* Chapman means by "application" the application of the subject of the masque to the persons and occasion for whom it has been devised. What he means by "supplied" and how all this relates to Jones's "invention" remains obscure. Beaumont's *Masque of the Inner Temple and Gray's Inne* (1613) was *Written by Francis Beaumont Gentleman.*

In the thirties we have a variety of authors—this was the period of Jones's predominance, when he presumably looked for authors to suit him. Shirley claims that *The Triumph of Peace* (1633)—not a masque prepared by the court—was *Invented and Written* by himself, while "The scene and ornament, was the act of Inigo Jones Esquire, Surveyor of his Majesty's works" (*Dramatic Works and Poems*, ed. Gifford and Dyce, London 1833, VI, p. 254). Carew's *Cælum Britannicum* (ed. 1640) has simply *The Inventors. Tho Carew. Inigo Jones.* Davenant's *The Temple of Love* and *Britannia Triumphans* (1634, 1637) are simply by Inigo Jones and Davenant. The *Triumphs of the Prince d'Amour* (1635), we learn, was "devis'd and written in three days" (*Dramatic Works*, ed. Maidment and Logan, Edinburgh and London, 1872, I, p. 327). *Salmacida Spolia* (1639) is interesting: "The invention, ornament, scenes and apparitions, with their descriptions, were made by Inigo Jones . . . What was spoken or sung, by William D'avenant . . . The subject was set down by them both." (II, p. 327.) Apart from the statement in *Tempe Restor'd* this is the most explicit statement we have.

When Davenant says that he and Jones collaborated in setting down the subject he means that they were together responsible for the argument of the masque which is printed under the heading *Subject*—as it is in *Britannia Triumphans*. In *The Temple of Love* it is called *Argument*. Chapman prints his as *The Applicable Argument*. Beaumont heads his *The Deuise or Argument of the Masque*. In *The Masque of Flowers* (1614) it appears as *The Devite of the Masque*. The extent to which the moral theme of the masque is set out varies.

II. The Pageant

In that the pageant demands the co-operation of visual and verbal elements, the same problems arise in connexion with it. We know little or nothing about the figure of the designer in connexion with the pageants. We do know that the company responsible had, naturally, to approve the subjects.

Jonson could use the same language about pageants as he used about masques. Thus describing one of the shows for James's procession through the City (1604) he calls it an "Invention"—because it gives a subject—and says "To which bodie . . . we were to apt our soule." (*Works*, VII, p. 106.)

Webster's *Monuments of Honour* (1624) appears as *Invented and Written by Iohn Webster*. Dekker's *Britannia's Honour* (1628) as invented by him; but his *London's Tempe* (1629) simply as written by him. All of Heywood's have "written by." Middleton is not consistent. *The Triumphs of Truth* (1613) is "*Directed, written, and redeem'd into Forme*" by him. *The Triumphs of Love and Antiquity* (1619) and *The Triumphs of Honour and Virtue* (1622) are simply "by" him. Only the hack, Antony Munday, is consistent: all of his pageants—and they stretch from 1605 to 1618—have *Deuised and Written*.

Appendix II:
Poet and Architect

Jonson's Sources for the Story of Eros and Anteros

Jonson had already used the story of Eros and Anteros in the earlier entertainment *A Challenge at Tilt* with its sequel *The Tilting*, produced over New Year 1613–4. Here the story is used to provide a framework for a "Barriers." We see two Cupids struggling and disputing about which is the real Cupid. A challenge is issued and accepted. The Cupids reappear with their champions. After the conflict Hymen appears and tells the children who they really are. He tells the story as it appears in *Love's Welcome*, gives them a branch of palm and says they must struggle for this and divide it between them. The little drama is emblematic of mutual love and the true concord of marriage—the entertainment is part of marriage celebrations. The story and its application are those of *Love's Welcome*.

The story of the two boys is common in the sixteenth century and was told in slightly varying forms by the mythographers whom Jonson commonly used, Giraldi and Cartari. There were two traditional views of how it was to be interpreted. Some held that Anteros was the enemy of Cupid, spiritual as opposed to earthly love. This tradition was however rejected by the better informed antiquarians, who knew the classical interpretation of Anteros as "Love in return." (On this see E. Panofsky, *Studies in Iconology* (N. Y. 1939), pp. 126–7.) Alciati represents Anteros as *amor virtutis* and as celestial love opposing earthly love. The story of Venus and the oracle, Themis, and the birth of Anteros, is told in the commentaries; but the "mutual love" interpretation is rejected (see Alciati, 1621, Emblems *cx* and *cxi*, and pp. 458, 460, 462, where the story of the struggle for the palm is told). The whole point of Jonson's use of the story is that it should be about mutual love, but he also knew the other interpretation. Thus in *Cynthia's Revels*, V, iii, Anteros is called "Love's enemy" and in *Love Restored* he is called "Anti-Cupid, the loue of vertue."

The versions in Giraldi, Cartari and in the Alciati commentaries are not enough to account for Jonson's version. Giraldi tells the story briefly, gives both interpretations, accepting that of "mutual love," reports from Pausanias the image of the struggle for the palm, and from "Porphyrius" the story of Venus consulting Themis, her reply, and the sequel. (L. G. Giraldi, *De Deis Gentium*, Basel 1565, pp. 348-9.) Cartari rejects the idea that Anteros is Cupid's enemy, reports the Pausanias story at greater length, as he does with that of "Porphyrius." He also illustrates the struggle of the Cupids (see Figure 62). (V. Cartari, *Imagines Deorum*, Lyons 1581, pp. 323-6. This is the Latin translation of the *Imagini* used by Jonson.) Details given by Jonson—the part played by the Graces, the note that Apollo had not yet come to Delphi—are not accounted for. A. H. Gilbert (*The Symbolic Persons in the Masques of Ben Jonson*, 1948, p. 43 n. 24) finds that Jonson contradicts himself by making the Graces nurses of Eros in *A Challenge at Tilt* and of Anteros in *Love's Welcome*. Herford and Simpson, however, in their text of the latter (*Works*, VII, p. 811), have found from the MS. that Anteros is the speaker of lines attributed in the folio text to Eros: so we have Anteros saying that the Graces were the nurses of Eros, not Eros giving them to Anteros. In the same note Gilbert points out that the story is told and illustrated by Bocchius in his *Symbolicarum Quæstionum* (Bologna, 1574, Symbol LXXX and pp. clxxx-i) and that Bocchius shows the Graces acting as nurses to Anteros. I should say that the image shows both children being nursed by the Graces, and certainly in the accompanying poem Bocchius writes "Olim cupidinem editum Venus dedit / Blandis alendum gratijs mater dolens."

We must go behind such authors to the source from which they themselves took the little apologue of Venus and her visit to Themis. The story has been fully set out by R. V. Merrill in his excellent article, "Eros and Anteros" (*Speculum*, XIX, 1944, pp. 265-84). The myth is found for the first time in one of the orations of Themistius, the fourth century rhetorician; and seems to have been his invention. Aldus in 1534 printed eight orations by Themistius, including the προτρεπτικός which contains our myth. Before this, however—presumably from a MS. source—Marico Equicola had found and used it in his *Libro de Natura d'amore* (first printed 1525). It is fully treated in Celio Calcagnini's *Anteros sive de mutuo amore* (1544)—and he for some reason attributes it to "Porphyrius." Giraldi probably took it over from Calcagnini. Jonson was clearly using one of the full versions, either by Themistius or Equicola or Calcagnini. They have the details he gives—including the note on Apollo and the part played by the Graces—and in all of them Themis's speech is verbally closer to his versions of it than is that given by Giraldi or Cartari. Equicola and Calcagnini give literal translations of Themistius. Which of the three Jonson was using I cannot determine.[a] I give Equicola's version, because he gives the detail about Anteros being the son of Mars. And Jonson has added, from Giraldi or Cartari, probably, the struggle for the palm.

[a] A. H. Gilbert, *Symbolic Persons* . . . , p. 43, quotes an epigram of Calcagnini's from the 1553 edition of his *Carmina*, of which Jonson had a copy. But this cannot have been Jonson's effective source.

Due sono le cupidini un detto Heros, l'altro Antheros. Questo M. Tullio dice essere stato figliulo di Venere & Marte . . . Di Themistio poneremo le parole nell'idioma nostro conuerse. Nel tempo che Venere generò Cupido, bello & uenusto si uedea quel fanciullo molto piu bello che la bella madre, ma non cresceua in grandezza & statura, laquale correspondesse alla bellezza. Perlaqual cosa anxia non sapende quel che fare la madre, tutta si affligeua, similmente le gratie del putto nutrici, perilche andarno al oracolo di Themis (non era ancora Apollo in Delphi) pregando supplici che qualche remedio si trouasse a quella insolita & degna di misericordia, infelicità. Themis disse. Io ui leuarò di questa sollecitudine. Certamente non me par habbiate ben compresa la natura & ingegno del putto, perche o Venere questo tuo uero amore, forse puo nascer solo, crescere non puo solo, pero se desideri che cresca, ti è necessaria l'opera di Antherote, il quale con reciproco amore risponde alla beneuolentia. Sera cosi la natura delli fratelli che l'uno a l'altro sera authore di farse crescere, riguardandosi mutuamente, germinando da equal pianta. Se l'uno mancarà, sera necessario manchino ambidue. In questo modo uenere parturi Antherote, il quale a pena nato subito Cupido crebbe in alto & esplicò le penne: gia caminaua grande, essendo addito a questa sorte molte uolte è uessato da male, mo cresce, mo decresce: cosi sempre ha bisogno della presentia del fratello, quale sel uede diuentar grande, esso se sforza diuentar maggiore, & se conosce quello esser picciolo, ello diuenta di mala uoglia & languido. Denota Themistio che chi uol esser amato, bisogno amare, che lo amore se non è mutuo, tosto manca.

Libro di Natura d'Amore di Mario Equicola. Di nuouo . . . ristampato e corretto da M. Lodovico Dolce. Venice, 1554, pp. 123–4.

Appendix III:
The Renaissance Poet as Classicist

Illustrative passages from Giulio Pace, *Aristoteles de anima libri tres, Graece et Latine, Ivl. Pacio a Bergia interprete, Hanover,* MDCXI.

a. Expositurus singulos sensus merito incipit ab aspectu, qui est omnium nobilissimus, & quo solo sentimus etiam res coelestes, ac ne recedat a methodo antea praescripta, incipit ab obiecto, quod est aspectabile seu visibile: quod ita definit . . . (pp. 290–1). Comment on II, vii. (1) (418a).

b. . . . nunc animae definitionem colligit & primo ait eam esse substantiam, vt incipiat a summo genere. Deinde addit eam esse formam . . . Quod sit substantia, non supponitur vt Auerroes existimat, sed probatur, ex quo quod dictum fuit in part. 7. Corpus viuens esse substantiam compositam ex anima & corpore, omnis enim pars substantiae est substantia. Cum igitur anima sit pars substantiae, id est corporis viuentis, necessario est substantia. Quod autem sit forma, colligitur ex particula octaua, vbi probatum fuit, corpus non esse animam: nam corpus est materia, vt ibidem dictum fuit: anima vero est in corpore, tamquam in materia & subiecto: proinde est eius forma . . . (p. 235). Comment on II, i. (4) (412a).

c. Secunda praemunito est subdiuisio substantiae in materiam, formam, & compositam ex materia & forma. ponit autem inter materiam & formam duplex discrimen, quod pertinet ad essentiam animae intelligendam. Vnum est: quod materia non est hoc aliquid, id est, per se non subsistit, sed per formam: forma autem est, quae facit hoc esse aliquid, id est quae facit rem consistere, & esse id quod est. Obserua, aliter accipi in praesentia hoc aliquid, aliter in categoriis cap de substantia. ibi namque solae substantiae indiuiduae vocantur hoc aliquid, vt Socrates, Plato: hic vero omnes substantiae compositae. Alterum discrimen est: quod materia est potentia, forma vero est actus. Cum autem actus a Graecis non vno nomine appelletur, sed modo ἐνέργεια, modo ἐντελέχεια: Aristoteles hoc loco vocat ἐντελέχειαν: quod verbum ponet etiam in definitione animae. non est autem cur existimemus esse hic aliquid singulare, aut arcanum, cum anima vocatur, ἐντελέχεια: sed eodem modo vocatur ἐντελέχεια, quo cetere naturales formae, vnde & alibi saepe Arist. hoc verbo vtitur ἐντελέχεια autem nihil aliud significat, quam perfectionem sine actum perficientem. nam ἐντελὴς, perfectum significat: propterea quod nihil est τέλειον, id est, perfectum, nisi habeat τὸ τέλος, id est, finem, vt ait Phylosophus 3. Physic. cap. 9 partic. 3. Hinc igitur est, quod forma vocatur ἐντελέχεια, quia est τέλος, id est, finis, vt Arist. exponit 2 Phys. cap. 7. part. 3. & cap. 8. part. 8 . . . . vt & ex multis aliis locis, apparet Aristoteles omnem formam vocare ἐντελέχειαν, non tantum animam. ponetur quidem ἐντελέχεια in definitione animae; sed vt genus in definitione speciei; quoniam anima est forma, & omnis forma est ἐντελέχεια (pp. 232–3).

Comment on II, i. (3) (412a).

d.   Inquit ergo colorem esse id, quod est inaspectabili per se, id est, in superficie visibili. nam superficies colorata videtur per se: corpus autem per se non videtur: tantum enim cernimus superficiem: non videmus autem altitudinem, vel latitudinem corporis, nisi quatenus videmus plures superficies, superiorem, & ad latus. Praeterea etiam lumen non videtur per se . . . .

. . . superficies non dicitur per se visibilis: quia visibile non ponitur in definitione superficiei, sed accidit. in alio igitur sensu dicitur per se visibilis, id est, non per aliud: quia in seipsa habet causam cur videatur, nempe colorem. corpus autem non videtur per se, sed per aliud, id est, per superficiem. Item lumen non videtur per se, sed per terminum siue extremum, id est, superficiem coloratum, vt paulo post explicabitur (pp. 290–1).

Comment on II, vii. (3) (418b).

Appendix IV:
The Imagery of *Blacknesse and Beautie*

1. The ancients induc'd *Oceanus* alwayes with a Bulls head: *propter vim ventorum, à quibus incitatur, & impellitur: vel quia Tauris similem fremitum emittat, vel quia tanquam Taurus furibundus, in littora feratur*, Euripid. *in* Oreste. Ὠκέανος ὅν ταυρόκρατος ἀγκάλαις ἑλίσσων κυκλεῖ χθόνα.

   Jonson, *Blacknesse*, p. 170, note h.

Taurinum autem caput Oceano tribuerunt antiqui propter vim ventorum, à quibus excitatur & impellitur, vel quia tauris similem fremitum emittat, vel quia tanquam tauris furibundus in litora feratur, cuiusmodi finguntur esse etiam fluuij.

Conti, Lyons 1602, p. 812.

Huic (Oceanus) tauri caput esse censuerunt antiqui, quare illum ita ταυρόκρανον appellauit Euripides in Oreste: Ὠκέανος ὅν ταυρόκρανος ἀγκάλαις ἑλίσσων κυκεῖ χθόνα. *Oceanus quem Tauriceps vlnis Se flectens ambit terram.*

Conti, pp. 809–10.

2. All riuers are said to be the sons of the *Ocean*: for, as the Ancients thought, out of the vapours, exhaled by the heat of the *Sunne*, riuers, and fountaines were begotten. And both by *Orph. in Hymn. & Homer Iliad* ξ *Oceanus* is celebrated *tanquam pater, & origo, dijs, & rebus, quia nihil sine humectatione nascitur, aut putrescit.*

   Jonson, *Blacknesse*, p. 172, note k.

Oceani filij tam multi & filiæ fuisse dicuntur, quia ex vaporibus, qui calore Solis sublimes tolluntur, gignuntur fluuiorum aquæ & fontes, vt putarunt antiquorum nonnulli.

Conti, p. 813.

Hunc eundem Oceanum tradidit Orpheus, & omnes antiquorum theologi principium ortus Diis & rebus extitisse, quia, vt sensit Thales, nihil sine humectatione nascitur aut putrescit . . .

Conti, p. 812.

3. Inde verò natam fuisse hanc opinionem scripserunt antiqui, quòd specula quædam rotunda ita parabantur, vt in his Luna omnino appareret è cœlo deducta. Atque Pythagoræ ludicrum fuit quodam, Luna plena existente, vt quis in speculo quodam

sanguine, quæcunque collibuisset, scriberet: atque alteri prædicens à tergo illi assisteret, ea quæ scripsisset Lunæ ostentans: atque ille deinde intenta acie oculorum in Lunam, vniuersa quæ forent in speculo scripta perlegeret, tanquam in Luna scripta fuissent. Inde existimo artificium Cornelij Agrippæ originem coepisse, qui in occulta philosphia videtur rationem quandam attingere, vt qui maximè à nobis distant, possint quæ volumus in Luna descripta perlegere.

Conti, pp. 252–3.

4. Aquam verò Isocaëdri figuram tenere dixerunt. Est autem Isocaëdrum, Euclide autore, figura solida, quæ viginti triangulis æqualibus & æqualium laterum, continetur: proptereà quòd aqua sua natura mobilis sit, & diuisioni flexuique perfacilis . . .

Valeriano, Lyons 1595, p. 585.

5. Si verò pedes altiùs in aquam mersos effinxissent, purificatorem significabant. Nam & alibi aqua & ignis in defecationis significatum accipiuntur, quòd rebus his labes omnis eleuatur & eximatur. Hic verò de iis sermo est, quæ leui sint maculata contaminata, quibus vnda satis supérque sit ad depurandum.

Valeriano, p. 337.

6. Salamandra: animal enim sine squamis & cute esse, corpus habere frigidum, & maximè humidum, quo singula quæcunque contigerit humectet multò magis, quam Limaces faciant, humorémque illum à corpore tam longè diffluentem, vim eam habere, vt ignem extinguat quem attigerit . . .

Valeriano, p. 152.

7. Vti igitur profati sumus, cœlum Ægyptij rore pluuium cùm pinxissent, disciplinam institutionisque laborem & operam intelligebant: mira etenim est vtriusque rei similitudo. Nam veluti ros in herbas, frutices, plantasque omnes decidens, ea omnia quæcunque molliri apta sunt, humectat, pascit & liberaliter educat . . . .

Valeriano, p. 369.

8. Questa bellezza (bellezza sensibile), si come la intelligibile, & come vniuersalmente ogni natura, ha tre modi di essere cioè, Causale, Essentiale, ò vero Formale & Participato. la causa sua e il Cielo, sensibile, animato di quelle virtu chel muoue, cosi come la causa della bellezza & Venere intelligibile era quel primo & vero Dio intelligibile. Questa virtu motiua del Cielo, è la infima potentia dell' anima celeste, secondo laqual potentia è congiunta al cor del cielo, come è la virtu nostra motiua & progressiua congiunta à musculi & à nerui, liquali vsa per instrumenti & organi ad essequire questa sua operatione, che è il moto, cosi la virtu motiua dell'anima del cielo, atto corpo & organo al moto celeste circolare et sempiterno, come i piedi sono atti al moto del caminare delli animali, mediante esso corpo del cielo transmuta questa materia inferiore & formale di tute le forme, che sono in lei non altrimenti, che la mano dell'artefice mediante el pennello forma la sua materia di questa Venere volgare, che è la bellezza di queste forme materiali sensibili, è quella virtu motiua dell'anima celeste, & in quella ha essa Venere lo essere causale. Lo essere suo formale & essentiale è in essi colori dalla luce del sole visibile illuminati, cosi come sono illuminate le Idee dalla luce di quel primo inuisibile sole.

Pico, Basel 1601, pp. 505–6.

9. ... Amor autem simile ad simile trahit. Terrae partes singulae amore mutuo copu-
lante, ad partes alias terrae sui similes sese conferunt. Tota etiam terra ad simile sibi
mundi centrum illius auiditate descendit. Aquae partes ad sese inuicem similiter & ad
locum sibi conuientiem cum toto aquae corpore perferuntur. Idem partes aeris
ignisque faciunt, ac etiam duo haec elementa ad supernam regionem sibi congruam &
similem regionis illius amore trahuntur ... Vnitatem vero partium mutuus earun-
dem efficit amor. Quod in humoribus nostrorum corporum & mundi elementis
intueri licet, quorum concordia, vt ait Empedocles Pythagoreus, & mundus & corpus
nostrum constat, discordia dissipatur. Concordiam vero illis pacis atque amoris
praestat vicissitudo.

   Ficino, Or. 3, Cap. 2, p. 1329.

10. Veneri, Floræ, Proserpinæ, fontium nimphis Corinthio genere constitutæ aptas
videbuntur habere proprietates, quod his dijs propter teneritatem gracilora & florida
foliisque & uolutis ornata opera facta augere uidebantur uistum decorem ...

   ... TERTIVM uero quod Corinthium dicitur, uirginalis habet gracilitatis imita-
tionem, quod uirgines propter ætatis teneritatem gracilioribus membris figuratæ,
effectus recipiunt in ornatu uenustiores.

   Vitruvius, *De Architectura Libri Decem Cum Commentariis Danielis Barbari* ...
   Venice, 1567, lib. 1, Cap. 2, p. 22; lib. 4, Cap. 1, p. 124.

11. Iridem Thaumantis & Electræ filiam fuisse tradiderunt, quia Thaumas sit Ponti filius,
Electra vero Cœli siue Solis; nam id nomen serenitatem significat: est enim ἥλιος Sol,
αἴθριος serenus. nascitur igitur Iris ex aqua & serenitate, è refractione radiorum
scilicet, vt voluit Aristoteles in meteorologicis.

   Conti, p. 901.

12. Harum verò fundamentum est elementorum quatuor temperata complexio: vt corpus
nostrum cœlo, cuius est temperata substantia, sit simillimum ... Sic enim & cœlestis
fulgor facile lucebit in corpore cœlo persimili: & forma hominis illa perfecta, quam
habet animus in pacatam obedientemque materiam, resultabit expressior.

   Ficino, Or. 5, Cap. 6, pp. 1337–8.

13. ... ogni volta che piu cose diuerse concorrono ad constitutione d'una terza, laquale
nasca della debita mistione & temperamento fatto di quelle cose varie, quello decore &
quella Harmonia & quella temperantia che resulta di quella proportionata commis-
tione, si chiama bellezza.

   Pico, lib. 2, Cap. 21, p. 505.

14. ... Hinc & Plato postquam Pythagoricæ successione doctrinæ, & ingenij proprij
diuina profunditate, cognouit nullam esse posse sine his numeris ingabilem compe-
tentiam, in Timæo suo mundi animam per istorum numerorum contextionem
ineffabili prouidentia Dei fabricatoris instituit ... Ergo mundi anima, quæ ad motum, hoc quod videmus vniuersitatis corpus impellit, contexta numeris musicam de se
creantibus concinentiam, necesse est vt sonos musicos de motu quem proprio impulsu
præstat, efficiat, quorum originem in fabrica suæ contextionis inuenit ...

   Macrobius, lib. II, Cap. II, pp. 153–4; p. 158.

Appendix V:
Hymenæi

The Epithalamium

The epithalamium was one of the well established poetic kinds and was much attempted by Renaissance poets; the models Jonson used and how he used them are topics which have been adequately studied. On the Renaissance epithalamium, on Jonson and his debts to his predecessors, James A. S. McPeek, *Catullus in Strange and Distant Britain* (Harvard, 1939), Chapter VII can be consulted: this is the most comprehensive treatment. The primary classical models were the two poems by Catullus, *Carmen* lxi (to use the modern numbering of the *Carmina*) which Jonson and his contemporaries knew as the Epithalamium for Manlius and Julia, and *Carmen* lxii, the Chorus of Youths and Maidens, together with Statius' *Epithalamium in Stellam et Violentillam* and Claudian's *Fescennina de nuptiis Honorii Augusti*. These, and perhaps others, Jonson knew and used in *Hymenæi*, particularly in the last songs and in the epithalamium itself. Catullus' influence is most marked, in words, imagery and verse form. Spenser's *Epithalamium* too was drawn on; and Jonson must have known the epithalamium that Chapman introduced into the fifth sestiad of *Hero and Leander*, with the description of marriage ritual that precedes it, a description that has the same background of scholarship as Jonson's. (See my note on "Chapman's use of Cartari in the Fifth Sestiad of *Hero and Leander*," *Modern Language Review*, XXXIX, pp. 280–5.)

Julius Caesar Scaliger devoted a chapter to the epithalamium in his *Poetices* (*Poetices Libri Septem*. Editio Tertia, 1586. Lib. III, Cap. CI, pp. 381–392). One of the topics that can be brought into such a poem, he says, is Love's place in the beginnings and makings of the world; much useful material in praise of Love, he adds, is to be found in Plato's *Symposium*. He also advises the prospective poet that such a poem gives admirable opportunities for displaying a widely ranging and far from contemptible erudition. To illustrate his point Scaliger then gives a cursory account of the ritual of the Roman marriage, of the *auspices*, the sacrifice, the personages in the procession, the dresses: almost all the items in fact that we find in Jonson. And Jonson knew this chapter of Scaliger's and quotes from it in *Hymenæi* (p. 225, note on Epithalamium. Cf. Appendix VI).

Appendix VI:
Hymenæi

The Sources and the Footnotes[a]

Jonson supports his text with some ninety-five references; we are directed to more than forty works by more than thirty authors. We are not however to suppose that each reference indicates an independent reference to an authority. Jonson was, as has been pointed out, working with secondary authorities. There is Scaliger; there are Landus, Alexander, Brisson and Hotman, and Robertus Stephanus. There are Ripa, Giraldi, Conti, Cartari. To his study of these works, and to his memories of the epithalamia of Catullus, Claudian and Statius, of an elegy by Propertius and the second book of Lucan's *Pharsalia* Jonson owes the various erudition of his footnotes and the references he gives. By far the greatest number of the references come from the three accounts of the Roman marriage, and from the mythographers, particularly from Giraldi. Few of the references to Catullus are independent of the secondary authorities; it is doubtful whether the references to Claudian, Statius and Propertius are really independent; and there is only the one independent reference to Lucan. "The Scholiast on Pindar," "Theoph. Phurnut. and the Grammarians on Homer"—such allusions come from less remote sources: from the sources scarcely mentioned. Alexander, Brisson, Hotman are mentioned once each, and the mythographers not at all. And not only the more exotic references are supplied in this way. The author most frequently referred to is Sextus Pompeius Festus whose *De Verborum Significatione* Jonson may well have known, as most scholars of his time did.

[a] Details of the works and editions referred to have already been given and are not repeated.

Martianus Capella and Plutarch come next; we know he had read the *De Nuptiis* and the *De Placitis Philosophorum*, and it is difficult to imagine that he had not also read Plutarch's life of Romulus and his *Conjugalia Praecepta*, and also the *Quaestiones Romanae* which turn up everywhere at this period. Ovid, Virgil and Servius' commentary on the *Aeneid* share the third place; this last Jonson had probably consulted from time to time, and no one is likely to question his familiarity with the works of the masters. In his references to and quotations from these texts, from the familiar as from the less familiar, Jonson is following his secondary authorities. A line from the *Aeneid* or the *Metamorphoses*, a sentence from Martianus—Jonson quotes them not because he has remembered them in the first place or has looked them up specially, but because they are adduced as evidence by the scholars he is following. Even with Catullus it is often difficult to say whether he is drawing directly on his memory or following someone else's lead. Jonson was not attempting to deceive anybody. The conventions of his age did not demand that obligations to secondary authorities be scrupulously recorded; and books of the kind he is using were regarded as compendiums of sources rather than as independent personal investigations.

A word about how Jonson used these sources. How they ran together in his mind can be seen from the analysis of his image of Juno. And often in one footnote he will quote from more than one source. He will combine Alexander and Brisson, or Giraldi and Brisson, or two separate passages in Giraldi, or quote Martianus in Giraldi's words but add the book reference himself. The explanation of this is, I am sure, that Jonson did his annotating from memory. In an autograph dedication to the Queen written in a copy of *The Masque of Queenes* he speaks of adding "this second labor of annotation to my first of Invention."[b] And I believe that once he had done the reading involved in the process of working out his scheme, he worked from memory; and that it was from memory that the footnotes, with the quotations in them, were later added.

The following is a detailed analysis of the sources of Jonson's footnotes. The page references are to the *Works*, VII, followed by the reference to the footnote. (Jonson's footnotes are sometimes marked with asterisks, but usually with letters.)

p. 210, *   Alexander, p. 134: "Ab aliis est vsurpatum, vt vitta purpurea candido distincta, aut veste versicolori, sicut apud Latinos vsus erat, noua nupta sponsusque amiciantur, aut iugum pariter subeant: quare Iuno iugalis dicta, quasi aequissimo iure & concordibus animis inuicem necterentur, societasquae & communicatio vitae coita foret." (This may also have suggested details for the bridegroom's dress as described by Jonson.) Also *ibid.*, note *x*: "nam Festus Pompeius lib. 9. Iugarius, inquit, vicus dicitur Romae, quia ibi fuerat ara Iunonis iugae, quam putabant matrimonia iungere . . ." And Giraldi, p. 160: "Iugae Iunonis ara fuit Romae in uico, qui ideo Iugarius dictus erat, ut Festus ait. Scribunt alij, quod ad hanc aram ueteri ritu nubentes uinculis iungebantur, in omen futurae concordiae."

p. 210, a   Brisson, p. 35.

[b] *Works*, VII, p. 279.

p. 210, b   A. Hotman, Cap. XVII, p. 546: "Ornatus autem sponsi in eo precipue notabatur quôd tonderetur. Iuuenal. Satyr. 6. Iam a tonsore magistro pecteris": also p. 547: "Quod à Catone neglectum fuisse notauit Lucanus his versibus:

Intonsas rigidum in frontem, descendere comas
Passus erat, moestámque genis increscere barbam."

Jonson's "And *Lucan l. 2* where he makes *Cato* negligent of the *ceremonies* in marriage, saith, *Ille nec horrificam sancto dimouit ab ore Caesariem*" is an independent reference to the passage which Hotman refers to, *Pharsalia*, Lib. II, 370–6.

p. 211, c   This quotation from Catullus is given by Brisson, p. 24 and by Alexander, p. 135, note *n*.

p. 211, d   The material here is complicated. The question was whether in Catullus, Carmen LXII,[c] line 15, *Pineam* or *Spineam* should be read; in reading *Pineam* and in the authorities he cites in support of this reading, Jonson is again dependent on the earlier scholars. Brisson, pp. 33, 34, discusses the question, and though he seems to prefer *Spineam* he gives the arguments against it, including the quotations from *Virg. in Ciri* and *Ouid. Fast. lib. 2*, which Jonson cites. Jonson admits the existence of *Spinea taeda* "which Plinie calls *Nuptiarum facibus auspicatissimam, Nat. Hist. l. 16, c. 18.*" Brisson, *loc. cit.*, gives the words but not the reference. This however Jonson found in Alexander, p. 137, note *e*, where there is another discussion of the problem. The commentator decides in favour of *Pineam* and he too quotes the lines from Ovid and Virgil, but divergencies in the texts show that here Jonson had Brisson in mind.

p. 211, e   Here again Jonson has combined Alexander and Brisson. The quotation from *Sex. Pompei* is in Alexander, p. 137, note *d*. The quotation from Varro and the second one from Sextus Pompeius Festus, come from Brisson, p. 40. The wording suggests that Jonson has consulted a later page of his Alexander, where we read (p. 552, note *n*): "(Servius) scribit, Ministros & ministras impuberes, Camillos & Camillas in sacris vocatos fuisse; vnde & Mercurius Hetrusca lingua Camillus dictus est, quasi minister deorum."

p. 211, f   Jonson's information about auspices is derived from A. Hotman, Caps. II, III, IV. The quotations from Juvenal and Lucan are in Cap. II, but do not have the references as Jonson gives them; they occur as Jonson gives them in Brisson, p. 22, and Alexander, p. 132, note *a*.

p. 211, g   Brisson, pp. 48, 49, has these quotations and references, discussing the playing of the *tibia* at marriage festivities; but he attributes the Terence quotation to *Adelphi*, Act. VI.

p. 214, a   See above, p. 163.

---

[c] Carmen LXI in modern editions.

p. 214, a   In Giraldi, p. 667, except that he gives the quotation from Virgil without saying that it comes from Aeneid IV.

p. 214, b   See above, pp. 163–4.

p. 215, a   A. Hotman, Cap. XXXI, p. 562.

p. 215, b   Brisson, p. 34. Jonson's explanation in the text is based on Brisson's "spinae albae ad maleficia depellenda vim inesse, antiquitas credidit." And a few sentences before he has quoted Sextus Pompeius as saying that it is in honour of Ceres that torches are carried at nuptials; this probably explains Jonson's "In token of encrease." In the same section, later (p. 35), Brisson talks of the *taeda*, which provides Jonson's *Tead*.

p. 215, c   Brisson, p. 47 (this is misnumbered; it is p. 46).

p. 215, d   Brisson, p. 31; Alexander, p. 136 and note *o*.

p. 215, e   Brisson, p. 23; A. Hotman, Cap. XVI, 544. Brisson has the reference to Pompeius Festus.

p. 215, f   Brisson, p. 40.

p. 215, g   The fact that Jonson's bride wears the fleece shows that here he is following Brisson, p. 45, rather than A. Hotman, Cap. XVI, 545, (both have the reference to Festus) or Alexander, p. 136.

p. 215, h   Brisson, p. 37; A. Hotman, Cap. XVI, 545; Alexander, p. 137. Hotman gives the reference to Plutarch's *Romulus*; Brisson and Alexander (note *c*) to the *Quaestiones Romanae*.

p. 216, i   Brisson, p. 24.

p. 216, k   Brisson, p. 25 and Alexander, p. 136, note *t*.

p. 216, l   Cartari, p. 129.

p. 216, m   Martianus Capella, pp. 239–40, and see above, pp. 163–4.

p. 216, n   Giraldi, p. 105. The reference to Martianus is here and again at p. 106; Macrobius is cited but the specific reference to the text is wanting, and was presumably supplied by Jonson himself.

p. 216, o   Ripa, p. 57, has the quotation from the *De Arte Amandi*, with the reference; Conti, p. 136, has that from the *Metamorphoses*, and the reference. Conti, p. 138, also provides Jonson's explanation of why the peacock is sacred to Juno: "vtpote aereo temperamento."

p. 216, p   Giraldi, p. 109.

p. 216, q   Giraldi, p. 106, or Cartari, p. 125. See above, p. 175.

p. 217, r   Martianus, p. 18; Cartari, p. 123; Ripa, p. 57. See above, pp. 174–5. The quotation from Virgil, with the reference, is in Conti, p. 136.

p. 217, s   Giraldi, p. 106, who does not however repeat the story of the infant Hercules, or Cartari, p. 132, or Conti, p. 133, who do. Jonson's "the *Rose* was also called *Iunonia*" is a mistake: he has misread either Giraldi's "Iunonis enim flos lilium & rosa Iunonia uocabatur..." or Cartari's "Iunonem veteres candidis liliis coronabant, quae Iunonias rosas appellabant..."

p. 217, a   Giraldi, p. 105, or Cartari, p. 132; the wording is closer to Giraldi.

p. 217, b   These quotations, in whole or in part, are the common property of all who write about Juno: but Conti, p. 132, has them all together, just as Jonson gives them, and in the same order.

p. 219, a   Giraldi, p. 111, with Brisson, p. 24. The quotation from Ovid, with the reference, is in Alexander, p. 135, note *l*.

p. 219, b   Giraldi, p. 108, or Brisson, pp. 43–4. The reference to Martianus Capella is probably from Brisson, p. 43.

p. 219, c   "She was named *Iuga, propter Iugum* (as *Seruius* sayes) for the yoke which was impos'd, in *Matrimony*, on those that were maried, or (with *Sex. Pomp. Fest.*) *quod Iuges sunt eiusdem Iugi Pares, vnde & Conjuges*, or in respect of the *Altar* (to which I haue declar'd before) sacred to *Iuno, in Vico Iugario*." Giraldi, p. 107: "Iuga Iuno appellata, uel quod Iuges, ut ait Pompeius, sunt eiusdem iugi pares, unde & coniuges. uel ut scribit Seruius in quarto Aen. super ea Didonis uerba, Ne cui me uinclo uellem sociare iugali: iugali, inquit, propter iugum quod imponebatur matrimonio coniungendis, unde etiam Iuno Iugalis dicitur." And see above on p. 210, note *. The passage from Giraldi quoted there follows immediately on this.

p. 219, d   Giraldi, p. 107.

p. 220, e   Both from Giraldi, p. 108 and p. 106. Giraldi does not give the book reference
and f   to Martianus, but the wording nevertheless shows that Jonson is following him. Thus Martianus, lib. II, p. 37, has: "Interducem & Domiducam ... mortales puellae debent in nuptias conuocare, vt earum & itinera protegas, & in optatas domos ducas ..." And Giraldi: "Interduca, & Domiduca Iuno, uocabantur a Romanis, quod ad sponsi aedes sponsa comitabatur, uel earum iter protegeret. meminit Martianus ..." (p. 108); and on p. 106 he quotes verbatim the above passage from Martianus, but with the reading *Iterducam* for his author's *Interducam*.

p. 220, g   Brisson, pp. 25–6, has the quotations from Festus and Arnobius and the reference to Martianus; but Jonson is again following Giraldi, as is shown by his wording. The phrase "a man most learned in their *Ceremonies*," applied to Arnobius has been supplied by Giraldi's "Arnobius, uir antiquitatis doctissimus" (p. 111, article on *Juno Curis*).

p. 220, h   A good example of Jonson's method of combining his authorities: "*Telia* signifies *Perfecta*, or, as some translate it, *Perfectrix*; with *Iul. Pol. libr. 3. Onomast.* ʽΗρα Τελεία valewes *Iuno Praeses Nuptiarum*: who saith, the *Attribute* descends of τέλειος, which (with the *Ancients*) signified Mariage, and thence, were they called τέλειοι that entred into that estate. *Seruius* interprets it the same with *Gamelia, Aeneid. 4. ad verb. Et Iunone secunda*: But it implies much more, as including the facultie to mature and perfect; See the Greeke *Scholiaste* on *Pind: Nem. in Hym. ad Thyaeum Vliae filium Argi.* τέλειος δέ ὁ γάμος δια τὸ κατασκευάξειν τὴν τελειότητα τοῦ βίου that is, *Nuptialls are therefore calld* τέλειοι *because they effect Perfection of Life*, and do note that maturity which should be in Matrimony. For before *Nuptialls*, she is called *Iuno* παρθένος, that is, *Virgo*; after *Nuptialls*, τελεία which is *Adulta*, or *Perfecta*."

Giraldi, pp. 107–8:

"Τέλεια ἥρα, hoc est perfecta Iuno, uel ut Poggius uertit apud Diodorum, Perfectrix, uel potius Nuptialis: nam Iul. Pollux in tertio ait, & matrimonium uocari τέλειος, & τέλειοι qui matrimonium ineunt. quin & ipsa coniunctionis actio ἡρατέλεια, ab Iunone preside nuptiarum, quam in primis uirgines ante nuptias sacrificijs placabant. Pindarus in Nem. in hymno ad Thiaeum Vliae filium Argiuum, de Hebe Herculis uxore loquens, τέλειαν, id est Iunonem Hebes matrem uocat. ubi graecus enarrator inter cetera & hoc ponit: τέλειος δε ὁ γάμὄς διά τό τελειότητα βίου κατασκενάζειν. hoc est, τέλειος autem nuptiae, propterea quod perfectionem vitae preparant."
Nam παρθένος, id est uirgo primùm uocata est: dein Ioui nupta fuisset, τέλεια id est adulta & perfecta."

Brisson, p. 26:

"Iunonem plane nuptiarum presidem Dio Chrysostomus . . . vocat. Eaque ratione τελεία cognomine a Graecis Juno ornatur. (A quotation from Plutarch follows.) Non enim adulta Juno eo verbo exaudienda est, quemadmodum illic perperam interpres vertit, sed nuptiarum praes: Epitheton namque hoc a voce τέλος descendit quae antiquis nuptias significabat. Pollux, libr. 3. Onomast . . . (The appropriate quotation follows, in Greek.) And later: Itaque τέλεια Juno nihil aliud quam γαμήλιον significat. quod epitheton Iunoni tributum Seruius in IIII Aeneid. ad verbum, *Et Iunone secunda*, notat."

p. 221, i   Valeriano, pp. 582–3, and Macrobius, pp. 70–71. And see above, p. 167.

p. 222, *   "*Stella Veneris*, or Venus, which when it goes before the *Sunne*, is call'd *Phosphorus*, or *Lucifer*; when it followes, *Hesperus*, or *Noctifer* (as *Cat.* translates it). See *Cic. 2 de Nat. Deor. Mar. Cap. de Nup. Phi. & Mer. l. 8.* The nature of this starre *Pythagoras* first found out: and the present office *Clau.* expresseth in *Fescen. Attollens thalamis Idalium iubar dilectus Veneri nascitur Hesperus*."
Catullus, Carmen LXIII,[d] has: "Nimirum Aetaeo se ostendit noctifer imbre."
On which Antonius Parthenius comments (Catullus, ed. cit., p. 192): "Hesperus Veneris stella vespertinum tempus ferens: & pro occiduo caelo sumitur . . . . Igitur *nocifer*, id est vesper seu Hesperus: hoc est occiduum caelum vbi sit Hesperus, qui latinè noctifer interpretatur. Veneris enim Stella, vt docet Cicero, phosphoros graece dicitur, latine lucifer, quum antegreditur Solem: quum autem subsequitur Hesperos: qui à Catullo latinè noctifer interpretatur. Huius sideris naturam deprehendit Pythagoras Samius. Legito Plinium libro secundo, cap. octavo." And Achilles Statius (*ibid.*, p. 194) writing on:

> Vesper Olympo,
> Exspectata diu vix tandem lumina tollit

says: "Eodem propè modo Claudian. in Honori & Mariae Epithalamio,

> Attollens thalamis Idalium iubar.
> Dilectus Veneri nascitur Hesperus.

[d] Carmen LXII in modern editions.

Giraldi on Phosphorus (p. 344) supplies the reference to "Cic. secundo de Nat. deor." The specific book reference to Martianus I have not found in these secondary authorities; in *op. cit.*, lib. VIII, p. 298, we have: "At Venus, quae ab aliis Phosphoros nominatur, à Pythagora Samio cum suis ostensa est terris rationibus peruestigata . . . . Nunc faciens ortum, vt in Luciferum, nunc post occasum Solis effulgens. Vesper vel vesperugo nominatur." Jonson may well have seen Robertus Stephanus under "Venus," "Stella" and "Hesperus."

p. 222, *   A. Hotman, 545. In this note Jonson refers to Hotman as his source.

p. 222, a   Part of the quotation is in Alexander, p. 132, note *b*; the other part in Brisson, p. 45. Both have the reference.

p. 223, *   Giraldi, p. 345, cites Statius, Claudian and Propertius as saying that there were many Cupids, but does not quote from the first two; nor does he give the full reference to Propertius.

p. 223, b   On Venus and nuptials see Conti, pp. 380–1; I have not found a source which refers to Statius and Claudian for this.

p. 224, *   Conti, p. 381: "Cum his praesset Venus, illi merito baltheum iniunxerunt, siue cestum discolorem, in quo suavitas, & dulcia colloquia, & beneuolentia, & blanditiae, suasiones, fraudes, veneficiàque includebantur, de quo ita scripsit Homerus Iliad ξ."

p. 224, a   Brisson, p. 21.

p. 224, b   Catullus, LXII (LXI), ll. 77–78; 109.

p. 225, *   Scaliger, p. 381: see above, App. I.

p. 225, *   Cf. Scaliger, p. 391.

p. 226, a   Brisson, p. 31.

p. 226, b   See on p. 222: on *Stella Veneris*.

p. 226, c   Brisson, p. 45.

p. 226, d   Jonson refers to "*Christ. Landus* vpon *Catul.*" and to Alexander. Landus (Catullus, ed. cit., p. 168) has the material of the note, including the reference to Servius, and to Alexander; Brisson, p. 44, provides the Plutarch reference, and also has the Servius.

p. 227, *, a, b   Alexander, p. 138, note *1*.

p. 228, *   "A frequent *surname* of *Venus* not out of place, as *Cypria*: but *quod parere faciat Theop. Phurnut.* and the *Grammarians* vpon *Homer*. See them."
"Cypris Venus frequenti cognomine dicta, ut ait Theophilus, quod parere faciat, ἡ τὸ κυέιν παρέχουσα: quod & Phurnutus innuit, idemque fere in Homerum grammatici dicunt." Giraldi, p. 341.
See also the rest of his note.

p. 228, a   The material is to be found in Giraldi's chapter on Genius; see p. 369 and p. 372.

p. 228, b   This is vague. Jonson seems to have had in mind Conti, p. 395, where he talks of Venus as "rerum omnium procreatricem" and quotes the *Georgics* book 2, and Lucretius. Can the reference to *Iliad*–which, as Wheeler notes,[c] is not accurate–be a reminiscence of *Iliad* 4 which Conti quotes at p. 381? And the passage from the *Georgics* is only appropriate if one has in mind Conti's interpretation of the allegory of Venus.

^c C. F. Wheeler, *Classical Mythology in the Plays, Masques and Poems of Ben Jonson* (Princeton 1938), pp. 192–3. Many corrections have to be made in this work.

Notes

Notes to "*Roles and Mysteries*"

1. Quotations are from the text of the work in Stephen Orgel and Roy Strong, *Inigo Jones* (London and Berkeley 1973); line numbers refer to this edition.
2. The translation is by S. G. Middlemore (London 1944), p. 245.
3. *Ibid.*, p. 246.
4. *Ibid.*, p. 247.
5. *Ibid.*, p. 248.
6. "I Costumi Teatrali per gli Intermezzi del 1589," in *Gesammelte Schriften* (Leipzig 1932) I, 277.
7. *Ibid.*, p. 283.
8. *The Magnificent Entertainment Given to King James*, in *Dramatic Works*, ed. F. Bowers (Cambridge 1955) II, 254-5, lines 55-67.
9. *Works*, ed. C. H. Herford, P. and E. Simpson, VII (Oxford 1941), p. 91. (This edition is hereafter cited as *Works*.)
10. Middleton, *Works*, ed. A. H. Bullen (London 1886) VII, 245; and cf. Jonson, *Hymenaei*, lines 885 ff.
11. Camillo Camilli, *Imprese Illustri* (Venice 1586), part 2, pp. 12-14.
12. P. 240.
13. *Journal of the Warburg & Courtauld Institutes* XI, pp. 163-92.
14. P. 173.
15. Torquato Tasso, *Il Conte overo de l'Imprese*, in *Dialoghi*, ed. E. Raimondi (Florence 1958) II, 1045.
16. *Ibid.*, p. 1046.
17. *Works*, VII, 209.
18. [The account from this point on significantly qualifies that given in *Poet and Architect.*—Ed.]
19. *Dialoghi* II, 1041-2.
20. *Laws* IV.i.3. *Works*, ed. Keble, Church and Paget (Oxford 1888) I, 418-9.
21. *Timber or Discoveries*, line 1526, in *Works* VIII.
22. E.g. *In Philebum Platonis*, I, xi-xii (*Opera* [Basel 1576] II, 1217-8); and see the discussion by E. Wind, *Pagan Mysteries in the Renaissance*, 2nd ed. (London 1967), p. 127.

23. *Timber*, line 2128.

24. C. Ruelens and M. Rooses, *Correspondence de Rubens et Documents Epistolaires* (Antwerp 1887–1909) III, 454.

Notes to "Rubens and the Whitehall Ceiling"

Bibliographical note: Annotation has been kept to the minimum. There is not much specifically on the ceiling since my original lecture was written, with two notable exceptions. One is Oliver Millar's lecture *Rubens: The Whitehall Ceiling*, Oxford University Press, 1958. The other is Per Palme, *Triumph of Peace: A Study of the Whitehall Banqueting House*, Stockholm, 1956. I have not referred to this in my text because I disagree so radically with Palme's interpretation of the political context of the ceiling, and therefore—and for other reasons, too—with his reading of the iconography, that to discuss his thesis at all would have meant making my lecture into a running argument; and I have preferred simply to state my own conclusions. See also the chapters on "Aspects of Taste" and Inigo Jones, in Margaret Whinney and Oliver Millar, *English Art, 1625–1714*, Oxford, 1957; and on Inigo Jones, John Summerson, *Architecture in Britain, 1530–1830*, Penguin Books, London, 1953. On the ceiling see also Edward Croft-Murray, *Decorative Painting in England, 1537–1837*, Vol. I, London, 1962. For Rubens and politics, Otto von Simson's "Rubens and Richelieu," *The Review of Politics*, VI, 4, Oct., 1944, pp. 422–51, is stimulating if rather perplexing; see also the same author's *Zur Genealogie der weltlichen Apotheose in Barock*, Strassburg, 1936. The volume in the L.C.C. *Survey of London* is still essential, but see note 16. Essential reference books on Rubens on which I have depended are:

M. Rooses. *L'oeuvre de P. P. Rubens: histoire et description de ses tableaux et dessins*. Antwerp, 1886–92. 5 vols.

R. Oldenbourg. *P. P. Rubens, Des Meisters Gemälde*. 4th ed. Stuttgart / Berlin, 1921 (Klassiker der Kunst).

C. Ruelens and M. Rooses. *Correspondence de Rubens et Documents Epistolaires*. Antwerp, 1887–1909. 6 vols. Here called *Correspondence*.

R. S. Magurn, ed. *The Letters of Peter Paul Rubens*. Harvard, 1955.

Julius S. Held. *Rubens: Selected Drawings*. London, 1959. 2 vols. (with admirable notes).

Rubens and the Whitehall Ceiling: Notes

1. *Anecdotes* (London 1862) I, 293.

2. Mary F. S. Hervey, *Arundel* (Cambridge 1921), p. 501.

3. R. and M. Wittkower, *The Divine Michaelangelo* (London 1964), pp. 44 ff.

4. *Ibid.*, p. 29.

5. *Ibid.*, pp. 42ff.

6. G. P. Bellori, *Le Vite de' Pittori . . .* (Genoa 1968) I, 300.

7. Van de Wouwer (Woverius), quoted in Frans Baudouin, *Rubens House* (Antwerp 1967), p. 3.

8. *Vite*, I, 271.

9. *Erinnerungen aus Rubens* (Basel 1898), pp. 23–4. The translation has kindly been supplied by Professor F. P. Pickering.

10. Rubens was writing to Justus Sustermans, Antwerp, March 12, 1638. R. S. Magurn, *Letters of Rubens* (Cambridge, Mass. 1955), pp. 408–9. This volume is hereafter cited as Magurn.

11. A letter to Peiresc, Antwerp, December 18, 1634. Magurn, p. 392.

12. A. W. Ward, *Cambridge Modern History*, IV (Cambridge 1934), p. 364.

13. Magurn, pp. 184–5 and 178 respectively.

14. The best account of the sketches and the progress of the composition is that of Oliver Millar, *Rubens: The Whitehall Ceiling* (Oxford 1958).

15. A letter to Peiresc, Paris, May 13, 1625. Magurn, pp. 109–10.

16. L. C. C. *Survey of London*, Vol. XIII, ed. M. H. Cox and P. Norman, (London 1930). The account of the iconography given here depended on a plan which used to hang in the Banqueting House. This document has now disappeared. It was probably—it is thought—eighteenth century; and so may well have depended

on the titles given by Gribelin in his engraving (which have no known authority). Unfortunately, too, the L. C. C. account was "revised" without any statement of sources and authorities. For Joseph Spence, see *Polymetis* (London 1747), Dialogue xviii, pp. 297–8. Spence probably refers to Gribelin.

17. William Laud, *Memorables*, in *Works* (Oxford 1857) VI, part 1, p. 5.
18. *Great Britains Salomon. A Sermon Preached at the Magnificent Funerall, of the most high and mighty King James,* etc., by John Williams, Bishop of Lincoln, London, 1625, in *A Collection of Scarce and Valuable Tracts . . .* (The Somers Tracts), 2nd ed., II (London 1809), p. 43.
19. Laud, *Memorables*, p. 5.
20. *The Basilicon Doron of King James VI*, ed. James Craigie (Scottish Text Society 1944), pp. 29–39.
21. *Memorables*, p. 6.
22. Private communication, 1956. [Sir Oliver Millar informs me that he still considers it fanciful, though not therefore necessarily incorrect.–Ed.]
23. From an unpublished lecture delivered at the Institute of Historical Research, March 8, 1945. I am indebted to the librarian of the Warburg Institute for permission to quote from this material.
24. On John Thornborough, Bishop of Bristol, and his propaganda tracts for James's Union, see my "*Hymenaei*: Ben Jonson's Masque of Union," *infra*, pp. 171–72. I am quoting here from a reissue of the tracts, inspired by obvious motives, *The Great Happinesse of England and Scotland, by Being reunited into one great Brittain* (London 1641), pp. 129–30, 192.
25. I believe that it was Dr. Burchard who first made–orally–the point about Rubens' use of the Veronese composition in San Sebastiano in Venice. I think he was right, particularly in view of the general relationship of the ceiling to Venetian models. Dr. Burchard was basing his opinion on the pose of the soldier, and the figure of the throned king gesturing forwards with his sceptre, and on their relationship. See Teresio Pignatti, *Le Pitture di Paolo Veronese nella chiesa di S. Sebastiano in Venezia* (Milan 1966).
26. August 8, 1626. *Correspondence*, III, Letter ccccvii, p. 454.

Notes to "Ripa's Fate"

1. *L'Art Réligieux du XVIIIe Siècle*, 2nd ed. (Paris 1951), p. 384.
2. *Ibid.*, pp. 386–7.
3. Joseph Spence, *Polymetis* (1747), pp. 292–4.
4. P. 295.
5. Pp. 296–7.
6. P. 4.
7. P. 5.
8. *Miscellaneous Works*, ed. A. C. Guthkelch (London 1914) II, 289.
9. Paris, 1719, I, vi. References to Montfaucon are to this edition, but I have used the contemporary English translations of David Humphreys, *Antiquity Explained* (London 1721).
10. *Polymetis*, p. 290.
11. For a detailed discussion, see Arnaldo Momigliano, "Ancient History and the Antiquarian," *JWCI* XIII (1950), pp. 285–315.
12. I, 45.
13. *Miscellaneous Works*, II, 282.
14. *Ibid.*, p. 295.
15. *Ibid.*
16. *Ibid.*, p. 296.
17. *Polymetis*, pp. 285–6.
18. *Ibid.*, p. 5.
19. *Ibid.*, pp. 11–2.
20. *Ibid.*, p. 15.
21. *Ibid.*
22. *Ibid.*, p. 28.
23. *Reflexions* (Paris 1733) I, 184.

24. *Polymetis*, p. 299.
25. *Ibid.*, p. 297.
26. *Ibid.*, pp. 296–7.
27. *Ibid.*, p. 144.
28. *L'Art Réligieux*, pp. 391–2.
29. *Polymetis*, p. 306.
30. *Ibid.*, p. 304.
31. *Ibid.*, p. 302.
32. *Ibid.*, pp. 302–3.
33. *Spenser's Faerie Queene* (London 1758) II, 505.
34. *Observations* (London 1754), p. 74.
35. (London 1762) I, 103.
36. The passage is on p. 30.
37. J. L. Jules David, *Le Peintre Louis David* (Paris 1880), p. 389.
38. *Observations*, p. 224.
39. A. Cunningham, *Lives* (1830) III, 86.
40. P. 58.
41. *Versuch einer Allegorie besonders für die Kunst*.
42. Notes to Ovid, in *Works* (London 1721) I, 229.
43. *L'Art Réligieux*, p. 384.
44. "*Veritas Filia Temporis*", in R. K. Litausky and H. J. Paton, edd. *Philosophy and History* (1936), pp. 197–222.

Notes to "Poet and Architect: The Intellectual Setting of the Quarrel between Ben Jonson and Inigo Jones"

1. See R. Brotanek, *Die Englischen Maskenspiele* (Vienna and Leipzig 1902), pp. 243 ff., P. Reyher, *Les Masques Anglais* (Paris 1909), pp. 193–200, and Ben Jonson, [*Works*,] edd. Herford and Simpson, I (Oxford 1925), pp. 60–2, 96–8, 100–1. These remain the best accounts. The documents of the quarrel are these: Epigram CXV, published in the 1616 folio, but to be dated earlier; references in the *Conversations with Drummond* (1619); *Underwoods*, xlvii, "An Epistle answering to one that asked to be Sealed of the Tribe of Ben" (published in the 1640 folio but to be referred to 1623–4? according to Brotanek, pp. 251–2); *Neptune's Triumph* (1623–4), for the figure of the Cook; this material transferred to *The Staple of News* (1626), III, 1, IV, 1; *An Expostulation with Inigo Jones, To Inigo Marquess Would be. A Corollary, To a Friend. An Epigram of him*, presumably connected with the quarrel over *Love's Triumph* and to be dated 1631; Jones's poem, a reply to Jonson's attacks and presumably of the same year, printed from the MS. by J. A. Gotch in his *Inigo Jones* (London 1928), pp. 254–5; *A Tale of a Tub*, 1633, for the figure of In-and-In Medlay; *Love's Welcome at Bolsover*, for Colonel Vitruvius. This is based on Brotanek and Herford and Simpson; but I have included only those works which I am convinced are, or contain, references to Jones. Thus I am not sure that Epigram CXXIX, "To Mime" is directed against Jones, as Herford and Simpson hold (I, pp. 61–3), nor am I certain that Lantern Leatherhead in *Bartholomew Fair* reflects on Jones (cf. Herford and Simpson, II, p. 146 ff.). I agree with Brotanek (pp. 248–9) that Vandergoose in *The Masque of Augurs* cannot be intended to represent Jones, but disagree with him when he argues (p. 250) that the Cook in *Neptune's Triumph* cannot reflect on him either. He argues that as Jones worked on *The Fortunate Isles*—the revised version of *Neptune's Triumph*—he must have worked on the earlier masque too and would not have tolerated an attack on himself. But the mere fact that the Cook is dropped in the amended version would indicate that the matter was taken to be offensive and had to be deleted. In fact the Cook's words are so clearly an attack on the architect's pretensions that no other evidence is needed; and that Jonson incorporated them into a later play shows that he thought them of importance. I shall seek to show that Jones's designs for Townshend's—and his own—*Albion's Triumph* and *Tempe Restored* belong with the documents of the quarrel.
2. *Conversations with Drummond, Works*, I, p. 145. (All references to the text of Jonson are to the volumes of the Herford and Simpson edition.)
3. *Works*, VIII, pp. 74–5.

4. *Works*, VIII, pp. 402–8. The source for the story of this quarrel and the connexion of the satire with it is a letter from Pory to Sir John Puckering. It is printed in Gotch, pp. 149–50.

5. *Works*, I, p. 100.

6. *Works*, VIII, pp. 403–4. (Scribal conventions in the passage, and in subsequent citations, have been normalised.) There is an unmistakable reference to *Chloridia* in the first lines.

7. *Works*, VII, pp. 209–10.

8. *Ibid.*, p. 169.

9. *Ibid.*, p. 172.

10. *Ibid.*, p. 260.

11. See Appendix I.

12. ". . . it [the *Impresa*] must haue a posie which is the soule of the body," and "you shall vnderstand that the body and soule aboue mentioned, is meant either by the mot or by the subject, and an *Impresa* is accounted vnperfect when the subject or body bear no proportion of meaning to the soule, or the soule to the body." S. Daniel, *The Worthy tract of Paulus Iouius*, etc. (London 1585), Sig. B. iii, v; Sig. B. iiii. r.

13. *Andreae Alciati Emblemata cum Commentariis Claudii Minois*, etc. (Padua 1621), p. LXI. How common the terms were can be seen from this reference of Lomazzo's in his *Idea del Tempio della Pittura* (1590): "nelle imprese significati, e simili, la virtu delle parole che gli s'aggiunge che dimandano motto ovvero anima ajuta sommamente a dimostrar palese il concetto dell'inventore come minutamente dichiarano 'Alciato, il Bocchio, il Costa, il Paradino, il Simeoni, Gioan Sambuco, il Giovio, ed ultimamente Girolamo Ruscelli, provandolo con autorita, tolte da Greci, da Latini, e da altri scrittori antichi" (ed. Bologna 1785, p. 107).

14. V. iii, *Works*, IV, pp. 298–9.

15. *Works*, VII, p. 282.

16. *Ibid.*, p. 312.

17. *Ibid.*, pp. 318–9. And see Appendix I.

18. *Ibid.*, pp. 685–6.

19. *Ibid.*, pp. 749–50.

20. *Ibid.*, pp. 283, 313.

21. *The Masque of Augurs*, *Works*, VII, p. 625.

22. *O.E.D.* definition. J. H. Atkins, *Literary Criticism in Antiquity* (Cambridge 1934), I, pp. 134–5, 137, 154, traces the origins of the term to the distinctions in Aristotle's *Rhetoric*, I, II: Aristotle's εὕρησις becomes in Latin *inventio*. On the terms used in Roman manuals of Rhetoric, cf. Atkins, II, pp. 16–18. On Cicero's use, cf. *De Oratore*, I, xxxi; *Orator*, XIV, xliii; *Partitiones Oratoriae*, I, iii, II, v. Quintilian's statement is a *locus classicus*: "Omnes autem orandi ratio, ut plurimi maximique auctores tradiderunt, quinque partibus constat, inventione, dispositione, elocutione, memoria, pronuntiatione sive actione, utroque enim modo dicitur." (*Institutio Oratoria*, III, 3, i.) An English writer of a manual of rhetoric in the middle of the sixteenth century—to give only one English example—repeats Quintilian's list and defines invention thus: "The finding out of apt matter, called otherwise Invention, is a searching out of things true, or things likely, the which may reasonablie set forth a matter, and make it appeare probable." (Thomas Wilson, *The Arte of Rhetorique*, ed. G. H. Mair, Oxford, 1909, p. 6). Information on the rhetorical terms in mediaeval and Renaissance poetics can be found in J. W. H. Atkins, *English Literary Criticism: the Medieval Phase* (Cambridge 1943), and D. L. Clark, *Rhetoric and Poetry in the Renaissance* (N. Y. 1922).

23. Cf., for example, the discussion by Gascoigne, *Elizabethan Critical Essays*, ed. G. Gregory Smith (Oxford 1904), I, pp. 47–8. It is interesting to note that Chapman, in the Epistle Dedicatory to *Ovid's Banquet of Sense*, talks of "high and hearty invention" in poetry; perhaps Jonson unconsciously echoes the phrase.

24. Cf. Gascoigne's discussion, already referred to.

25. Cf. Harington, in the *Brief Apology for Poetry* which he prefixed to his translation of the *Orlando Furioso*, Gregory Smith, II, pp. 204 ff.

26. *Works*, VIII, p. 635. M. Castelain, in his commentary (Ben Jonson, *Discoveries*, Paris, 1906, pp. 119–20) suggests as source only the familiar passage in the *Poetics*. On invention see further, *Discoveries*, pp. 565, 609, 615, 619, 628, 629.

27. Cf. *Discoveries*, *Works*, VIII, p. 621: "In all speech, words and sense, are as the body, and the soule. The sense is as the life and soule of Language, without which all words are dead."

28. Cf. also *Discoveries*, p. 636: "*Poesy* is his skill, or Crafte of making: the very Fiction itselfe, the reason or forme of the worke." Castelain, p. 121, compares with Scaliger, *Poetices*, Lib. I, Cap. ii, *ad fin*: "Poesis autem, ratio ac forma poematis."

29. One of the basic tenets in the Renaissance doctrine of the "learned poet."

30. *Cynthia's Revels*, V, v, 59 ff (*Works* IV, p. 160).

31. "An Ode to James Earle of Desmond," *Works*, VIII, p. 176.

32. *Expostulation*, *Works*, VIII, p. 404.

33. V, ii, *Works*, III, pp. 78–9.

34. V, vii, *Works*, III, pp. 85–6.

35. Gregory Smith, p. 48.

36. Jonson gives as his reference (*Works*, VII, p. 683), "*Athenae. Deipnosop. lib. i ex Euphr. Comico.*" The quotation is *A poeta nihil sane differt coquus:* / *Est enim utriusque ars mentis solertia, Athenaei Deipnosophistarum Libri Quindecim* (Cologne 1612), p. 7. This was Casaubon's great edition, with Dalechamp's translation. Jonson possessed a copy.

37. *Works*, VII, pp. 684–5.

38. Jonson's copy of *M. Vitruvii Pollionis de Architectura libri decem . . . Accesserunt, Guglielmi Philandri Castilionij, ciuis Romani, annotationes castigatiores, & plus tertia parte locupletiores . . .* M.D.LXXXVI . . . Reg. Lvgd., with his name and motto on the title-page, turned up during the war in a London bookshop, when photographs of the title-page and the annotated pages were taken by the Warburg Institute.

39. Vitruvius, p. 2.

40. This, from *Tempe Restor'd*, shows clearly the nature of the collaboration, and illustrates the meaning of "Invention": "All the verses were written by Mr. *Aurelian Townesend*. The subject and Allegory of the Masque, with the descriptions, and Apparatus of the Sceanes were invented by *Inigo Iones*, Surveyor of his Maiesties worke." *Aurelian Townshend's Poems and Masks*, ed. E. K. Chambers (Oxford 1912), p. 99.

41. See above, note 4.

42. Many drawings survive. See S. Orgel and R. Strong, *Inigo Jones* (London and Berkeley 1973), nos. 190–215.

43. *Townshend's Poems and Masks*, p. 99.

44. *Op. cit.*, p. 119.

45. *Op. cit.*, p. 68.

46. *Works*, VIII, p. 568. For the source in Vives see Castelain, ed., *Discoveries*, pp. 12–3.

47. On the defence of the arts, cf. A. Blunt, *Artistic Theory in Italy, 1450–1600* (Oxford 1940), chap. IV; N. Pevsner, *Academies of Art* (Cambridge 1940), chap. II.

48. *L'Idea della Architettura Vniuersale, di Vincenzo Scamozzi Architetto Veneto*, Venice 1615. Jones's copy is at Worcester College, Oxford. He met Scamozzi during his visit to Italy in 1613–14. Cf. Gotch, *Inigo Jones*, p. 76, and R. Wittkower, *Pseudo-Palladian Elements in English Neo-Classical Architecture*, in *JWCI*, VI (1943), p. 155.

49. *I dieci libri dell'Architettura di M. Vitruvio tradutti et commentati da Monsignor Barbaro*, Venice 1556. Jones possessed a copy of the edition of Venice, 1567; it is now at Chatsworth, and I have to thank Mr. Francis Thompson for information about it, and photographs. G. P. Lomazzo's books are *Trattato dell'Arte della Pittura*, Milan 1584, *Idea del Tempio della Pittura*, Milan 1590. Jones quotes from Lomazzo in his MS. sketchbook. For an account of Barbaro's theories see R. Wittkower, *Principles of Palladio's Architecture*, in *JWCI*, VII (1944), pp. 107–8. See Barbaro (ed. Venice 1629), p. 4; Scamozzi, Lib. I, Cap. XXIII; and Lomazzo's *Tempio, passim*.

50. Cf. Barbaro, *Vitruvio*, pp. 6–7; Scamozzi, *Architettura, Proemio della prima parte*, p. 1 ff., and especially p. 7.

51. For this and what follows, cf. Ripa, *Iconologia* (Padua 1625), p. 522 ff., 666 ff.

52. Cf. Ripa, p. 667.

53. *Ibid.*, p. 43.

54. *Ibid.*, p. 580.

55. *Op. cit.*, Lib. I, Cap. VIII.

56. On the learned artist and on the connections between literary and artistic theory, cf. R. W. Lee, "Ut Pictura Poesis: the Humanistic Theory of Painting," *The Art Bulletin*, XXII (1940), pp. 197 ff.

57. Cf. R. W. Lee, *op. cit.*, App. 2, pp. 264–5, on *Inventio, Dispositio, Elocutio*; Schlosser-Magnino, *La Letteratura Artistica* (Florence 1935), pp. 197, 278, 283; the quotation is from Vasari, *Vita di Lippo, Pittore Fiorentino, Vite*, ed. Milanesi (Florence 1878) II, p. 11.

58. Ripa, p. 331.

59. Scamozzi, p. 11.

60. Cf. Scamozzi, pp. 5, 8, 42, 46, 55; Barbaro, *Vitruvio*, p. 11.

61. Lomazzo's *Trattato dell'Arte della Pittura* had been in part translated by Richard Haydocke and published in Oxford in 1598. On the knowledge of Lomazzo shown by Hilliard and his circle, cf. John Pope-

Hennessy, *Nicholas Hillard and Mannerist Art Theory*, in *JWCI*, VI (1943), pp. 90 ff. On Lomazzo and this whole movement in art theory, cf. E. Panofsky, *Idea* (Studies of the Warburg Institute, V), (Leipzig 1924), pp. 39 ff.

62. On "Disegno" see Schlosser-Magnino, *loc. cit.*; Dolce, *Dialogo della Pittura* (Milan 1863), p. 30; Vasari, *Della Pittura, Vite*, (Florence 1878), I, pp. 168–9.

63. F. Zuccari, *L'Idea de'scultori, pittori e architetti* (Turin 1607). See again Panofsky, *Idea*, pp. 47 ff.; also Blunt, *Artistic Theory*, chap. IX.

64. Zuccari, *L'Idea*, Lib. I, p. 52.

65. *Ibid.*, Lib. II, p. 83.

66. Ripa, p. 180.

67. Scamozzi, *Architettura*, p. 43; Zuccari, *L'Idea*, Lib. II, p. 9.

68. *Works*, VII, pp. 807–14.

69. The implied distinction between a banquet of the senses and a banquet of love is found elsewhere in Jonson, cf. *The New Inn*, III, ii, *Works*, VI, p. 455: "I relish not these philosophicall feasts; / Gue me a banquet o'sense, like that of *Ovid*"—an aside during a highly Platonic discussion of love. On the one hand the reference is to the *Symposium*, on the other, perhaps, to Chapman's poem, Ovid's *Banquet of Sense*. In connection with this poem D. Bush (*Mythology and the Renaissance Tradition in English Poetry*, Minneapolis, 1932, p. 204) refers to Ficino, *Commentary on the Symposium*, V, 2, where Ficino treats of the five senses. No especial significance is to be seen in Jonson's putting Taste last, instead of Touch.

70. Cf. on the *Symposium*, Or. II, Cap. ii, Marsilio Ficino, *Supra La Amore ovvero Convito di Platone*, ed. Rensi (Lanciano 1914), p. 26.

71. Cf. *ibid.*, Or. II, Cap. viii, p. 37 ff. On the importance of mutual love for Ficino, see P. O. Kristeller, *The Philosophy of Marsilio Ficino* (N. Y. 1943), pp. 276–7.

72. Cf. Appendix II.

73. Cf. Loue is a spirituall coupling of two
             soules,
         So much more excellent, as it least
             relates
         Vnto the body; circular, eternal . . .
     (*The New Inn*, III, ii, *Works*, VI, p. 454.)

74. On this see the exhaustive treatment by R. Wittkower, in his *Principles of Palladio's Architecture*, in *JWCI*, VIII, pp. 68 ff., which I am following here.

75. *La Republica di Platone, Tradotta . . . Dall'Eccellente Phisico Messer Pamphilo Fiorimbene . . .* (Venice 1554), p. 93. Jones's copy of this, and of the Plutarch mentioned above, are in the library of Worcester College, Oxford. I have to thank Col. C. H. Wilkinson, the Librarian, for permission to examine them.

76. *Opuscoli Morali, di Plutarcho Cheronese . . . Tradotti in volgare Dal Sig. Marc' Antonio Gandino, & da altri Letterati . . .* (Venice 1614), Pt. II, p. 334.

77. This is not to claim that Jonson was not perfectly well aware that there was no conflict between the mathematical vision of the ordered unity of the universe and the vision of the universe bound together in a unity of love. For the Platonist philosophers these were both aspects of the one reality. But it suits Jonson to imply a conflict here.

Notes to "The Renaissance Poet as Classicist: Chapman's *Hero and Leander*"

1. The best studies of the "Ovidian" poem are those by M. C. Bradbrook in *Shakespeare and Elizabethan Poetry* (London 1951), and Hallett Smith in *Elizabethan Poetry* (Cambridge, Mass. 1952). Douglas Bush's pioneering *Mythology and the Renaissance Tradition in English Poetry* (Minneapolis 1932) remains useful.

2. All references to Chapman's text are to *The Poems of George Chapman*, ed. Phyllis B. Bartlett (New York 1941). Particularly useful for its comments on Chapman's syntax is L. C. Martin's commentary in his edition of Marlowe's *Poems* (London 1931). The standard studies are by Bush, *op. cit.*, by Bradbrook, *op. cit.*, and by Jean Jacquot, in his *George Chapman* (Paris 1951). F. L. Schoell's *Etudes sur l'Humanisme Continental*

en Angleterre à la fin de la Renaissance (Paris 1926), is still an essential reference book. Of the earlier studies, Miss Bradbrook's is closest in approach to the present essay, and raises some of the points developed here.

3. Cf. Martin, Marlowe's *Poems*, p. 27, note on *Sestiad*.

4. E.g., by Scaliger, *Poetices* (Geneva 1561), p. 114 (Lib. III, Cap. XCVI). Scaliger notoriously preferred Musaeus' style to Homer's: see *Poetices*, p. 215. And cf. George Puttenham, *The Arte of English Poesie*, ed. Willcock and Walker (Cambridge 1936), pp. 6, 9, 41. As late as 1616, when Chapman published his translation of Musaeus, he still believed, as appears from his note on Musaeus, that the poem was the work of the legendary poet, although by this time scholars had realised that there was more than one Musaeus. In 1627 Daniel Pareus quotes and accepts Casaubon's opinion that the author was Musaeus the grammarian: see his *Musaei Erotopaegnion Herus et Leandri* (Frankfurt 1627), in the *Praefatio*.

5. Cf. Bush, *Mythology*, p. 208, note 23. Bush thinks that Chapman read the story in Servius' commentary on the *Aeneid*, but notes that it is told by Boccaccio in the *Genealogia*, and by Cartari. L. G. Giraldi also told the story in much the same terms as Cartari; cf. his *De Deis Gentium* (Lyons 1565), p. 117.

6. D. J. Gordon, "Chapman's Use of Cartari in the Fifth Sestiad of *Hero and Leander*," *Modern Language Review* 39 (July 1944), pp. 280–5. I was, however, wrong in thinking that Chapman was using Verderius' Latin translation of Cartari's book: the evidence for Chapman's dependence on the Italian text is much stronger. The circulation of Verderius' translation is attested by the fact that it is to this, and not to the Italian, that Marston refers in a passage in his *Satire II*: "Reach me some poet's index that will show. / Imagines deorum, Booke of Epithetes . . . ." See Jean Seznec, *La Survivance des Dieux Antiques* (London 1940), pp. 281–2. Cartari's *Imagini* was first published in Venice in 1556. Illustrations by Zaltieri first appear in 1571 (see Seznec, *Survivance*, p. 217, n. 4).

7. See Cartari, *Le Imagini de i Dei* (Lyons 1581), pp. 160–1.

8. *Ibid.*, pp. 157, 165.

9. Cartari, p. 148, and plate on p. 149.

10. Cartari, p. 447. Giraldi mentions Peristera (Lyons 1565, p. 329), but does not give this detail.

11. Cartari, pp. 447–8; the plate accompanies this text (p. 446). Cf. Giraldi, p. 329; and N. Comes (or Conti), *Mythologiae* (Lyons 1602), p. 381.

12. Cf. L. C. Martin, Marlowe's *Poems*, pp. 101–2, notes.

13. Cartari, pp. 218–9.

14. Jean Jacquot, *Chapman*, p. 70, n. 21. Cf. *Inferno* XVII.

15. Cf. Boccaccio, *Genealogia*, Lib. I (Fraud, seventh daughter of Erebus); Giraldi, p. 38; Cesare Ripa, *Iconologia* (Rome 1603), p. 173.

16. Cartari, pp. 396–7. This gives us a clear proof that Chapman used the Italian text, not Verderius' translation; for Verderius leaves out the detail about the scorpion tail, and gives a condensed version, in Latin, of the Dante lines, omitting details that Chapman used.

17. Cartari, p. 396.

18. *Inferno* XVII, 14–5. The text is Cartari's.

19. Spenser, *Epithalamium*, lines 154–5.

20. Shakespeare, sonnet 130.

21. Donne, *Satire IV*, line 195.

22. Cf. D'Arcy Thompson, *A Glossary of Greek Birds* (Oxford 1936). The *Thesaurus* of Henri Estienne (or Stephanus), Basel 1572, gives under ἀκανθίς: "Auis quae Spinus à Gaza dicitur apud Aristot. item Ligurinus. Virg. Georg. 3. Littoràque: halcyonè resonant & acanthida dumi. Vbi Seruius, Per dumos verò [resonat] acanthis, quam alii lusciniam esse volunt alii vero cardulem, quae spinis & carduis pascitur." He also gives ἀκανθυλλίς as "eadem auis quae & ακανθίς." Schoell believes (*Etudes*, pp. 150ff.) that Chapman knew only the abbreviated form of the *Thesaurus* by Scapula. Certainly this was very widely circulated, and a far more manageable volume. The proof that Chapman never used Stephanus is, however, I think, not absolute. I have constantly checked Stephanus with Scapula (using for the latter the edition of Basel 1580), and have not posited for Chapman information that could only have come from Stephanus.

23. The only source is in the *Metamorphoseon* of Antonius Liberalis, Cap. VII. This was translated into Latin by the great *vulgarisateur*, Xylander, in 1568, and published at Basel. It was known in England. Dr. I. R. F. Calder informs me that John Dee possessed a copy. I have used Muncker's edition, Amsterdam 1676.

24. Ovid, *Metamorphoses*, V. Chapman's *Adolesche* comes from ἀδολέσχης or ἀδόλεσχος, "verbosus, loquax, garrulus." This suits well Ovid's "Nunc quoque in alitibus facundia prisca remansit / raucaque garrulitas studiumque immane loquendi" (lines 677–8). There is an attractive possible link between Chapman's two metamorphoses. Thompson's *Glossary* gives ἀκαλανθίς as a third name for the gold-finch. Antoninus

Liberalis, *Metamorphoseon*, Lib. IX, gives Acalanthis as the name of one of the Pierides. Unfortunately neither of the lexicons records ἀκαλανθις at all. But if it is given in a source Chapman was using, we should have a pretty example of how his mind worked.

25. Stephanus, *sub* τέρας; also Scapula.

26. On the study of comets in this period, see Lynn Thorndike, *A History of Magic and Experimental Sciences* (New York 1941) VI, chap. 32; C. D. Hellman, *The Comet of 1577 and its Place in the History of Astronomy* (New York 1944); Francis R. Johnson, *Astronomical Thought in Renaissance England* (Baltimore 1937).

27. De la Primaudaye, *The French Academie* (London 1618), pp. 745–6. (The series of partial English translations began in 1586.)

28. Virgil, *Aeneid*, VI, 45–8.

29. Stephanus (and Scapula), *sub* κομὴ, κομήτης.

30. Cartari, p. 52.

31. Cartari, pp. 51–2.

32. Cf. my analysis of this figure in "*Hymenaei*: Ben Jonson's Masque of Union," *infra*.

33. On this aspect of the sixteenth-century mythologies cf. Jean Seznec, *Survivance*, bk. II, chap. I.

34. Cf. Alessandro Perosa, "*Febris*: a Poetic Myth Created by Poliziano," in *JWCI*, IX (1946), pp. 74–95

35. Richard Hooker, *The Works*, ed. Keble, Church and Paget (Oxford 1888) I, pp. 418–9.

36. George Puttenham, *The Arte of English Poesie*, edd. Willcock and Walker, pp. 261–2.

37. As Martin noted, Marlowe's *Poems*, p. 70.

38. Stephanus, vol. III, col. 1524, B *et seq.* gives θεσμός as synonymous with νόμος, but notes a possible distinction: "Forsan θεσμός est quod Latini Institutum dicunt: quod vocabulum itidem cum voce Lex solet copulare. Veluti à Cic. quum ait. Qui eius civitates non leges, non instituta, non mores, non iura noritis." Further, he refers to a note by Budé that the phrase θεσμόις ἱερόις means "ritus sacrorum diuinitus institutos." Scapula, under θεσμός, gives "positae et constitutae leges, siue in tabulis, siue in animis hominum, siue etiam consuetudine diuturna confirmatae"; and retains a reference to the distinction.

39. *Iliad* VIII, 17–27.

40. Cf. Ben Jonson, *Hymenaei*, line 320, note i (Herford and Simpson, VII, p. 221), who gives the Macrobius reference. Spondanus in his note on this passage records the Macrobius passage, but dismisses the conjectures of the commentators, holding that Homer intended only to indicate the omnipotence of Jove. (*Homeri quae exstant omnia . . . Perpetuis iustisque . . . Io. Spondani Mauleonensis Commentariis* etc. [Basel 1606], p. 132.) Cf. also Spenser, *Faerie Queene* IV, i, 30; and Natalis Comes (or Conti), *Mythologiae* (Lyons 1602), p. 138.

41. Pico della Mirandola, *Conclusiones nongentae, in omni genere scientiarum* (Paris 1532), p. 146. I owe this reference to Dr. I. R. F. Calder.

42. Cf. Cornelius Agrippa on the number 5: *De Occulta Philosophia* (Lyons 1531), II, cap. 8, pp. 173–4.

43. Cf. Cornelius Agrippa on the pentacle, *De Occulta Philosphia*, pp. 534–5: ". . . sunt autem ipsa Pentacula tanquam signa quaedam sacra, à malis eventibus nos praeseruantia, et ad malorum daemonum constrictionem et exterminationem, nos adiuuantia, bonosque spiritus allicientia, nobisque conciliantia.'

44. There is another source which may have influenced Chapman's conception of Ceremony. He must have known that the usual personification of law was Themis. If he consulted Giraldi, a mythographer whose work he knew well, he would have found standing in the forefront of the article on Themis a passage from Ammianus Marcellinus which Giraldi considered *cognitione digna*. (*De Deis Gentium*, 1565, p. 380.) His quotation is from Ammianus Marcellinus' *Rerum Gestarum*, XXI, 1, 8: "The spirit pervading all the elements, seeing that they are eternal bodies, is always and everywhere strong in the power of prescience, and as the result of the knowledge which we acquire through varied studies makes us also sharers in the gifts of divination; and the elemental powers, when propitiated by divers rites, supply mortals with words of prophecy, as if from the veins of inexhaustible founts. These prophecies are said to be under the control of the divine Themis, so named because she reveals in advance decrees determined for the future by the law of the fates, which the Greeks call τυθειμενα; and therefore the ancient theologians gave her a share in the bed and throne of Jupiter, the life-giving power. (The translation is from J. C. Rolfe's Loeb edition of Ammianus [London 1935–39] II, pp. 93–4.) Stephanus, vol. III, col. 1527, H, gives θέμις as *idem quod* θεσμος; Scapula follows.

45. Cf. Giraldi, p. 37, and Cartari, pp. 72–3.

46. Hooker, *Works*, I, p. 285.

47. This passage from Puttenham, p. 39, helps to explain the introduction of memory: "There is nothing in man of all the potential parts of his mind (reason and will except) more noble or more necessary to the

active life than memory: because it maketh most to a sound iudgement and perfect worldly wisedome, examining and comparing the times past with the present, and by them both considering the time to come, concludeth with a stedfast resolution, what is the best course to be taken in all his actions and aduices in this world . . . ."

48. Dr. I. R. F. Calder informs me that the 'Mathematique Christall' was certainly the crystal ball used as lens and burning glass in contemporary experiments in optics.

49. Ficino, *De Vita*, lib. III, cap. XVII (Basel 1576), I, p. 555. Cf. *infra*, pp. 123–24.

50. Cf. Martin, *Marlowe's Poems*, p. 76.

51. On the 'Rainbow' portrait of Elizabeth at Hatfield and the significance of the serpent see Frances A. Yates, *Allegorical Portraits of Queen Elizabeth I at Hatfield* (Hatfield House Booklet No. 1). This portrait has been attributed to Federico Zuccaro, but there is no need to take this attribution seriously. The origin of the serpent allegory is, of course, the scriptural injunction "Estote ergo prudentes sicut serpentes" (*Matthew*, X.16).

52. For the story of how the word 'policy' took on a bad sense through its association with Machiavellianism, see Mario Praz, "Machiavelli e gl'Inglesi dell'epoca elisabettiana," in *Machiavelli in Inghilterra ed altri Saggi* (Rome 1942), pp. 101–7. (This is a revised version of the British Academy lecture of 1928.) See also Napoleone Orsini, "*Policy* or the Language of Elizabethan Machiavellianism," *JWCI* IX (1946), pp. 122–34.

53. Cartari, p. 466: "le Gratie tengono i mortali insieme raccolti, perche i beneficij, che à vicenda si fanno gli huomini l'un con l'altro, sono cagione, che l'uno all'altro è caro e grato, onde stanno congiunti insieme del bel nodo della amicitia: senza laquale non è dubbio alcuno, che gli huomini sarebbono inferiori di gran lunga à gli altri animali, e le città diverrebbono spelonche, anzi pure non sarebbono. Per laquale cosa potrebbesi quasi dire, che meglio fosse stato à mortali non essere, che essendo, vivere senza le Gratie."

54. Cf. my "*Hymenaei*: Ben Jonson's Masque of Union," *infra*.

55. Hymenaei, lines 198 ff. Cf. Cornelius Agrippa, *De Occulta Philosophia*, pp. 173–4: "ex primo pari, et primo impari, tamquam ex foemina et masculo. impar numerus mas est, par verò foemina," and "numerus connubij appellatur à Pythagoricis." See also D. J. Gordon, "Chapman's Use of Cartari . . . ," *MLR* 39, p. 282.

56. Cf. Hooker, *Works*, I, p. 285. The position is extremely familiar. Aristotle in both the *De Anima* and *De Sensu* takes sight as the first of the senses to be discussed. Renaissance Platonists put sight first in a hierarchy of the senses because it is "the most pure spirit of sense." Ficino elaborates this in his *Commentary* on the *Symposium, Or.* V. cap. 2, *Opera Omnia* (Basel 1576), p. 1334. Cf. also Appendix III, a.

57. Hooker, I, pp. 417–8.

58. Jonson, VII, p. 213.

59. Hooker, II, p. 259.

60. The fundamentals of Aristotle's position are entirely familiar and are set out in many studies. As a general guide I have used W. D. Ross, *Aristotle* (5th ed. revised, London 1953); the modern edition of the *De Anima* that I have relied on is that by R. D. Hicks (Cambridge 1907). Of the translations and commentaries available in Chapman's time I have used that by Giulio Pace, *Aristotles de anima libri tres, Graece et Latine* (Hanover 1611). The first edition was published in Frankfurt in 1596. Pace (1550–1635), *Vicentino* by birth, was internationally famous as jurist, philosopher and heretic, though he was finally reconciled to the church. He visited many European universities. Garin numbers him among "i compilatori, i professori," as distinct from those Aristotelians who, like Zabarella, had ideas of their own to expound. (E. Garin, *La Filosofia* [Milan 1947] II, 61–2.) Cf. also Tiraboschi, *Storia della Letteratura Italiana* (Venice 1796) VII, 698–702. Here, see Appendix III, b.

61. See Appendix III, c.

62. *Theologia Platonica*, Lib. X, cap. 8, in *Opera Omnia* (Basel 1576), I, p. 235.

63. That Time follows Motion is a statement of Aristotelian doctrine (see Ross, *Aristotle*, pp. 89–91) which had passed into current thought. Cf. de la Primaudaye, *The French Academie* (London 1618), pp. 641–2: "And here the definition which *Aristotle* maketh of *Time*, serueth to our purpose, to wit, that it is the measure of motion . . . . For that which giueth time his course is the changing of things, when they giue place one to another, and one succeed another, because they cannot consist all at once together."

64. Pace, *De Anima*, p. 235. *Subiectum* and the English *subject* which translates it are translations of the Aristotelian τὸ ὑποκείμενον. Cf. *OED* under *subject*.

65. This is in Aristotle, as, for example, in his famous instance of the sculptor who imposes form on his

material. Cf. Ross, *Aristotle*, p. 74. We can see the possibilities in Stephanus' translations of εἶδος as *Facies*, *Forma*, *Species* (I, col. 1105). Scapula repeats this.

66. Cf. P. O. Kristeller, *The Philosophy of Marsilio Ficino* (New York 1943), pp. 37–46.

67. For Democritus' conception of the soul as fire see *De Anima*, 404a, 405a; for the criticism of the Platonic notion of the circular movement of the soul as set out in the *Timaeus*, see 406b–407b.

68. Cf. *De Anima*, 431a, b. And see note 84, below.

69. Cf. Aristotle, *De Sensu*, 438a.

70. Hooker, II, pp. 323–4.

71. Hooker, p. 323, note 2, cites three sentences from *De Anima*: (1) from *De Anima* 403a (in which, however, Hooker seems to be running two sentences together in his mind), rendered thus by Pace (*De Anima*, p. 5): "maximè autem proprium videtur [sc. anima] intelligere. quod si hoc est phantasia quaedam, aut non sine phantasia: certè neque hoc potest esse sine corpore." Cf. Pace's commentary, pp. 163–64, where he explains that Aristotle's difficulty is to separate *intellectus* from *phantasia*, the ground of the difficulty being "quia sicut sensibilia sunt obiecta sensus, ita phantasmata sunt obiecta intellectus, vt lib. 3. explicabitur." (2) From *De Anima*, 434a (given with minor omissions), rendered by Pace (*op. cit.* p. 130), "ergo sensitiua phantasia . . . etiam brutis animalibus inest: deliberatiua autem in iis dumtaxat, quae sunt ratione praedita." (3) From *De Anima*, 431b (given accurately). In Pace's rendering it reads, "Species igitur intellectiuum in phantasmatibus intelligit. & vt in illis definitum ei est, *quod est* persequendum et fugiendum, etiam quod est extra sensum, quando est in phantasmatibus, monetur" (p. 120).

72. Cf. Kristeller, *Ficino*, p. 39.

73. Cf. *Sestiad* IV, 146–40.

74. *In Convivium Platonis, De Amore, commentarius*, Or. V, Cap. IV, in *Opera Omnia* (Basel 1576) II, pp. 1336–7. (See also references in note 78, below.) On Chapman's reading in this text of Ficino's, see Schoell, *Etudes*, chap. I.

75. I have to thank Dr. I. R. F. Calder for notes on the study of optics during the Renaissance.

76. I am much indebted to E. H. Gombrich's exposition in "Icones Symbolicae," *JWCI* XI (1948), especially pp. 175–78.

77. Ficino, *De Vita*, Lib. III, cap. XVII, in *Opera Omnia* (Basel 1576), I, p. 555.

78. *Opera Omnia* (Basel 1576), II, p. 1323 (*Or.* I, cap. IV). Also, *ibid.*, "Pulchritudo verò gratia quaedam est, quae vt plurimum in concinnitate plurium maxime nascitur. Ea triplex est: siquidem ex plurimum virtutum concinnitate in animis gratia est. Ex plurium colorum linearumque concordia in corporibus gratia nascitur. Gratia item in sonis maxima ex vocum plurium consonantia." (Later, Ficino will argue that this is not enough, in his endeavour to prove that beauty is finally incorporeal.)

79. *De Deis Gentium* (Lyons 1565), p. 147. Schoell first demonstrated Chapman's familiarity with this book, *Etudes*, chap. 2.

80. See Kristeller, *Ficino*, pp. 37 f., and S. R. Jayne, *Marsilio Ficino's Commentary on Plato's Symposium* (Columbia, Mo. 1944), p. 127, note 27.

81. Ficino, II, 1322 (*Or.* I, cap. III, *Origo Amoris ex Chaos*). Cf. also, "Quis igitur dubitabit, quin amor statim chaos sequatur, praecedatque mundum: & deos omnes, qui mundi partibus distributi sunt? Cum mentis ille appetitus ante sui formationem sit, & in mente formata dij mundusque nascantur." (*Ibid.*)

82. *De Deis Gentium* (Lyons 1565), p. 228.

83. Kristeller, pp. 233–4.

84. Cf. *Sestiad* III, 85–6: "And as the colours of all things we see, / To our sights powers communicated bee . . . ." See *De Anima*, 418b ff., and Appendix III, d.

85. *Sestiad* III, 343–50.

86. As Bush points out, *Mythology*, p. 126, Abraham Fraunce in his *Countesse of Pembroke's Yvychurch* (1592) gives Fulgentius' moral.

87. Caspar von Barth (1587–1658), the immensely prolific German scholar, poet, translator. It does not seem possible to find absolutely reliable bibliographical information about Barth's works. I have, however, no reference to the publication of his *Leandridos* before its appearance in his *Opuscula Varia* ("nunc primum edita") (Hanover 1612), nor to his translation and commentary on Musaeus before the edition of Amberg, 1608.

88. *Leandridos*, Lib. III, *ad fin.*, in Daniel Pareus, *Musæi . . . Erotopaegnion Herus et Leandri* etc. (Frankfurt 1627), p. 208. This is an extremely useful volume. It contains not only Pareus' own text, version, and elaborate commentary on Musaeus' poem, but also de Mara's *paraphrasis*, Barth's *Leandridos*, the Ovid

epistles, and Marot's *Histoire de Leandre, et Ero.*

89. Commentators on Marlowe and Milton have adduced many 'parallels' for the speeches of Leander and Comus (see, e.g., L. C. Martin's notes, pp. 37 f.). The idea of parallels is, however, misleading in this connexion: we are dealing with a rhetorical complex which requires study as a whole. See M. C. Bradbrook, *Shakespeare . . .* , p. 252, note 13. Miss Bradbrook says "the whole has the flavour of the medieval *suasio.*"

90. On the Aristotelian–or pseudo-Aristotelian–sources of Marlowe's "Women receaue perfection euery way," see Martin's note to lines 267–68 (p. 42). Miss Bradbrook also, in the note already quoted, remarks that "some of his arguments are Aristotelian." The Aristotelian phraseology of the lines on virginity is obvious.

91. "Amusing as parodies," Miss Bradbrook says of Leander's arguments (p. 58).

Notes to "The Imagery of Ben Jonson's *Masques of Blacknesse and Beautie*"

1. Jones's debt to Italian sources is well known now. See Enid Welsford, "Italian Influence on the English Court Masque," *Modern Language Review* XVII (1923), pp. 934 ff.; Percy Simpson and C. F. Bell, *Designs by Inigo Jones for Masques and Plays at Court* (Walpole Society XII, 1924), Introduction, pp. 29–31; Stephen Orgel and Roy Strong, *Inigo Jones* (London and Berkeley 1973), chap. III, and the indications in the Catalogue; Allardyce Nicoll, *Stuart Masques and the Renaissance Stage* (London 1937), *passim*.

2. On these manuals see Jean Seznec, *La Survivance des Dieux Antiques* (London 1940) II, chap. 1.

3. My references are to the following editions: Lilius Gregorius Gyraldus (or Giraldi), *De Deis Gentium Libri siue Syntagmata XVII* (Lyons 1565); Natalis Comes (or Conti), *Mythologiae, siue explicationis fabularum, libri decem* (Lyons 1602); Vincentius Chartarius (or Cartari), *Imagines Deorum, qui ab Antiquis colebantur* (Lyons 1581)–Antoine du Verdier's translation from Cartari's Italian. On the Elizabethan use of the manuals, see F. L. Schoell, *Etudes sur l'Humanisme Continentale en Angleterre à la fin de la Renaissance* (Paris 1926), pp. 21 ff.; C. W. Lemmi, *The Classical Deities in Bacon* (Baltimore 1933). References are also to be found in Douglas Bush, *Mythology and the Renaissance Tradition in English Poetry* (Minneapolis 1932). C. F. Wheeler, *Classical Mythology in the Plays, Masques and Poems of Ben Jonson* (Princeton 1938) has little value as an account of Jonson's sources, because the author omits any mention of the intermediary sources.

   Jonson refers explicitly to Giraldi in his *Part of the Kings entertainment in Passing to his Coronation*, Jonson, *Works*, ed. C. H. Herford, Percy and Evelyn Simpson, VII (Oxford 1941), p. 85. (All my references to the text of the masques is to this edition.) Seznec quotes an interesting passage from Marston's *Second Satire*. Marston is complaining of the obscurity of his contemporaries and exclaims,

   > Reach me some poet's index that will show.
   > *Imagines Deorum*, Book of Epithets,
   > Natalis Comes, that I know recites,
   > And makest anatomy of poetry;
   > Help me to unmask the satire's secrecy . . . .
   >   (Marston, *Works*, ed. Bullen, 1887, III, 269–70)

4. References are to Cesare Ripa, *Iconologia overo Descrittione di Diverse Imagini cauate dall' antichita, & di propria inuentione . . .* (Rome 1603). A certain amount of material for the study of the influence of Ripa on the English masque has been assembled by P. Reyher, *Les Masques Anglais* (Paris 1909), chapter VI, and for Ripa, and the general repertory of imagery, by Allardyce Nicoll, *Stuart Masques*, chap. VI.

5. G. P. Valeriano, *Hieroglyphica, seu de sacris Aegyptiorum aliarumque gentium literis commentarii. Quibus etiam duo alii a quodam eruditissimo vivo sunt annexi* (Lyons 1595). All references are to this edition unless otherwise stated.

6. Jonson, *Works*, VII, 209–10.

7. *In Conuiuium Platonis, De Amore, Commentarius*, in Ficino, *Opera* (Basel 1576), II, 1320 f.; and *Commento sopra vna Canzona de Amore, composta da Girolamo Beneuieni . . .* , in Pico della Mirandola, *Opera* (Basel 1601), I, 496 f. All references are to these texts.

8. In spite of all that has been said about the influence of Platonism and Italian Neo-Platonism on English literature of the sixteenth and seventeenth centuries, surprisingly little work has been done on the subject, except so far as Spenser is concerned. The standard book, J. S. Harrison, *Platonism in English Poetry of the Sixteenth and Seventeenth Centuries* (New York 1903), is not satisfactory. Schoell has, however, shown that Chapman knew Ficino's *Commentary* (*Etudes*, p. 7 f.).

9. Conti, p. 817.

10. p. 818.

11. See Appendix IV. In order to lighten the text many of the quotations from the sources have been put in the Appendix.

12. See Appendix IV, 2, and for the references to the tenth book of the *Iliad* and the Orphic hymns, Conti, p. 809. Nicoll thinks that Jonson may have been indebted to Ripa for his presentation of Oceanus "in spite of the reference to the ancients" (*Stuart Masques*, p. 69). Ripa's "Oceano" is not horned. It is just as likely that Jonson took his figure from Cartari (cf. pp. 162–3).

13. Jonson (VII, p. 176) explains why he calls the moon Æthiopia: "The *Æthiopians* worshipd the *Moone* by that surname. See Stepha. περὶ πόλεων in voce ΑΙ'ΘΙΟΠΙΟΝ and his reasons." Cf. Giraldi, p. 320: "Aethiopia Diana cognominata, teste Stephano, qui & eius varias opiniones recenset . . . ."

14. See Appendix IV, 3.

15. Jones's drawing of one of these nymphs survives and shows her holding a white fan in her left hand; see Orgel and Strong, *Inigo Jones*, no 1.

16. Valeriano, p. 585. See Appendix IV, 4. This symbol is indeed a famous one: the Icosaedron is one of the five "Platonic Bodies."

17. Valeriano, p. 337. See Appendix IV, 5.

18. On the importance and influence of this book see Mario Praz. *Studies in Seventeenth Century Imagery* (London 1939), pp. 19–20.

19. Valeriano, pp. 151–2.

20. See Appendix IV, 6.

21. See Appendix IV, 7.

22. Valeriano (ed. Cologne 1614), p. 476.

23. The *OED* interprets Jonson's phrase to mean an urn filled with wine; but this reading seems for various reasons (one of which is the difficulty of representing visually an urn full of wine) less convincing than the one adopted.

24. Ripa, p. 125.

25. Valeriano (ed. Cologne 1614), pp. 478–9. See also the end of Blaise de Vigenère's commentary on Philostratus' picture of the Nile (*Les Images . . . des deux Philostrates* [Paris 1629], pp. 39–40).

26. Cf. Conti, p. 310; Cartari, pp. 354–5; Giraldi, p. 356.

27. Giraldi, p. 357.

28. See *infra*, p. 149.

29. Jonson, *Works*, VII, p. 234, ll. 727–8.

30. *Genesis* II, verses 9–14.

31. For example, the names of the twelve Oceaniæ who accompany the twelve nymphs as light-bearers have not been taken into account. These were Doris, Petraea, Ocyrhoe, Cydippe, Glauce, Tyche, Beroe, Acaste, Clytia, Ianthe, Lycoris, Plexaure. (Jonson, *Works*, VII, pp. 171, 178.)

32. Jonson, *Works*, VII, p. 181.

33. The Moon, in the last speech in *Blacknesse*, had told them that they must "this night, the yeare gone round," "againe salute this ground" (lines 347–8). The return of the daughters of Niger was in fact delayed because in the winter of 1606, "and again in the winter of 1606–7, great Court weddings intervened, for which specifically wedding masques were desired" (Jonson, *Works*, II, p. 267).

34. For the presentation of January and the Winds Jonson uses Ripa, as Allardyce Nicoll (*Stuart Masques*, pp. 163–4) points out, and indeed Jonson gives Ripa as his authority for January (cf. Ripa, p. 320). January has "the signe *Aquarius* and the *Character*"; "Character" here means the appropriate astrological symbol, in this case ♒ . The "*Anademe*" of laurel which January wears may have been suggested by the wreath of palm carried by Ripa's *Mese in Generale*. For Boreas and Euro (Jonson's Vulturnus) see Ripa, pp. 496–7. For Boreas Jonson has also used another source. He follows Ripa in giving Boreas serpents' tails for feet, and adds in a footnote (note *a*, p. 181):

> So *Paus. in Eliacis* reports him to haue, as he was carued *in arcà Cipseli*

(The quarto and folio texts read *Cipselli*). Certainly this reference points to Cartari (p. 177):

> ... hunc (Boreas) Pausanias in Eliacis scribit in Cypselli arca exculptum fuisse, Orythiam rapeintem; non tamen eius effigiem designat, nisi quod eum pro pedibus anguium caudas habuisse dicit.

And when Jonson refers to Boreas and Orythia he has also Conti in mind (cf. ll. 101–3, and accompanying note *a* with Conti, p. 859). Cartari's illustration of the Winds shows very clearly the tradition in which Jonson was working. (See Figure 50.)

35. This personification of the Thames is fully in harmony with the accepted mode of representing rivers, cf. Cartari, p. 179, and Ripa's descriptions of various rivers.
36. Cf. *Blacknesse*, lines 253–7 (quoted above), line 349; *Beautie*, lines 31–3.
37. Pico begins his *Commentary* by defining these terms, *Opera* (1601) I, p. 496.
38. See Appendix IV, 8. Pico compares the "anima celeste" working through the medium of the sky to the craftsman using his pencil to create shapes. There seems to be an echo of this image in Jonson's lines.
39. Jonson's phrase; it is used in *Chloridia*, *Works*, VII, p. 750, l. 13.
40. Giraldi, p. 345. The description is given by Cartari too, pp. 328–9.
41. Valeriano (ed. Cologne 1614), pp. 154–5.
42. Erwin Panofsky, *Studies in Iconology* (New York 1939), on Blind Cupid, pp. 95 ff. For the Cranach, see *ibid.*, p. 128 and Figure 106.
43. Jonson adds this note:

> So he is faind by *Orpheus*, to haue appear'd first of all the *Gods*: awakened by *Clotho*: and is therefore call'd *Phanes*, both by him, and *Lactantius*.

Here Jonson is following Giraldi (p. 347):

> Phanes etiam dictus est Amor, quod ex Chao primus apparuerit, quod Orpheus & Lactantius aiunt.

Jonson's reference to Love being awakened by Clotho is rather puzzling. I have found no classical sources for this, nor have I found it in any 16th-century authority. But Spenser in his *Hymne in Honour of Love* had written:

> Loue, that had now long time securely slept
> In Venus lap, vnarmed then and naked,
> Gan reare his head, by Clotho being waked.

(ll. 107–9) With reference to this Lotspeich quotes from Boccaccio's *Genealogia*:

> Clotho interpretari *euocationem*, eo quod suum sit, iacto cuiuscumque rei semine, illud adeo in crementum trahere, ut aptum sit in lucem emergere.

That this could be associated with the beliefs about the part played by Love in the ordering of the world which are expressed in Spenser's poem—drawn from Platonic and Neo-Platonic sources—is fairly obvious. Spenser himself may have bridged the gap and connected Clotho with the awakening of Love. Jonson, who was dealing with the same theme as Spenser, may well have had the elder poet in mind here.

Giraldi is cited in yet another note on this song:

> It was for *Beauty*, that the World was made,
> And where she raignes, *Loues* lights admit no shade,
> (ll. 289–90)

which is annotated thus:

> Alluding to his name of *Himerus*, and his signification in the name, which is *Desiderium post aspectum*: and more then *Eros*, which is onely *Cupido, ex aspectu amare*.

Giraldi has:

> Hesoidus Erota & Himerum, quo vtroque nomine Amor significatur, Veneris sectatores facit. quo loco scholiastes philosophatus, differentiamque inter eos ponit. Erota enim, id est, Cupidinem, ex aspectu amare: 'ίμερον verò: id est desiderium post aspectum desiderare facere ait ... (p. 345).

44. Ficino, *Commentary*, Or. 3, Cap. 2 (Basel 1576) II, p. 1329.
45. Pp. 406–7.
46. See Appendix IV, 9. The concluding lines of this song are:

> And then a *motion* he them taught,
> That elder then himselfe was thought.
> Which thought was, yet, the child of earth,
>   For *loue* is elder then his birth.

(Note) a

> That is, borne since the world, and, out of those duller apprehensions that did not thinke hee was before.

The "motion" is either the movement described by Ficino in the passage cited above, or a reference to Ficino's concept—a cardinal one in his system—of the *circuitus spiritualis*, that "self-reverting current from God to the world and from the world to God, the generating power of which is Love: in Love God created the world, and in Love every creature aspires to return to Him." Cf. Panofsky, *Studies in Iconology*, p. 141; E. Cassirer, *Individuo e Cosmo nella Filosofia del Rinascimento* (It. transl. of *Individuum und Kosmos in der Philosophie der Renaissance*, Studien der Bibliotek Warburg, 10), (Florence, 1935), pp. 211-3; and Ficino, Or. 2, Cap. 2, p. 1324. This is suggested by the context, for the last three lines of the song seem to be a reference to the belief that Love was both the youngest and the oldest of the gods, a theme discussed at length by Ficino, Or. 5, Caps. 10, 11, p. 1340. The idea of the *circuitus spiritualis* enters this discussion, cf. Pico, *Commentary*, lib. 2, Cap. 19, pp. 504-5, and Giovanni Semprini, *La Filosofia di Pico della Mirandola* (Milan 1936), p. 91.

47. That fountains of Youth and Pleasure should be associated with an image expressing Beauty and Love is appropriate enough. Jonson seems to have associated the "Fons Amoris" and "Fons Iuventutis" of medieval tradition with the classical figures.

48. When Jonson says that these figures "being females had the Corinthian order" he is following Vitruvius (see Appendix IV, 10), though it is not clear from his description how they were linked with this order within the structure of the machine.

49. Ficino, Or. 2, Cap. 9, p. 1328.

50. Ficino, Or. 5, Cap. 4, p. 1336.

51. Ripa, pp. 40-2. Jonson gives *Splendor* roses because "The *Rose* is call'd, elegantlie, by Achil. Tat. lib. 2. φυτῶν ἀγλάισμα the splendor of plants, and is euery where taken for the *Hieroglyphick*, of Splendor." This suggests that Jonson is again beginning a scheme with *Aglaia*, the first of the Three Graces, whose name means "splendour" and who has the rose as her attribute. See Cartari, pp. 356-7, and fig. p. 358.

52. Ripa, p. 356.

53. See Appendix IV, 11.

54. "*Electra* signifies Serenitie it selfe, and is compounded of ἥλιος, which is the Sunne, and αἰθριος, that signifies serene" (note c). "She is also faind to be the mother of the rainebow. *Nascitur enim Iris ex aqua & serenitate, è refractione radiorum scilicet. Arist. in Meteorol.*" (note d) Jonson, *Works*, VII, p. 107.

55. Conti, p. 901.

56. Works, VII, p. 107.

57. "As this of *Serenity*" is to be read as following on from "is euery where taken as the *Hieroglyphick*, of Splendor" in note a.

58. Conti, p. 902.

59. On all this see Ficino, Or. 1, Cap. 3, p. 1321; Or. 2, Cap. 3, pp. 1324-5, 1326-7; Or. 6, Cap. 7, pp. 1344-5. And Panofsky, *Studies in Iconology* pp. 131 ff.

60. Ficino, p. 1326. Secunda Venus (i.e. *Venus Vulgaris*), quae in mundi anima ponitur, ex Ioue & Dione genita. [The 1576 ed. has her born of Jove and Diogenes!] Ex Ioue, id est, ex ea virtute ipsius animae, quae coelestia mouet. Ea siquidem istam creauit potentiam, quae inferiora haec generat . . . Denique . . . Duplex est Venus . . . altera (*Venus Vulgaris*) vis generandi animae mundi tributa. Cf. Pico, *Commentary*, II, ix.

61. Ripa, p. 473.

62. Ficino, Or. 5, Cap. 2, p. 1334. Cf. Giraldi, p. 357, for whom Euphrosyne is "hilaritas, iucunditas, laetitiaque."

63. Ripa, pp. 10-12.

64. Ripa, p. 482.

65. Ficino, Or. 1, Cap. 4, pp. 1322-3.

66. See Appendix IV, 12.

67. Ficino, Or. 5, Cap. 3, p. 1335.

68. Ficino, Or. 5, Cap. 6, p. 1338: . . . pulchritudinem esse gratiam quandam vivacem & spiritalem, Dei radio illustrante Angelo primum infusam: inde & animis hominum, corporumque figuris, & vocibus: quae per rationem, visum, auditum, animos nostros movet atque delectat, oblectando rapit, rapiendo ardenti inflammat amore.

69. Pico, *Commentary*, III, x, pp. 514 ff.

70. Ripa, p. 195.

71. Valeriano, p. 404.

> Vniones tamen cum ad ornatam praecipue comparentur, venustatis significatum sibi ante alias vsurparunt . . . . in vnione nitor & laeuor tantam expetitur.

The pearls, the silver robe, and the veil are all to be found, however, in Ripa's presentation of "Età dell'Argento," p. 138. And silver was associated with Venus, cf. Giraldi, p. 342, where he recalls that she was called by Pindar "silver-footed."

72. Valeriano (Cologne 1614), p. 689.

73. Jonson's *Dignitas* very closely resembles Spenser's personification of *Sapience* in the *Hymne of Heavenly Beautie*:

> There in his bosome Sapience doth sit,
> The soveraine dearling of the Deity,
> Clad like a Queene in royall robes, most fit
> For so great powre and peereless majesty,
> And all with gemmes and jewels gorgeously
> Adornd, that brighter than the starres appeare,
> And make her native brightnes seem more cleare.
> And on her head a crowne of purest gold
> Is set, in signe of highest soveraignty;
> And in her hand a scepter she doth hold,
> With which she rules the house of God on hy,
> And menageth the ever-moving sky,
> And in the same these lower creatures all
> Subjected to her powre imperiall.
>   (Lines 183–96)

On the background of *Sapience*, see Joseph B. Collins, *Christian Mysticism in the Elizabethan Age* (Baltimore 1940), p. 222 f. The *Sapientia* of Solomon had indeed already been identified with the *Venus Cœlestis* of Plato, for example, by Blaise de Vigenère, *Les Images . . . de Philostrate* (Paris 1602), p. 99.

74. Pico, II, xxi, p. 505.

75. Ficino, Or. 5, Cap. 1, p. 1334.

76. Ripa, pp. 391–2.

77. See Appendix IV, 13.

78. Pico, II, vi, p. 501.

79. Ripa, p. 25. Ripa's figure is taken from that designed by Buontalenti for the first of the *Intermezzi* conceived by Giovanni de'Bardi for the wedding of the Grand Duke Ferdinand I of Florence with Christine de Lorraine in 1589. See Aby Warburg, "I Costumi Teatrali per Gl'Intermezzi del 1589," *Gesammelte Schriften* (Leipzig 1932), I, pp. 261 ff., and plate XLVI, Figure 80. The *Intermezzo* in question represented the Music of the Spheres.

80. Macrobius, *In Somnium Scipionis*, etc. (Lyons 1585), Lib. 2, Cap 1, p. 147. (The passage cited is a chapter heading found only in the Renaissance editions.)

81. See Appendix IV, 14.

82. Spondanus, *Homeri quae extant omnia . . . cum Latina versione . . . perpetuis item . . . in Iliada simul & Odysseam . . . commentariis* (Basel 1606), p. 223. On Chapman's use of Spondanus see Schoell, *op. cit.*, p. 162.

83. Macrobius, Lib. 1, Cap. 14, pp. 97–8. (In the Teubner edition, Leipzig 1893, the passage is on p. 544.) The translation is by W. H. Stahl.

84. From the series of the so-called "Finguerra Planets," cf. A. M. Hind, *Early Italian Engraving* (London 1938), A III, 7 b.

85. Information communicated to me by Fritz Saxl. Jonson departs from the type by introducing Scorpio. This sign has no relevance to the time of year when the masque was produced, and it does not seem likely that the introduction of the moon in Scorpio is intended to carry an involved and esoteric astrological meaning applicable in some way or other to the occasion of the masque. Dr. Saxl suggested that as a well-known and quite definite formula for the representation of the moon is being followed, a formula which always includes the sign Cancer–for Cancer is the House of the Moon–the most likely reason for the unexpected appearance of Scorpio here is simply that Jonson or the designer in a moment of carelessness mistook Cancer for Scorpio, a mistake which is by no means difficult to make. The "character" in question here is the crescent moon which is the symbol of this planet.

86. Jonson alludes to the *Poeticon Astronomicon* in *The Masque of Queènes, Works*, VII, p. 309, note d, and in *Part of the Kings Entertainment, ibid.*, p. 107, note b.

87. Reyher, p. 391, and *pièce justificative* no. 12, p. 512.
88. *An Expostulation with Inigo Jones*, lines 42–56.
89. *Works*, VII, p. 213, note a.
90. *Ibid.*, p. 91, lines 263–7.

Notes to "*Hymenaei*: Ben Jonson's Masque of Union"

1. S. R. Gardiner, *History of England from the Accession of James I to the outbreak of the Civil War* (London 1883), II, p. 166; *CSP Venetian*, Jan. 6, 1606.
2. Jonson, *Works*, VII, p. 232. These acknowledgements are in the quarto (1606) but were omitted in the folio (1616). None of Jones's designs for this masque survives. There are however three portraits which seem to be connected with *Hymenaei*: a portrait at Welbeck Abbey of a woman wearing a dress almost identical with that worn by the lady masquers, whose costume is elaborately described by Jonson; a portrait at Berkeley Castle which is believed to be a replica of the Welbeck portrait; a portrait at Woburn Abbey of Lucy, Countess of Bedford, wearing a dress which somewhat resembles the *Hymenaei* costume. See S. Orgel and R. Strong, *Inigo Jones*, nos. 8–10.
3. P. 210, note on the inscription. The inscription, though it clearly follows the well-known formula of dedication to Jupiter, has no basis in antiquity and has no parallel among the Humanist fakes. Such a departure is due to Jonson's desire to stress the word *Vnio*. I have to thank Fritz Saxl for allowing me to draw on his knowledge of classical and Humanist epigraphy.
4. Here, in this last stanza, Jonson is speaking with the voice of the Renaissance Platonist. In the *Symposium* Plato had given Agathon eloquent words to describe the birth of Love and the order he brought to the warring elements: the passage, with Ficino's commentary on it, was echoed by many Renaissance poets, and by Jonson among them, here and elsewhere—in, for instance, *The Masque of Beautie*, written two years later. On the Neo-Platonism of this masque, see my "The Imagery of Jonson's *Masques of Blacknesse and Beautie*," above.
5. *Batman vppon Bartholome, his booke De Proprietatibus Rerum* . . . (London, 1582), Lib. III, Chap. 6, pp. 13*v*–14*r*.
6. To illustrate and explain ideas Jonson uses in his masque I refer to de la Primaudaye's *The French Academie*, the great Protestant (and Platonizing) encyclopædia of the late sixteenth century. All my references are to the complete English edition of 1618 (here to p. 14).
7. Cf. de la Primaudaye, p. 533. Jonson says (pp. 213 and 230) that these masquers were distinguished by "Ensignes" and colours; they were arranged in four pairs, each pair consisting of one Humour and one Affection, who wore silk mantles of the same symbolic colour; the colours being, sky, pearl, flame and tawny. It is easy to find from the handbooks an "Ensign" for each Humour and each Affection; but I cannot say which Humour went with which Affection nor which colour would be appropriate for which pair, because I cannot find that the theorists definitely and strictly related one particular Affection to one particular Humour or that there is a precise relationship between these colours and the Humours and Affections. Such writings as exist on Elizabethan colour symbolism have not proved very helpful; this is a subject which might well be investigated further.
8. De la Primaudaye, pp. 447–8.
9. *Ibid.*, p. 449.
10. For Jonson's use of Ripa, and on topics that will be discussed later—his acquaintance with the Pythagorean-Platonic tradition, his use of Giraldi, Conti, Cartari, Valeriano—see my article cited above. It is no longer necessary to prove Jonson's knowledge of this range of sources.
11. *Iconologia* (Rome 1603), pp. 425–6.
12. *Ibid.*, p. 441.
13. De la Primaudaye, p. 528.
14. "matrimony, which is an honourable estate . . . signifying unto us the mystical union, that is betwixt Christ and his church . . .": *Book of Common Prayer*, 1559.
15. Cf. Hooker, *Laws*, V, chap. LVIII, opening sentence.
16. In Xylander's *Plutarch* (Frankfurt 1599), the most popular Latin version, the reference is to vol. 2, pp. 876–77. I quote from Philemon Holland's version of *The Morals* (London 1603), pp. 806–7.

17. For Unity meaning One see *O.E.D.* Jonson refers to *Mac. in som. Scipion. lib. I.* The passage he has in mind is in Bk. I, Chap. VI: "Vnum autem, quod μονὰς, id est, unitas dicitur, et mas idem et foemina est: par idem, atque impar: ipse non numerus, sed fons et origo numerorum. Haec monas initium finisque omnium, neque ipsa principij aut finis sciens, ad summum refertur Deum" (Macrobius, ed. Lyons 1560, p. 30).

18. The phrase is Ficino's: "ac supra multitudinem omnem vnitas sit opportet, quae est numeri totius origo: necesse est eam ab vno rerum omnium principio, quod ipsum vnum vocamus, effluere." *In Convivium Platonis De Amore Commentarius,* Or. VI, Cap. 18, *Opera* (Basel 1576), II, p. 1354. Jonson would find material similar to that in Macrobius in Martianus, *De Monade,* in Lib. VII. I have no doubt that Jonson used the most up-to-date edition of Martianus–that done by the young Grotius: *Martiani Minei Felicis Capellae . . . Satyricon, in quo De Nuptiis Philologiae & mercurij libri duo, & de Septem Artibus Liberalibus Libri Singulares.* Omnes & amendati & Notis, sine Febrius Hvg. Grotii illustrati. Leyden. 1599.

19. Holland, *Morals,* p. 806.

20. Based on Ficino, Or. III, Cap. 2, p. 1329.

21. Jonson, *The Masque of Beautie, Works,* VII, p. 190, note o. See my article, *infra,* p. 145.

22. De la Primaudaye, pp. 699–700.

23. King James, *The Works,* edited by James, Bishop of Winchester (London 1616), p. 464 and p. 148.

24. Martianus, (Leyden 1599), p. 238.

25. Cornelius Agrippa did this, *De Occulta Philosophia,* Lib. II, Cap. 4, *De Vnitate, et eius scala, Opera* (Lyons N.D.), I, pp. 124–5. Martianus is used here. Jonson could have found the whole story of *Unitas* in Petrus Bungus, *Numerorum Mysteria,* etc.; I have used the edition of Paris, 1618, but there were later sixteenth-century editions. His first chapter is *De Unitate:* fifty pages of it, where the whole tradition is summed up; the Bible, the Fathers, Plato, Aristotle, Pythagoras, Hermes Trismegistus–alchemy, Neo-Platonism, Mysticism–all are pressed into service. There is, however, no trace of direct borrowing from this source.

26. George Marcellin, *The Triumphs of King James the First . . . Published vpon his Majesties Advertisement to all the Kings . . . of Christendome* (1610), p. 62. (See Appendix VI, on Jonson, p. 216, notes l and m.)

27. The phrase is Batman's *Bartholome,* p. 29.

28. The authorities were by no means agreed on the details of the constitution of the cosmos. Jonson's account of the regions of air (pp. 231–2) is however in line with the general body of opinion. Cf. Sylvester, *Du Bartas, His Deuine Weekes and Workes Translated* (London, 1611), p. 35 ff. and de la Primaudaye, p. 736 ff. In making the rainbow appear in the lowest region of the air Jonson disagrees with de la Primaudaye, who puts it in the middle region; but Conti's discussion of Iris–a passage which Jonson uses later in *The Masque of Beautie*–would give him authority for so doing (cf. *Mythologiæ,* Lyons, 1602, p. 901).

29. In later editions of Ripa "Right and True Order" carries a *squadra* or "square" for determining angles and levels; this goes back to Valeriano (*Hieroglyphica,* Lib. XLIX) and the *perpendiculum* and *amussis* which signify *rectus tenor.*

30. Cf. E. M. W. Tillyard, *The Elizabethan World Picture* (London 1943), pp. 94 ff.

31. Valeriano (*Hieroglyphica,* Lyons 1595, pp. 582–3) has the explanations from the *Theætetus* and Macrobius; but Jonson has gone to the *In Somnium Scipionis* for his quotation.

32. For the history of this concept see A. O. Lovejoy, *The Great Chain of Being,* (Harvard 1936); and for its ubiquity in Elizabethan writing, E. M. W. Tillyard.

33. On the circle and the sphere, cf. Valeriano, pp. 376–9.

34. See my article on *The Masques of Blacknesse and Beautie,* p. 149, with reference to Ficino.

35. J. Nichols, *The Progresses of King James the First* (London 1828) II, p. 33: John Pory to Sir Robert Cotton.

36. King James, *The Workes,* p. 488.

37. *Journals of the House of Commons,* I, p. 315; James, *Workes,* p. 513.

38. *Rapta Tatio. The Mirrour of his Majesties present Gouernment, tending to the Vnion of his whole Iland of Brittonie* (London 1604), last page. The authorship remains uncertain.

39. *The Miraculous and Happie Vnion of England and Scotland* (Edinburgh 1604), Sig. C. 1. r.

40. This pamphlet was published under the initials "I.H."; the attribution to Hayward is commonly accepted, and need not be questioned. Elizabeth had been gravely displeased by Hayward's account of the deposition of Richard II in a work which he dedicated to Essex. Cf. the *D.N.B.* article on Hayward.

41. Hayward, chap. I, pp. 1–2. Among his sources Hayward names Plutarch's *De Placitis Philosophorum.*

42. S. T. Bindoff in "The Stuarts and their Style," *English Historical Review,* LX (1945), pp. 192–216, gives an adequate account of the steps leading to the adoption of the style, but does not cover the historical and theological-philosophical justifications of it. But he sees the importance of the occurrence of the name "Britain" in the *Masque of Blacknesse,* which I had failed to do.

43. The text of the proclamation is in Rymer's *Foedera* (1742), VII, pp. 125 ff. For the proclamation on the coinage cf. *ibid.*, p. 127. Cf. Oman, *The Coinage of England* (Oxford 1931), pp. 291–2, and plate XXXIII.
44. EVΩTIKOV *Or a Sermon of the Vnion of Great Britannie, in antiquitie of language, name, religion, and Kingdome: Preached by Iohn Gordovn Dean of Sarvm, the 28 day of October 1604, in presence of the Kings Maiestie at Whitehall.* London, 1604.
45. On Gordon see the *D.N.B.* article.
46. *Panegyrique de Congratulation . . . par Jean de Gordon Escossais, sieur de Long-orme, Gentilhomme ordinaire de la chambre du Roy Tres-Chrestien* etc. (La Rochelle 1603). In England: *A Panegyrique of congratulation* (London 1603); *The Union of Great Britaine* (London 1604); *England and Scotlands happinesse in being reduced to unitie of religion* (London 1604).
47. Gordon, pp. 2, 8–14; the last quotation is from p. 12.
48. See the *D.N.B.* article on Thornborough. Sir John Harington thought him important enough to be included in his catalogue of eminent divines prepared for Prince Henry, but says nothing about these activities. Harington, *Nugæ Antiquæ* (London 1804), II, pp. 210–3.
49. *Journals of the House of Commons,* I, pp. 188–9.
50. *Journals of the House of Commons,* I, pp. 226–7, 236, 238; *Journals of the House of Lords,* II, pp. 306, 308–10, 314; *Hist. MSS. Comm. Buccleuch,* III, pp. 88–9.
51. *A Discourse plainely prouing the euident utilitie and vrgent necessitie of the desired happie Vnion of the two famous Kingdomes of England and Scotland: by way of answer to certaine obiections against the same* (London 1604), sig. A3.r: "Your most excellent Maiestie being graciously pleased to reade and approoue the written Copie of that I haue now printed, and withall to declare your princely pleasure (sufficient warrant) for publishing the same . . . ." There is a reprint of this tract in *Harleian Miscellany, Miscellaneous Pieces* (London 1812), I, p. 95 ff.
52. p. 15.
53. Published at Oxford in 1604 or 1605.
54. Based on Thornborough, pp. 5–8; with the last phrase, cf. Jonson: *The perfect'st figure is the round. / Nor fell you in it by aduenter, / Where REASON was your guide, and center.*
55. Pp. 11–14.
56. Pp. 18–20.
57. Thornborough cites Macrobius as his authority for identifying Pallas with the μονας. This is a mistake. It is *seven* with which Macrobius identifies Pallas (Lyons 1560, pp. 19–20). I have not found any source justifying Thornborough's equation.
58. *Journals of the House of Commons,* I, p. 315.
59. I should like to express my gratitude to the Librarian and the College Council of St. John's College, Cambridge, who generously deposited for my use in the Harold Cohen Library of the University of Liverpool a volume containing *Rapta Tatio,* Hayward's tract, the pamphlets of Gordon and Thornborough, and other relevant works, all rare and difficult to find, especially in these days. This one volume constitutes a contemporary collection of tracts on the union.
60. Here I am concerned only with Jonson's treatment of ritual and mythology. His imitation of the Epithalamium is a fairly familiar subject; a note on it will be found in Appendix V.
61. Study of Jonson's sources starts from the footnotes with which he so lavishly supports his text. In Appendix VI, I present a detailed analysis of these footnotes and their sources, with illustrative material. My comments here are based on these findings.
62. These are the editions used: Lilius Gregorius Gyraldus, *De Deis Gentium* (Lyons 1565); Natalis Comes (Conti), *Mythologiae, siue explicationis fabularum libri decem* (Lyons 1602); Vincentius Chartarius (Cartari), *Imagines Deorum, qui ab Antiquis colebantur* (Lyons 1581).
63. For details see Appendix VI, on Jonson's p. 216, notes n, o, p, q, and on p. 217, notes r, s, a, b.
64. *C. Val. Catulli, Albii, Tibulli, Sex. Avr. Propertii, Opera Omnia quae exstant. Cum Doctorum Virorum Commentariis* etc. Lutetiae . . . M.D,CIIII. Costanzo Landi–or Landus–Conte di Compiano was born in Piacenza in 1521, and died in Rome in 1564. He was a jurist and seems to have been a pupil and friend of Alciati. From internal evidence (e.g. p. 173) his commentary seems to have been written after Alciati's death, that is after January 1550. On Landi, cf. Tirabeschi, *Storia della Letteratura Italiana* (Milan 1824), VII, pp. 1250–5. I can trace no earlier edition of his commentary. Jonson gets his Christian name wrong.
65. *Alexandri ab Alexandro . . . Genialivm Diervm Libri Sex. Illustrati & Locupletati, Semestribvs, eruditissimis, & plane iucundis. Andreae Tiraqvelli . . . Cui accessit Avctarivm variarvm notarvm atque obseruationvm & pensiculata recognition. Christophori Coleri Franci . . . Francoforti . . . M.D.XCIIII.*

66. *B. Brissonii I. C. Et in Svprema Parisiensi Cvria Advocati, De Ritv Nvptiarvm Liber Singularis* . . . (Parisiis 1564). So far as I know this was the first edition.
67. The edition used is that included in the collected edition of the works of his better known brother François Hotman, edited by the latter's son Jean: *Franc. Hotmani Ivrisconsulti Opervm Tomus Primus* . . . (Geneva) M.D.XCIX. The Bibliothèque Nationale has a copy of Antoine's treatise published in Paris in 1585, the earliest I have traced.

   On the scholars mentioned in this paragraph see *Dictionnaire de Biographie Universelle; Vitae Clarissimorum Auctorum* . . . *Ex Recensione et cum Notis Frider. Jac. Leickheri,* Lipsiæ, 1687; Teissier, *Eloges des Hommes Savants* (1715). On Tiraqueau there is the ample monograph by Jacques Brejon, *André Tiraqueau,* Paris, 1937.
68. Some details may come from the *Thesaurus Linguae Latinae* of Robertus Stephanus. Jonson's use of this dictionary was pointed out by E. W. Talbert in his valuable article "New Light on Ben Jonson's Workmanship," *Studies in Philology,* XL, 1943, pp. 154 f. As far as *Hymenæi* is concerned I disagree with Mr. Talbert on points of detail. I do not think Jonson used Charles Stephanus' *Dictionarium Historicum Geographicum Poeticum,* though in the *Barriers* he took one note from it: the note of the river Euripus (p. 235, note c). This, and the information about the Euripus in the text, come from Charles Stephanus' article on this river.
69. References are to the text in Tucker Brooke, *The Shakespeare Apocrypha,* Oxford, 1908 (impression of 1929). He finds it "excessively improbable" that the play was acted as early as 1614 (p. xli, note 2).
70. On Boccaccio see F. Saxl, "Pagan Sacrifice in the Italian Renaissance," *JWCI,* II (1938-9), p. 359.
71. Act I, scene i, p. 309.
72. Act V, scene ii, p. 342.
73. On this see E. Panofsky and F. Saxl, "Classical Mythology in Medieval Art," *Metropolitan Museum Studies,* IV, Part II (March 1933), pp. 266-8.
74. On the development of this attitude see Panofsky and Saxl, p. 274 f.
75. *Works,* V, pp. 444-5, and 450-1.
76. Jonson would find the blood drinking episode in Dion, in Plutarch, and in Sallust (who, however, doubts the authenticity of the story). The sixteenth-century historian Constantius Felicius Durantinus, whose *Historia Coniurationis Catilinariæ* was included in the Basel Sallust of 1564 and used by Jonson, says (pp. 466-7), after mentioning the sacrifice of the slave: "cum furoris sui socios omni foedere et iureiurando sibi ad hoc scelus astringeret, vinum humano sanguine perfusum in crateris, cum primum ipsi libasset, hoc deinde socijs degustandum dedisse." (I owe these references to the kindness of Miss Ellen Duffy.) Saxl, "Pagan Sacrifice," pp. 364-5, draws attention to the revival of interest in human sacrifice during the Renaissance, and its association with stories of human sacrifices offered by Jews and by the savage peoples in the newly discovered lands.
77. Ripa (1603), p. 499.
78. Jonson has consulted Giraldi as well as Ripa on Truth and Opinion. He writes: *"Truth* is fained to be the daughter of *Saturne:* who, indeed, with the Ancients, was no other then *Time,* and so his name alludes, Κρόνος, *Plut. in Quaest.* To which conferre the *Greeke Adage* ἄγει δὲ πρὸς ψῶς τὴν ἀλήθειαν χρονὸs"(p. 233, note a), and *"Hippocrat.* in a certaine epistle to *Philopoem.* describeth her, *Mulierem, quae non mala videatur, sed audacior aspectu concitatior.* To which *Cesare Ripa* in his *Iconolog.* alludeth, in these words, *Faccia, ne dispiaceuole,* . . ." For Ripa on Opinion, see p. 370. Talbert believes that the source of the first note is Charles Stephanus, but I cannot follow him here. Giraldi, p. 29, discussed *Veritas* and *Opinio* in the same paragraph: here is all Jonson's material on Truth, and also the reference to *Hippocrates uero in quadam ad Philopoemenen epistola,* with the quotation describing Opinion, for his second note (neither the quotation nor the precise reference is to be found in Ripa).
79. On Jonson's use of Catullus in the *Barriers,* cf. McPeek (reference given in App. I), pp. 201-5.
80. Charron, *Of Wisdome,* trans. Samson Lennard (London 1640), p. 77.
81. *French Academie,* p. 430.
82. *Ibid.,* pp. 454-5.
83. De la Primaudaye, p. 416.
84. *Ibid.,* pp. 409-10.
85. *Ibid.,* p. 455.
86. De la Primaudaye, pp. 414-5.
87. To make this figure Jonson may simply have been combining as many attributes as he needed—and some of them come from Ripa's representations of Truth—or he may have been following a single visual source

which I have not found. The general pattern he is following, a Virtue triumphing over the opposing Vice, is clear enough, and was commonly represented. Middleton in his pageant *The Triumphs of Truth* (1613) either copied this figure in almost every detail–which is likely enough–or drew on a common source or sources. Cf. Middleton, *The Works*, ed. Bullen (London 1886), VII, p. 244.

88. My account of the symbolism is largely based on Ripa. He makes doves symbols of Purity, Simplicity, Sincerity (pp. 421, 455-6); the serpent the symbol of Prudence, quoting *Estote prudentes sicut serpentes* (*ibid.*, p. 417); Sincerity offers her heart for the reason given (*ibid.*, pp. 455-6); his Authority or Power carries keys which symbolize spiritual power–they are of course the Pope's keys, and Ripa quotes *Et tibi dabo claves Regni Coelorum* (*ibid.*, p. 36); on Truth's sun, mirror and splendid attire cf. *ibid.*, pp. 499, 501. I have found no source for the significance Jonson gives to Truth's hair: but he may well be thinking of the famous fore-lock of *Occasio* or *Fortuna*.

89. Jonson probably found this out in the first place from Valeriano, but he may well have gone on to look at the Platonic text; although Valeriano cites Macrobius' explanation of the golden chain, Jonson went to Macrobius independently.

90. These translations of the Platonic terms are Cornford's. See F. M. Cornford, *Plato's Theory of Knowledge* (London 1935).

91. *Divini Platonis Opera Omnia. Marsilio Ficino Interprete* (Basel 1532), p. 135.

92. De la Primaudaye, p. 426.

Notes to "Jonson's *Haddington Masque*: The Story and the Fable"

1. Arthur Wilson, *The History of Great Britain, being the Life and Reign of King James the First* (London 1653), p. 12.

2. Jonson says that Camden, writing of the Earls of Sussex, spells the name in this way. This is so (*Britannia* [1600], p. 279). But Camden does not give this etymology.

3. Cf. Jonson, *Works*, VII, pp. 211, 215-6.

4. Cf. Cartari, *Imagines Deorum* (Lyons 1581), p. 343. Myrtle has power to rouse and maintain love; it is the symbol of peace; it grows near the sea. For these reasons it is sacred to Venus.

5. Jonson would find Greek text and Latin translation in the copy of *Poetae Graeci Veteres Carminis Heroici Scriptores, Qui extant, omnes* . . . (Augsburg 1606), p. 605, which we know he owned. I see no evidence that Jonson was influenced by earlier handlings, either Lyly's or Tasso's (in the epilogue to the *Aminta*) or Spenser's (*Faerie Queene*, III, vi, 11 ff.), as is suggested by Reyher, *Les Masques Anglais* (Paris 1909), pp. 140, 143.

6. Jonson's footnote here reads, "*Aeneas*, the sonne of *Venus*, *Virgil* makes through-out the most exquisite patterne of *Pietie, Iustice, Prudence*, and all other Princely vertues, with whom (in way of that excellence) I conferre my Soueraigne, applying in his description, his owne *word*, vsurped of that *Poets Parcere subiectis, & debellare superbos*." Authority for taking this as James's motto is given in the last sentence of the *Basilicon Doron*: "Let it be your chiefest earthlie glorie, to excell in your own craft: according to the worthie counsell & charge of *Anchises* to his posterity, in that sublime & heroicall Poet, wherein also my dicton is included . . . ." The relevant lines from Virgil are then quoted. (From the Waldegrave text, 1603, in *The Basilicon Doron of King James VI*, ed. Craigie, Scottish Text Society, 1944, p. 207.) Contemporary writers made considerable use of this motto of the King's. On the conception of Aeneas as the pattern hero, see Sidney, *Apology for Poetry*, in Gregory Smith, *Elizabethan Critical Essays* (Oxford 1937), I, 179-80. Piety is the main theme of the first book of James's treatise; Justice is stressed at the beginning of the second book. With the last lines of this eulogy:

> . . . is vow'd
> To spare his subiects, yet to quell the proud,
> And does esteeme it the first fortitude,
> To haue his passions, foes at home, subdued,
> (lines 220-3)

compare also the opening words of the first book of *Basilicon Doron*: "As he cannot be thought worthie to rule and command others, that cannot rule and dantone his owne proper affections and vnreasonable appetites . . ." (p. 25).

7. On Jonson's use of such handbooks, see my article "The Imagery of Ben Jonson's *Masque of Blacknesse* and *Masque of Beautie*," and my "*Hymenaei*: Ben Jonson's Masque of Union," above. E. W. Talbert discusses another range of sources in "New Light on Ben Jonson's Workmanship," *Studies in Philology* XL (1943).

8. Conti, Mythologiae (Lyons 1602), pp. 381–2. Jonson's reference to *Metamorphoses* XI is wrong: Conti gives, correctly, XV. This is the traditional way of representing the car; cf. Cartari, pp. 341–2.

9. Conti, p. 380.

10. *Ibid.*, pp. 401–2.

11. Cf. *Luciani Samosatensis Dialogi selectiores* . . . (Paris 1582), pp. 40–2, 57 ("Veneris et Cupidinis").

12. Cartari, p. 262.

13. *Ibid.*, pp. 262, 259.

14. Jonson of course knew this passage, but Conti, referring to it for material on the Cyclopes, also quotes the verses Jonson gives in his note on the Cyclopes (note on l. 319).

15. Jonson's use of Spondanus in *The Masque of Beautie* is noted in my article above. On Chapman and Spondanus, see F. L. Schoell, *Etudes sur l'Humanisme Continentale en Angleterre à la fin de la Renaissance* (Paris 1926).

16. Chapman's rendering of *Iliad* XVIII, lines 330–5. Vulcan was also attended by "Handmaids of gold," "resembling in all worth Living young damsels." *Ibid.*, lines 372–6.

17. *Homeri quae exstant omnia* . . . *Io. Spondani Mauleonensis Commentariis* (Basel 1606), p. 340.

18. Cf. *Hieronymi Cardani Mediolanensis, Medici, De Rerum Varietate Libri XVII* (Lyons 1580), Lib. XII, Cap. 58, pp. 562 ff.

19. Spondanus, p. 344.

20. Chapman, *Iliad*, XVIII, lines 430–4.

21. Spondanus, p. 344.

22. *Ibid.*

23. Cartari, p. 259.

24. Conti, pp. 145–6, and especially p. 147: "Atque Orpheus in hymnis Vulcanum, Solem et Lunam, et astra et lumen purissimum atque aethera ipsum nominauit."

25. Conti, p. 145, and especially p. 152. The reference to the *Cratylus* of Plato is from this passage: this dialogue has no independent relevance to the masque. Note that while Conti's text has "Hunc Deum facem ferre in nuptiis inquit Euripides," Jonson's phrase "Facifer in nuptijs" is actually given in the *index* to the 1602 edition; similarly, although the text gives the sense, it is only in the index that Jonson's phrase "Vulcanus calor est naturae" occurs. Turning to Conti, Jonson would naturally consult the index first, and these sharper phrases would have stuck in his memory.

26. Conti, p. 152.

27. *Ibid.*, p. 391; Cartari, p. 340.

28. Cf. lines 161–2 and 209, note a.

29. Conti, p. 393; Cartari, p. 344.

30. Note on *loue* in line 87. The warning is not unnecessary, for, as Conti says (p. 397), there has been no little dispute about Cupid's parentage; he goes on for several pages to give the various accounts. And the 'explanation' of Cupid varies according to the parents chosen for him.

31. Conti, p. 406.

32. Cartari, p. 353.

33. *Hymenaei*, line 295, note h. On the source of this see Appendix VI.

34. On the sphere and the circle see Valeriano, *Hieroglyphica* (Lyons 1595), pp. 376–80. Jonson had already used these symbols in *Hymenaei*.

35. See my article on *The Masques of Blacknesse and Beautie* above, p. 152 and Fig. 68.

36. Conti, p. 393.

Notes to "Chapman's *Memorable Masque*"

1. The text used is that of T. M. Parrott, *The Plays and Poems of George Chapman*, II (London 1914).

2. Cartari, *Imagines Deorum* (Lyons 1581), p. 246.

3. *Of Honour*, ed. V. B. Heltzel (San Marino, Calif. 1947), p. 37.

4. *The Philosophy Commonly Called, The Morals*, trans. Philemon Holland (London 1603), pp. 374–5.

5. "Dell'Honore Universale," in *Dialoghi Piacevole* (Venice 1604), p. 349.

6. Lines 23–4.

7. Peter Ure, "The Main Outline of Chapman's Byron," *SP*, XLVII (1950), pp. 571–2. And see also Ennis Rees, *The Tragedies of George Chapman* (Cambridge, Mass. 1954), p. 202, n. 36.

8. Ficino, "De Sole," in *Opera* (Basel 1576), p. 970.

9. *Ibid.*, p. 968.

10. *Ibid.*, p. 973.

Notes to "Name and Fame: Shakespeare's *Coriolanus*"

1. The basis of my work has been the great dictionaries, concordances, and indexes, especially the articles *fama* and *gloria* in the *Thesaurus linguae latinae*. I have also found the following studies important: U. Knoche, 'Der romische Ruhmesgedanke', *Philologus* LXXXIX (NF XLIII), 1934, pp. 102–24; A. D. Leeman, *Gloria. Cicero's waardering van de roem en haar achtergrond . . .* (with English summary) (Rotterdam, 1949); A. J. Vermeulen, *The semantic Development of Gloria in early-Christian Latin* (Nijmegen, 1956); C. Mohrmann, 'Note sur Doxa' in her *Études sur le Latin des Chrétiens* (Rome, 1958); J. Daniélou, *Théologie du Judéo-Christianisme* (Paris, 1958); C. Bailey, Commentary on Lucretius *De natura rerum*, cited in note 79 above; Arnold Williams, *The Common Expositor: An account of the Commentaries on Genesis 1527–1633* (Chapel Hill, 1948); P. Villey, *Les Sources et l'evolution des Essais de Montaigne* (Paris, 1933), Vol. I; P. Ure, 'A note on "Opinion" in Daniel, Greville and Chapman', *Modern Language Review*, Vol. XLVI (1951), pp. 331–8 (a particularly valuable study of the topic); P. Ure, ed., *King Richard II* (Arden edn.), 1956 etc.; V. B. Heltzel's edn. of Robert Ashley's *Of Honour* (San Marino, 1947), which has a very useful introduction and commentary. Curtis Brown Watson, *Shakespeare and the Renaissance Concept of Honor* (Princeton, 1960), I conceive to be mistaken in method and conclusions. I should like to thank my colleagues in the Department of Classics in the University of Reading for their readiness to answer questions, and Dr. Whitney Bolton and Mr. J. B. Trapp for help with the text.

2. *Plutarch's Lives of the Noble Grecians and Romans, Englished by Sir Thomas North . . .* with an introduction by G. Wyndham (Tudor Translations, London 1895), II, p. 144.

3. II. ii. 81–83. References to act, scene and line number are given as in William Shakespeare, *The Complete Works*, ed. P. Alexander (London, 1951).

4. I. ix. 58–66.

5. II. i. 153–7.

6. II. i. 163–5.

7. *Tusculan Disputations*, I. XIV. 31 (Loeb Classical Library, pp. 38–39).

8. V. iii. 126–7.

9. V. iii. 142–8.

10. IV. v. 52–64.

11. IV. v. 65–78.

12. North's Plutarch, II, p. 170.

13. *Hamlet*, V. ii. 347–8.

14. E.g. *Les Vies des hommes illustres, grecs et romains, comparées l'une avec l'autre, par Plutarque de Choeronée, translatées . . . par Jacques Amyot . . .* 2nd edn., printing of 1572, fol. 128ʳ, 130ʳ; North's Plutarch, II, pp. 158, 166–7.

15. fol. 130ʳ.

16. Vol. II, p. 166.

17. J. E. Neale, *The Elizabethan House of Commons* (London, 1949), Chaps. 3–6, esp. pp. 87 ff. The quotation is from p. 88.

18. III. iii. 8–10.

19. Neale, p. 87.

20. II. iii. 122–8.

21. III. iii. 122–3.
22. IV. vi. 147–8.
23. IV. vi. 97–9.
24. *Richard II*, III. ii. 54–57.
25. II. ii. 147–8.
26. II. i. 225–6.
27. *Epistulae morales*, CII (Loeb Classical Library, Vol. III, pp. 172–7).
28. *The Workes of Lucius Annaeus Seneca, newly inlarged and corrected by Thomas Lodge* (London, 1614), p. 428.
29. *Brutus*, 281 (Loeb Classical Library, pp. 242–3).
30. *Nicomachean Ethics*, 1095b (Loeb Classical Library, pp. 14–15).
31. *Ibid.* 1123a (Loeb Classical Library, pp. 214–15).
32. *Rhetoric*, 1361a (Loeb Classical Library, pp. 52–53).
33. Seneca, *loc. cit.*
34. Cicero, *De inventione* II. 166 (Loeb Classical Library, pp. 332–3).
35. I. i. 28–29.
36. I. i. 30–32.
37. Quintilian, *Institutio oratoria*, v. iii. I (Loeb Classical Library, Vol. II, pp. 162–3). The translation is by H. E. Butler.
38. *Metamorphoses*, XII. 47 ff. (Loeb Classical Library, Vol. II, pp. 184–5). The translation is by F. J. Miller.
39. Juvenal, VII. 71 (Loeb Classical Library, pp. 142–3).
40. *Aeneid*, IV. 188 (Loeb Classical Library, Vol. I, pp. 408–9).
41. *Aeneid*, XI. 708 (Loeb Classical Library, Vol. II, pp. 282–3).
42. *Aeneid*, VII. 645–6 (Loeb Classical Library, Vol. II, pp. 46–47).
43. *Romeo and Juliet*, I. i. 87.
44. *Troilus and Cressida*, I. iii. 244; III. iii. 210; I. iii. 144.
45. II *Henry IV*, Ind. 15–20.
46. *Tusculan Disputations*, V. 46 (Loeb Classical Library, pp. 472–3).
47. *Of Glory*, in *The Essaies . . . done into English by John Florio* . . . with an introduction by G. Saintsbury (Tudor Translations, London, 1893), Book II, Chap. 16, Vol. II, pp. 354–5.
48. I *Henry IV*, v. i. 130–2.
49. II. i. 166.
50. IV. ii. 19–20.
51. II. ii. 70.
52. II. iii. 122–5.
53. II. iii. 73.
54. II. ii. 142–3.
55. III. i. 257–8.
56. III. ii. 54–57.
57. III. ii. 120–3.
58. *Of Glory, Essaies*, Vol. II, p. 353. The quotation from St. Paul is 2 Cor. i. 12. Cf. St. Augustine, *Hom.* XXXV (*Patrologia Latina*, XXXVIII, col. 213 f.).
59. *Troilus and Cressida*, v. ii. 139–40.
60. Cicero, *De inventione*, I. 34 (Loeb Classical Library, pp. 70–71).
61. North's Plutarch, II, pp. 154–5.
62. II. i. 164.
63. IV. v. 73.
64. v. i. 11–15.
65. v. ii. 12–13.
66. v. ii. 91–92.
67. *Romeo and Juliet*, II. ii. 38–49.
68. *Of Glory, Essaies*, Vol. II, p. 348.
69. D. P. Walker, *Spiritual and Demonic Magic from Ficino to Campanella*, (Studies of the Warburg Institute, XXII, London, 1958), pp. 80–81.
70. *Julius Caesar*, III. iii. 32–34.
71. *Richard II*, III. ii. 85–87.
72. *Richard II*, IV. i. 255–7.
73. *Richard II*, v. v. 36–38.

74. *Of Glory, Essaies*, Vol. II, p. 358.
75. III. iii. 125.
76. Cf. e.g. Montaigne, *Of Glory, Essaies*, Vol. II, p. 357.
77. v. i. 13.
78. *Of the Interpretation of Nature*, I (*Works*, eds. Ellis and Spedding, Vol. III, London, 1859, p. 222).
79. Lucretius, *De rerum natura*, V. 1011 ff. (Loeb Classical Library, pp. 412–15); Vitruvius, *De architectura*, II. 1 (Loeb Classical Library, Vol. I, pp. 76–79); cf. Cicero, *De inventione* I. 2–3 (Loeb Classical Library, pp. 4–7). For other ancient accounts see Lucretius, *De rerum natura*, ed. C. Bailey, Oxford, 1947, Vol. III (Commentary), pp. 1487 ff.
80. IV. v. 37, 42.
81. v. iii. 35–37.
82. III. i. 80–81.
83. North's Plutarch, II, p. 144.
84. v. vi. 114–17.

Notes to *"Veritas Filia Temporis*: Hadrianus Junius and Geoffrey Whitney"

1. "Veritas Filia Temporis," *Philosophy and History. Essays presented to Ernst Cassirer* (Oxford 1936), p. 203 f.
2. I have used the edition by L. A. Magnus. (Early English Text Society. London. 1905) It was also edited by Alois Brandl. (*Quellen des Weltlichen Dramas in England vor Shakespeare.* Quellen und Forschungen etc. LXXX. Strasbourg, 1898.) On this play see also W. R. Mackenzie, *The English Moralities from the point of view of allegory* (Boston 1914), pp. 226 f.
3. Magnus (Introduction, xxiv) takes these two lines as a possible reference to Bishop Gardiner. This seems highly improbable.
4. P. 202.
5. They had appeared in the early morality *The Castle of Perseverance* (1400–1425?) after 'Mankind's' death, to struggle for his soul which had been claimed by the Devil. Mercy and Pes wish to rescue him, but Rytwysnes and Trewthe argue that he damned himself, of his own free-will. They take the question to God, who decides in favour of Mercy and Pes. So here Mercy pleads for the guilty (V,x) and is opposed by Iustice. Veritee and Peace think the demands of both can be satisfied. Nemesis agrees.
6. An edition of Junius' letters, prefaced with a Vita, was published by his son in 1652 (Dordrechti, Apud Vincentium Caimax, Bibliopolam). There is a *Diatribe in Hadriani Junii vitam, ingenium, familiam, merita literaria* by P. Scheltema, Amsterdam, 1836 (an unsatisfactory work). In 1839 Scheltema published (at Amsterdam) some letters of Junius', not included in the 17th century volume. There are notes on Junius in G. F. Nott's edition of Wyatt and Surrey (London 1815–16), in Bapst's study of Surrey in his *Deux Gentilshommes-poètes de la cour de Henry VIII* (Paris, 1891) and in Edwin Casady, *Henry Howard, Earl of Surrey* (New York, 1938). But there is as yet no full treatment, especially of his relations with England, and there is not space here for one. There is also a note in Green's edition of Whitney, which tells us little. Hadrianus comes off badly at Sandys' hands. When we consider the enormous amount of work he covered (vide the B.M. catalogue and the catalogue of the University Library, Cambridge, and the lists in the Vita, and Scheltema) it seems a little hard that this should be his epitaph: "Hadrianus Junius (Adriaan de Jonghe) a physician at Haarlem, Copenhagen, and Delft (1511–1575), is in good repute as an early editor of Nonius Marcellus (1565)." Even although a note adds "Also as the author of a Greek and Latin Lexicon (Basle, 1548, 1577)." Sandys, *History of Classical Scholarship* (Cambridge, 1908), vol. 2, p. 216. [See now J. A. van Dorsten, *The Radical Arts* (Leiden 1970) pp. 131 ff.–Ed.]
7. Scheltema, p. 12.
8. The last paragraph quoted from Casady, pp. 111–2. See also Scheltema, p. 13.
9. Casady, p. 55.
10. Scheltema (p. 13) is quite wrong when he says: "Duce enim Nordfolciae mortuo, ejus filius . . . Capite multatus est."
11. *Epistolae*, p. 392. Casady does not quote this, though it is an exact summary of the argument of his book.

12. This dedication is reprinted, *Epistolae*, pp. 508 ff.
13. P. 63.
14. *Epistolae*, p. 390 ff.
15. *Epistolae*, pp. 393–4. He used this last argument in a letter to "Antonio Perenotto Cardinali" (i.e. Antoine Perrenot de Granvelle) asking for help in having his name removed from the Index. (*Epistolae*, p. 469 ff.) This letter is followed by the quotation from the Appendix under Hadrianus' name, cited above, but without any indication of its exact provenance (p. 471). Scheltema does the same (*op. cit.*, p. 52). Scheltema had not attempted to trace the occasion or date of the 1569–70 letter to the Commissioners.
16. *Philippeis, seu, in nuptias Divi Philippi, Aug. Pii, Max. & Heroinae Mariae Aug. Felicis, Invictae, Regum Angliae*–etc. Londini 1554. The British Museum copy of this book is inscribed "Lumley" indicating that it came from the library of John, Lord Lumley (1534?–1609). The orbits of Lumley and Hadrianus intersected at one or two points. Lumley was a Catholic, educated at Cambridge and the Court of Edward VI. He took an active part in public affairs, especially those connected with the law, in Mary's reign and at the beginning of Elizabeth's. He married a daughter of Henry Fitzalan, twelfth Earl of Arundel, and thus became a brother-in-law of Thomas Howard, eldest son of the Earl of Surrey, a pupil of Hadrianus, and later fourth Duke of Norfolk. Lumley, Arundel and Norfolk were deeply implicated in schemes for the re-establishment of Catholicism in England and the marriage of Norfolk to Mary Queen of Scots. When the 'Ridolfi' plot was discovered in 1571, Arundel was imprisoned and was not released for more than a year; he lived in retirement till his death (1579–80). Norfolk was imprisoned, tried for treason in 1572, and executed the same year. Lumley, who seems to have been implicated largely through his friendliness with the two others, spent some time in prison. But he seems to have cut his connections with political intrigue. He was one of the Commissioners at Mary's trial, and later at the trials of Essex and Southampton. He also held various offices under James. He collected portraits and books, and was interested in antiquities–and in medicine. In 1582–3, along with Richard Caldwell, he founded and endowed a lectureship in surgery at the Royal College of Physicians.
17. Pp. 14–17.
18. For this dedication see *Ep.*, p. 520 ff.
19. *Epistolae*, p. 544 ff.
20. London, Richard Iohnes.
21. We have a minor puzzle here. This epistle is signed H.I.H. which immediately suggests Hadrianus Iunius Hornanus. But Hadrianus died in 1575, four years before the publication of this translation. And Sir Thomas Bromley did not become Lord Chancellor till April 1579 (according to the *D.N.B.* article). There is no indication of who the translator was; and it has not, to my knowledge, ever been attributed to anyone.

    The translator may have written this second dedication himself as a *réclame* for his work and to flatter Bromley. The text certainly implies that Hadrianus is speaking. But if Hadrianus had anything to do with it we must suppose that it was done at latest in 1575, that he did it before the translation had actually been finished or that there had been a long delay in publishing it, that he had decided to dedicate it to Bromley who was then an eminent figure in the legal world, that, as at the time of publication Bromley had become Lord Chancellor, the translator then made the necessary adjustments. This is rather complicated. That Bromley had been one of the Counsel for the Crown at the trial of the Duke of Norfolk in 1571 and had largely made his name through his successful handling of this case, is not, unfortunately, evidence that Hadrianus would not have approached him. I do not really see any answer to the riddle. And it is of little importance.

    Again, does the phrase "brought it over into England" mean that Hadrianus had actually come to England in 1568 to present his book to Elizabeth, as he had done to Philip and Mary? Or does it simply mean that by dedicating the book to Elizabeth he had "brought it over into England"? There is a letter dated from London in 1568 to which Scheltema (p. 17, note 2) refers as follows:

    > Annum 1568. Epistola Jano Douzae. p. 200 spurium esse, verosimile est, nullum certe vestigium alibi in litteris hujus itineris in Angliam inveni.

    But Scheltema, who dismissed this letter on those grounds, must have overlooked the letter "Gregorio Martino Britanno" which is dated "Londino. Julio Mense. anno 1568." (*Epistolae*, pp. 201–3) I do not think we can doubt that Hadrianus actually made this journey in 1568.

    Martin Gregory was at this time in the household of Thomas, fourth Duke of Norfolk, as tutor to his eldest son. See the *D.N.B.* article on him, also *Recusant Poets*, ed. Guiney, Vol. I (London 1938), p. 167 ff.

22. *Epistolae*, pp. 255–6.
23. London, 1585. There were several later editions.
24. *A Choice of emblemes, and other Devises, For the most parte gathered out of sundrie writers, Englished and Moralized. And Divers newly devised*, by Geoffrey Whitney. Imprinted at Leyden, In the house of Christopher Plantyn, by Francis Raphelengius M.D. LXXXVI. Whitney's connection with the Netherlands seems to have begun when he was a town offical at Yarmouth (? 1580–1586). In 1586 he became a student of the newly founded University of Leyden.
25. Geoffrey Whitney, *A Choice of Emblems*. A facsimile reprint. Ed. H. Green (London, 1866).
26. *Hadriani Iunii Medici Emblemata, ad Arnoldum Cobelium. Eiusedem Aenigmatum Libellus, ad D. Arnoldum Rosenbergum*. Antwerpiae ex officina Christophori Plantini. M.D. LXV. The emblem in question is no. 53, and is to be found on p. 59; in Whitney on p. 4.
27. Saxl, in dealing with Aretino's use of the motto, has shown how Calumny was associated with the theme of the Liberation of Truth by Time (*op. cit.*, pp. 200–1). The figure of Calumny here is nearer the traditional *Calumnia Apellis* than are the monsters in Saxl's illustrations. This is achieved at the expense of putting Calumny in no direct relation with the figure of Truth. I suggest that our Inuidia is derived from the Inuidia which appears in most of the editions of Alciati, beginning with that of Lyons, 1550. Here she is represented as a very tall and ugly woman, striding along, her right foot forward (as in our illustration); she is naked to the waist and in her right hand, which is clasped over her bosom, she holds her heart; in her left hand, she has a rough stick; a viper issues from her mouth and is striking back at her; her head is covered with a shapeless arrangement of folded cloth. The verse is:

> Squallida viperas manducans femina carnes,
>   Cuique dolent oculi, quaeque suum cor edit,
> Quam macies & pallor habent, spinosaque gestat
>   Tela manu: talis pingitur Inuidia.

In the comments later added to Alciati's emblems, this verse is buttressed by lavish quotations from the Roman poets. A modification of this figure, rather closer to ours, appeared in the edition of Alciati ("Adiectis commentariis & scholiis . . . Per Claudium Minoem") which Plantin published at Antwerp in 1573, nine years after he had published Hadrianus' emblems. The association of Envy and Discord with the theme is new to me with Hadrianus, but it seems an obvious extension. The attributes of the three furies are shared: Calumnia and Lis have both fire, Lis and Inuidia have both snakes.
28. Green (p. 250) cites this emblem as "Envy etc. imprison Truth."
29. *Middleton's Works*, ed. Bullen (London 1886) VII, which I use; it is also included in Nichols' *Progresses of King James*, II.
30. In Middleton's masque *The World Well Lost at Tennis* (1620; Bullen, VII), Time appears weeping to complain to Jupiter of the wrongs done to him by men. These lines are relevant:

> O, but my wrongs they are innumerable!
> The lawyer drives me off from term to term,
> Bids me—and I do't—bring forth my Alethe,
> My poor child Truth, he sees and will not see her;
> What I could manifest in one clear day,
> He still delays a cloudy jubilee.

Notes to "Giannotti, Michelangelo and the Cult of Brutus"

1. The evidence for the connexion of Giannotti and Ridolfi with the bust is a statement by Vasari in his life of Michelangelo, *Vite*, ed. Milanesi (Florence 1906) VII, 262.
2. We are gravely handicapped by the lack of lives and studies of the *fuorusciti*. There is no full life of Giannotti, no modern edition of his works and no edition of his letters (though parts of his correspondence have been published in periodicals). [But now see R. Starn, *Donato Giannotti and his Epistolae* (Geneva 1968).–Ed.] The best account of his life is in R. Ridolfi's introduction to Donato Giannotti, *Lettere a Piero Vettori*, ed. R. Ridolfi and Cecil Roth, Florence 1932: on this I, in general, rely. The critical

edition of Giannotti's *Dialogi, de' giorni che Dante consumò nel cercare l'Inferno e 'l Purgatorio* is by Deoclecio Redig de Campos, Florence 1939. All my references to the text of the *Dialogi* are to this edition. De Campos gives full references to the literature on the *Dialogi*. H. Thode, for example, long ago discussed the connexion between the *Dialogi* and the bust, in his *Michelangelo und das Ende der Renaissance*, Berlin 1902–13, vol. I, pp. 125–6. *Cf.* also Charles de Tolney, "Michelangelo's Bust of Brutus," in *Burlington Magazine*, LXVII (1935), pp. 23 ff. Tolnay argues that the fibula which holds the drapery on the shoulder of the bust is the work of Michelangelo himself and is a kind of "preliminary study" for the bust; and that the head on the brooch reproduces the pose of the head of Brutus on antique coins, and may be a portrait of Giannotti.

3. *Opere Politiche e Letterarie di Donato Giannotti*, ed. F. L. Polidori (Florence 1850), vol. I, p. 59. This is the only attempt at a critical edition of Giannotti's works and replaces the first collected edition by Giovanni Rosini (Pisa 1819), 3 vols.

4. "Recitazione del caso di Pietro Paolo Boscoli e di Agostino Capponi, scritta da Luca della Robbia, l'anno MDXIII," in *Archivio Storico Italiano*, I (1842), pp. 289–90.

5. *Discorsi*, I, p. 10.

6. *cf.* H. A. Grueber, *Coins of the Roman Republic in the British Museum* (London 1910), vol. II, p. 480, nos. 68, 69, 70.

7. I use the text of the *Apologia* in *Lorenzino de' Medici: Aridosia, Apologia*, etc., ed. F. Ravello (Turin 1921), which reproduces the only critical text, by G. Lisio, in *Orazioni Scelte del Secolo XVI* (Florence 1897). A good modern study of Lorenzino is lacking. The standard work is still L. A. Ferrai, *Lorenzino de' Medici e la Società Cortigiana del Cinquecento* (Milan 1891).

8. Benedetto Varchi, *Storia Fiorentina*, LIB. XV (ed. Milanesi [Florence 1888] III, pp. 190–1). Varchi's account of the whole affair, and of the personality of Lorenzino, is by far the best of all the contemporary accounts.

9. *cf.* Filippo de' Nerli, *Commentari de' Fatti Civili occorsi dentro la Città di Firenze dall' Anno MCCXV al MDXXVII* (Augusta 1728), p. 288.

10. As Ravello, *op. cit.*, p. 8, suggests (following A. Borgognoni, *Lorenzo di Pier Francesco de' Medici*, in *Studi di Letteratura Storica* [Bologna 1891], p. 9).

11. A. F. Doni, *La Fortuna di Cesare tratta da gl' Autori Latini* (Venice 1550), in the address *Ai lettori*, sig. A iiii^{r-v}.

12. *cf.* Bernardo Segni, *Storie Fiorentine* (Milan 1805) II, p. 132. Varchi, *Storia Fiorentina, ed. cit.*; III, p. 210.

13. *cf.* F. Martini, *Lorenzino de' Medici e il Tirannicidio nel Rinascimento* (Florence 1882), pp. 9, 58.

14. Martini, pp. 59–62 cites these compositions from a Strozzi MS (now in the Archivio di Stato, Florence). For the rest, it may be noted, this is not a very satisfactory book.

15. Varchi, *ed. cit.*, III, p. 210.

16. Quoted from Giorgio Spini, *Cosimo I de' Medici e la Indipendenza del Principato Mediceo* (Florence 1945), p. 62, *n.* 2 (or in Varchi, *ed. cit.*, III, p. 212).

17. *Ibid.*, p. 75, *n.* 2.

18. I quote the text given by Spini, p. 172, from the copy sent to the Emperor and preserved in the Simancas archives.

19. Thode, I think, was wrong in relating the bust too strictly to the particular figure of Lorenzino, *cf.* I, p. 35.

20. *cf.* I. Sanesi, *La Vita e le Opere di Donato Giannotti* (Pistoia 1899), p. 11 (a work now out of date).

21. On the interlocutori *cf.* Giannotti, *Dialogi*, pp. 8–18.

22. Ed. F. L. Polidori (Florence 1850).

23. *Dialogi*, pp. 27–9.

24. Giannotti, *Dialogi*, p. 25: "l'argomento più decisivo, e finora non mai invocato da alcuno."

25. This and the following quotations are from *Dante con l'Espositione di Christoforo Landino, et di Alessandro Vellutello*, etc., ed. Francesco Sansovino (Venice 1564), fol. 160.

26. *Dialogi*, pp. 92–3.

27. Dante (Venice 1564), fols. 69^v, 70^{r-v}.

28. *Dialogi*, pp. 38–9, 47–8.

29. *cf.* for example the following commentaries: Iacopo Alighieri's *Chiose alla Cantica dell' Inferno di Dante Alighieri*, edd. Jarro, G. Piccini (Florence 1915), pp. 161–2; *Chiose sopra Dante*, ed. Lord Vernon (Florence 1846), p. 279; Francesco da Buti's *Commento sopra la Divina Commedia di Dante Alighieri*, ed. C. Giannini (Pisa 1858–62), I, p. 855; and especially the *Anonimo Fiorentino*, ed. Fanfani (Bologna 1866–74), I, p. 711. It seems clear that Dante, like most of his contemporaries, regarded Caesar as the first of the Roman emperors; they were probably influenced by Suetonius who began his *Lives of the Caesars* with Julius. *Cf.* A. Graf, *Roma nella Memoria e nella Immaginazione del Medio Evo* (Turin 1882), I, pp. 248–9.

30. Translation in E. Emerton, *Humanism and Tyranny* (Cambridge, Mass. 1925), pp. 110–15.
31. This was Stefano Talice da Ricaldone. See *La Commedia di Dante Alighieri, col Commento Inedito di Stefano Talice da Ricaldone*, edd. V. Promis and Carlo Negroni (Milan 1888), pp. 456–7. The authority he is generally following is Benvenuto da Imola, whose great commentary on the *Comedy* is of the late fourteenth century.
32. Dante (Venice 1564), fol. 160ʳ. For Michelangelo's reference to this comment, *cf.* Giannotti, *Dialogi*, p. 23.

Notes to "Academicians Build a Theatre and Give a Play: The Accademia Olimpica, 1579–1585"

1. For most of our knowledge of the academies we still have to turn to the work of those admirable eighteenth- and nineteenth-century antiquaries and cultivators of *storia patria*. The fundamental work is still M. Maylender, *Storia delle Accademie d'Italia*, Bologna, 1926–30: but it is a list, not a history. See, still, the important suggestions in Frances Yates, *The French Academies of the Sixteenth Century*, London, 1947, Chap. I; and N. Pevsner, *Academies of Art, Past and Present*, Cambridge, 1940. Recently, on one important aspect, Bernard Weinberg, "Argomenti di Discussione Letteraria nell'Accademia degli Alterati (1570–1600)", *Giornale Storico della Letteratura Italiana*, CXXXI, 1954, pp. 75–94; and indications in the same author's *A History of Literary Criticism in the Italian Renaissance*, Chicago, 1961 (to which reference will be made later). The solidest and best study of a single academy that I know is still Giuseppe Turrini, *L'Accademia Filarmonica di Verona dalla fondazione (maggio 1543) al 1600 e il suo patrimonio musicale*, Verona, 1941 (*Atti e memorie della Accademia di Agricoltura Scienze e Lettere di Verona*, series V, XVIII).
2. *Documents in the Biblioteca Bertoliana*, Vicenza. Two sets of contemporary minutes of the academy meeting in council. These documents do not seem to have been used before. They record, it is important to remember, only certain kinds of business: and are often irritating by silence–e.g. about the decision to build Palladio's theatre and no other, and about the role of Scamozzi (not that that is any longer in much doubt). Nor do they tell us about the educational and social activities of the academy. Other kinds of records were kept, now, unfortunately lost. These minutes, from which most of my material comes, are: 1) *Bib. Bertoliana, ms. Accademia Olimpica*, O.9.2.4.D. *Libro delle creationi de prencipi* etc. May 1579–April 1582. 2) *Bib. Bertoliana, ms. Accademia Olimpica*, O.9.2.4.E. *Atti ordinarij et straordinarij dell'Academia*, April 1582–April 1586. Unfortunately it is not possible to work only from original sources. In the 18th century a local antiquary, the Abbé Ziggiotti, started to compile an annals of the academy. He had at his disposal very many documents which have not been available since his death in 1763. Students refer only to *Bertoliana, ms. Ziggiotti*, 2916: a fair copy made of what may have been Ziggiotti's final (but not inclusive) summary of his notes and containing material from other sources, including selections, calendared, from our D and E. But there is much Ziggiotti material in the shape of notes and drafts among the academy documents in the Bertoliana: it is very confused and difficult to sort out. However, two drafts: 1) *Bib. Bertoliana, ms. Accademia Olimpica*, O.9.2.11.(M) 2) O.9.2.13.(O) lie behind and are fuller than Ziggiotti 2916; they do not exactly coincide, each being richer than the other at certain points. 11.(M) is more coherent. These I have used. There is also in Venice, in the Correr library, a Ziggiotti ms. which I have not been able to collate: Cod. Cic. 3251 / IV. I use Ziggiotti with the greatest reluctance. I do not believe that it is always certain how he is handling the documents he had, whether he is quoting or summarising with interpolations of his own. Sometimes he clearly has not understood a name; and I wonder whether his dating is always consistent. He has been used too uncritically. For other important mss. see notes 3 and 33. I have to thank Dr. Antonio M. Dalla Pozza, Librarian of the Bertoliana, authority on Palladio and the Vicenza of those times, for his continued welcome; and the Signorina Cristofori of the same library for much friendly help.
3. For the theatre see, of modern studies, Liciso Magagnato, "The Genesis of the Teatro Olimpico", *Journal of the Warburg and Courtauld Institutes*, XIV, 1951, and in his *Teatri italiani del Cinquecento*, Venice, 1954. Two recent studies are Leo Schrade, *La Représentation d'Edipo Tiranno au Teatro Olimpico*, Paris, 1960; Lionello Puppi, "La rappresentazione inaugurale del teatro Olimpico", *Critica d'arte*, L, LI, 1962 (written, apparently, without knowledge of Schrade's book). The later essay by Puppi, *Il Teatro Olimpico*, Vicenza, 1963, adds little. Schrade is important for the discussion of the translation, and of the music for the chorus, and the publication of music and text. He does not know the Bertoliana mss; and I am not always quite

sure what secondary authorities he is following for the history of the academy. Puppi is concerned with theatre and production in terms of a certain theory of "spectacle"; he publishes for the first time three drawings by G. B. Maganza which may well be sketches for costume for the *Oedipus*; he makes much use of Ziggiotti 2916. Both Schrade and Puppi use a document of fundamental importance for the production: Milan, Ambrosiana, Cod. R. 123 sup. This is a sort of dossier put together by or for the Paduan dilettante and collector, G. V. Pinelli. It contains, among other material, an elaborate incomplete producer's programme for the production (I do not here enter into the question of how much was by Paolo Teggia, and how much by Angelo Ingegneri), and the letters about the production by F. Pigafetta (which have been published twice and gave the only account generally known), G. Dolfini, and Antonio Riccoboni. For this ms. see also B. Weinberg, *History*, vol. II, pp. 942–945. This ms. has not, however, been fully exploited.

4. Of the general milieu there is no modern study. For Trissino and Vicenza we still have to turn to Bernardo Morsolin, *Giangiorgio Trissino*, Vicenza, 1878. On the Accademia Olimpica the received works are principally O. Bertotti-Scamozzi, *Origine dell'Accademia Olimpica*, etc., Vicenza, 1790; A. Magrini, *Il Teatro Olimpico*, etc., Padua, 1847 (with whose sharp words about Ziggiotti one has much sympathy); by far the best is F. Lampertico's genial account in his "Ricordi academici", *Scritti storici e letterari*, Florence, 1882, vol. I (but he deliberately does not deal with the theatre or the production). G. Crovato, *La Drammatica a Vicenza nel Cinquecento*, Turin, 1895, which is still quoted, is not reliable in detail. Behind all lies Ziggiotti 2916.

5. Fol. 3v. References for O.9.2.4.D and (later) O.9.2.4.E are given in this form. I have given references only where I have made significant quotations. The date given in my text will permit any passage to be looked up in these two mss. very easily. The minutes of meetings are, naturally, arranged chronologically. I have, however, given all references to the Ziggiotti mss.

6. Fol. 4r.

7. Fol. 8v. I am altogether uncertain of the status of the passage now generally quoted from ms. Ziggiotti 2916 (p. 31) and perhaps purporting to be in the words of the request to the city: "disegnando essi di venir alla fondazione del Teatro secondo il modello già fatto dal loro conaccademico Palladio, e disegno parimenti delle Prospettiue".

8. Fol. 12r.

9. Fol. 15r–v.

10. Fol. 18r.

11. Fol. 23r. There is perhaps a mistake in the ms. about the dates of this and the last meeting.

12. And see a document quoted by G. Montanari, *Del Teatro Olimpico etc.*, Padua, second edition, 1749 p. 3. Montanari (who knew Ziggiotti) refers to "memorie, che sono nell'Archivio della Città".

13. The authority is Ziggiotti ms. 2916, p. 160. According to this source it was granted on January 28th, 1582.

14. Fol. 26v.

15. Fol. 33r.

16. Fol. 33v.

17. Fol. 33v.

18. Fols. 34r–36r.

19. Paolo Chiappino, who from now on signs the minutes. From this point we pass to 0.9.2.4.E.

20. Fol. 8r.

21. For Leonardo Valmarana, see S. Rumor, *I Conti di Valmarana*, Vicenza, 1908.

22. O.9.2.13.(O), III, p. 8. For much material, not recorded in our minutes, we now have to rely on Ziggiotti.

23. O.9.2.11.(M), *sub* 1581.

24. O.9.2.11.(M), *sub* 1581.

25. On Pace, see Calvi (Angiolgabriello di Santa Maria), *Biblioteca e storia di quegli scrittori così come del territorio di Vicenza*, Vicenza, 1772–82, V, pp. 123–34.

26. On Pagello, see Calvi, V, pp. 181–90. Some mss. are in the Bertoliana, notably a collection of prose writings, including academic addresses, Bertoliana, ms. 171 (Gonzati, 25.7.4, 1–73), and Bertoliana ms. 170 (Gonzati 26.1.29), an imperfect autograph of his tragedy *L'Eraclea*. See also Crovato, *Drammatica*, pp. 45–51, 131–35.

27. O.9.2.11.(M), *sub* 1583.

28. I am not happy about the dating of events not recorded in the minutes. O.9.2.11.(M) makes it appear that everything was happening in 1583 (including the decision to go to Giustiniano); and 13.(O) does not seem to disagree. The Vatican ms. (see note 33) attributes the learned opinions on the tragedies to "l'anno

1583"; but M. A. Muret's letter about *L'Eraclea* in that ms. is dated April 27th 1584; however Ziggiotti records its reception by the academy (along with a letter from Guarini and one from Speroni) under 1583 (13.(O), p. 35—which cannot be right, unless the Vatican ms. is wrong and it is wrong elsewhere). It may be that we are dealing with differing methods of dating for the difficult period, January-March. It would make better sense if the discussions took about a year; Muret's letter would fall into place, and also the resolution of May 28th, 1584.

29. The list is Ziggiotti's and depends on combining O.9.2.11.(M) (*sub* 1583) and O.9.2.13.(O), III, p. 34. It was transmitted by Magrini, *Teatro Olimpico*, p. 60; and it was plainly from Magrini that, for example, it was taken over by Schrade, p. 46.

30. This is how Magrini interpreted the reference: "l'*Achille* ... prima tragedia scritta nella lingua del Latio ... come più tardi la *Sofonisba* nel l'italiana del Trissino".

31. Alessandro Massaria (died 1598), Vicentine, very well known as a doctor and writer on medical topics, is credited with an Italian translation of the *Andria* performed by the academy in 1557. Calvi, who writes of him at length, *Biblioteca*, V, pp. 82-94 makes no reference to another play nor can I find it mentioned elsewhere.

32. This is odd, as the family is so well known, and Ziggiotti is so specific (O.9.2.11.(M), *sub* 1583): "La Tragedia del Luigi Valmarana, Padre d'Accademia, Principe dell'accademia dei Costanti". The title is in 13.(O), III, p. 34. The reference books give us no help. Seb. Rumor, *I Conti di Valmarana*, Vicenza, 1907, p. 46, refers to a certain Odorico Valmarana, who was for some time a Jesuit, and wrote verse in Latin and Italian, as being the author of the tragedy *Placidia*. But I do not know how much this is worth.

33. Muzio Manfredi's *dossier* is in the Vatican Library, in ms. Vat. Lat. 8745 (I have to thank the appropriate authorities for a microfilm). This ms. was discovered by Bernard Weinberg and studied by him in his *History of Literary Criticism in the Italian Renaissance*, Chicago, 1961, vol. II, pp. 937-941. See also his bibliography, p. 1132, under Ingegneri. On fol. 23v. there is a note by Muzio Manfredi saying he had these three "discorsi" from Giulio Poggiana in Vicenza, 1589, and has copied them "con l'ortografia, e puntatura dell'Autor loro". He also says that he has had one "contro la mia Semiramis" "che più innanzi sarà scritto su questo libro"—but which is not included in this ms. I am sure Weinberg—who would have modified what he says about the context of the ms. if he had known the academy documents—is right when he attributes the second piece on *L'Eraclea* given to Ingegneri by the ms. to Riccoboni: the internal evidence he offers combined with the attribution of the same piece to Riccoboni in another ms. (ms. Vat. Lat. 6528, which I have not seen) and with Ziggiotti's evidence that Riccoboni was involved at this stage seem pretty conclusive. But if Manfredi was wrong about this, was he also wrong about giving *L'Alessio* to Vincenzo Giusti—which is, like the Ingegneri attribution, a matter of a headline description? It is possible.

34. See notes 28, 33.

35. Still dependent on the narrative in O.9.2.11.(M), *sub* 1583.

36. Fol. 25v.

37. Fol. 22v. This must be what lies behind the passage from Ziggiotti 2916 (p. 46) often quoted in connexion with Scamozzi's work, e.g., F. Barbieri, *Vincenzo Scamozzi* (Vicenza 1952), p. 131; Puppi, *Critica d'Arte*, LI (1962), p. 60. These minutes do not in fact mention Scamozzi—not that there is any doubt that the Academy did call him in.

38. O.9.2.13.(O), pp. 39-40. Giangiorgio Zorzi's identification is therefore confirmed. See his "Tre Scultori lombardi e le loro opere nel Teatro Olimpico di Vicenza (Ruggero Brascapè, Cristoforo Milanese e Domenico Fontana)", *Arte Lombarda*, V (1960), pp. 231-42.

39. O.9.2.11.(M), *sub* 1584. Teggia's paper is preserved in the Pinelli dossier, already referred to: ms. Ambrosiana, Cod. R. 123 sup. On Teggia see, principally, G. Tiraboschi, *Biblioteca Modenese* (Modena, 1784) V, p. 224ff.

40. O.9.2.11.(M), *sub* 1584.

41. O.9.2.11.(M), *sub* 1584. The discourse by Teggia is presumably that in the Ambrosiana ms. which also contains a letter from Scamozzi about lighting, and brief notes about the production by Speroni.

42. O.9.2.13.(O), IV, pp. 1-2.

43. O.9.2.11.(M), *sub* 1584, 1585.

44. Fol. 34^{r-v}.

45. O.9.2.11.(M), *sub* 1585.

46. The hard evidence for the date is Pigafetta's letter (Ambrosiana, Cod. R. 123 *sup.*, pp. 322r-325r) which is dated from Vicenza, March 4th, and refers to the production as having happened "yesterday". The

so-called "memoria" of "Arnaldi" cited by Ziggiotti, O.9.2.13.(O), IV, p. 1, and 2916, p. 48, and printed, and so diffused by Crovato, *Drammatica*, pp. 146–7, speaks of the performances as being on "Domenica 28 Febraro, et il giorno ultimo di carnovale"; February 28th fell on a Thursday. Sunday was March 3rd. There is some confusion among the Ziggiotti mss. about the number of performances; but I think we may take it that there were two; and that the second was on the last day of Carnival, March 5th.

47. For details, except for those shewn as deriving from Ziggiotti, I am relying in this paragraph on the Pigafetta letter. Very full use of it is made by Schrade, pp. 47–50. The times are those given by Pigafetta, which do not disagree with those given by Dolfini (Ambrosiana, ms. R. 123 *sup.*, f. 304r); and I have assumed a twenty-four hour clock starting at our 6 p.m.

48. O.9.2.11.(M), *sub* 1585.

49. O.9.2.11.(M), *sub* 1585.

50. O.9.2.11.(M), *sub* 1585.

51. O.9.2.11.(M), *sub* 1585.

52. Fol. 38v–39r.

Index